To H.D.
from Bill
8-30-76

# THE RAILROAD CAR BUILDER'S PICTORIAL DICTIONARY

BY

## Matthias N. Forney

WITH A NEW INTRODUCTION BY JOHN F. STOVER,
PROFESSOR OF HISTORY, PURDUE UNIVERSITY

DOVER PUBLICATIONS, INC.
NEW YORK

# A Note on the Pagination

———————◆———————

In the original edition several double-page spreads were left blank, although included in the page numbering. To avoid confusion, unsightliness and the suspicion that material has been omitted, the present edition eliminates these blank spreads, pointing out the situation each time. For instance, on page 307 will be found the indication "308 & 309 blank," and the next page will be 310. Moreover, in three places material has been shifted from left-hand pages to right-hand pages to avoid blanks on the right. NO MATERIAL HAS BEEN OMITTED.

Published in Canada by General Publishing Company, Ltd., 30 Lesmill Road, Don Mills, Toronto, Ontario.
Published in the United Kingdom by Constable and Company, Ltd., 10 Orange Street, London WC 2.

This Dover edition, first published in 1974, is an unabridged republication of the work originally published by *The Railroad Gazette*, New York, in 1879. The original title page read as follows: *The Car-Builder's Dictionary: an illustrated vocabulary of terms which designate American railroad cars, their parts and attachments. Compiled for the Master Car-Builders' Association by Matthias N. Forney, Mechanical Engineer, assisted by Leander Garey, Sup't of the Car Dep't, N. Y. Central & Hudson River Railroad, And Calvin A. Smith, Secretary of the Master Car-Builders' Association. Published by The Railroad Gazette, No. 73 Broadway, New-York. 1879.*
A new introduction has been written specially for the present edition by John F. Stover.

*International Standard Book Number: 0-486-22974-2*
*Library of Congress Catalog Card Number: 74-78972*

Manufactured in the United States of America
Dover Publications, Inc.
180 Varick Street
New York, N.Y. 10014

# INTRODUCTION

## TO THE DOVER EDITION

Barely a century ago, in the first decades after the Civil War, the whistle of a steam locomotive was perhaps the most exciting sound to be heard in America. Few other countries have had a railroad history so vital to the national development. The new rail lines in western Europe generally served towns and industrial cities long in existence—in America the railroad often created the towns, filled in the frontier, and made possible the full maturing of an industrial society. The generation after Appomattox was the golden age of railroading. The appearance of *The Car-Builder's Dictionary,* in 1879, came at a time when the future of American railroads indeed seemed bright.

Railroads were booming in America in 1879. That year marked the tenth anniversary of the Golden Spike ceremony of 1869, when the newly completed Union Pacific-Central Pacific had provided the first rail service out to the West Coast. In 1879 the railways of the nation were on the threshold of a decade of record-breaking new construction. More than 70,000 miles of new road were to be built in the decade of the 1880's, an increase which exceeded any other ten-year period in our history.

The recovery from the depression seventies was indicated by the 4,800 miles of new track completed in 1879. The year 1880 saw 6,700 miles built; 1881 saw 9,800 miles completed, a record promptly passed by the 11,500 miles constructed during 1882. Construction slowed a bit in the middle eighties, but in 1887 an all-time high of 12,878 miles was laid in twelve months. For the ten years as a whole, the rate of construction averaged better than 19 miles of new line completed each and every day of the decade. At the end of the eighties only five nations in the world, Germany, Great Britain, France, Russia and Austria-Hungary, had even a tenth of the trackage found in the United States.

In the same years there was also a marked growth and expansion in both railroad employment and total revenue. During the seventies and eighties railroad workers, in both number and influence, ranked high in the labor force of the nation. Between 1870 and 1890 railroad labor more than quadrupled, growing from 163,000 to 749,000 workers. Railroad employees in 1890 accounted for more than three per cent of the gainfully employed in America, and many thousands of additional workers were directly or indirectly dependent upon the industry.

Rail revenue grew more slowly, because of the general price deflation, and particularly because railroad rates and fares declined markedly during the period. Between 1871 and 1879 total rail revenue grew only from $403 million to $529 million, reflecting the general hard times of the decade. Annual gross revenues nearly doubled during the next ten years, and by 1889 stood at a record high of just over a billion dollars.

The first edition of *The Car-Builder's Dictionary* itself illustrates still another facet of the vigorous railroad industry. These were years of rapid technological change for railways, and this volume displays the latest innovations and advances in the art of car building. Priced at two dollars, the dictionary was published by *The Railroad Gazette*, a weekly illustrated journal of railroad news. Matthias N. Forney, who was editor of the *Gazette*, compiled the volume under the sponsorship of the Master Car-Builders' Association.

Forney, who had served an apprenticeship under Ross Winans, was a skilled draftsman and machinist, and had earlier worked for the Baltimore & Ohio, the Illinois Central and the Hinkley Locomotive Works. Forney was also an inventor, and held patents for innovations or improvements in railway seats, furnace doors, signal equipment, steam boilers and interlocking switches. The most important of his 33 patents was one issued in 1866 for an "improved tank locomotive," known as the Forney engine, and designed for suburban service. Five years before the *Dictionary*, in 1874, Forney had written the standard text *Catechism of the Locomotive.*

The years before and after 1879 were indeed years of hectic and active railroad invention. A substantial fraction of the twenty to thirty thousand patents issued annually in the seventies and eighties were railroad-oriented. In the pages of this book, both in the section of "Engravings," and in the concluding advertisements, there are dozens of illustrations of patents issued in the years just after the Civil War.

In these years the variety of railway innovation and technological advance seemed to be almost infinite. During the 1870's changes were being made, in the North at least, toward the adoption of a single standard track gauge of 4 feet 8½ inches. The Grand Trunk of Canada in 1874, and the Delaware, Lackawanna and Western in 1876, shifted to standard gauge. And the six-foot-broad-gauge Erie finally got in step by the early summer of 1880. In the same years many lines were putting down steel rail in the place of iron. By 1880 probably a quarter of all track in the nation was steel, and annual production of the new-type rail had climbed to the million-ton mark.

Standard time, sponsored by the industry, was adopted across the nation by the railroads on November 18, 1883.

Block signaling and a manual interlocking system by this time were permitting improved and safer train control. More powerful locomotives were pulling longer and heavier trains, which often included new types of freight equipment. A few fortunate passengers were able to enjoy steam-heated cars after 1881, and even read by the new electric lights after 1887. By the early eighties more and more companies were installing automatic couplers and air brakes, inventions originally patented a dozen years before.

*The Car-Builder's Dictionary* is of course limited to freight and passenger equipment. The "Dictionary of Terms" found in the first two-fifths of the volume includes more than 2400 notations covering a broad range and spectrum of subjects. In the following section of "Engravings" more than 800 illustrations and figures cover the same general material.

In the section of illustrations and drawings there is far more material on passenger equipment than on freight. After all, one does not find such items as seat hinges, berth springs, towel rods, spittoons, water coolers, lamps or car stoves in the freight equipment of a century ago. This emphasis on passenger facilities was in marked contrast to the railroad revenue dollar in the 1870's and 1880's. In annual dollar revenue during these two decades freight traffic was generally two and a half to three times as large as that produced by the passenger service.

Some relatively new kinds of freight equipment are included in the volume. Shown in the grouping of freight-car bodies is a horizontal tank car, a type of equipment first introduced about a decade earlier. Shortly after the appearance of *The Car-Builder's Dictionary* additional improvements in stock-car design were to be made by Alonzo C. Mather, a young Chicago businessman. Mather became interested in providing a more humane treatment of livestock being shipped to market.

Much of the material described or illustrated in Forney's work is of course common to both freight and passenger equipment. Wheels, axles, trucks, brakes, draw-gear equipment and couplers are all necessary to the entire roster of rolling stock. Such items are found on the car carrying pigs to market, or the smoking car filled with traveling salesmen and drummers. The volume also contains brief sections on horse-drawn streetcars, baggage and freight trucks, hand cars and simple bridge trusses.

A great variety of railway products are presented in the concluding section, "Advertisements." Anvils, brakes, journal bearings, locomotives, refrigerator cars, paper car wheels, narrow-gauge rolling stock, barbwire fencing and padlocks are among the items displayed in the 84-page supplement. There is even some humor included in the ad of a Newark, New Jersey, maker of railroad car varnish. In defining a "misplaced switch" the manufacturer writes: "The schoolboy's notion of a birch rod applied in the rear. The switchman should also remember that the locomotive has a tender behind."

Throughout Forney's volume particular attention is given to two very important technical innovations which were being introduced in these years: the automatic coupler and the air brake. Perhaps a tenth of all the figures and illustrations deal with these two inventions. The seventies and eighties were years in which most forward-thinking railroad men were looking for improvements in the braking and coupling of railroad equipment.

In the early years after the Civil War all trains—fast freights, local mixed trains, even the new mail or express trains—were plagued by a pair of devices, the link-and-pin coupler and the hand brake, which seemed to make all railroad service slow and dangerous. Slowing a train with hand brakes was always hazardous. As larger cars were built the clearances beneath bridges and overpasses were reduced. When the locomotive engineer's whistle for "down brakes" sent the freight brakemen up to the top of the moving cars, the risk to life and limb was the greater if the work was being done in snow, ice or darkness.

The old link-and-pin coupler was just as dangerous. This old-style coupler was so arranged that, in practice at least, the average brakeman could steer the "link" into the socket and drop the "pin" only if he stood between the cars to be coupled. This was so hazardous that train brakemen of that day were often recognized by their crippled hands or missing fingers. When a boomer brakeman was seeking employment, often the yard master or railroad official would be satisfied that the applicant was qualified if he could show a hand with one or two fingers missing.

In the postwar years dozens of inventors were issued hundreds of patents for new or improved couplers. One of these inventors was a Confederate veteran, Major Eli H. Janney. Using a penknife, Janney carved out his first model coupler while working in a dry-goods store near Alexandria, Virginia. Janney's coupler, which he patented in 1868, worked like the hooked fingers of two hands. He improved his device by 1873, and by the late seventies Tom Scott was approving the Janney coupler for use on the passenger cars of the Pennsylvania Railroad. But many railroad presidents were slow to adopt the coupler because of the cost, and in the first years few orders came to the Janney Car Coupling Company.

About the same time a young Union Army veteran, George Westinghouse, was inventing the air brake. The young New Yorker got his idea from French tunnel engineers who were cutting rock with compressed air. He obtained a patent for his brake in 1869, and that same year saw his invention dramatically tested when the new brake saved from destruction a farmer's wagon stalled on a railroad crossing track. But railroad officials were still hard to sell. When the young inventor approached the president of the New York Central, the old Commodore reportedly roared: "Do you pretend to tell me that you could stop trains with wind?" Men like Vanderbilt were hard to convince, but by 1879 the Pennsylvania was using the Westinghouse air brake on its passenger locomotives. And before many more years Federal legislation would require that all trains be equipped with both air brakes and automatic couplers.

Several illustrations of the Janney car coupler in its 1879 version, along with other contemporary couplers, are included in the section of "Engravings." A number of pages are also devoted to the Westinghouse air brake and its use on both locomotives and rolling stock.

The new coupler, the air brake, and the other innovations and technological improvements being introduced in these years, all made possible a marked improvement in the total railroad service. During the seventies and eighties there were drastic reductions made in nearly all railroad rates. The end of each new rate war rarely saw a full return to the earlier, higher rate structure. As a result railroads were obtaining a growing monopoly of domestic transport at the very time that American industry was expanding. In the generation after the Civil War the average American came to rely more and more upon the expanding rail network. Total railroad freight traffic seemed to simply explode in these years. The per capita annual rail freight service increased from 285 ton-miles in 1867 to 1,211 ton-miles by the year 1890. Merchants waiting for a new consignment of notions and groceries, farmers sending their hogs to market, traveling salesmen offering a new product, families moving their household goods to a new home in a distant town—all were patrons of the American railroad.

Clearly the view of American railroading presented in this 1879 edition of *The Car-Builder's Dictionary* is a picture of hope and confidence. The railroads of that day were enjoying a golden age of growth and expansion, an era now long gone. In the 1870's Matthias Forney and his fellow railroaders were serving a more expansive America.

JOHN F. STOVER

# PREFACE.

Ever since the general interchange of cars among different railroads. a great deal of inconvenience, confusion, and delay has been caused to those who build and repair them by the want of common names for the different parts of cars. One part is known by one name at one place and by quite different names at other places; and, what causes still worse confusion, a term often means one thing on one road and quite a different thing on another. A *Draw-bar* is called a "Pull-iron" in one section, a "Shackle-bar" in another, and in some of the Middle and Southern states it is known by the euphonious name of a "Bull-nose." A *Journal-box* in one place means the brass-bearing which rests on, and is exposed to, the friction of the axle-journal; at other places, it means the cast-iron box which incloses the journal and its bearing and holds the lubricating material. Numberless examples of a similar kind might be given. The art of car-building, in fact, has grown more rapidly than the language relating to it. Early in the history of the Master Car-Builders' Association this subject attracted attention, and in 1871 a Committee was appointed to prepare a "Dictionary of Terms used in Car-building." This Committee originally consisted of eight or ten members, who held a number of meetings without accomplishing much, and it soon became apparent that it was too unwieldy to do the work which had been undertaken. It was finally narrowed down to those members of the Association whose names appear on the title page of this book, who were courageous enough to undertake the task of com pleting the work, probably, only because they were then quite ignorant of its magnitude.

The first plan was to give, as far as possible, the names of all the parts of cars and their synonyms in use in different parts of the country. This, it was soon found, would make the book much larger and the vocabulary more cumbersome than seemed desirable, and, at the same time, would rather add to than diminish the existing confusion. The Committee, therefore, determined to confine its labors chiefly to selecting and assigning appropriate terms to those parts and objects which *are in common use*, and which pertain to railroad cars.

It should be noticed, too, that, to supply the want which demanded such a vocabulary, what might be called a double dictionary is needed. Thus, supposing that a car-builder in Chicago received an order for a *Journal-box;* by looking in an alphabetical list of words he could readily find that term and a description and definition of it. But suppose that he wanted, himself, to order such castings from the shop in Albany and did not know their name : it would be impracticable for him to commence at A and look through to Z, or until he found the proper term to designate that part. It was therefore necessary, in a dictionary of this kind, to provide the most copious illustrations and arrange them in some systematic way so that a person could find a representation of any part of a car he might have in mind, and from that illustration find the name. The manner in which this want has been met is fully described in the DIRECTIONS FOR USING THE DICTIONARY which follow the preface.

The system of cross-references employed in " Knight's Mechanical Dictionary" has also been adopted here. Thus, under the term *Axle* there are references to *" master car-builders' standard axle, muley axle, street-car axle,"* etc. Under the word *Bar* a list of various kinds of bars, such as " *arch-bar, draw-bar, guide-bar,*" etc., is given. This will often aid very materially in finding terms.

Of the defects of the book, and its incompleteness, no one can be so well informed as the Committee who are its sponsors. Several years' time would be too little to devote to the compilation of such a dictionary, if completeness were aimed at ; and if more care could have been given to the preparation of the material in the book, it could have been confined within considerably smaller limits, but at the same time more thorough investigation would have increased the vocabulary very much in other directions. In fact, there is hardly a limit to the scope which such a book might cover. It was at one time intended to include the names of all the different materials used in car-building, and a good deal of data was collected for that purpose ; but it was found that to do so would involve more time and labor than the Committee could devote to it, and therefore that part of the work had to be omitted.

Of the philological qualifications of the Committee for their work, it perhaps need only be said, to disarm criticism, that none of its members knows any other language than the one he inherited, and that very imperfectly. Two of them are practical car-builders, one of them in charge of the cars of one of the largest and most fully equipped roads in the country ; and the compiler, during all the time that the book was in preparation, was actively engaged in editing a weekly technical paper. The only time any of the members of the Committee could give to the work was that which could be eked out from his other duties. They are, therefore, compelled to submit their work to the public, knowing its imperfection and how much it might be improved if the requisite labor could be devoted to it. They trust, however, it will prove useful in establishing a common language where now there is well nigh a Babel of confusion.

One word more must be added to this long preface. Possibly some persons may be found who will object to the advertisements appended to the end of the book. The reason for these is that the cost of preparing the engravings was so great that no publisher would have undertaken to issue the book for the proceeds of its sale alone, and the treasury of the Car-Builders' Association was empty. In this condition of things *The Railroad Gazette* proposed to undertake the publication of the Dictionary at its own expense, if the Car-Builders' Association would give the privilege of publishing the advertisements. The proposition was accepted, and it is thought that readers and users of the book will not find the advertisements any detriment to its usefulness, but rather an advantage.

# DIRECTIONS

*For Using the Car-builder's Dictionary.*

When it is desired to find the meaning of a given word or term, refer to it in the alphabetical list printed on tinted paper, where a definition or explanation, similar to those contained in ordinary dictionaries, and a reference to some engraving illustrating the object—if it is capable of such illustration—will usually be found.

To find the name of a car or part of a car, let the reader examine the list of the different classes of engravings, in the index which follows these directions, until he finds the class to which the object he is looking for belongs. By referring to the engravings included in that class, he will usually find a representation of the object. If the engraving is of a single object, its name will be found underneath, but if it consists of several or many parts, these will each be numbered, and a list of the names of the parts arranged consecutively by their numbers is given at the beginning of the class to which the engraving belongs. If the list is not on the same page, a running line over the engraving usually refers to the page on which it can be found.

Thus, suppose a reader wants the name of the longitudinal timbers under the floor of a freight car nearest the centre. These form part of a freight-car body. He therefore refers to "Freight-car Bodies" in the index, and finds that they are represented in figs. 55–87. In looking over these, it will be seen that the timbers referred to are represented in the plan, fig. 57, and the end view, fig. 58, and are numbered **4.** The running line on top reads, "*For list of names of the parts designated by the numbers in the engravings, see page* 216." Turning to 216, he will learn that the name given to the parts numbered **4** is " *Centre Floor-timbers.*" If he wants the name of the piece of metal which rests on top of the journal of an axle and resists its wear, he finds "Axles, Journal-boxes, etc.," and refers to figs. 138 to 153. In figs. 138 and 139 the part he is looking for is numbered **7,** and in the list on page 278 its name is given as "*Journal-bearing.*" If the name of the attachment to car window-sashes for holding them up is sought, the reader would know that it belongs to the class designated "Window-furnishings," in the following index. By looking over the engravings representing this class of objects, figs. 308 and 309, which represent this attachment, would soon be found, with its name, " *Window-latches,*" in the title below. The several parts of a window-latch are also numbered in the engravings, but as there are so few of them, the list is given under the engraving.

Terms can also be found, if the general word under which it is classed is known, by referring to the latter in the alphabetical list. Thus, to find the name of the bearing which supports a car-body on each side of the king-bolt of a truck, look under " Bearing," and in the list will be found " *Truck Side-bearing.*" In a similar way, other terms may often be found from these cross references.

It must be remembered, though, that this book does not contain all the terms used by car-builders to designate the parts of cars. If it did, it would be many times its present size. All that was aimed at, in compiling it, was to assign appropriate names to the appliances and to the parts of cars in *common use.*

# INDEX.

xvii

# AN INDEX TO ADVERTISEMENTS

*In the added pages of the Car-builder's Dictionary.*

# A DICTIONARY OF TERMS

USED IN

## CAR-BUILDING.

**Adjustable-globe Lamp.** A lamp with a globe-chimney, which can be raised or lowered so as to adjust its position to suit the height of the globe. See fig. 475.

**Air-brake.** A system of continuous brakes which are applied and operated by compressed air. The air is compressed by some form of pump on the locomotive, and is conveyed, by pipes and flexible hose between the cars, to cylinders and pistons under each car, by which the pressure is transmitted to the brake levers, and thence to the brake-shoes. See *Westinghouse Air-brake. Westinghouse Automatic Air-brake. Loughridge Air-brake.*

**Air-cylinder,** *for Engine and Air-pump of Westinghouse Brake.* A hollow cast-iron cylinder, which is accurately bored out on the inside to receive a piston, the action of which compresses the air required to operate the brakes. The piston in the air-cylinder is connected with and is worked by the piston in the steam-cylinder. See **5**, figs. 664, 665, and fig. 669.

**Air-cylinder Head,** *for Engine and Air-pump for Westinghouse Brake.* A cast-iron cover for the lower end of

the air-cylinder of an air-pump for a Westinghouse Brake. See **6**, figs. 664, 665, and fig. 670.

**Air-gauge,** *for Westinghouse Brake.* An instrument for indicating the pressure of air in the reservoir of a Westinghouse Brake. It is similar to an ordinary steam-pressure gauge. See fig. 738.

**Air-piston,** *for Air-pump of Westinghouse Brake.* An arrangement of a cast-iron disk, with packing rings, etc., made so as to fit air tight and work up and down in the air-cylinder of a pump for a Westinghouse Brake. The air-pistons and steam-pistons of engines and air-pumps are generally alike in size and construction. See **8**, fig. 665 and fig. 672.

**Air-piston Head,** *for Air-pump of a Westinghouse Brake.* A short cast-iron solid cylinder or disk, with grooves turned in the edge to receive packing-rings, and which forms the main portion of a piston of an air-pump of a Westinghouse Brake. Same as **7'**, fig. 665.

**Air-pump and Engine complete,** *for Westinghouse Brake.* See *Engine and Air-Pump.*

**Air-strainer,** *of Air-pump for Westinghouse Brake.* A funnel-shaped mouth-piece on the end of the air-receiving pipe, with a wire netting, or a perforated plate over its mouth to exclude dirt, insects, etc., from the pump. See **5,** fig. 655 and fig. 698.

**Aisle.** A longitudinal passage way through a passenger car, between the seats. See figs. 216 and 220.

**Aisle Seat-end.** The end or arm of a transverse seat of a passenger car next the aisle. See **123,** figs. 215–229 ; **2,** fig. 400 and **3,** fig. 401. See also *Wall Seat-end.*

**Alcove.** A recess. See *Faucet-alcove. Lamp-alcove. Water-alcove.*

**Alcove Cup-holder.** A metal receptacle in a faucet-alcove to hold a drinking-cup or tumbler. See **5,** fig. 426.

**Alcove-faucet.** A faucet placed in a water-alcove, and which is connected with a water-cooler, from which water may be drawn for drinking. See **3,** fig. 426.

**Alcove-front.** See *Water-alcove Front.*

**Alcove-lamp.** A lamp placed in a recess in the side of a car. Also called a *Panel-lamp,* as it is sometimes covered by a panel. They are used chiefly in sleeping-cars. See **27,** fig. 492.

**Alcove-lamp Reflector.** A plate with a polished surface placed at the side or back of an alcove-lamp, to reflect the light into the car. See **25,** fig. 492.

**Alcove-pan or Bottom.** See *Water Alcove-pan or Bottom.*

**Anti-clinker Car-heater.** See *Spear Anti-clinker Car-heater.*

**Anti-clinker Grate.** A stove grate placed below the fire-pot so as to leave an annular opening between the two through which the clinkers can be raked out from the fire. See **18,** fig. 554.

**Apron.** See *Door-apron. Roof-apron.*

**Arbor.** See *Door-latch Arbor.*

**Arch.** See *Truss-arch.*

**Arch-bar.** A bent wrought-iron bar which forms the compression member of a truss of an iron side-frame of a truck. See **14,** figs. 95–114.
See *Auxiliary Arch-bar.*    *Centre-bearing Inverted-Centre-bearing Arch-bar.*    *arch-bar.*
*Inverted Arch-bar.*

**Arched Roof.** A roof, the surface of which is of an arched or curved form. See figs. 58 and 59.

**Arm.** See *Berth-arm.*    *Seat-back Arm.*
*Lamp-arm.*    *Striker-arm.*
*Seat-arm.*    *Top-arm.*

**Arm-cap.** A metal-plate wooden-cap, or piece of upholstery with which the top of a seat-end, arm-rest or chair-arm is covered and intended to afford a comfortable rest for the arms of passengers. See **16,** fig. 401 and fig. 410.

**Armor.** See *Brake-hose Armor.*

**Armored Brake-hose.** Brake-hose covered with a woven wire fabric, to protect it from injury or abrasion. See fig. 726.

**Arm-pivot.** See *Seat-back Arm-pivot.*

**Arm-plate.** See *Seat-back Arm-plate.*

**Arm-rest.** A wooden or metal bar or ledge attached to the side of a car for passengers to rest their arms on. See, also, *Seat-back Arm-rest.* See **26**, fig. 298; **39**, fig. 299.

**Ash-pit.** The space into which the ashes of a stove or heater fall. See **1**, fig. 544; **13**, fig. 554.

**Ash-pit,** *for a Baker Heater.* An annular iron casting or plate which rests on top of the bottom plate, and forms a chamber for receiving the ashes in a Baker heater. See **2**, fig. 581 and fig. 583.

**Ash-pit Base,** *for a Spear Heater.* A cast-iron case or vessel upon which the fire-pot rests, and which forms the ash-pit or receptacle for the ashes. See **13**, fig. 554, and fig. 568.

**Ash-pit Door,** *for a Baker Heater.* A small sheet-iron plate with a suitable handle and which forms a door for an ash-pit of a Baker heater. See fig. 588.

**Ash-pit Door,** *for a Spear Heater.* One of a pair or doors for closing the opening leading to an ash-pit base. See **24**, figs. 551–553 and fig. 565.

**Ash-pit Door-handle,** *for a Baker Heater.* A wrought-iron bar, bent so as to form a handle for an ash-pit door, to which it is riveted. See fig. 598.

**Ash-pit Front,** *for a Spear Heater.* A cast-iron plate which covers the opening in the front of an ash-pit base, and which has suitable doors attached, for admitting air to the fire and for removing the ashes. See **23**, figs. 551, –553 and fig. 565.

**Atmospheric-brake.** See *Air-brake.*

**Automatic Air-brake.** See *Westinghouse Automatic Air-brake.*

**Automatic Lubricator,** *for Steam-pump of Westinghouse Brake.* A metal cup with automatic feeding apparatus, attached to the steam-cylinder of a Westinghouse air-pump for lubricating its piston. See fig. 741.

**Automatic Ventilator.** A ventilator which is self-adjusting, so as to exhaust air from a car if the train runs in either direction. See figs. 347 and 348.

**Auxiliary Arch-bar.** A wrought-iron bar attached to the under side of the journal-boxes, and which forms the lower member of an iron truck side-frame. In some cases such arch-bars are made with transverse pieces which extend across from one frame to the other under the transoms as shown at **16**, figs. 108–111.

**Auxiliary Buffer-spring.** A spring placed back of a draw-spring to give greater resistance to compression on the draw-bar in buffing. See **6**, figs. 257 and 259.

**Auxiliary Draw-bar Follower-plates.** Iron plates which bear against the ends of an auxiliary buffer-spring. One plate of this kind bears against each end of the auxiliary buffer spring. Part of the pressure on the draw-bar is transmitted to the auxiliary spring by these plates. See 15, figs. 257 and 259.

**Auxiliary Reservoir,** *for Westinghouse Automatic Air-brake.* A cylindrical reservoir made of sheet iron, which is attached to the under side of a car or tender to hold a supply of compressed air to operate the brakes of that car. See 1, figs 661 and 663.

**Auxiliary Reservoir-bands,** *for Westinghouse Automatic Brake.* Iron bands by which the auxiliary reservoir is attached to the under side of a car. See 21, fig. 661.

**Auxiliary Reservoir-beams,** *for Westinghouse Automatic Brake.* Short wooden timbers, bolted to the under side of the longitudinal floor-timbers of a car, and to which the auxiliary reservoir is attached. See 22, figs. 661 and 663.

**Auxiliary-reservoir Nipple,** *for Westinghouse Automatic Brake.* A short pipe by which the triple valve is connected with the auxiliary reservoir. See 23, fig. 661.

**Axle.** See *Car-axle.*
  *Hammered Axle.*    *Master Car-builders'*
              *Standard Axle.*

  *Muley-axle.*       *Standard Car-axle.*
  *Rolled Axle.*      *Street-car Axle.*

**Axle-box.** A *Journal-box,* which see.

**Axle-collar.** A rim or enlargement on the end of a car-axle, which takes the end thrust of the journal-bearing. Sometimes called a *button.* See 5, fig. 143.

**Axle-packing.** A *Dust-guard,* which see. The waste and oil or grease or *journal-packing* is often called *axle-packing.*

**Axle Safety-bearing.** A bar of iron bent into a shape resembling somewhat an inverted letter ∩, and bolted to a safety-beam of a truck above an axle so as to act as a bearing for the latter in case it should break. See 54, figs. 115, 118 and 120.

**Axle-safety-bearing Thimbles.** Cast-iron thimbles which serve the purpose of distance pieces for attaching a safety-strap to a safety-beam. They are used in place of safety-beam blocks. See 56, figs 118, 120 and 123.

**Axle Safety-strap.** A bar of iron attached to a safety-beam of a truck, underneath an axle, so as to hold it in its place and prevent accident in case of the breakage of the latter. See 55, figs 106, 115, 118, 120, 123, 128 and 129.

**Axle-seat.** The hole in a car-wheel which receives the axle. More properly, it is the inside surface of this hole which comes in contact with the axle, and not the hole itself.

**Back.** See *Seat-back. Slat Seat-back.*

**Back-arm.** See *Seat-back Arm.*

**Back Cylinder-head,** *for Westinghouse Car-brake.* A circular cast-iron plate or cover for the end of a brake cylinder and which has an opening in the centre through which the piston-rod works. See **4,** figs. 729 and 730. For convenience of designation, the end of the cylinder opposite to the piston-rod is called the front end, and that adjoining the piston-rod the back end.

**Back Cylinder-head,** *for Westinghouse Tender-brake.* Same as above for cylinder of tender-brake. See **4,** figs. 727 and 728.

**Back Seat-bottom Rail.** A horizontal wooden strip at the back edge of a longitudinal seat, to which a wooden seat-bottom is attached. See **38,** fig. 752. See also *Front Seat-bottom rail.*

**Back Seat-rail.** A longitudinal strip of wood which extends along the back edge of the seats of street-cars and is fastened to the window-posts. See **39,** fig. 752.

**Baggage Barrow-truck.** A vehicle which runs on two wheels, and with a long sloping or curved back for carrying baggage and moving it by hand about railroad stations. See figs. 53 and 54.

**Baggage-car.** A car for carrying the baggage of passengers on railroads. Such cars are therefore adapted to carrying heavy loads at high speeds in passenger trains.

See figs. 6, 7 and 8. Also see *Combined Baggage and Express or Mail Car, Push Baggage-car.*

**Baggage-truck.** See *Baggage Barrow-truck,* fig. 53 and 54. *Baggage Wagon-truck,* fig. 52.

**Baggage Wagon-truck.** A four-wheeled vehicle with a suitable frame or rack for carrying baggage, and used for moving the latter by hand about railroad stations. See fig. 52.

**Baker Car-heater.** A stove invented and patented by Mr. Wm. C. Baker for warming cars. It is arranged so as to heat water in a coil of pipe in the inside of the stove, and cause it to circulate through a series of pipes laid near the floor of the car. See figs. 580 and 581.

**Ball.** See *Safety-valve Ball for Baker Car-heater.*

**Band.** See *Auxiliary Reservoir-band.*    *Guard-band.*
*Belt-rail Band.*    *Platform-timber Band.*
*Corner-band.*    *Seat-back Band.*
*Door-guard Band.*    *Spring-band.*
   *Tank-band.*

**Bar.** See *Body-bolster Compression-bar.*    *Center - bearing Arch-bar.*
*Body-bolster Tension-bar.*    *Center-bearing Inverted Arch-bar.*
*Bolt Draw-bar.*    *Compression Bar.*
*Buffer-bar.*    *Cross-bar.*

| | |
|---|---|
| *Draw-bar.* | *Rocking-bar.* |
| *Draw-timber Tie-bar.* | *Shackle-bar.* |
| *Equalizing-bar.* | *Side-bearing Arch-bar.* |
| *Grate-bar.* | *Tension-bar.* |
| *Guide-bar.* | *Tie-bar.* |
| *Pedestal Tie-bar.* | *Transom Tie-bar.* |

*Truck-bolster Guide-bar.*

**Bar-lift.** See *Window Bar-lift.*

**Barrel Door-bolt.** A door-bolt made of a round metal bar and held on its slide in a round tube or "*barrel.*" It is constructed so that when it is either engaged or disengaged from its keeper, it can be turned by a short lever or knob, and held in either position by suitable stops. See fig. 516.

**Barrel Seat-lock.** A lock contained in a cylindrical case or barrel, which is attached to a seat-end to prevent the seat from being reversed. See fig. 422.

**Barrow-truck.** This term has been adopted to designate two-wheeled vehicles used about railroads for moving freight and baggage by hand. See *Freight Barrow-truck*, fig. 51, and *Baggage Barrow-truck*, figs. 53 and 54.

**Base.** See *Ash-pit Base. Revolving-chair-stand Base. Window-moulding Base.*

**Base-plate,** *for a Spear Heater.* A cast-iron cylindrical ring, which forms the bottom part of the heater. It has suitable openings through which cold air enters or warmed air escapes, and other openings with doors to admit air to the fire and remove the ashes from the ash-pit. See **21**, figs. 550–554, and figs. 558 and 573.

**Base-plate Screen,** *for a Spear Heater.* A perforated cast-iron plate or grating for covering the air opening of a base-plate. See fig. 569.

**Base-washer,** *for Platform-post.* A metal ring or plate at the bottom of a platform-rail post of a passenger or street-car, and which forms a bearing for the post on the plat-form timber. See **40**, figs. 215, 217, 219, 223 and 228 ; **109**, figs. 750, 751 and 753.

**Basin.** A hollow vessel made of porcelain or metal, and in cars usually fixed in a suitable stand with pipes and other attachments for filling it with water and emptying it. Such basins are used as lavatories in sleeping and other passenger cars. See **5**, fig. 424.

**Basin-chain.** A chain by which a basin-plug is fastened to the wash-stand. See **4**, fig. 383.

**Basin-chain Holder.** A staple or stanchion by which a basin-plug and chain are fastened to a wash-stand. See **3**, fig. 383.

**Basin-couplings.** A socket and ring or nut for attaching a pipe to the bottom of a wash-basin. See fig. 384.

**Basin-plug.** A plug or stopper for closing the opening in the bottom of fixed or stationary wash-basins. See **5**, fig. 383.

**Basket-rack.** A frame or receptacle made of metal rods or a combination of rods and wire netting for holding parcels or other light articles. Such *racks* are attached to the sides of passenger cars above the heads of the passengers, so as to be out of the way. See **145**, figs. 215, 218, and fig. 430.

**Basket-rack Bracket.** A light metal or wooden support for the end or centre of a basket-rack. See **1**, fig. 430.

**Basket-rack Netting.** Wire netting with very large meshes which forms part of a basket-rack for holding small articles. See **2**, fig. 430.

**Basket-rack Rod.** A small round metal bar which is attached to brackets and forms the main portion of a basket-rack and to which the netting, when it is used, is fastened. See **3**, fig. 430.

**Basket-rack Tip.** An ornamental knob or boss attached to the end of a basket-rack rod. See **4**, fig. 430.

**Batten.** " A piece of board or scantling of a few inches in breadth."—*Webster*.

**Beam.** " The term *Beam* is generally applied to any piece of material of considerable scantling, whether subject to transverse strain or not ; as for example, ' Collar-beam,' ' Tie-beam,' ' Bressummer-beam,' the two former being subject to longitudinal strains of compression and tension respectively, and the latter to transverse strain."—*Stoney*.

1. " Any large piece of timber, large in proportion to its thickness, and squared or hewed for use."—*Webster*.

2. A bar of metal of similar proportions is also called a *beam*.

3. " A bar supported at two points and loaded in a direction perpendicular or oblique to its length is called a *beam*."—*Rankine*.

By analogy, the term has of late years come to be applied to similar pieces or bars of iron. Thus we have I-*beams*, and *deck-beams* made out of iron, to take the place of wooden beams in buildings. The term is also used to designate such things as the *beam* of a balance or scales, a *plow-beam*, the *walking-beam* of a steam-engine, *brake-beam*, etc.

| See *Auxiliary-reservoir* | *Middle Safety-beam.* |
| *Beam.* | *Needle-beam.* |
| *Brake-beam.* | *Platform-truss Beam.* |
| *Buffer-beam,* | *Safety-beam.* |
| *Buffer-spring Beam.* | *Spring-beam.* |
| *Centre-beam.* | *Suspender-beam.* |
| *Compression-beam.* | *Swing-beam.* |
| *Drop-door Beam.* | *Truss-beam.* |
| *Floor-beam.* | *Trussed Brake-beam.* |

**Bearing.** That which supports or rests on something, and is in contact with it. Thus a block or stone on which the end of a timber rests is called a *bearing* The metal block or bushing in contact with a journal is called a *bearing*.

   See *Axle Safety-bearing.*    *Master Car-builders'*
   *Body Truss-rod Bearing.*      *Standard Journal-bear-*
   *Brake-hanger Bearing.*      *ing.*
   *Brake-shaft Bearing.*     *Rocker-bearing.*
   *Centre-bearing.*     *Rocker Side-bearing.*
   *Crank-shaft Bearing.*    *Safety-beam Truss-rod*
   *Cup Side-bearing.*      *Bearing.*
   *Dust-guard Bearing.*    *Side-bearing.*
   *Half-elliptic-spring Bear-*  *Spring-plank Bearing.*
    *ing.*       *Stop Journal-bearing.*
   *Hopkins' Journal - bear-*  *Stop - key Journal - bear-*
    *ing.*        *ing.*
   *Journal-bearing.*    *Swing-hanger-pivot Bear-*
   *Lead-lined Journal-bear-*   *ing.*
    *ing.*       *Truck - bolster Truss - rod*
   *Lever-shaft Bearing.*    *Bearing.*
   *Lower Brake-shaft Bear-*  *Truck Side-bearing.*
    *ing.*       *Truss-rod Bearing.*
        *Upper Brake-shaft Bearing.*

**Bearing-block.**  See *Transverse Bearing-block.*

**Bell.**  See *Recording-bell. Signal-bell. Smoke Bell.*

**Bell-cord.**  A rope, one end of which is attached to a signal-bell on the engine, and which extends along the tops of the cars the whole length of the train, and is used for signaling to the locomotive runner.  On freight trains, it is placed on the outside, and on top of the roofs of the cars, but in passenger trains it is attached to the rafters or purlins by suitable supports, on the inside of the cars. On passenger trains, the *bell-cord* is made of lengths equal to that of each car, and is fastened together with suitable couplings.  Bell-cord is made of flax, hemp and sometimes of leather, and is known by the following names in trade : *Bell-cord, brass-wire covered ; Bell-cord, fancy braided ; Bell-cord, Flaxen ; Bell-cord, Italian hemp ; Bell-cord, solid leather.*

**Bell-cord, Bevelled-bushing.**  A thimble for lining a hole in an inclined surface through which a bell-cord passes. See fig. 456.

**Bell-cord Bushing.**  A thimble for lining a hole through which a bell-cord passes.  See figs 454–456.

**Bell-cord Bushing,** *with Pulley.*  A bell-cord bushing with a sheave or pulley attached, over which the bell-cord runs.  See fig. 455.

**Bell-cord Coupling.**  A hook which is attached to the end of a bell-cord, for the purpose of connecting it to the end of another cord having a similar hook.  See fig. 467.

**Bell-cord Double Strap-hanger.**  A bell-cord strap-hanger with two straps as shown in fig. 453.

**Bell-cord End-hook.**  A metal hook with a screw-shank by which it is attached to the end of a car.  The hook is used to fasten the end of a bell-cord to the last car and thus hold it in its place, and prevent it from being drawn out of its guides. See fig. 469.

**Bell-cord Fixed-hanger.** A rigid metal bar or bracket attached to the ceiling of a car, and by which a bell-cord is suspended from the roof. See fig. 450.

**Bell-cord Guide.** A metal eye or ring attached to the roof or ceiling of a car, or to the end of a bell-cord hanger, and by which a bell-cord is carried or conducted. See figs. 450–465.

**Bell-cord Guide,** *for Strap Hanger.* A bell-cord guide which is attached to the end of a strap-hanger. See **1**, fig. 452.

**Bell-cord Guide,** *with centre Pulley.* A bell-cord guide made in the shape of a ring or loop, with a pulley in the centre. See fig. 465.

**Bell-cord Guide,** *with Flange.* A bell-cord guide, with one or more flanges or lugs attached to it, by which it is fastened to the ceiling of a car, usually with screws. See fig. 457.

**Bell-cord Guide,** *with Flange and Pulley.* A bell-cord guide with a pulley for carrying a bell-cord, and with one or more flanges or lugs by which it is fastened to the ceiling of a car, usually with screws.

**Bell-cord Guide,** *with Flange and side Pulley.* A bell-cord guide with a flange and a pulley on one side to conduct a bell rope in an oblique line. See fig. 459.

**Bell-cord Guide,** *with four Pulleys.* A bell-cord guide with pulleys above and below and on each side of the cord. They are used when a bell-cord must be carried in oblique line. See fig. 461.

**Bell-cord Guide,** *with Pulley.* A bell-cord guide with a sheave or pulley attached to it, over which the bell-cord runs. See figs. 458–461, 463–465.

**Bell-cord Guide,** *with Pulley, for Strap-hanger.* A bell-cord guide which is attached to a strap-hanger, and has a pulley on which the bell-cord runs. See **4**, figs. 451 and 453.

**Bell-cord Guide,** *with Screw.* A bell-cord guide to which a screw is attached and by which the former is fastened to the ceiling of a car. See fig. 462.

**Bell-cord Guide,** *with Screw and Pulley.* A bell-cord guide with a pulley on which the bell-cord runs, and with a screw attached for fastening it to the ceiling of a car. See fig. 463.

**Bell-cord Guide,** *with side Pulley and Flange.* A bell-cord guide, which has flanges by which it is attached to the car, and a pulley on the side. See fig. 459.

**Bell-cord Guide,** *with side Pulley and Screw-top.* A bell-cord guide which has a screw top. by which it is attached to the car, and a pulley on the side. See fig. 464.

**Bell-cord Guide,** *with two Pulleys, top and bottom.* A bell-cord guide with a pulley above and below the rope, for the latter to run on. See fig. 460.

**Bell-cord-guide Washer.** An ornamental washer for making a finish for a bell-cord guide where it is attached to a car roof. See fig. 466.

**Bell-cord Hanger.** A metal bar or bracket, or a strap made of leather or some textile material, and attached to the ceiling of a car, and by which a bell-cord is suspended from the roof of a car. See figs. 450-453; also, *Bell-cord Fixed-hanger. Bell-cord Strap-hanger.*

**Bell-cord Hanger Screw-top.** A screw attached to a metal clip for fastening a bell-cord hanger to the ceiling of a car. It is screwed into one of the rafters and the bell-cord hanger is fastened in the clip with screws or rivets. See 3, fig. 452.

**Bell-cord Pulley or Sheave.** A wheel in a bell-cord guide over which a bell-cord runs. See 1, figs. 451, 453, 455, 458, 459, 463, 464 and 465.

**Bell-cord Sheave.** A *Bell-cord Pulley,* which see.

**Bell-cord Splice.** A metal coupling with right and left-hand screws for splicing the ends of a broken bell-cord. See fig. 468.

**Bell-cord Strap.** The narrow piece of leather, woven or flexible metallic fabric, of a bell-cord strap-hanger, by which a bell-cord is suspended. See 2, figs. 451-453.

**Bell-cord Strap-hanger.** A support made of leather, or some textile material which is attached by a screw-top, flanges, or brackets to the ceiling of a car, and by which a bell-cord is suspended from the roof. See figs. 451-453.

**Bell-cord Strap-hanger Bracket.** A metal bracket which is attached to the ceiling of a car, and with a suitable clip to which the upper end of a strap-hanger is fastened. See 3, figs. 451 and 453.

**Bell-cord Strap-hanger Screw-top.** A metal clip which holds the upper end of a strap-hanger, and which is fastened to the ceiling of a car by a screw attached to the clip. See 3, fig. 452.

**Bell-cord Thimble.** A *Bell-cord Bushing,* which see.

**Bell-crank,** *for Hand-car.* A short iron crank attached to the shaft which forms the fulcrum of the levers of a hand-car. It is connected by a rod with another crank, which is geared into one of the axles of the car. The bell-crank has a reciprocating motion, whereas the other crank revolves. See 23, figs. 773 and 775.

**Bell-punch.** An instrument for punching a hole on a recording slip of paper or tickets so as to register the fares collected by a conductor. The instrument has a bell attached which is rung every time a fare is recorded by punching the paper or ticket. The bell is intended to indicate or announce to the passengers that the conductor has recorded the fares collected. These instruments are made in a variety of forms.

**Bell-rope.** A *Bell-cord*, which see.

**Bell-strap.** A leather strap which extends along the under side of the rafters, from a signal bell on one end of a street-car over the platform to one on the other end. The strap is used by the conductor on the rear platform to ring the bell in front and thus signal to the driver, and by the driver in front to signal to the conductor. See **98**, fig. 750.

**Bell-strap Bracket.** A *Bell-strap Guide*, which see.

**Bell-strap Guide.** A metal loop or bracket attached to the ceiling of a street car for carrying a signal-strap. See **99**, figs. 750 and 752, and figs. 754 and 755.

**Bell-strap Guide**, *with Roller.* A metal loop or eye with a roller attached which carries a signal-strap. See fig. 757.

**Bell-strap Guide**, *with Screw-end.* A bell-strap guide with a screw attached to it by which it is fastened to the car. See fig. 756.

**Belt.** See *Belt-rail*.

**Belt-rail.** A strip of wood on the outside of a passenger or street-car frame below the windows extending the whole length of the car-body and attached to each post. See **65**, figs. 215–226, and **19**, fig. 752. Also, *Upper Belt-rail*.

**Belt-rail Band.** An iron band on the outside of a belt-rail of street-cars, and which covers the joint of the latter with the panel. It extends around each corner of the car to the door posts. See **20**, figs. 750 and 753.

**Belt-rail Cap.** A thin strip of wood nailed to the top of a belt-rail, and which forms a seat for the window sill. See **81**, figs. 225 and 226.

**Bend**, *for iron pipes.* A short cast or malleable iron tube of **U** shape for uniting the ends of two wrought-iron pipes. The latter are screwed into the casting. See figs. 617 and 618. Also, *Close-return Bend. Open-return Bend. Return Bend.*

**Berth.** A bed in a sleeping-car. The term is also used to designate the shelf or support on which a sleeping-car bed rests. Usually there are two such beds in the space occupied by two double seats which is called a section. The lower berth is made upon the seats as shown at **1, 1**, figs. 296 and 297, and the upper one on a shelf, **2, 2**, which can be raised or folded up out of the way in day time, as shown at **3, 3**. See *Lower berth. Upper-berth.*

**Berth-arm.** A *Berth-brace*, which see.

**Berth-bolt.** See *Berth-latch Bolt.*

**Berth-brace.** A metal rod, chain or wire rope attached to the side and near the top of a sleeping-car, and which extends down diagonally and is fastened at the other end near the outer edge of a berth, which is supported by the brace. When a metal rod is used, it usually has a joint so that it can fold up like an ordinary two-feet rule, when the berth is raised up, See **4**, figs. 296 and 297.

**Berth-brace Eye.** A metal plate with suitable lugs for fastening the brace to the top of the car, or to the berth. The brace is attached to the lugs by a pin, and the plate is screwed fast either to the side or roof of the car or to the berth. The former is called a *Berth-brace Upper-eye*, and the latter a *Berth-brace Lower-eye*. See **5**, fig. 297.

**Berth-bracket.** A bracket on which an upper-berth of a sleeping-car rests when lowered and the bed is made and in use. See fig. 356.

**Berth-chain.** A chain by which an upper sleeping-car berth is supported when it is lowered. The chain is usually wound on a spiral spring-case by which the weight of the berth is counter-balanced. See **6**, fig. 298.

**Berth-chain Pulley.** A pulley attached to the roof of a sleeping-car, and over which a berth-chain runs. See **7**, fig. 298.

**Berth-curtain.** A cloth of some kind of textile material hung in front of a sleeping-car section to hide the occupants from sight. See **13**, fig. 298.

**Berth-curtain Hook.** A metal hook attached to a berth-curtain of a sleeping-car, and by which the latter is hung on a rod above the berths. Such hooks are usually covered with leather or other soft material to prevent them from rattling on the metal rod on which they are hung. See fig. 374.

**Berth-curtain Rod.** A rod or bar usually made of metal tubing, fastened above a section of a sleeping-car and to which a berth-curtain is hung. See **14**, figs. 296–298.

**Berth Curtain-rod Bracket.** A metal bracket attached to the side of the clear-story of a sleeping-car, and which forms a support for a berth-curtain rod. Such brackets often have a coat and hat hook attached to them. See **15**, figs. 296–298 and fig. 371.

**Berth Curtain-rod Coupling.** A fastening by which a berth-curtain rod of a sleeping-car is secured to a bracket. It usually consists of a bolt or screw. See **1**, fig. 371.

**Berth Curtain-rod Socket.** A metal flanged ring which is fastened to some part of a sleeping-car, and which forms the attachment for a berth-curtain rod. See fig. 373.

**Berth Curtain-rod Tip.** A metal ornament at the end of a berth curtain-rod. See fig. 372.

**Berth-handle.** A *Berth-latch Handle*, which see.

**Berth Head-board.** A light partition which separates one berth in a sleeping-car from that next to it. See **16**, figs. 296–298.

**Berth-hinge.** A hinge or joint by which the back edge

of an upper berth of a sleeping-car is attached to the side of a car, and on which the berth turns. See figs. 351 and 352. See *Loose Berth-hinge. Fast Berth-hinge.*

**Berth-hinge Bushing.** A hollow metal socket which forms a bearing on which the spindle of a loose berth-hinge of a sleeping-car works. See fig. 353.

**Berth-latch.** A spring bolt for holding the upper berth of a sleeping-car up in its place when not in use. See figs. 357 and 358.

**Berth-latch Bolt.** The bar or pin of a berth-latch which engages in a corresponding catch, plate or keeper, and which holds the berth up. See fig. 358.

**Berth-latch Face-plate.** A metal plate attached to the under side of a berth with a suitable hole or bearing in which the spindle of a berth-latch works. See **1**, fig. 357.

**Berth-latch Handle.** A projecting metal bar or knob which is connected with a berth-latch bolt and of convenient form to take hold of, and by which the latch is disengaged from its catch. See **12**, fig. 296 ; fig. 357.

**Berth-latch Keeper.** A metal plate attached to a part of of sleeping-car either above or on the side of an upper-berth, and which forms a catch in which a berth-latch bolt engages, and which holds up the berth. See fig. 359.

**Berth-latch Shell.** A metal covering made in the form of a sea shell for covering and protecting the handle of a berth-latch in a sleeping-car.

**Berth-lock.** A *Berth-latch*, which see.

**Berth-numbers.** Figures or numbers, usually made of metal or porcelain, for numbering the berths or sections of sleeping-cars. See fig. 360.

**Berth-rest.**—See *Upper-berth Rest.*

**Berth Safety-rope.** A wire rope which is attached to an upper-berth of a sleeping-car, by one end, and to the seat under it by the other, so as to prevent the berth from closing up in case of an accident if the car should overturn. See **11**, figs. 296–298.

**Berth Safety-rope Fastener.** A metal lug which is fastened to the upper-berth of a sleeping-car, and to which one end of a safety-rope is attached. See fig. 363.

**Berth Safety-rope Holder.** A metal catch attached to a seat-frame or other part of a sleeping-car, to which a safety-rope is fastened so as to hold the upper-berth in its place in case of an accident, and prevent it from closing up and thus injuring the occupant of the berth. See fig. 364.

**Berth Safety-rope Knob.** A metal attachment to the end of a berth safety-rope by which one end of the latter is fastened so as to hold the berth down in its place in case of an accident. The knob engages with a catch called a *Berth Safety-rope Holder.*

**Berth-spring.** A spring usually made in a spiral form like a watch spring, and attached to the upper berth of a sleeping-car by a cord or chain, so as to counteract the weight of the latter and make it easy to raise and lower it. See **8,** figs. 296–298 ; figs. 361 and 362.

**Berth-spring Frame.** A metal support which holds a berth-spring and fusee in its place in a sleeping-car. See **9,** figs. 296–298 ; **1,** fig. 361.

**Berth-spring Fusee.** A cone, or conical metal shell, resembling the fusee of a watch, on which a berth-spring rope is wound, and which incloses a berth-spring of a sleeping-car. See **2,** fig. 361.

**Berth-spring Rope.** A cord, usually made of wire, which is connected to an upper-berth of a sleeping-car at one end, and to the berth-spring at the other, and by which the tension of the spring is transmitted to the berth, thus counteracting its weight. See **10,** figs. 296 and 297; **3,** fig. 361.

**Berth Striker-plate.** A *Berth-latch Keeper,* which see.

**Bevelled-bushing.** See *Bell-cord Bevelled-bushing.*

**Bevelled-washer.** A washer used on truss or other rods which stand at an acute angle to the surface on which the nut or head on the rod bears. Such washers are used so that the bearing for the nut or head may be brought at right angles to the bolt. See fig. 786. Sometimes two such washers which come near together are cast in one piece, and are then called double-bevelled washers.

**Bibb.** A curved nozzle for conveying water or other liquids and changing the direction of their flow usually from a horizontal to a vertical current as from the end of a pipe or cock. See figs. 427–429.

**Bibb-cock.** A cock with a curved nozzle or spout. See figs. 427–429.

**Blind.** A *Window-blind,* which see. See also
*Double Window-blind.*     *Single Window-blind.*
*Lower Window-blind.*     *Upper Window-blind.*

**Block.** 1. " A heavy piece of timber or wood, usually with one plane surface ; or it is rectangular and rather thick than long."—*Webster.*

2. " A pulley or system of pulleys mounted on its frame or shell, with its band or strap. A block consists of one or more pulleys or sheaves, in a groove of which the rope runs, fastened in a shell or frame by pins, on which they revolve ; of a shell or frame inclosing the pulley or pulleys; and of a strap or band, consisting of a rope, encompassing the shell, and attached by an eye of rope or a hook to some object."—*Ed. Ency.* See fig. 803. See

*Body-bolster Truss-block.*     *Bumper-block.*
*Brake-block.*     *Centre-plate Block.*
*Buffer-block.*     *Dead-block.*

*Distance-block.*
*Floor - timber Distance-block.*
*Guide-block.*
*Safety-beam Block.*
*Spring-block.*
*Stirrup-block.*
*Stop-block.*

*Swing - hanger Friction-block.*
*Transom Bearing-Block.*
*Transom Truss-block.*
*Truck-bolster Guide-block.*
*Truck-bolster Truss-block.*
*Truss-block.*

**Board.** " A piece of timber sawed thin, and of considerable length and breadth, compared with the thickness, used for building and other purposes."—*Webster.*
See

*Berth Head-board.*
*Brake Foot-board.*
*Clear-story Soffit-board.*
*Eaves Fascia-board.*
*Fender-board.*
*Inside-cornice Fascia-board.*
*Inside-cornice Sub-fascia-board.*

*Letter-board.*
*Roof-boards.*
*Roof Running-board.*
*Running-board.*
*Seat-back Board.*
*Soffit-board.*
*Splash-board.*
*Tread-board.*

**Boarding-car.** A car fitted up for cooking and serving meals to men at work on the line of a road.

**Bob-tail Street-car.** A term used to designate a street-car with a platform in front only and a small step behind. Such cars are usually drawn by one horse only. See fig. 41.

**Body.** The main or principal part of a car, in or on which the load is placed. American cars for steam railroads usually consist of a body carried on two trucks. Street-cars are usually carried on four wheels only. See *Cylinder-body, for Westinghouse Car-brake.*

**Body-bolsters.** Cross beams attached near the ends of the under side of a car-body which is supported on two trucks. The body centre-plate and side-bearings, which rest on the truck, are fastened to these bolsters. Such beams are made of wood, or of iron trussed, or of wood and iron combined. See **12,** figs. 55–76 · **10,** figs. 215–231 and figs. 233–241. See *Iron Body-bolster. Double Iron Body-bolster.*

**Body-bolster Compression-bar.** The bottom bar of an iron body-bolster which is subjected to a strain of compression. See **1.** fig. 235.

**Body-bolster Tension-bar.** The top bar of an iron body-bolster which is subjected to a strain of tension. See **2,** fig. 235.

**Body-bolster Thimble.** A small casting used as a distance-piece between the upper and lower truss-bars of an iron body-bolster. See **3,** fig. 235.

**Body-bolster Truss-block.** A block of wood or distance-piece, on the top of a wooden body-bolster, between the centre floor-timbers and underneath the bolster truss-rods. See **15,** figs. 58, 72 ; **13,** figs. 218–222 ; **4,** fig. 233.

**Body-bolster Truss-rod.** A rod attached to the ends of a wooden body-bolster, usually with nuts, and which extends lengthwise to it and passes above it at its centre so as to form a truss ; generally two or more such rods are used for each bolster and are intended to strengthen it. See **13,** figs. 55–59, 69–72 ; **11,** figs. 218, 220, 222; **6,** fig. 233.

**Body-bolster Truss-rod Bearing.** An iron plate or casting, placed on top of a body-bolster truss-block, to prevent the truss-rods from crushing into the wood. See **5,** fig. 233.

**Body-bolster Truss-rod Washer.** An iron bearing for a nut on the end of a truss-rod of a body-bolster. This is often made in the form of a long plate so as to take two or more rods. See **14,** figs. 55–59 ; **12,** figs. 215, 218, 219 and 222 ; **7,** fig. 233.

**Body-brace.** An inclined beam or strip of timber in the side or end frame of a car-body which acts as a brace. See *Body-counterbrace, End Body-brace* and *Side Body-brace.*

**Body Brace-rod.** An inclined iron rod in the side or end of a car-body frame, which acts as a brace. See **34,** fig. 61; **52,** fig. 221. See also

*Body-counterbrace-rod.* *End Body Brace-rod.*
*Brace Straining-rod.* *Side Body Brace-rod.*

**Body Centre-plate.** A metal plate attached to a body-bolster of a car, and which rests in a corresponding plate on the centre of a truck. The weight of the car-body usually rests on the centre-plates, and they form a pivot about which the truck turns. A king-bolt passes through the centre of the two centre-plates. See **17,** figs. 55–72; **15,** figs. 216, 219, 229, 230–232; **8,** figs. 233 and 235.

**Body Check-chain Eye.** An eye-bolt, clevis or other similar attachment for fastening a check-chain to the car-body. See **19,** figs. 218–224. See also *Truck Check-chain Eye.*

**Body Check-chain Hook.** An iron hook or similar means of attachment, by which check-chains are fastened to a car-body.

**Body Counter-brace.** A brace in the side frame of a car-body between the bolsters and end of the car. These braces are inclined in a direction opposite to those between the bolster and centre of the car. See **37,** figs. 56, 61, 69; **55,** figs. 215 and 229. See also *Body Counter-brace Rod.*

**Body Counter-brace Rod.** An inclined iron rod in the side-frame of a car-body, between the bolster and the end of the car. See **56,** fig. 221.

**Body Hand-rail.** An iron rod or bar attached to the end of passenger and street cars for persons to take hold of in getting on or off the cars. See **44, figs.** 215, 219, 223; **113,** figs. 750, 753.

**Body-post.** An upright timber which is framed into the sill and plate of a freight car. The posts form the vertical members of the frame of the sides of a car-body. See **42,** figs. 56–82. In passenger cars such posts are called *Window-posts,* which see.

**Body Queen-post.** An iron rod, bar, or casting, on the under side of a car-body and against which the truss-rods bear. See **22,** figs. 215, 216, 228 and 229. See also *Queen-post.*

**Body Queen-post Stay.** An iron bar attached to the lower end of a body queen-post and extending diagonally upward to the cross-frame tie-timber to which it is fastened. The purpose of the brace is to hold the queen-post and prevent it from bending sideways. See **2,** fig. 242.

**Body Side-bearings.** Plates or castings which are attached to the body-bolsters, one on each side of the centre-pin, and which bear on corresponding plates on the truck. See **13,** figs. 57, 58, 63, 70, 72 ; **14,** figs. 222, 230 and 231.

**Body-spring.** A *Bolster-spring,* which see.

**Body Truss-rod.** A rod under a car-body to truss or strengthen it, and prevent it from sagging in the centre between the body-bolsters or points at which it is sup-ported on the trucks. See **19,** figs. 55, 56, 60, 61, 69 ; **20,** figs. 215, 216, 219, 228, 229. See also *Inverted Body Truss-rod. Centre Body Truss-rod. Outside Body Truss-rod.*

**Body Truss-rod Bearing.** A cast or wrought-iron plate, on the under side of a truss-block or of a cross-frame tie-timber, and against which the truss-rod bears. See **21,** figs. 55, 56, 60, 61, 69.

**Body Truss-rod Saddle.** A block of wood or casting which forms a distance-piece on the top of a bolster, and on which a body truss-rod bears. See **20,** figs. 61, 62, 64, 69, 70, 72 ; **21,** fig. 215.

**Bogie.** A term used in England to designate a *Car-truck,* which see.

**Bogus-plate.** A horizontal timber attached to the posts of a refrigerator-car, on the inside of the car, a short distance below the plate. The *bogus-plates* support horizontal cross-timbers to which hooks are attached for hanging meat and other articles to be transported.

**Bolster.** A cross timber or trussed beam on the under side of a car-body, and in the centre of a truck. The body-bolster rests on the truck-bolster.

See *Body-bolster.* *Iron Body-bolster.*
*Compound Bolster.* *Swing-bolster.*
*Double Iron-body-* *Truck-bolster.*
 *bolster.*

**Bolster-bridge.** *A Side-bearing Bridge*, which see.

**Bolster-plates.** Wrought-iron plates bolted or riveted to the sides of wooden body-bolsters to strengthen them.

**Bolster-springs.** Springs which are carried on the transverse beams of a truck and on which the truck-bolster and the weight of the car-body rests. See **80**, figs. 91–104, 108–129.

**Bolster-spring Cap.** A cast or wrought-iron plate or socket attached to the under side of a truck-bolster, and which bears on top of a bolster-spring and holds the latter in its place. See **75**, figs. 111, 121, 126.

**Bolster-spring Seat.** A cast or wrought-iron plate or socket on top of a spring-plank, on which a bolster-spring rests or bears. See **74**, figs. 111, 121, 126.

**Bolster-truss Block.** See *Body-bolster Truss-block. Truck-bolster Truss-block.*

**Bolster Truss-rod.** See *Body-bolster Truss-rod. Truck-bolster Truss-rod.*

**Bolster Truss-rod Washer.** See *Body-bolster Truss-rod Washer. Truck-bolster Truss-rod Washer.*

**Bolt.** Generally a pin, rod or bar of metal used to hold or fasten anything in its place ; ordinarily a bolt is a metal rod, having a head on one end and usually a screw and nut on the other end, as shown in figs. 776–784.

See *Barrel Door-bolt.*          *Brake Safety-chain Eye-*
   *Berth-latch Bolt.*          *bolt.*

*Carriage Bolt.*                    *King-bolt.*
*Cupboard-bolt.*                    *Lug-bolt.*
*Discharge-valve Stop-bolt.*        *Machine-bolt.*
*Door-bolt.*                        *Piston-follower Bolt.*
*Door-latch Bolt.*                  *Reversing-valve-plate*
*Door-lock Bolt.*                      *Bolt.*
*Door-sash Bolt.*                   *Seat-lock Bolt.*
*Draw-bar Bolt.*                    *Sofa-bolt.*
*Eye-bolt.*                         *Stake-pocket U-bolt.*
*Flush-bolt.*                       *Stop-bolt.*
*Head-board Bolt.*                  *Strap-bolt.*
*Hub-bolt.*                         *Tire-bolt.*
*Joint-bolt.*                       *U-bolt.*
*Journal-box-cover Bolt.*           *Window-blind Bolt.*
*Key-bolt.*                         *Window-latch Bolt.*

**Bolt Draw-bar.** A draw-bar to which the draw-spring is attached by a bolt. See figs. 251–253, 266, 267.

**Bonnet.** A *Platform-hood*, which see.

**Bottom.** " The lowest part of anything; as, the bottom of a well, vat, or ship."—*Webster.*

See *Alcove-bottom.*               *Fire-proof Bottom.*
   *Candle-lamp Bottom.*        *Lamp-bottom.*
   *Drop-bottom.*               *Seat-bottom.*

**Bottom Arch-bar.** See *Inverted Arch-bar.*

**Bottom-chord.** See *Lower-chord.*

**Bottom Cylinder-head,** *for Westinghouse Driving-wheel*

*Brake.* A circular cast-iron plate or cover for the lower end of a cylinder. It has an opening in the centre through which the piston-rod works. See **4**, fig. 749.

**Bottom Door-rail.** The lower transverse piece of a door-frame.

**Bottom Door-track.** A door-track below a sliding-door. It is usually a metal bar which supports the door and on which the latter moves. Such doors are usually provided with rollers or slides which rest on the track. See **66**, figs. 55, 59, 69, 72.

**Bottom-rail.** The lowermost horizontal bar or member of a frame, as of a sash or door. See **147**, figs. 218, 222, 223, 230: **5**, fig. 502.

**Bottom-ratchet of Drum,** *for Creamer Brake.* A ratchet on the under side of the drum of a Creamer brake. The side pawl engages into the ratchet to retain the tension on the brake produced by the momentum of the drum when the spring is released. See **15**, fig. 646.

**Bottom Stove-plate,** *for a Baker Heater.* An iron casting shaped somewhat like a dinner plate and which forms the under side of a Baker stove or heater. See **1**, fig. 581; fig. 582.

**Bottom Stove-plate,** *for a Spear Heater.* A circular casting which rests on the floor of a car and forms the base or pedestal of the stove. See **14**, figs. 550–554: fig. 575.

**Bow.** See *Platform-hood Bow.*

**Bowl.** See *Wash-bowl.*

**Box.** See *Journal-box.*
    *Master-car-builders Stand-*    *Top-reservoir Journal-box.*
    *ard Journal-box.*        *Wheel-box.*

**Box-car.** A freight car which is covered with a roof, and inclosed on the sides to protect its contents from the weather and from being stolen. See *Four-wheeled Box-car*, fig. 13. *Eight-wheeled Box-car*, fig. 12. *Combined Box-car*, fig. 14. *Four-wheeled Box-car.*

**Box Cattle-car.** A cattle-car of which the sides are boarded up tight and which has grated doors and windows, similar to figs. 14 and 16. See *Slat Cattle-car.*

**Box-cover.** See *Journal-box Cover.*

**Box-cushion.** A cushion for passenger-car seats, made on a wooden frame. Box-cushions are sometimes stuffed with hair or other elastic material alone, and sometimes steel springs are used in addition to the hair or other elastic material. Fig. 414 shows a frame for a box-cushion.

**Box-guide.** See *Journal-box Guide.*

**Box-packing.** *Journal-packing,* which see.

**Box-room,** *on Axle.* A *Dust-guard Seat,* which see.

**Box-steps.** Passenger-car steps made with wooden stringers or sides. See fig. 244.

**Brace.** An inclined beam, rod or bar of a frame, truss, girder, etc., which unites two or more of the points, where other members of the structure are connected together, and which prevents them from turning about their joints. A brace thus makes the structure incapable of altering its form from this cause, and it also distributes or transmits part of the strain at one or more of the joints toward the point or points of support, or resistance to that strain. A brace may be subjected to either a strain of compression or tension. If the former, in car construction, it is called simply a *brace ;* in the latter it is called a *brace-rod.* See **8,** figs. 805, 807, 809.

See *Berth-brace.*     *Door-brace.*
*Body-brace.*     *End Body-brace.*
*Brake-lever-bracket Brace.*     *Floor-timber Brace.*
*Brake-shaft Brace.*     *Pedestal-brace.*
*Brake-shaft-step Brace.*     *Roof-brace.*
*Compression-beam Brace.*     *Seat-bracket Brace.*
*Corner-post Brace.*     *Side-lamp Brace.*
        *Stop-brace.*

**Brace-pocket.** A casting which forms a step or socket for holding the ends of braces, especially of car-bodies. See **39,** fig. 61; **40,** fig. 69; **41,** figs. 69, 71. See also
*Double-brace Pocket.*     *Left-hand Brace-pocket.*
      *Right-hand Brace-pocket.*

**Brace-rod.** An inclined iron rod which acts as a brace. See **34,** fig. 61; **52,** fig. 221; **10,** fig. 808.
See *Body Brace-rod.*     *Side Body-brace-rod.*
*Counterbrace-rod.*     *Side Counterbrace-rod.*

**Brace-rod Washer.** An iron plate which forms a bearing for the nut or head of a brace-rod. Such washers are sometimes made of triangular or bevelled shape and in other cases are made of a flat bar of iron bent to fit into a notch cut into the timber, as shown at **38,** figs. 61, 69. See also **57,** fig. 221; and also *Triangular Washer. Bevelled Washer.*

**Brace Straining-rod.** A vertical iron rod in the side or end frame of a car-body by which the upper end of a brace is connected, or tied to the sill of the car. The brace-rods are members of the truss of which the sill, braces, posts or plates, etc., form parts. Such rods often have hook-heads at the upper ends against which the braces bear, and nuts at the lower ends by which they are screwed up, and are thus brought into a state of tension and the braces into compression. See **53,** figs. 215, 229.

**Bracket.** "An angular stay in the form of a knee to support shelves and the like."—*Webster.*
See *Basket-rack Bracket.*     *Brake-shaft Bracket.*
*Bell-cord Strap-hanger Bracket.*     *Brake-step Bracket.*
     *Coupling-spring Bracket.*
*Bell-strap Bracket.*     *Cylinder-lever Bracket.*
*Berth-bracket.*     *Door-track Bracket.*
*Berth-curtain-rod Bracket.*     *Inside-hand-rail Bracket.*
*Brake-lever Bracket.*     *Lamp-bracket.*

*Lamp-chimney Bracket.*
*Longitudinal-step Bracket.*
*Post-bracket.*
*Release-spring Bracket.*
*Roof Running-board Bracket.*
*Running-board Bracket.*

*Seat-bracket.*
*Side-lamp Bracket.*
*Sliding-door Bracket.*
*Tender-spring Bracket.*
*Towel-bracket.*
*Window-curtain-rod Bracket.*

**Bracket Gas-burner.** A gas-burner attached to the side of a car by a suitable pipe or metal bracket.

**Bracket-lamp.** A *Side-lamp*, which see.

**Braided Bell-cord.** See *Bell-cord.*

**Brake.** The whole combination of parts by which the motion of a car is retarded or arrested.

See *Air-brake.*
*Atmospheric Brake.*
*Automatic Air-brake.*
*Compression-rod Brake.*
*Continuous-brake.*
*Creamer Safety-brake.*
*Double-lever Brake.*
*Driving-wheel Brake.*
*Eames Vacuum Brake.*
*Elder's Brake.*
*Hodge Brake.*
*Inner-hung Brake.*

*Loughridge Air-brake.*
*Outer-hung Brake.*
*Single-lever Brake.*
*Smith's Vacuum Brake.*
*Stevens Brake.*
*Tanner Brake.*
*Tyler Brake.*
*Vacuum Brake.*
*Westinghouse Air-brake.*
*Westinghouse Automatic Air-brake.*

**Brake for Drop-bottom Car.** A brake arranged so that none of the rods or levers will interfere with the drop doors through which the contents of the car are emptied. See figs. 77–80, 640.

**Brake-beam.** A transverse iron or wooden bar to which the brake-block and shoes are attached. It is suspended near the wheels so that the brake-shoes can conveniently be applied to the treads of the wheels. See **143**, figs. 77–84 ; **84**, figs. 88–125 ; **4**, figs. 629–631, **1**, figs. 637–645 ; **133**, figs. 750–753. See also *Trussed Brake-beam.*

**Brake-beam Chafing-plate.** A plate attached to a brake-beam and against which a brake-spring bears. The object of the plate is to resist the wear due to the action of the spring.

**Brake-beam Eye-bolt.** An eye-bolt for fastening a lower brake-rod to a brake-beam on trucks having but one brake-lever. These bolts have threads cut nearly their entire length and usually a nut is placed on each side of the brake-beam, which can be screwed up so as to take up the wear of the brake-shoes. See **85**, figs. 89, 93, 116.

**Brake-beam Fulcrum.** See *Brake-lever Fulcrum.*

**Brake-beam King-post.** A post or distance-piece, which forms a bearing for the truss-rods of a brake-beam. Sometimes the brake-lever is attached to it and it then forms also a fulcrum for the latter. See **6,** fig. 631.

**Brake-beam Truss-rod.** A rod used to truss or strengthen a brake-beam. See 5, fig. 631.

**Brake-block.** A piece of wood or metal which carries a removable shoe which bears directly against the tread of the wheel when the brake is applied. The brake-blocks are attached to the ends of a transverse beam extending from one wheel to the one opposite and called a brake-beam. See 82, figs. 100, 105, 115, 118, 122, 127, 128, 129; 1, figs. 629–631, fig. 633.

**Brake-block,** *for Westinghouse Driving-wheel Brake.* An iron casting to which a brake-shoe is attached and which acts as a support for the latter. They are made separate from each other so that when the shoe is worn out it can be replaced without destroying the block. See 17, fig. 747.

**Brake-block Pin,** *for Westinghouse Driving-wheel Brake.* A pin by which the suspending and supporting links are attached to a brake-block. See 26, fig. 747.

**Brake-block Suspending-link,** *for Westinghouse Driving-wheel Brake.* An iron bar attached to a locomotive frame and to which a brake-block is hung. See 23, fig. 747, 748.

**Brake-block Suspending-plates,** *for Westinghouse Driving-wheel Brake.* A wrought-iron plate bolted to a locomotive frame and which forms a support or means of attachment for the upper end of a brake-block suspending-link. See 24, figs. 747, 748.

**Brake-block Suspending-stud,** *for Westinghouse Driving-wheel Brake.* A bolt or pin by which the upper end of a brake-bolt suspending-link is attached to a suspending plate. See 25, figs. 747, 748.

**Brake-block Tie-rod,** *for Westinghouse Driving-wheel Brake.* A rod by which the brake-blocks on opposite sides of the engine are tied together and prevented from spreading apart. The lower ends of the supporting-links are attached to the *tie-rod.* See 27 figs. 747, 748.

**Brake-carrier.** See *Brake-hanger Carrier.*

**Brake-chain.** See *Brake-shaft Chain.*

**Brake-chain Worm.** A conical casting attached to the brake-shaft with a screw-shaped groove on it, in which a brake-chain is wound. The object of it is to produce a rapid motion in first applying the brakes, and to increase the power when the brake-shoes are brought in close contact with the wheels. See 160, figs. 215, 217; 1, fig. 244.

**Brake-clevis.** A *Brake-lever Fulcrum,* which see.

**Brake-cylinder,** *for Westinghouse Automatic Car-brake* A hollow cast-iron cylinder which is usually attached to the under side of a car-frame. It is accurately bored out and fitted with two heads and a piston, against which the compressed air exerts its pressure and thus applies the brakes to the wheels. The piston-rod is connected with a lever (**5**, fig. 661; **12**, fig. 729), which is provided with a spiral spring, **15**, which is compressed by the action of the piston, and the movement of the lever, so that when the air which has forced out the piston is allowed to escape the elasticity of the spring forces the piston back to the end of the cylinder and thus releases the brakes. See **2**, figs. 660, 661, 663, 729, 730. The main casting, **2**, figs. 729, 730, is called the *cylinder-body for Westinghouse car-brake.* The whole arrangement of cylinder, springs, lever, etc., represented in figs. 729, 730, is designated as a *brake-cylinder with releasing apparatus complete, for Westinghouse automatic car-brake.*

**Brake-cylinder,** *for Westinghouse Automatic Tender-brake.* A cylinder similar to the above which is used on tenders, but without a releasing-lever and spring. See **2**, figs. 655–657, 727, 728.

**Brake-cylinder,** *for Westinghouse Driving-wheel Brake.* A hollow cast-iron cylinder which is attached to a locomotive in a vertical position between the driving-wheels. It is accurately bored out and fitted with two heads and a piston, against which the compressed air exerts its pressure, the force of which is transmitted to two eccentric-levers, which act against the brake-heads and thus apply the brakes. The main casting, **2**, fig. 749, of the cylinder is called the *cylinder-body for Westinghouse driving-wheel brake.* See **12**, fig. 655; **1**, fig. 747, and fig. 749.

**Brake-cylinder Pipe,** *for Westinghouse Automatic Brake.* A pipe which connects a brake-cylinder with the triple-valve. See **25**, figs. 661, 663.

**Brake-dog.** A *Brake-pawl*, which see.

**Brake-drum.** A *Brake-shaft Drum*, which see.

**Brake Foot-board.** A *Brake-step*, which see.

**Brake-hanger.** A link or bar by which brake-beams and attachments are suspended from a truck-frame or car-body. See **144**, fig. 77; **86**, figs. 88–129; **7**, figs. 629, 630; **134**, fig. 750. See also *Parallel Brake-hanger.*

**Brake-hanger Bearing.** A casting which is held by a Brake-hanger carrier, and which forms a bearing for a brake-hanger. See **14**, figs. 629, 630.

**Brake-hanger Carrier.** An eye or **U** bolt, a casting or other fastening by which a brake-hanger is attached to the truck or body of a car. See **87**, fig. 129; **8**, figs. 629, 630. See also *Parallel Brake-hanger Carrier.*

**Brake-hanger Timber.** A short transverse timber between the floor-timbers of a car-body, and which is framed into them, and to which the brake-hangers, which are hung from the body of a car, are attached. See **6**, figs. 62, 64, 78.

**Brake-head.** A piece of iron or wood attached to a brake-beam and which bears against the wheels, and combines both a brake-block and brake-shoe in one piece. See **142**, fig. 77 ; **83**, fig. 91 ; fig. 632 ; **135**, figs. 750-753.

**Brake-hose**, *for Westinghouse Car-brake.* Flexible tubes made of india-rubber and canvas by which the different vehicles in the train are connected together and by which the compressed air which operates the brakes is conducted from the engine to the cars, and from one car to another. The hose is made in two pieces with a coupling between each two vehicles, so that they can readily be connected or disconnected. See **30**, figs. 660, 661 ; fig. 725. See *Armored Brake-hose.*

**Brake-hose Armor.** A woven wire covering on the outside of brake-hose to protect it from injury or abrasion. See fig. 726.

**Brake-hose Clutch-coupling**, *for Westinghouse-brake.* A brake-hose coupling formed by two parts which lap over each other, as shown in figs. 715, 716.

**Brake-hose Coupling.** A contrivance for coupling or connecting the ends of a pair of brake-hose together so that the air by which the brakes are operated can pass from one vehicle in a train to another. See figs. 715, 716.

**Brake-hose Coupling-cap**, *for Clutch-coupling of Westinghouse-brake.* A screw-plug which is screwed into a coupling-case and which holds the coupling-valve in its place. See **4**, figs. 715, 716, and fig. 718.

**Brake-hose Coupling-case**, *for Clutch-coupling of West-*inghouse-brake. A hollow casting which joins the main part of one piece of a pair of couplings and to which the hose is attached. See **3**, figs. 715, 716.

**Brake-hose Coupling Packing-expander**, *for Clutch-coupling of Westinghouse-brake.* A metal bushing or cage which is inserted in a coupling-case to expand the packing when the valves are removed. This is used in place of the valves in the ordinary brake. See fig. 724.

**Brake-hose Coupling-valve**, *for Clutch-coupling of West-inghouse-brake.* A puppet-valve which is contained in a chamber in a coupling-case to prevent the escape of air from the hose when the latter are uncoupled. See **5**, fig. 715, and fig. 719.

**Brake-hose Coupling-valve Spring**, *for Clutch-coupling of Westinghouse-brake.* A spiral-spring in a coupling-case which bears on the valve to close it promptly when the hose are uncoupled. See **6**, fig. 715, and fig. 720.

**Brake-hose Nipple**, *for Westinghouse-brake.* A tubular elbow which is attached by one end to the hose and by the other to a car or engine. See fig. 723.

**Brake-lever.** A lever by which the power employed to apply the brakes is transmitted to the brake-beams. The brake-levers are connected to the brake-beams at or near the short ends of the former, and the brake-chains, or rods, are connected to the opposite end. See **145**, figs. 77, 78, 82, 84 ; **92**, figs. 88-129 ; **11**, figs. 629, 630 ; **15**, fig. 661. In some cases the upper end of one of the brake-levers on each truck is attached to a brake-lever stop. Such levers are called fixed brake-levers to distinguish them from those which are movable. See *Centre Brake-lever. Fixed Brake-lever*

**Brake-lever Bracket.** A wrought-iron knee fastened to the under side of a car, and to which the fulcrum of a brake-lever is attached. See **148** figs. 77, 78.

**Brake-lever-bracket Brace.** A diagonal wrought-iron brace, attached to a brake-lever-bracket to stiffen it. See **149**, fig. 77.

**Brake-lever Clevis.** A *Brake-lever Fulcrum*, which see.

**Brake-lever Fulcrum.** A forked iron attached to a brake-beam by means of which a brake-lever is connected to the beam. Usually it consists of a bolt which passes through the beam and is fastened with a nut, and at the other end it has a forked end or clevis in which the lever is fastened with a pin or bolt. In some cases a casting is used for this purpose. See **146**, figs. 77–80 ; **93**, figs. 88–129 ; **12**, figs. 629, 631.

**Brake-lever Guide.** A bar of wood or iron which holds or supports the upper end of a brake-lever in its place. See **147**, figs. 77, 79 ; **94**, figs. 101, 102, 123, 124.

**Brake-lever Sheave.** A pulley attached to a brake-lever, over which a chain by which the brakes are applied runs. See **96**, fig. 102, 103.

**Brake-lever Stop.** An iron bar or loop attached to a truck or car frame, and which holds the upper end of a fixed brake-lever. It usually has holes in it in which a pin is inserted against which the end of the lever bears. By moving the pin from one hole to another the position of the lever is adjusted so as to take up the wear of the brake-shoes. See **95**, figs. 92, 118, 123, 124 ; **13**, fig. 630.

**Brake-pawl.** A small pivoted bar for engaging in the teeth of a brake ratchet-wheel to prevent the latter from turning backward. It is usually placed in such a position as to be worked by the foot. See **159**, figs. 216, 220; fig. 636.

**Brake-pipe,** *for Westinghouse Automatic-brake.* An iron pipe attached to the under side of a car-body and extending from one end of the car to the other, and connected to the pipes on the adjoining cars by flexible hose. The purpose of these pipes is to convey the air from the air-pump on the engine to the auxiliary reservoirs attached to the cars. These pipes are filled with compressed air when the brakes are not on. When the latter are to be applied, the air is allowed to escape from the pipes which causes the triple-valves to open communication between the auxiliary reservoirs and the brake-cylinders, so that the compressed air stored up in the reservoirs acts on the pistons and brake-levers. See **20**, figs. 661, 663.

**Brake Ratchet-wheel.** A wheel attached to a brake-shaft

having teeth shaped like saw teeth, into which a pawl engages, thus preventing the wheel and shaft from turning backward. See **103**, figs. 55–84; **158**, figs. 215, 216, 217, 219, 220, 223; fig. 636; **125**, fig. 750.

**Brake-rod.** See *Lower Brake-rod. Secondary Brake-rod. Main Brake-rod.*

**Brake-rod Guide.** A hook, eye, roller or other contrivance attached to a car-truck or body for supporting a brake-rod.

**Brake-rubber.** A *Brake-shoe*, which see.

**Brake Safety-chain or link.** A chain attached to a brake-beam, and to the truck or body of a car. It is intended for the same purpose as a brake safety-strap; that is, to hold the brake-beams in case a brake-hanger should break. Sometimes these are made of a single link or bar. See **88**, figs. 94, 101, 103, 105; **9**, figs. 629, 630.

**Brake Safety-chain Eye-bolt.** An eye-bolt attached to a truck or car-body, and which holds a brake safety-chain. See **89**, figs. 103, 105; **10**, figs. 629, 630.

**Brake Safety-strap.** A strap of iron fastened by its ends to the end-piece or transom of a truck and bent into such a shape as to embrace the brake-beam. In case any of the hangers should give way the safety-strap is intended to catch and hold the beam, and prevent it from falling on the track. Sometimes it is made of steel, and

used as a brake-spring for throwing off the brake. See **90**, figs. 88–90, 115–129.

**Brake-shaft.** A vertical or horizontal shaft on which a chain is wound and by which the power of a hand-brake is applied to the wheels. See **94**, figs. 55–84; **95**, figs. 55, 56, 69, 72; **152**, figs. 215, 217, 219, 223; **122**, figs. 750, 753. See *Horizontal Brake-shaft. Long Brake-shaft.*

**Brake-shaft Bearing.** A metal eye by which a brake-shaft is held in its place, and in which it turns. See *Brake-shaft Step. Lower Brake-shaft Bearing. Upper Brake-shaft Bearing.*

**Brake-shaft Brace.** A brace on the Miller platform which holds the bottom of the brake-shaft, and forms a step for it. See **1**, figs. 282, 285.

**Brake-shaft Bracket.** A support made in the form of a bracket for holding a horizontal brake-shaft in its place, used mostly on freight cars. See **99**, figs. 55, 56, 69.

**Brake-shaft Bracket, for Creamer-brake.** A cast-iron bracket attached to the hand-rail, and which forms a support or bearing for the upper end of the brake-shaft. See **13**, fig. 646.

**Brake-shaft Bushing.** A thimble on a brake-shaft on a Miller platform.

**Brake-shaft Chain.** A chain connected with the brake-levers, and which is wound up on a shaft, called the brake-shaft. The force exerted on the shaft is transmitted to the other connection of the brake by this chain. See **150**, fig. 77; **3**, figs. 637–645; **127**, figs. 750, 751. See *Horizontal Brake-shaft Chain*.

**Brake-shaft-chain Sheave.** A roller over which a brake-shaft chain passes. See **105**, figs. 55, 56, 69.

**Brake-shaft Connecting-rod.** A rod which is attached at one end to a brake-chain, and at the other to a brake-lever, or to the centre-lever of the Tanner or Elder brake or to a floating-lever of the Hodge brake. See **151**, figs. 77, 80; **4**, figs. 637–645; **13**, fig. 661; **128**, figs. 750, 751, 753.

**Brake-shaft Crank.** An elbow attached to the upper end of the brake-shaft of street-cars for turning the brake-shaft and operating the brakes. See **120**, figs. 750, 753.

**Brake-shaft Crank-handle.** That part of a brake-shaft crank which is held in the hand, when the crank is used. See **121**, figs. 750, 753.

**Brake-shaft Drum.** The part of a brake-shaft on which the brake-chain is wound, in applying the brakes. The shaft is sometimes enlarged at this part, and sometimes a cast-iron sleeve is put on it to increase the diameter of the part on which the chain is wound. See *Brake-chain drum*.

**Brake-shaft Hanger.** A *Brake-shaft Bracket*, which see.

**Brake-shaft Holder.** A *Brake-shaft Bearing*, which see.

**Brake-shaft Step.** A bearing which holds the lower end of a brake-shaft. It usually consists of a U-shaped bar of iron, the upper ends of which are fastened to the car-body, and a hole in the curved part of the bar, which receives the end of the shaft. See **98**, figs. 60–84; **153**, figs. 215, 217, 223. See also *Brake-shaft Holder*.

**Brake-shaft-step Brace.** A wrought-iron brace attached to a brake-step to resist the pull of the brake chain.

**Brake-shaft Thimble.** An iron bushing attached to some portion of the car to form a bearing for a brake-shaft. See **44**, fig. 285.

**Brake-shoe.** A piece of metal or wood shaped to fit the tread of a car-wheel and attached by a key or otherwise to a brake-block. It rubs against the tread of the wheel when the brakes are applied. Such shoes are made of wood, cast, wrought, or malleable iron, and sometimes of a combination of cast and wrought iron. See **98**, figs. 88, 89, 105, 107, 115, 118; **2**, figs. 630, 631; fig. 633. See *Congdon Brake-shoe*. *Malleable Brake-shoe*.

**Brake-shoe,** *for Westinghouse Driving-wheel Brake*. A wrought, cast, or malleable iron plate attached to a brake-block, and which bears against the driving-wheel. Such shoes are sometimes made of a combination of cast and wrought iron. See **16**, fig. 747.

**Brake-shoe Key.** A key or wedge by which a brake-shoe is fastened to a brake-block. See fig. 633.

**Brake-spring.** A *Release-spring*, which see.

**Brake-staff.** A *Brake-shaft*, which see.

**Brake-step.** A small shelf or ledge on the end of a freight-car near the top, on which the brake-man stands when applying the brake from the top of a car. Also called a *brake foot-board*. See **100**, figs. 55–71.

**Brake-step Bracket.** An iron bracket to support a brake-step. See **101**, figs. 55–71.

**Brake-windlass.** A shaft with a hand-wheel attached by which the former is turned, and a chain, connected with the brake-levers, is wound up on a part of the shaft called a drum. The shaft also has a ratchet-wheel and a pawl to prevent it from being turned backward by the tension on the chain when it is wound up. The term windlass is used to designate all of these parts combined. See *Brake-shaft.*

**Brake-wheel.** A hand-wheel attached to a brake-shaft, and by which the latter is turned in applying the brakes. See **93**, figs. 55–84 ; **157**, figs. 215, 216, 217, 219, 220, 223 ; fig. 635.

**Brass.** " An alloy of copper and zinc. The term is commonly applied to the yellow alloy of copper with about half its weight of zinc, in which case it is called by engineers *yellow-brass ;* but copper alloyed with about one-ninth its weight of tin is the metal of brass ordnance or gun-metal. Similar alloys used for the ' brasses ' or bearings of machinery are called *hard* brass, and when employed for statues and medals they are called bronze." —*Tomlinson's Cyclopædia of Useful Arts.* The term *brass* is often used to designate a *Journal-bearing*, which see.

**Brass-wire-covered Bell-cord.** See *Bell-cord.*

**Bridge.** In car-construction the term *bridge* means a timber, bar, or beam which is supported at each end. See *Bolster-bridge. Centre-bearing Bridge. Side-bearing Bridge.*

**Bridging.** The cross-pieces or " nailers " in the floor, to which the flooring is nailed. See **6**, figs. 215, 216, 229, 231.

**Broad-gauge.** The distance between the heads of the rails, when it is greater than 4 ft. 8½ in. See *Gauge.*

**Broad-tread Wheel.** A wheel of which the periphery or tread is wider than usual so as to be able to run over tracks which vary somewhat in width such as 4-ft.-8½-in., 4-ft.-9-in., and 4-ft.-10-in. gauges. Also called *compromise-wheels.*

**Brush.** See *Car-window Brush.*

**Brush-and-comb Rack.** A metal or wooden receptacle fastened to the side of a car or a partition of a passenger or sleeping-car for holding a brush and comb. See fig. 385.

**Buffer.** An elastic apparatus or cushion attached to the end of a car to receive the concussions of other cars running against it. The term is generally applied to those attachments in which springs are used to give the apparatus elasticity. The Miller buffer is shown at **35**, figs. 282–285, and the Janney buffer at *F*. figs. 290–292. The term is often applied to a *Draw-bar*, which see.

**Buffer-arm.** A *Draw-bar Timber*, which see.

**Buffer-bar.** A wrought-iron bar at the end of a car to resist the concussions of one car against another. Such bars are usually provided with springs so as to offer an elastic resistance when two cars come in contact with each other. In this country they are used chiefly with the Miller and Janney platforms. See **2**, figs. 282, 285 ; *F.*, figs. 290–292.

**Buffer-beam.** A transverse timber bolted to the outside of an end-sill of a car and to which the *dead-blocks* are attached. See **32′**, fig. 78. This term is also used to designate a *platform end-timber* of a Miller platform.

**Buffer-block.** A wooden block or stick of timber attached to the end-sill or platform end-timber of a car above the draw-bar, and intended to protect persons between the cars from injury by preventing the cars from coming together in case the draw-bar or its attachments should be broken or fail in any other way. See **29**, figs. 60–65, and **1**, fig. 278. The terms *buffer-block* and *dead-block* are often confused in meaning. A *buffer-block* is a single peice of timber bolted to the end-sill of a car above the

draw-bar, as shown in fig. 278, while *dead-blocks* are used in pairs, one on each-side of the draw-bar, as shown at **2, 2**, fig. 279.

**Buffer-block Face-plate.** A metal plate bolted to the outside or face of a wooden buffer-block, and which forms a bearing for the buffer-blocks of other cars when they come in contact with each other. The object of the plate is to protect the wood from wear.

**Buffer-head.** The broad, flat part of the buffer which is used with the Miller platform, and which bears against another similar one on the adjoining car. See **35**, figs. 282–287.

**Buffer-plate.** An iron plate with which the buffer-beam on the Miller platform is faced, and through which the buffer-shank passes. See **3**, figs. 284, 285.

**Buffer-shank.** The square part of a Miller buffer, between the buffer-head and the buffer-stem. See **36**, fig. 287.

**Buffer-spring.** A spring used with the buffer of the Miller and Janney couplers to resist the concussions of one car against another, and which gives elasticity to the buffer-bar. See **5**, figs. 282, 283, 284.

**Buffer-spring Beam,** *for Miller Platform.* A short transverse piece of timber framed between the draw-timbers and against which the buffer-spring bears. See **24**, figs. 282, 283, 284.

**Buffer-spring Cup.** An iron washer or seat in which the

inside end of the Miller buffer-spring rests. Such cups are used with a volute spring; when a spiral spring is used the spring-cup is the same as the spring-washers. See **6**, figs. 282, 283, 284.

**Buffer-spring Washer.** A plate or washer on the buffer-stem of a Miller buffer which bears against the outside end of the buffer-spring. When spiral buffer-springs are used, washers of the same kind are used at each end. See **7**, figs. 282, 283, 284.

**Buffer-stem.** The round part of a Miller buffer-bar which passes through the buffer-springs. See **37**, fig. 287.

**Buffer-stem Washer.** A metal ring or plate on the inside end of a Miller buffer-bar, and which is intended as a bearing for a key in the end of the buffer-bar. See **8**, figs. 283, 284.

**Buffer-thimble.** A cast-iron thimble or bushing in a platform end-timber through which a Miller buffer-shank passes. The buffer-thimble and buffer-plate are now made in one piece. See **9**, fig. 284.

**Bull's-eye.** A convex glass lens, which is placed in front of a lamp, and which diffuses the light so as to make it more conspicuous for a signal. They are used to close the opening in fixed lamps at the ends of cars, and also in signal lanterns. See **26**, figs. 495, 496.

**Bull's-eye Lamp.** A lantern, with a bull's-eye lens, generally used for a signal-lamp. See figs. 495, 496.

**Bumper.** An indefinite term used to designate a *Buffer* or *Draw-bar*, or a *Buffer-block*, which terms see.

**Bumper-block.** A *Buffer-block*, which see.

**Bunk.** A *Berth*, which see.

**Burlaps.** A coarse canvas used for upholstering the seats of passenger cars.

**Burner.** "That part of a lighting apparatus at which combustion takes place."—*Knight.* See

> *Bracket Gas-burner.*      *Mineral-oil Burner.*
> *Dual Burner.*             *Screw Burner.*
> *Gas-burner.*              *Spring Burner.*
> *Hinge Burner.*            *Sun Burner.*
> *Lamp-burner.*

**Bushing.** "A lining for a hole."—*Knight.* Usually a metal cylindrical ring which forms a bearing for some other object, as a shaft, valve, etc., which is inserted in the hole. See

> *Bell-cord Bevelled Bushing.*      *Head-board-bolt Bushing.*
> *Bell-cord Bushing.*               *Lower Steam-valve Bushing.*
> *Berth-curtain-rod Bushing.*       *Reversing-valve Bushing.*
> *Berth-hinge Bushing.*             *Steam-valve Bushing.*
> *Brake-shaft Bushing.*             *Upper Steam-valve Bushing.*
> *Clear-story Window-pivot Bushing.*  *Window-latch Bushing.*
>                                    *Window-pivot Bushing.*

**Bushing,** *for Pipes.* A short tube with a screw cut inside and outside, and used to screw into a pipe to reduce its diameter when it is necessary to connect it with a smaller pipe. Generally, a bushing has a hexagonal head by which it is turned. Such bushings are sometimes called *reducers.* See fig. 624.

**Butt.** A contraction of *Butt-hinge,* which see.

**Butt-hinge.** A hinge for hanging doors, etc., which is fastened with screws to the edge of a door, so that when the latter is closed the hinge is folded up between the door and its frame. A hinge like that represented in fig. 509, the two parts of which are so fastened together that they cannot readily be detached, is called a *fast-joint butt-hinge.* See also *Loose-joint Butt-hinge,* and *Loose-pin Butt-hinge.*

**Button.** This term, besides its usual meaning, is sometimes used to designate an *Axle-collar,* which see. See

   *Door-button.*       *L-window Button.*
   *Door-case-sash Button.*   *V-window Button.*
   *Eccentric Window-button.*   *Wheel-box Button.*
        *Window-button.*

# C

**Cabin-car.** A *Conductor's Car,* which see.

**Caboose-car.** A *Conductor's Car,* which see.

**Cage.** See *Tank-valve Cage.*

**Camber.** The upward deflection or bend of a beam, girder, or truss.

**Candle.** See *Car-candle. Hydraulic-pressed Car-candle.*

**Candle-bottom.** A *Candle-lamp Bottom,* which see.

**Candle-holder.** The inside part of a candle-lamp bottom, which is provided with a spring to feed or push the candle up as it burns away. See fig. 486.

**Candle-holder Cap.** A thimble in a candle-holder against which the top of a candle bears. See **21,** fig. 2_6.

**Candle-holder Cup.** A metal cup which forms the bottom of a candle-holder. See **22,** fig. 486.

**Candle-lamp.** A lamp in which candles are burned. See fig. 470.

**Candle-lamp Bottom.** A tubular arrangement which holds the candle in a candle-lamp. It has suitable clips or catches so that it can easily be attached or detached to or from the under side of the lamp. It also has a spiral spring in the inside by which the candle is pushed up as it burns away. See fig. 485.

**Candle-rods.** Metal rods, which have a cup attached at one end and a cap at the other, the whole, with a spring, forming a candle-holder for a candle-lamp. See **23,** fig. 486.

**Candle-spring.** A spiral spring which is placed in a candle-holder to feed or push the candle up as it burns away. See engraving of candle-holder. See **24**, fig. 486.

**Cane-seat.** A seat made of woven strips of cane. See fig. 404.

**Cannon-car.** A car especially constructed for carrying heavy cannon. Also called *gun-car.*

**Canopy.** See *Lamp-canopy.* A platform-hood is sometimes called a *canopy.*

**Canvas.** A coarse cloth made of cotton, used for the outside covering of street-car roofs and for upholstering seats. See *Roofing-canvas.*

**Cap.** The top or covering of anything. See

*Arm-cap.*
*Belt-rail Cap.*
*Bolster-spring Cap.*
*Brake-hose Coupling-cap.*
*Candle-holder Cap.*
*Coupling-cap.*
*Equalizing - bar - spring Cap.*
*Inside-lining Cap.*
*Leakage-valve Cap.*
*Left-chamber Cap.*
*Lever-frame Cap.*

*Lower Cap of Triple-valve.*
*Main Cap of Triple-valve.*
*Reversing-cylinder Cap.*
*Reversing-valve Cap.*
*Right-chamber Cap.*
*Smoke-pipe Cap.*
*Spiral-spring Cap.*
*Spring-cap.*
*Tank-nozzle Cap.*
*Trimming Cap.*
*Truss-plank Cap.*
*Upper Cap of Triple-valve.*

*Window-sill Cap.*

**Car.** A term used in the United States to designate any vehicle or carriage for running on a railroad. As the term is usually employed it denotes any vehicle used for transportation and not belonging to the motive power of a railroad. See

*Baggage-car.*
*Boarding-car.*
*Bob-tail Street-car.*
*Box-car.*
*Box Cattle-car.*
*Cabin-car.*
*Caboose-car.*
*Cannon-car.*
*Cattle-car.*
*Coach.*
*Coal-car.*
*Coal Dump-car.*
*Coal-hopper.*
*Combined Baggage and Express or Mail Car.*
*Combined Box and Cattle Car.*
*Combined Passenger and Mail, Baggage, or Express Car.*
*Conductor's Car.*
*Crank Hand-car.*

*Derrick-car.*
*Double-deck Cattle-car.*
*Double-deck Street-car.*
*Drawing-room Car.*
*Drop-bottom Car.*
*Dump-car.*
*Eight-wheeled Box-car.*
*Eight - wheeled Gondola Coal-car.*
*Eight-wheeled Hopper-bottom Coal-car.*
*Excursion Street-car.*
*Express-car.*
*Express Hand-car.*
*Fare-box Street-car.*
*Ferry Push-car.*
*First-class Car.*
*Flat-car.*
*Folding-side Gondola-car.*
*Four-wheeled Box-car.*
*Four - wheeled Gondola-car.*

*Four-wheeled Hopper-bottom Coal-car.*
*Freight-car.*
*Gondola-car.*
*Grain-car.*
*Gravel-car.*
*Gun-car.*
*Hand-car.*
*Hay-car.*
*Hopper-bottom Coal-car.*
*Hopper-bottom Gondola Coal-car.*
*Horse-car.*
*Hotel-car.*
*House-car.*
*Ice-car.*
*Inclined-plane Car.*
*Inspection car.*
*Inspection Hand-car.*
*Iron-hopper Coal-car.*
*Lever Hand-car.*
*Lodging-car.*
*Mail-car.*
*Milk-car.*
*Mine-car.*
*Oil-car.*

*One-horse Street-car.*
*Ore-car.*
*Palace-car.*
*Passenger-car.*
*Post-office Car.*
*Push Baggage-car.*
*Push-car.*
*Postal-car.*
*Railroad-car.*
*Refrigerator-car.*
*Restaurant-car.*
*Reversible Street-car.*
*Second-class Car.*
*Slat Cattle-car.*
*Sleeping-car.*
*Steam-car.*
*Stock-car.*
*Street-car.*
*Suburban Excursion-car.*
*Summer Street-car.*
*Sweeping-car.*
*Tank-car.*
*Three-wheeled Hand-car.*
*Tip-car.*
*Top-seat Street-car.*
*Tool-car.*

*Train-car.*     *Wrecking-car.*

**Car-axle.** A shaft made of wrought-iron or steel to which a pair of car-wheels are attached. See **2**, figs. 88–129 and figs. 143, 144. In nearly all cases the wheels are both rigidly fastened to the axle, but sometimes one, or both of them, is made so that it can turn independently of the axle. The following are the names of the parts of an axle indicated by numbers in fig. 143.: **1**, *Centre of Axle;* **2**, *Neck of Axle;* **3**, *Wheel-seat;* **4**, *Dust-guard Bearing;* **5**, *Collar;* **6**, *Journal.* See *Hammered Car-axle. Master Car-builders' Standard Axle. Standard Car-axle.*

**Car-box.** A *Journal-box,* which see.

**Car-candle.** A candle made especially for lighting cars. Such candles are usually made of larger diameter than those ordinarily used. They are commonly burned in candle-lamps. See *Hydraulic-pressed Car-candle.*

**Car-coupler.** An appliance for connecting or coupling cars together. The term is used generally to designate an apparatus which acts automatically. See *Janney Car-coupler. Miller Car-coupler.*

**Car-door Lock.** A lock for a car-door. Usually the term is used to designate a lock for a passenger-car door. See fig. 522.

**Card-rack.** A small receptacle on the outside of a freight-car to receive cards on which the shipping directions for the freight, with which the car is loaded, is written. See **80**, figs. 55, 60.

**Car-fittings.** *Car-furnishings*, which see.

**Car-furnishings.** The hardware, upholstery materials, and other fittings, such as lamps, ventilators, water-coolers, etc., used in finishing a passenger-car.

**Car-gong.** A *Signal-bell*, which see.

**Car-heater.** Any apparatus for heating cars by convection, that is, by conveying hot water, steam, or warmed air into, or through, the car. It generally refers to any arrangement for warming cars other than stoves. See *Spear Anti-clinker Car-heater. Baker Car-heater.*

**Carline**, *or* **Carling.** A transverse bar of wood or iron which extends across the top of a car or from one side to the other, and which supports the roof-boards. See **81**, figs. **56, 58, 61, 62, 64, 69, 70, 72** ; **100**, figs. 215, 221, 225, 226, 229 ; **53**, figs. 750, 752. A carline is sometimes called a *Rafter*, which see. See

*Clear-story Carline.*　　*Platform-hood Carline.*
*Compound Carline.*　　*Platform-roof Carline.*
*End Carline.*　　　　*Platform-roof-end Carline.*
*Main Carline.*　　　　*Profile Carline.*
　　　　　*Short Carline.*

**Car-platform.** A floor at the end and on the outside of a car, and supported by projecting timbers below the car-body. On passenger and street cars such platforms are intended to facilitate the ingress and egress of passengers to and from the car. On freight-cars they are used for the convenience of train-men. See **34**, figs. 215, 216, 217, 219, 220, 223, 228, 229, 232; **104**, figs. 750—752.

**Car-pump.** A *Wash-room Pump*, which see.

**Carriage-bolt.** A bolt which is made square under the head so as to prevent it from turning when in its place, and which has a metal thread and nut on the opposite end. Such bolts usually have button-shaped heads and are used for fastening wooden objects together. See fig. 778.

**Carrier.** That which carries or supports something. See
*Brake-hanger Carrier.*　*Parallel Brake-hanger Car-*
*Foot-rest Carrier.*　　　*rier.*
　　　　*Spring-plank Carrier.*

**Car-roof.** A covering for a car, consisting of rafters or car-lines covered with boards or other material. See
*Corrugated-metal Car-*　*Plank Car-roof.*
*roof.*　　　　　　　　*Tin Car-roof.*
*Double-board Car-roof.*　*Winslow Car-roof.*

**Carry-iron.** See
*Draw-bar Carry-iron.*　*Inner Draw-bar Carry-iron.*

**Car-seal.** A disc of lead or other soft metal, with two holes through it to receive a piece of twisted wire, which is first passed through a hasp or ring in a car-door and another in the car-door post, so as to hold the door shut. The seal is then stamped with suitable dies so as to leave some device on it which must be defaced before the door can be opened unless the wire is cut. Either will reveal that the door has been opened. See figs. 539, 540. Seals made of glass, hard rubber and other material are also used. These are attached to some kind of latch or lock so that when the latter is fastened the car-door cannot be opened without breaking or defacing the seal.

**Car-seat.** This term is applied to the complete set of fixtures on which passengers sit in a car. It consists of a seat-frame, cushions, back, arm-rest, foot-rest, and their attachments. Ordinarily, the seats in American cars used on steam roads are placed cross-wise of the car; and are made so that two passengers can sit on one seat, and the backs of the seats are generally made reversible so that passengers can sit and face either way, and are sometimes called *reversible seats*. See **122**, figs. 215, 216, 218, 219, 220, 229, 230 ; figs. 400–407. The seats of street-cars are usually placed longitudinally on each side of the car as shown in figs. 750–752, extending its full length, and the passengers sit facing each other. See

| | |
|---|---|
| *Cane-seat.* | *Rattan Car-seat.* |
| *Perforated-veneer Seat.* | *Side-seat.* |

**Car-spring.** This a general term applied to springs on which the weight of a car rests, and also to draw and buffer springs. See

| | |
|---|---|
| *Auxiliary Buffer-spring.* | *Nest-spring.* |
| *Combination Elliptic-spring.* | *Paragon Spiral-spring.* |
| *Compound Spiral-spring.* | *Quadruple-coil Spiral-spring.* |
| *Couplet of Springs.* | *Quadruplet of Springs.* |
| *Cluster-spring.* | *Quintuplet of Springs.* |
| *Dinsmore Spiral-spring.* | *Round-bar Spiral-spring.* |
| *Double-coil Nest-spring.* | *Rubber-centre Spiral-spring.* |
| *Draft-spring.* | *Rubber-spring.* |
| *Draw-spring.* | *Set of Springs.* |
| *Edge-rolled Spiral-spring.* | *Sextuplet of Springs.* |
| *Elliptic-spring.* | *Spiral-spring* |
| *Equal-bar Nest-spring.* | *Spool-shaped Spiral-spring.* |
| *Equalizing-bar Spring.* | *Square-bar Spiral-spring.* |
| *Flat-bar Spiral-spring.* | *Triple-coil Nest-spring.* |
| *Group-spring.* | *Triplet of Springs.* |
| *Gum-spring.* | *Volute-spring.* |
| *Half Elliptic-spring.* | *Wool-packed Spiral-spring.* |
| *Hibbard-spring.* | |
| *India-rubber Car-spring.* | |
| *Journal-spring.* | |
| *Keg-shaped Spiral-spring.* | |

**Car-truck.** A group of two or more pairs of wheels and axles attached to a frame with suitable journal-boxes, springs, jaws, etc., to form a complete carriage, and intended to carry one end of a car-body. The latter is attached to the truck by a pair of centre-plates, and a centre-pin or king-bolt, about which the truck can swivel. Most American cars are carried on two trucks, one placed near each end of the car-body. In Europe, a truck is often called a *bogie*. Figs. 88–129 are illustrations of different kinds of car-trucks.

**Car-washer.** A brush made for washing the outside of passenger cars. They are made of bristles or feathers. See fig. 792.

**Car-wheel.** A wheel for a railroad car. Such wheels are usually made in this country of cast-iron with a chilled tread and flange. The portion of such wheels between the hub and tread generally consists of one or two cast-iron discs or plates. When one is used they are called *single-plate wheels*, and when two, *double-plate wheels*. When one disc is used, it is sometimes made flat, with ribs on the back, and sometimes corrugated, without ribs. The discs of double-plate wheels are generally corrugated. What is known as the Washburn pattern of wheel has two corrugated discs extending from the hub about half way to the tread, and a single plate, with curved ribs on the back, between the tread and the double plates. Cast-iron wheels are also made with spokes, which are either solid or tubular, with steel tires either welded or bolted to or shrunk on cast-iron centres, and also with wooden or paper discs, or centres, and steel tires. See **1,** figs. 88–127; **25–25,** fig. 138. The parts of wheels are the *flange, tread, rim, face of rim, tire, retaining rings, plate, ribs, spokes, centre, hub, and axle-seat.* See

*Broad-tread Wheel.*
*Combination Plate-wheel.*
*Combination-wheel.*
*Compromise-wheel.*
*Double-plate Wheel.*
*Elastic-wheel.*
*Hand-car Wheel.*
*Hollow-spoke Wheel.*
*Narrow-tread Wheel.*
*Open-plate Wheel.*
*Pair of Wheels.*

*Paper-wheel.*
*Plate-wheel.*
*Sax and Kear Wheel.*
*Single-plate Wheel.*
*Spoke-wheel.*
*Steeled-wheel.*
*Steel-tired Wheel.*
*Steel-wheel.*
*Street-car Wheel.*
*Washburn Wheel.*
*Wrought-iron Wheel.*

**Car-window Brush.** A brush used for washing car-windows. See fig. 793.

**Case.** "A covering, box, or sheath; that which incloses or contains: as, a case for knives; a case for books; a watch case; a pillow case."—*Webster.* See

*Brake-hose Coupling-case.*
*Coupling-case.*
*Door-case.*

*Lamp-case.*
*Leakage-valve Case.*
*Spring-case.*

*Triple-valve Case.*

**Casing.** That which forms a case. See

*Heater-pipe Casing.*    *Perforated Smoke-pipe*
*Inside-casing.*          *Casing.*
*Outside-casing.*      *Smoke-pipe Casing.*
        *Window-casing.*

**Casing,** *for Spear heater.* A cylindrical sheet-iron cover by which the fire-pot is inclosed so as to leave an air-space between the two. See **16,** figs. 550–554.

**Casting.** Any piece of metal which has been cast in a mould. See

*Corner-casting.*     *Roof Corner-casting.*
*Draw-bar Side-casting.*  *Side-casting.*
*Eccentric-lever Casting.*  *Transom-casting.*
   *Roller Side-bearing Casting.*

**Cast-iron Top,** *for Baker heater.* A plate which forms the top of the fire-chamber of a Baker heater. It is made with perforations around the outside, and has an opening in the centre through which the fire in the stove is supplied with coal. See **8,** fig. 581 ; fig. 589.

**Castor.** A small wheel on a swivel, attached to furniture, and on which it is rolled on the floor. See *Chair-castor. Sofa-castor. Socket-castor.*

**Catch.** See *Door-holder Catch. Sliding-door-holder Catch.*

**Catcher.** See *Mail-catcher.*

**Cattle-car.** A car made for transporting live-stock. Such cars are made with grated doors and windows as well as tight doors for closing in cold weather. They are also made with slats which leave about one-half the sides and ends open. The former are called *box cattle-cars,* and the latter *slat cattle-cars.* Cattle-cars are also called *stock-cars.* See figs. 15, 69–72. See *Double-deck Cattle-car. Combined Box and Cattle-car.*

**Ceiling.** The inside or under surface of the roof or covering of a room or car opposite the floor. This term is sometimes used to mean *sheathing,* which see. See also, *Deafening Ceiling.*

**Ceiling-veneers.** Thin boards with which the ceilings of passenger-cars are covered.

**Centre.** See *Wheel-centre.*

**Centre-bearing.** The place in the centre of a truck where the weight of a car-body rests. A plate attached to the car-body—called a *body centre-plate*—here rests on another fastened to the truck, called a *truck centre-plate.* The general term, *centre-bearing,* is used to designate the whole arrangement and the functions which it performs. See *Body Centre-plate. Truck Centre-plate.*

**Centre-bearing Arch-bar.** The upper or compression member of a centre-bearing bridge which supports the centre-bearing of a six-wheeled truck. See **66,** figs. 129, 130.

**Centre-bearing Beam.** A transverse beam which forms the centre member of a bolster for a six-wheeled truck, and to which the centre-plate is attached. See **65**, figs. 129, 130.

**Centre-bearing Bridge.** A longitudinal iron bar, truss, or wooden beam, the ends of which rest on the spring-beams of a six-wheeled truck, and by which the truck centre-beam is supported. See **66, 67**, figs. 129, 130.

**Centre-bearing Inverted Arch-bar.** The lower or tension member of a centre-bearing bridge which supports the centre-bearing block of a six-wheeled truck. See **67**, figs. 129, 130.

**Centre-block.** A *Centre-plate Block*, which see.

**Centre-body Truss-rod.** When two or more body truss-rods are used under each side of a car-body, those nearest the centre are called *centre-body truss-rods*.

**Centre Brake-lever.** A horizontal lever placed underneath the bottom of a car-body, and attached to the latter by a fixed fulcrum in the centre of the body and of the lever. It is connected to each of the brake-beams by rods attached to it near the fulcrum, and its ends by rods and chains, with a brake-windlass on each platform. See **9**, figs. 641, 644, 645; **129**, figs. 750–753.

**Centre Brake-lever Chain.** A chain used on the Elder-brake, which runs over pulleys on a lever attached underneath the centre of the car-body. See **10**, fig. 645.

**Centre-brake-lever Sheave.** A pulley attached to a centre-brake-lever of an Elder-brake, over which a chain runs which is used in applying the brakes. See **11**, fig. 645.

**Centre-brake-lever Spider.** A wrought-iron support, resembling the letter **H** in form, by which a centre-brake-lever is attached to a car-body. See **130**, figs. 750, 751.

**Centre Door-rail.** See *Middle Door-rail.*

**Centre-draft Draw-bar.** A draw-bar which is connected directly with the king-bolt of a truck. See **32**, figs. 229-232.

**Centre Floor-timbers.** The two main longitudinal timbers underneath the floor which are nearest the centre of the car. See **4**, figs. 55-84, 216-230.

**Centre-lamp.** A lamp suspended from the centre of the ceiling of a car. The term is used to distinguish *centre-lamps* from *side-lamps*; the latter being attached to the sides of cars. See **135**, fig. 218; figs. 470–473.

**Centre-piece,** *for Engine and Air-pump of Westinghouse-brake.* An iron casting which forms the lower head of a steam-cylinder, and the upper head of an air-cylinder, and which has suitable projecting recesses cast with it, which form stuffing-boxes for the piston-rod. See **4**, figs. 664, 665; fig. 668.

**Centre-pin.** A *King-bolt*, which see.

**Centre-plate.** One of a pair of plates, usually made of

cast-iron, which support a car-body on the centre of a truck. See

 *Body Centre-plate.* *Male Centre-plate.*
 *Female Centre-plate.* *Truck Centre-plate.*

**Centre-plate Block.** A piece of wood placed under a truck centre-plate to raise it up to the proper height. See **64**, figs. 109–111 ; figs. 119–126.

**Centre-shaft.** A *Winding-shaft*, which see.

**Centre-stop,** *for Tip-car.* An iron bracket or wooden block, which is attached to a draw-timber, and holds the body of a tip-car from moving longitudinally on the running gear. See **161**, fig. 81.

**Chafing-plate.** A metal plate interposed to resist wear between two surfaces which rub or wear against each other. Such plates are used on brake-beams, truck-transoms, and swinging spring-beams. See

 *Brake-beam Chafing-* *Draw-bar Chafing-plate.*
 *plate.* *Transom Chafing-plate.*
 *Check-chain Chafing-* *Truck-bolster Chafing-plate.*
 *plate.* *Coupling-pin Chafing-plate.*

**Chain.** " A series of links or rings connected, or fitted into one another, usually made of some kind of metal."— *Webster.* See

 *Basin-chain.* *Brake-shaft Chain.*
 *Berth-chain.* *Centre Brake-lever Chain.*
 *Brake Safety-chain.* *Check-chain.*

 *Coupling-chain.* *Man-hole-cover Chain.*
 *Coupling-pin Chain.* *Platform-railing Chain.*
 *Door-pin Chain.* *Railing-chain.*
 *Drop-bottom Chain.* *Safety-coupling Chain.*
 *Horizontal-brake-shaft* *Tank-nozzle-cap Chain.*
 *Chain.* *Uncoupling-chain.*
 *Lock-chain.* *Wedge-chain.*

**Chain Coupling-link.** Two or more coupling-links attached together like a chain. See **1**, fig. 271.

**Chain-holder.** See *Basin-chain Holder.*

**Chain-pulley,** *for Creamer-brake.* An inclined pulley on top of the iron pipe which guards the connecting-chain, and over which it runs.

**Chair.** See *Revolving-chair.*

**Chair-arm Cap.** An *Arm-shield*, which see.

**Chair-castor.** A small wheel and swivel attached to the legs of chairs so that they can be easily moved on the floor. See fig. 390.

**Chair-leg Socket.** A hollow casting which fits on the end of a chair-leg and forms a foot or shoe for the latter. Such sockets are sometimes provided with wheels on which the chair is rolled and sometimes they are without them. See fig. 392.

**Chamber.** See *Dust-guard Chamber.*

**Chamber-cap.** See *Right Chamber-cap.*

**Chaplet.** A piece of iron used in a mould for casting, to hold a core in its place.

**Check-chain.** A chain attached to a truck and the body of a car to prevent the former from swinging crosswise on the track in case the wheels leave the rails. Such chains are usually attached either to two, or to each of the four corners of a truck and to the sills of the cars. See **68**, fig. 122 ; **18**, figs. 215, 218.

**Check-chain Chafing-plate.** A plate attached to a truck-timber to resist the wear of a check-chain.

**Check-chain Eye.** See *Body Check-chain Eye. Truck Check-chain Eye.*

**Check-chain Hook.** See *Body Check-chain Hook. Truck Check-chain Hook.*

**Check-valve,** *for Westinghouse Driving-wheel Brake.* A valve which is placed in the pipe which connects a driving-wheel brake-cylinder with the air-reservoir. The pressure in the reservoir causes the valve to seat itself or close. The air must then flow through a small hole which is drilled in the valve, which prevents the brakes from being applied too suddenly. When the brakes are released, this valve unseats, and permits a quick escape of the air. See fig. 731. See *Double Check-valve.*

**Chill.** The state of hardness which is produced when some kinds of melted cast-iron are allowed to solidify in contact with a metal (usually iron) mould. The hardened part of a car-wheel is called the *chill.* The mould in which a chill is produced is sometimes called a *chill,* but the name *chill-mould* has been given to this, which see.

**Chill-mould.** A mould, as for the tread of a car-wheel, into which melted cast-iron is poured in order to chill or harden the portions which solidify in contact with the mould.

**Chilson's Stove.** A stove for heating cars, which is named after the manufacturer. See fig. 546.

**Chimney.** A passage, tube, or duct for conveying smoke and other volatile matter from a stove or lamp, etc. See

    *Globe-chimney.*     *Lamp-case Chimney.*
    *Lamp-Chimney.*     *Lamp-globe Chimney.*

**Chord.** The outside top or bottom member of a truss. See *Bottom-chord. Lower-chord Top-chord.*

**Circulating-drum,** *for Baker heater.* A cast-iron cylindrical vessel, with hemispherical ends, which is placed on top of a car and is filled with water. It is connected by a pipe with the coil in the stove, and also with the pipes which extend through the car to heat it. As the water in the coil becomes heated it ascends to the drum and from there it descends through the other pipe to the radiating pipes in the car, and after passing through them it is brought back by return pipes to the coil in the stove, when it is again heated, and thus a continuous current or circulation of the water is kept up. See **23**, fig. 581 ; fig. 602.

**Clamp.** 1. "In general, something that fastens or binds; a piece of timber or of iron used to fasten work together." —*Webster.*

2. (Joinery). "A frame with two tightening screws by which two portions of an article are tightly compressed together, either while being formed, or while their glue joint is drying."—*Knight.* See *Clear-story Window-sector Clamp. Platform-timber Clamp.*

**Clapper.** See *Signal-bell Clapper.*

**Clear-story.** "An upper story or row of windows in a church, tower or other erection, rising clear above the adjoining parts of the building."—*Webster.* Hence, the portion of a car-roof which rises above the main roof, with windows or openings for ventilation on the sides. This portion of a car has been called the *raised-roof, monitor-top, dome, upper-deck, texas,* and other incongruous names. See **110-110**, figs. 215–230; **56-56**, figs. 750, 752, 753.

**Clear-story Bottom-rail.** A horizontal timber running lengthwise of a car and fastened to the rafters or carlines of the main roof, or to the clear-story sill, and which forms the base into which the posts of the clear-story are framed. See **112**, fig. 227; **57**, figs. 750, 752.

**Clear-story Carline.** A timber on top of a clear-story, and which extends from one side to the other, and supports the roof boards. See **118**, fig. 215, 218, 219, 221, 222, 224, 227, 229, 230; **60**, figs. 750, 752.

**Clear-story Eaves-moulding.** A wooden moulding attached to the outside edge of the roof of a clear-story. See **119**, fig. 227.

**Clear-story End-panel.** A panel in the end of a clear-story. See **116**, figs. 218, 219, 221, 222, 224.

**Clear-story End-sill.** A horizontal timber running crosswise of a car and secured to the rafters or carlines or to the end of a car-body, and which forms the base for the end of the clear-story. See **113**, figs. 215, 219, 221.

**Clear-story End-ventilator.** An aperture in the end of a clear-story for the admission or escape of air. This aperture is usually opened or closed by a swinging panel. See **116**, figs. 215, 218, 219, 221, 222, 224; **61**, figs. 750, 753.

**Clear-story End-ventilator Hood.** A projecting screen, made of tin or sheet-iron, placed over the aperture of an end-ventilator of a street-car to prevent snow and rain from blowing into the car. See **63**, fig. 750.

**Clear-story Inside-cornice.** A moulding on the inside of a passenger-car, which fills the angle formed where the ceiling or roof of the clear-story joins the side. See **120**, fig. 227.

**Clear-story Plate.** A horizontal timber running lengthwise of the car on top of the clear-story posts, or mullions, and to which the clear-story carlines are attached. See **117**, figs. 215, 218, 219, 221,222, 224, 227. Also called a *Clear-story Top-rail.*

**Clear-story Post.** An upright piece of wood which connects the clear-story plate with the bottom-rail. In street-cars they are attached to the main rafters or car-lines at the lower end, and to the clear-story carlines at the upper end. See **115**, figs. 215, 219, 221, 229; **53**, figs. 750, 752.

**Clear-story Side.** A wooden frame, consisting of a plate, rail, posts and panels, or windows, which forms the side of a clear-story, and occupies the space between the main roof and that of the clear-story.

**Clear-story Side-panel.** A panel in the side of a clear-story between the windows or ventilators.

**Clear-story Side-ventilator.** An opening in the side of a clear-story for the admission or escape of air to or from a car. See **143**, fig. 215; fig. 348. This term is also used to designate the door or valves and their attachments for opening and closing the aperture.

**Clear-story Sill.** A horizontal timber attached to the inner ends of the roof, ribs, or short carlines, and on which the clear-story side rests. See **111**, figs. 215, 218, 221, 222, 224, 226.

**Clear-story-sill Facing.** Thin boards or mouldings at-tached to the inside of a clear-story sill, for ornament. See **114**, fig. 227.

**Clear-story Soffit-board.** A board on the under side of the overhanging cornice of a clear-story roof. See **121**, fig. 227.

**Clear-story Top-rail.** A *Clear-story Plate*, which see.

**Clear-story Ventilator.** A ventilator in the clear-story of a car. See *Clear-story End-ventilator. Clear-story Side-ventilator.*

**Clear-story Window** An opening covered with a glazed sash in the sides of a clear-story. See **144**, figs. 215, 219, 221, 228, 229; **59**, fig. 250.

**Clear-story Window-latch.** A spring-bolt attached to a clear-story window-sash to fasten it or hold it shut. See fig. 330.

**Clear-story Window-latch Keeper.** A plate attached to a clear-story window-frame with a suitable opening in which the bolt of a clear-story window-latch engages. See fig. 331.

**Clear-story Window-opener.** A lever or rod by which a window, ventilator, sash, or panel in a clear-story is held in any desired position. See fig. 333.

**Clear-story Window-pivot.** A metal stud or spindle at-tached to a suitable flange by which it is fastened to a clear-story window-sash, and on which the latter turns. See figs. 327, 770.

**Clear-story Window-pivot Bushing.** A ring or lining for the hole in a clear-story window-post in which a window-pivot works. Same as fig. 310.

**Clear-story Window-pivot Plate.** A plate attached to a window-post, or frame with a hole or eye in which a window-pivot works. Sometimes they are provided with springs so as to prevent the sash from rattling. See fig. 771.

**Clear-story Window-pull.** A screw-ring attached to a clear-story window-sash to open and close it. See fig. 332.

**Clear-story Window-sector.** A bar or plate of metal of the form of part of a circle, and which is used as a guide or stop to control the movement of a clear-story window. See 2, fig. 326.

**Clear-story Window-sector Clamp.** A metal band attached to a clear-story window, and which embraces a clear-story window-sector, and on which the latter slides. See 1, fig. 326.

**Cleat.** "1. A narrow strip of wood nailed on in joinery. 2. A term applied to small wooden projections in tackle to fasten ropes by."—*Webster.*

**Cleveland-truck.** A *Diamond-truck,* which see.

**Clevis.** "A stirrup-shaped metallic strap used in connection with a pin to connect a draft-chain or tree to a plow or other tool."—*Knight.* The term is applied to various kinds of irons resembling a plow clevis in shape, and also to bolts with forked ends. See *Brake-lever Clevis. Draw-clevis.*

**Clinch-nail.** A wrought-iron nail, so named because it can be bent or clinched without breaking.

**Closed-door-stop.** A block or strip of wood or piece of iron fastened to the side of a freight car to prevent outside sliding-doors from moving too far when they are closed. See **72,** fig. 55; 60.

**Close Return-bend.** A short cast-iron tube made of a **U**-shape, for uniting the ends of two wrought-iron pipes. It differs from an open return-bend in having the two branches in contact with each other. See fig. 617.

**Closet.** See *Water-closet.*

**Cluster-spring.** A *Group-spring,* which see.

**Clutch-coupling.** See *Brake-hose Clutch-coupling.*

**Coach.** This term is used to designate a first-class passenger-car in distinction from second-class, smoking, drawing-room, sleeping, and other cars for carrying passengers. See fig. 4.

**Coal-car.** A car especially designed for carrying coal. Ordinary platform-cars with sideboards are much used for that purpose. Four-wheeled cars, with drop-bottoms, and iron cars, with four, six and eight wheels, also with drop-bottoms, are made for that purpose. See
   *Coal Dump-car.*          *Coal-hopper.*

Eight-wheeled Gondola Coal-car.

Eight-wheeled Hopper-bottom Coal-car.

Four-wheeled Gondola Coal-car.

Four-wheeled Hopper-bottom Coal-car.

Hopper-bottom Coal-car.

Hopper-bottom Gondola Coal-car.

Iron-hopper Coal-car.

**Coal Dump-car.** A term applied to all coal-cars with drop-bottoms or tilting arrangements for unloading the coal which they carry. See figs. 24, 25, 26, 27.

**Coal-hopper.** See Hopper-bottom Coal-car. Iron-hopper Coal-car.

**Coal-oil Burner.** See Mineral-oil Burner.

**Coat and Hat-hook.** A metal hook with two prongs, one for hanging a coat on and the other for a hat. See fig. 446.

**Coat-hook.** A hook with one prong used for hanging a coat or other light article on. See fig. 444.

**Cock.** "A spout; an instrument to draw out or discharge liquor from a cask, vat, or pipe."—Webster. See

Bibb-cock.

Combination-cock.

Drain-cock.

Draw-off Cock.

Four-way-cock Plug.

Reservoir Drain-cock.

Self-closing cock.

Stop-cock.

Telegraph-cock.

Three-way Cock.

Vertical Telegraph-cock.

**Cocoa Floor-mat.** See Floor-mat.

**Coil,** for Baker Car-heater. An iron pipe which is bent into a spiral form and placed inside of a Baker heater next the fire, for heating water which circulates through the coil. See 20, fig. 581; 601.

**Cold-air Pipe,** for Spear Heater. A pipe by which cold air is conducted from a hood on top of the car to the bottom of the stove, and into the air-space between the stove and the stove casing. See 2-2, figs. 550, 551, 554.

**Cold-shot.** Small globules of iron resembling ordinary gun-shot, which are found in the chilled portion of cast-iron wheels.

**Collar.** "A ring or round flange upon or against an object."—Knight. See Axle-collar. Deck-collar. Dust-collar.

**Collar,** for Creamer-brake. A cast-iron ring which is fastened to the brake-shaft under the cross-bar by a set-screw to prevent the shaft from being lifted up by the action of the jointed-top pawl. See 11, fig. 646.

**Combination-cock,** for Baker Car-heater. A cock attached to the circulating drum of a Baker car-heater to fill it with water. See 25, figs. 581; 604.

**Combination Elliptic-spring.** An elliptic-spring with which auxiliary rubber bearings at the ends are combined. The load, instead of resting on the centre of the spring, bears on two rubber bearings each placed about one-third the length of the spring from the end. See fig. 188.

**Combination Plate-wheel.** A wheel with a single centre-plate, but with a recess cast around the hub as shown in the engraving. See figs. 159, 160.

**Combination-wheel.** A term applied by Mr. Lobdell to a wheel which he patented, and which has a projection cast on the inside of the rim opposite to the flange.

**Combined Baggage and Express or Mail-car.** A car divided into two or three compartments, one of them for carrying baggage and the other one or two for carrying either express or mail matter or both. See fig. 7.

**Combined Box and Cattle-car.** A car so constructed as to be suited for carrying either cattle or other kinds of freight and merchandise. See fig. 14.

**Combined Passenger and Mail, Baggage or Express-car.** A car divided into two or more compartments for carrying passengers in one, and baggage, mails, or express-matter in others. See fig. 8.

**Compound-bolster.** A bolster composed of one or more sticks of timber stiffened with vertical plates of iron. See fig. 239.

**Compound-carline.** A carline of which the main or central portion is made of wrought-iron with a piece of wood on each side. They are commonly used for cars with clear-stories, and either extend directly from one plate to the other, or are bent to conform to the shape of the clear-story. In the latter case, they are called *Profile-carlines*, which see. See **100**, figs. 215, 221, 229, 248.

**Compound Spiral-spring.** A spring made of a flat bar of metal coiled edgewise on a mandrel, and with the spaces between the coils filled with India-rubber. See fig. 207.

**Compression-bar.** A bar which is subjected to a compressive strain. See *Body-bolster Compression-bar.*

**Compression-beam.** A horizontal timber in the side of a car-body, which acts as the compression-member of a truss for strengthening the body. See **1**, fig. 245.

**Compression-beam Brace.** A brace used in connection with a compression-beam to form a truss in the side of a passenger-car. See **2**, fig. 245.

**Compression-member.** Any bar, beam, brace, etc., which is subjected to strains of compression, and forms part of a frame, truss, beam, girder, etc. *Struts, body-braces,* etc., are *compression-members.* See *Tension-member.*

**Compression-rod Brake.** An inner-hung brake with a single lever, which is connected with the brake-beam farthest from it by a rod or bar which is subjected to a strain of compression when the brakes are applied. See fig. 639.

**Compromise-wheel.** A *Broad-tread Wheel*, which see.

**Conductor's Car.** A car attached to freight trains for the accommodation of the conductor and train-men, and used for protecting them from undue exposure to the weather, and for carrying lanterns, flags, ropes and various stores, tools, etc., required on freight trains while on the road. Also called *caboose-car* and *cabin-car*. Such cars are often made with a clear-story, which is used for displaying train-signals which can be seen by the locomotive runner, and also by following trains. An elevated seat is arranged in the clear-story to give the conductor a good position to see the condition of the train. Conductors' cars are made with four or eight wheels. See figs. 10, 11.

**Conductor's Lantern.** A lantern with a large ring or bail attached to it, by which it can be held on the arm by a conductor while he is collecting tickets and attending to his other duties. See fig. 501.

**Conductor's-valve,** *for Westinghouse Automatic-brake.* A valve placed at some convenient point in a car and operated by a cord extending through the train within reach of the conductor. See fig. 734.

**Conductor's-valve Discharge-pipe,** *for Westinghouse Automatic-brake.* A pipe leading from the conductor's-valve down through the floor of the car. See **28,** fig. 661.

**Conductor's-valve Pipe,** *for Westinghouse Automatic-brake.* A pipe which connects a brake-pipe with the conductor's-valve. See **27,** fig. 661.

**Congdon Brake-shoe.** A brake-shoe invented and pat-

ented by Mr. J. H. Congdon, Master of Machinery of the Union Pacific Railroad. It consists of a cast-iron shoe, with pieces of wrought-iron cast in it in the face or rubbing surface, so as to give it greater endurance than it would have if made of cast-iron alone. See fig. 634.

**Connecting-rod.** A rod which connects two or more parts or objects together. See *Brake-shaft Connecting-rod.*

**Connecting-rod,** *for Creamer brake.* A vertical rod connected at the lower end to the tripping lever and at the upper end with a branch line to the bell-cord, and by which the side-pawl is disengaged from the drum and the brakes are applied. See **8,** fig. 646.

**Connecting-rod,** *for Hand-car.* An iron rod which connects the bell-crank and crank-shaft of a hand-car together, and by which the latter is operated. See **24,** figs. 772, 773, 775.

**Continuous-brake.** A system of brakes so arranged that by connecting together the brake apparatus on the different vehicles forming a train it can be operated on all of them from one or more points on the train, as from the engine or from any of the cars. See

| | |
|---|---|
| *Air-brake.* | *Smith's Vacuum-brake.* |
| *Eames' Vacuum-brake.* | *Vacuum-brake.* |
| *Empire Vacuum-brake.* | *Westinghouse Air-brake.* |
| *Loughridge Air-brake.* | *Westinghouse Automatic Air-brake.* |

**Continuous-frame Truck.** A car-truck with an iron frame, the sides and ends of which are all made in one piece. Figs. 105–107 are engravings of such a truck.

**Continuous Truck-frame.** An iron bar which is welded together in a rectangular shape so as to form the sides and ends of a truck-frame. See **9**, figs. 105–107.

**Cooler.** See *Water-cooler*.

**Corner-band.** See *Corner-plate*.

**Cope.** The upper portion of a mould or flask used in making metal castings.

**Cord.** "A string or small rope, composed of several strands twisted together."—*Webster*. See *Hat-cord*. *Window-curtain Cord*.

**Corner-casting.** A *Knee-iron*, which see. See also *Roof Corner-casting*.

**Corner-handle.** A handle attached at or near the corner of a freight-car for men to take hold of in climbing on and off cars. Such handles are usually made of iron bars bent into a suitable shape. See **102**, figs. 60, 65, 69, 71, 82, 84.

**Corner-plate.** A wrought or cast iron angle-plate or knee on the outside corner of a freight-car body to strengthen it at that point and to protect the side and end sills and sheathing from injury in case the car should come into collision with another car or other object.

See *Upper Corner-plate. Lower Corner-plate. Middle Corner-plate*.

**Corner-post.** The upright stick of timber at the corner of a car-body which forms the corner of the frame. See **43**, figs. 55–84 ; **61**, figs. 215–229 ; **17**, figs. 750–753.

**Corner-post Brace.** A bar of wrought-iron which is attached to the corner-post, and extends diagonally from it to the sill, which projects beyond the body. See **163**, fig. 81.

**Corner-post Ornament.** An ornamental casting on the outside corner of a passenger-car.

**Corner-post Pocket.** A casting on top of the sills of a car-body to receive a corner-post. See **45**, figs. 69, 71, 72 77, 78, 79.

**Corner-seat.** A seat for the corner of a car, the back of which is not reversible. See figs. 406, 407. See *Left-hand Seat. Right-hand Seat*.

**Corner Seat-end.** A seat-end which forms a bracket that is secured to the wall of a passenger-car for supporting the outer end of a corner-seat. See figs. 406, 407. They are of two kinds: *right-hand* and *left-hand*. A *right-hand end* is one which would be on the right-hand side of a person when seated in the corner-seat. See figs. 406, 408. A *left-hand end* is one which would come on the left-hand side of a passenger in a similar position. See figs. 407, 409.

**Corner-urinal.** A urinal shaped so as to fit into the corner of a car or room. See fig. 438.

**Corner Urinal-handle.** A handle attached in the corner of a water closet. See fig. 443. See *Urinal-handle*. *Side Urinal-handle*.

**Cornice.** The mouldings at the eaves of the roof outside of a car, and where the ceiling joins the sides and ends of the car inside. There is, therefore, an inside and outside cornice. See **93** and **94**, figs. 225, 226. See *Clear-story Inside-cornice*. *Window-cornice*.

**Corrugated-metal Car-roof.** A roof for freight-cars, consisting of iron, steel, or zinc plates or sheets which extend across the car and are fastened to the rafters and carlines. The plates are covered with boards, which run lengthwise, and rest on roof-strips on top of the rafters and carlines. See fig. 67.

**Counter-brace.** A brace which transmits strains in an opposite direction to a main-brace. See **9**, figs. 807, 809. In car-building a counter-brace is a brace in the side of the body, between its ends and the body-bolster. See *Body Counter-brace*.

**Counter-brace Rod.** An inclined rod which acts as a counter-brace in a frame, truss, girder, etc. See **11**, figs. 806, 808. See also *Body Counter-brace-rod*.

**Coupler.** That which couples. In relation to cars the term usually designates the appliances for coupling or connecting cars together. See *Car-coupler*. *Janney-car Coupler*. *Miller Car-coupler*.

**Couplet of Springs.** Two elliptic springs, placed side by side, and united in such a way as to act as one spring. See **80**, figs. 100, 108. Three springs united in this way form a *triplet*, four a *quadruplet*, five a *quintuplet*, six a *sextuplet*.

**Coupling.** "That which couples or connects, as a hook, chain, or bar."—*Webster*. A coupling-link is often called simply a *Coupling*. See

    *Basin-coupling*.         *Brake-hose Coupling*.
    *Bell-cord Coupling*.      *Clutch-coupling*.
    *Berth Curtain-rod Coupling*.     *Coupling-link*.
       *ling*.               *Head-board Coupling*.
    *Brake-hose Clutch-coupling*.     *Hose-coupling*.
       *ling*.              *Pipe-coupling*.
        *Reducing Pipe-coupling*.

**Coupling-cap.** See *Brake-hose Coupling-cap*.

**Coupling-case.** See *Brake-hose-coupling Case*.

**Coupling-chain.** See *Safety-coupling-chain*.

**Coupling-hose.** *Brake-hose*, which see.

**Coupling-hook.** A hook for coupling cars together. See *Draw-bar Coupling-hook*. *Draw-hook*.

**Coupling-link.** A wrought-iron link or open bar by which cars with ordinary draw-heads are connected or coupled together. The links are fastened to the draw-heads by coupling pins. Coupling-links are often called simply *links* or *couplings*. See **2**; figs. 267, 269, 272. See

*Chain Coupling-link.*    *Fast Coupling-link.*
*Crooked Coupling-link.*    *Triple Coupling-link.*

**Coupling-link Rivet.** A pin by which a fast coupling-link is attached to a draw-bar. The pin is riveted fast in the bar. See **1**, figs. 267, 269.

**Coupling-pin.** A short bar of iron with which a coupling-link is connected to a draw-bar. See **140**, figs. 56, 60, 69, 73 ; figs. 274–277. See

*Eye-head Coupling-pin.*    *Flat Coupling-pin.*
*Fast-Coupling-pin.*    *Oval Coupling-pin.*
*Solid-head Coupling-pin.*

**Coupling-pin Chafing-plate,** *for Miller-platform.* An iron plate attached to the outside of a platform end-timber opposite the hole which receives the coupling-link when it is not in use. The purpose of the plate is to protect the timber from being worn or chafed by the chain by which the pin is fastened to the platform. See **40**, figs. 283, 285.

**Coupling-pin Chain.** A small chain for fastening a coupling-pin to the car-body to prevent the pin from being lost. See **41**, fig. 285.

**Coupling-pin-chain Eye.** An iron eye attached to the end of a car for fastening a coupling-pin chain. See **42**, fig. 285.

**Coupling-pin Plate,** *for Miller-platform.* An iron plate which is attached to the top of a platform end-timber near the outside end, and which forms a guard or shield for a hole in the timber to hold the pin when it is not in use. See **39**, figs. 283–285.

**Coupling-spring,** *for Miller-coupler.* A steel spring made of two or more flat and nearly straight plates of steel which bear against the back of a Miller draw-bar coupling-hook so as to cause it to engage with the hook of the adjoining car. See **49**, fig. 282.

**Coupling-spring Bracket,** *for Miller-platform.* A cast-iron lug attached to one of the draw-bar timbers, and to which a bolt is fastened for drawing up or increasing the tension on the coupling-spring. See **50**, figs. 282, 283.

**Coupling-valve.** See *Brake hose-coupling Valve.*

**Coupling-valve Spring.** See *Brake-hose Coupling-valve Spring.*

**Cover.** See

*Drum-cover.*    *Urinal-cover.*
*Journal-box Cover.*    *Window-moulding-joint*
*Man-hole Cover.*    *Cover.*
*Moulding-joint Cover.*

**Crank.** "Literally a bend or turn; hence an iron axis with a part bent like an elbow, for producing a horizontal or perpendicular motion by means of a rotary motion or the contrary."—*Webster.* See *Bell-crank. Brake-shaft crank. Door-shaft crank.*

**Crank Hand-car.** A hand-car which is worked by one or

two cranks connected by gearing with the axles of the car. See figs. 43, 45.

**Crank-shaft,** *for Hand-car.* A short wrought-iron shaft to which a crank of a hand-car is attached, which is turned by suitable levers and is connected by gear-wheels with one of the axles of the car. See **6,** figs. 772–775.

**Crank-shaft Bearings,** *for Hand-car.* Iron boxes or clamps which hold the crank-shaft of a hand-car in its place, and in which it turns. See **7,** figs. 772–775.

**Creamer Safety-brake.** A brake represented by figs. 646–648, invented by William G. Creamer, of New York, and which consists of an involute spring which is attached to and acts on the brake-shaft. This spring is contained in a case, or drum, **1,** fig. 646. Before a train starts on a trip the spring is wound up and held in a state of tension by a pawl, **6.** In case of danger, the pawl is disengaged by a lever, **7,** connected to the rod **8,** which is operated by the bell-cord. By this means the locomotive-runner, conductor, or brakemen can at any time apply all the brakes, or they will be applied by the separation of the train.

**Cricket-iron.** A *Seat-stand,* which see.

**Crooked Coupling-link.** A coupling-link bent in such a way as to couple draw-bars which vary considerably in height. See fig. 273.

**Crooked End-piece,** *of Truck-frame.* An outside end-piece of a truck which is bent or hollowed out on top so as to clear the draw-timbers and draw-bar fixtures. See **17,** figs. 90, 94.

**Cross-bar,** *for Creamer-brake.* A horizontal cast-iron bar fastened to the platform-posts, and to which the bearings for the brake-shaft and the pawls which hold the spring are attached. See **2,** figs. 646, 647.

**Cross-bearer.** A *Cross-frame Tie-timber,* which see.

**Cross-frame King-post or Truss-block.** A bearing for a cross-frame truss-rod at the centre of the cross-frame tie-timber.

**Cross-frame Tie-timber.** A transverse timber bolted to the under side of the longitudinal sills and floor timbers of a car-body between the bolsters, and to which the body, king or queen posts, or truss-blocks are attached when truss-rods are used under a car-body. See **22,** figs. 55–72 ; **26,** figs. 215, 216, 219, 221, 228, 229.

**Cross-frame Truss-rod.** A rod with which a cross-frame tie-timber is trussed. See **3,** fig. 242.

**Cross-frame Truss-rod Washer.** A plate on the end of a cross-frame tie-timber which forms a bearing for a nut on the truss-rod. See **6,** fig. 242.

**Cross-head,** *for Westinghouse Driving-wheel Brake.* A wrought-iron **T**-shaped head attached to the lower end of a piston-rod of a driving-wheel brake, and to which two links are attached, which connect the piston-rod with the eccentric-levers which work the brake-heads. See **6**, figs. 747, 749.

**Cross-head,** *for Westinghouse Car-brake.* A forked casting attached to the outside end of a piston-rod for Westinghouse car-brake, and to which one of the brake-levers and also the releasing-lever are connected. See **3**, figs. 660, 661 ; **6**, figs. 729.

**Cup.** "A small vessel of capacity used commonly to drink out of, but the name is also given to vessels of like shape used for other purposes."—*Webster.* See

    *Buffer-spring Cup.*      *Drinking-cup.*
    *Candle-holder Cup.*      *Oil-cup.*
    *Drain-cup.*      *Side-bearing Cup.*

**Cupboard-bolt.** A *Flush-bolt,* which see.

**Cupboard-latch.** A small metal lift-latch attached to a cupboard-door to hold it shut. See fig. 538.

**Cup-holder.** A stand or rack for holding a drinking-cup. See *Alcove Cup-holder.* See fig. 425.

**Cup Side-bearing.** A side-bearing for trucks, with a receptacle for holding oil and waste for lubricating the two bearings. See **61**, figs. 89, 112, 113, 116, 117, 124–126.

**Cup-washer.** A *Socket-washer,* which see.

**Curled-hair.** Hair from the tails or manes of cattle, horses, etc., which is first spun into ropes, then wound into coils, and either steeped or boiled in water. After this the coil is dried and the hair unwound, which

leaves it in a curly and elastic state. suited for stuffing cushions, etc.

**Curtain.** A cloth hanging in front of or around any space or object, as a window or sleeping-car berth, and which may be contracted or spread at will. See *Berth-curtain. Summer Street-car Curtain. Window-curtain.*

**Cushion.** A soft pad to be placed on a seat. See *Box-cushion. Seat-cushion. Squab-cushion.*

**Cushion-frame.** A wooden frame to which the seat-springs and upholstery of a car-seat are attached. See fig. 414.

**Cuspador.** A vessel to receive discharges of spittle, and having a wide rim so that if it is upset its contents will not be spilled. See fig. 388.

**Cylinder.** A chamber or vessel whose ends are circular, and with straight parallel sides, as the cylinder of a steam-engine. The cylinders used in connection with cars and locomotives are made oi cast-iron, and have pistons fitted so as to work air-tight in them. See

    *Air-cylinder.*      *Reversing-cylinder.*
    *Brake-cylinder.*      *Steam-cylinder.*

**Cylinder-body,** *for Westinghouse Car-brake.* A hollow, cylindrical casting, which is accurately bored out and fitted with two heads or covers, and a piston and rod by which the car-brakes are operated. See **2**, figs. 729, 730.

**Cylinder-body,** *for Westinghouse Driving-wheel Brake.* Same as above for driving-wheel brake. See **2,** fig. 749.

**Cylinder-body,** *for Westinghouse Tender-brake.* Same as above for tender-brake. See **2,** figs. 727, 728.

**Cylinder-head.** A metal cover for the end of a cylinder. See

    *Air-cylinder Head.*      *Front Cylinder-head.*
    *Back Cylinder-head.*      *Steam Cylinder-head.*
    *Bottom Cylinder-head.*      *Top-cylinder Head.*

**Cylinder-levers,** *for Westinghouse Automatic Car-brake.* Two levers which are connected together by a rod attached near their centres. One end of the one lever is attached to the cross-head of the brake-cylinder and the corresponding end of the other lever is attached to a bracket on the brake-cylinder head at the opposite end of the cylinder. The other ends of the levers are connected with the floating levers by rods. See **11,** fig. 661.

**Cylinder-lever Bracket,** *for Westinghouse Car-brake.* A **T**-shaped piece of iron bolted to the front cylinder-head, and to which one of the brake-levers is attached. See **4,** fig. 661; **7,** fig. 729.

**Cylinder-lever Support,** *for Westinghouse-brake.* A wrought-iron bar bolted to one of the centre floor-timbers, and on which the ends of the cylinder-levers rest. See **19,** figs. 660, 661.

**Cylinder-lever Tie-rod,** *of Westinghouse-brake.* A rod by which the two cylinder-levers are connected together. See **18,** fig. 661.

**Cylindrical-gauges.** Gauges made for measuring the size of cylinders and cylindrical holes, and which were made by Whitworth, of England, and are therefore often called Whitworth gauges. They consist of steel cylinders and rings hardened and ground very accurately to standard sizes. These fit into each other. The first is used for measuring the size of holes and the last for measuring the outside of cylindrical objects, and they are called *internal* and *external cylindrical-gauges.* They are generally used as standards alone, from which other tools and gauges are made of the proper size. See *External Cylindrical-gauge. Internal Cylindrical-gauge.*

**Cylindrical-stove.** A stove made of the form of an upright cylinder. See fig. 544.

# D

**Damper.** See *Stove-pipe Damper.*

**Damper-handle.** See *Stove-pipe Damper-handle.*

**Dash-guard.** A plate or sheet of metal attached to the platform railing of street-cars to prevent water, mud, or snow from being thrown upon persons on the platform. See **111,** figs. 750–753.

**Dash-guard Straps.** Small clamps or iron bands which are

riveted to a dash-guard, and by which the latter is fastened to the platform-posts   See **112**, fig. 750.

**Dead-blocks.**  Two blocks of wood or iron, attached either to the end-sill or buffer-beam of a freight-car, and intended to resist the concussion of two cars when they come together after the buffer-springs are compressed. They are placed somewhat above the draw-bar and one on each side of it, with a space of about one or two feet between them, as shown at **32**, figs. 55–59, 69–84; fig. 278. The term *dead-blocks* and *buffer-blocks* are often confused with each other.  *Dead-blocks* are always used in pairs, one on each side of the draw-bar, as shown in the figs. referred to above, while a buffer-block is a single piece of wood directly over the draw-bar, as shown at **29**, figs. 60–65.  Dead-blocks have probably been so named because so many men have been killed by them. They are also called *man-killers*.

**Dead-block Face-plate.**  A metal plate bolted to the outside or face of a wooden buffer-block, and which forms a bearing for the buffer-blocks of other cars when they come in contact with each other.  The object of the plate is to protect the wood from wear.

**Dead-lock.**  A lock in which the bolt is thrown each way by the key, and not by a spring, in one direction, as is the case with a spring-lock or night-latch.  See fig. 523.

**Dead-padlock.**  A padlock in which neither the bolt nor hasp has a spring, but the former is thrown each way by the key and the hasp must be opened by the hand.

**Dead-wood.**  A *Buffer-block*, which see.

**Deafening-ceiling.**  Boarding on the under side of the floor-timbers of a passenger-car to exclude or deaden the noise of the car.  See **28**, figs. 215, 216, 218, 219, 221.

**Deafening-floor.**  See *Deafening-ceiling.*

**Deck-collar,** *for Spear Heater.*  A sheet-metal ring or collar with which the opening in the roof for the smoke or cold air pipes is lined, and through which these pipes pass.  It is large enough to leave an air space between it and the pipes, and thus protect the roof from the heat of the pipe and from danger of taking fire.  The collar has a flange or lip on top of the roof to exclude rain from leaking through the opening into the car.  See **6**, figs. 550–553.

**Deflector.**  See *Ventilator-deflector.*

**Derrick-car.**  A strong platform-car which carries a derrick, which is used for removing wrecked cars and engines, erecting bridges, or handling any heavy objects.  See fig. 31.

**Detachable Globe-holder.**  A globe-holder arranged so that a lamp-globe can readily be attached to or removed from the lamp.  See **7**, fig. 475.

**Diagonal Floor-timbers.**  Floor-timbers which are placed in an inclined position to the longitudinal floor-timbers   See **1**, fig. 249.

**Diagonal Roof-straps.** A band of hoop-iron placed diagonally on the top of the roof-boards of street-cars to stiffen the roof.

**Diamond-truck.** A car-truck with iron side-frames which are diamond-shaped. The journal-boxes are rigidly bolted to the sides, and have no vertical motion in the frame. Figs. 95–114 are illustrations of different kinds of diamond-trucks.

**Diamond-truck Side-frame.** A diamond-shaped frame, formed of two or more bars of iron to which the journal-boxes are bolted, and which is attached to the transoms or spring-beam of a diamond-truck. The bars of the side-frame form a truss which bears a part of the weight of the car-body and rests on the journals of the axles. Such frames are shown in figs. 95–114 ; also by fig. 133.

**Dinsmore Spiral-spring.** A spiral-spring invented and patented by C. Dinsmore in 1862, 1863, and 1871. It is formed of a bar of steel, whose section resembles the outline of a figure 8 which is wound flatwise on a mandrel to form the coil. They are used both singly or in nests. See figs. 201, 202.

**Discharge-pipe,** *of Air-pump for Westinghouse-brake.* A pipe by which the compressed-air is conveyed from the air-pump to the main air-reservoir. See **9, 9,** fig. 655 ; **48,** fig. 664, 665.

**Discharge-valve,** *of Air-pump for Westinghouse-brake.* See *Upper Discharge-valve. Lower Discharge-valve.*

**Discharge Valve-seat,** *of Air-pump for Westinghouse-brake.* A brass ring which is screwed into the chamber which receives the upper discharge-valve, and which forms a bearing for the latter. See **31,** fig. 665; fig. 693.

**Discharge-valve Stop-bolt,** *for Air-pump of Westinghouse-brake.* A bolt which is placed transversely across the discharge-passage above the lower discharge-valve to limit or stop its movement. See **26,** fig. 665; fig. 688.

**Dish.** See *Soap-dish.*

**Distance-block.** A short, thick piece of wood placed between two or more objects to keep them apart, or to preserve an interval of space between them. See *Floor-timber Distance-Block.*

**Distance-piece.** A piece of wood, metal, or other material placed between two or more objects to keep them apart or to preserve an interval of space between them. See *Draw-bar Distance-piece.*

**Division.** See *Seat-division.*

**Dog,** *for Pawl of Winding-shaft.* A disc or button which is pivoted in such a way as to hold the ratchet-wheel pawl connected with a winding-shaft in its place, and arranged so that the pawl can readily be detached from the ratchet wheel. See **132,** fig. 77. See also *Brake-dog.*

**Dome.** A *clear-story* is sometimes erroneously called a Dome. See *Tank-dome.*

**Dome-head.** The top of the dome of a tank-car. See **109**, figs. 73–76.

**Door.** A frame of boards for closing a doorway. See fig. 502. See

| | |
|---|---|
| *Ash-pit Door.* | *Grated-door.* |
| *Double-door.* | *Lamp-case Door.* |
| *Double Fire-door.* | *Overhung-door.* |
| *Dust Hand-hole Door.* | *Platform Trap-door.* |
| *Fare-wicket Door.* | *Sliding-door.* |
| *Feed-door.* | *Tip-car Door.* |
| *Fire-door.* | *Underhung-door.* |
| *Grain-door.* | *Ventilator-door.* |

**Door-apron.** A sheet-iron cover attached to a swinging door of a street-car to inclose the step. See **1**, fig. 42.

**Door-bolt.** A metal bar attached to a slide and fastened to a door so as to hold it shut from the inside. See figs. 514–517. See also

| | |
|---|---|
| *Barrel Door-bolt.* | *Square Door-bolt.* |
| *Neck Door-bolt.* | *Square-neck Door-bolt.* |

**Door-bolt Keeper.** A catch attached to a door-frame, in which the bolt engages to hold the door shut. See fig. 516.

**Door-brace.** A diagonal piece of timber framed in a freight-car door to stiffen it. See **69**, figs. 61, 69.

**Door-butt.** A *Butt-hinge*, which see.

**Door-button.** " A small piece of wood or metal swiveled by a screw through the middle, and used as a fastening for a door or gate."—*Knight.* See figs. 518, 519.

**Door-button on Plate.** A door-button attached by a rivet or pin to a metal plate which is fastened to a door with screws. See fig. 519.

**Door-case.** 1. A frame which incloses or surrounds the sides and top of a door.

2. A partition at the end of a street-car which incloses a sliding door when it is open. See *Fare-wicket Door-case.*

**Door-case Intermediate-rail.** A rail of a door-case above the window of a street-car. See **84**, fig. 752.

**Door-case Panel.** A panel in a partition which incloses a sliding-door at the end of a street-car. See *Door-case Top-panel. Door-case Seat-panel.*

**Door-case Sash.** A window-sash in the partition which incloses a sliding-door of a street-car. This sash opens on hinges and is placed opposite to another in the end of the car on the outside of the door. See **86**, fig. 752.

**Door-case Sash-button.** A fastening, consisting usually of an eccentric metal disc, used for holding the door-case sash shut. Sometimes the fastening is similar to an old-fashioned door-button. See **87**, fig. 752 ; fig. 768.

**Door-case Seat-panel.** A panel in a door-case next to the seat in the car. Similar to **43**, fig. 752.

**Door-case Top-panel.** A panel in a door-case of a street-car above the window. In some cases a mirror is used in place of a panel. See **85**, fig. 752.

**Door-case Top-rail.** An upper rail of a door-case which extends from one side of the car to the other. See **83**, fig. 752.

**Door-frame.** The structure in which the panels of a door are fitted. It is composed of the *stiles*, or upright pieces at the sides; the *mullions*, or central upright pieces; the *bottom-rail ;* the *lock*, or *central rails*, and the *top-rail.—Knight.* See fig. 502. See *Fire-door-frame for Spear Heater.*

**Door Friction-roller.** See *Sliding-door Friction-roller.*

**Door-guards.** Strips of wood which inclose the space occupied by sliding-doors in baggage, express, and freight cars to keep the baggage or freight from interfering with the movement of the doors. See **77**, figs. 56, 57, 58.

**Door Guard-band.** A metal band fastened crosswise on the middle rail of the door of a street-car to protect the door from being chafed in opening and closing. See **88**, fig. 753.

**Door-handle.** An attachment to a door to take hold of in opening or closing it. See **78**, figs. 55, 60, 63, 64. See *Sliding-door Handle.*

**Door Hand-rail.** A rail attached to the inside of a swinging-door of a street-car for passengers to take hold of in getting on and off the car. See **2**, fig. 42.

**Door-hanger.** A hook-shaped piece of metal by which a sliding-door is suspended at its top and which slides on an iron track at the top of the door. For freight-cars they are usually made of wrought-iron, but sometimes of cast-iron with friction rollers, or sheaves, on which the door rolls. They are also used in sleeping and drawing-room cars, and are then generally made of brass and plated. See **68**, figs. 60, 63, 64, 69, 72.

**Door-hasp.** A metal clasp attached to car-doors, and by which they are fastened to a staple or eye-bolt on the body of the car. They are used chiefly on freight-car doors when these are secured with padlocks. See **73**, fig. 55.

**Door-hinge.** A metal joint on which a door turns and by which it is connected to the jamb of a door, door-frame, or post. See **16**, figs. 502, 509, 513.

**Door-holder.** A catch or hook to hold a swinging passenger-car door open. It usually consists of two parts, one of which is attached to the door, and the other to the floor or other part of the car, so that one piece will hook into the other and thus hold the door open. See fig. 507. See also *Lamp-case Door-holder. Sliding-door Holder.*

**Door-holder Catch.** A metal bracket attached to the

floor or side of a car, with which a door-holder engages to hold a door open. See. fig. 508.

**Door-hook.** A *Sliding-door Holder*, which see.

**Door-jamb.** The side piece or post of a door opening. See **1**, fig. 502. Also see *Door-post*.

**Door-knob.** A ball attached to the end of a spindle of a door-latch to take hold of in moving the latch or opening the door. See **17**, fig. 502 ; **5**, figs. 524–531.

**Door-latch.** An attachment to a door to hold it shut. A door-latch usually consists of a spring-bolt, held in a suitable metal case, and a spindle and knobs by which the bolt is disengaged from a keeper attached to the door-post. See figs. 526–530. A door-latch is often made in combination with a lock, having a separate bolt and key to secure or fasten the door from the outside, as in figs. 522, 524, 529. See *Sliding-door Latch. Spring Door-latch.*

**Door-latch Bolt.** A metal pin or bar attached to a door or door-latch, and which engages with a keeper to hold the door shut. See **1**, figs. 522–528.

**Door-latch Arbor.** A *Door-latch Spindle*, which see.

**Door-latch Keeper.** A metal plate attached to a door-post, and into or with which a door-latch engages. See **9**, figs. 526, 530. Also see *Sliding-door-latch Keeper.*

**Door-latch Hook.** The part of a sliding-door latch which

engages with the keeper and holds the door shut. See **2**, figs. 529, 530.

**Door-latch Rose** *or* **Escutcheon.** A plate fastened to a door, and in which a door-latch spindle works. The escutcheon acts as a guard or bearing for the spindle. See **4**, figs. 524, 528, 529, 531.

**Door-latch Spindle.** A small metal shaft to which a door-handle or knob and the latch are attached, and by which the latter is turned by means of the power exerted on the former by the hand. See **10**, figs. 524. 531.

**Door-latch Spring.** A spring attached to a door-latch, and which acts on the latch-hook or bolt and causes it to engage with its keeper. The spring is usually made of a flat piece of cast-steel.

**Door-lintel.** The horizontal part of a door-frame above the door. This part is usually made of wood, but in passenger-cars it is sometimes made of a thin shell of cast-iron. See **99**, figs. 217, 219, 221, 222, 224, 229, 230 ; **18**, fig. 502.

**Door-lock.** An attachment to doors to fasten them, with a separate piece called a key. A door-latch is usually combined with a passenger-car door-lock. See **19**, fig. 502; figs. 522–530. See *Sliding Door-lock. Spring Door-lock.*

**Door-lock Bolt.** The piece in a lock which is moved or

"shot" out by the key, and which fastens that which the lock is intended to secure. See **7**, figs. 522–524, 529.

**Door-lock Bolt-spring.** A spring which moves and holds a lock-bolt in place.

**Door-lock Keeper.** A metal plate or catch into which the bolt of a lock protrudes, and which holds the door shut. See **8**, figs. 522–524, 529.

**Door-lock Nosing.** A *Door-lock Keeper*, which see.

**Door-mullion.** A vertical bar or partition of wood between the panels of a door. See **146**, figs. 218, 222, 223 ; **2**, fig. 502 ; **79**, fig. 753. See *Door-window Mullion.*

**Door Name-plate.** A metal plate placed on the inside of a passenger-car door with the name of the builder or manufacturer of the car inscribed on it. See **3**, fig. 502.

**Door-panel.** "A piece of board whose edges are inserted into the groove of a thicker surrounding frame of a door."—*Webster.* See **151**, figs. 218, 222, 223 ; **10** and **11**, fig. 502. See

    *Lower Door-panel.*      *Twin-door Panel.*
    *Middle Door-panel.*      *Upper Door-panel.*

**Door-pin.** A pin used in connection with a hasp and an eye-bolt or staple to fasten a freight-car door shut. Leaden seals are sometimes attached thereto. See **74**, figs. 55, 60.

**Door-pin Chain.** A chain by which a door-pin is attached to a car. See **75**, fig. 55.

**Door-plate.** See *Door Name-plate. Water-closet Door-plate.*

**Door-post.** A vertical post which forms the side of a doorway. See **44**, figs. 55–84 ; **62**, figs. 215–232 ; **1**, fig. 502 ; **18**, figs. 750, 752.

**Door-pull.** A **D**-shaped handle attached to a door to take hold of in opening or closing it. See figs. 520, 521.

**Door-rail.** A horizontal member or bar of the framing of a door. The upper one, **4**, fig 502, is called the *top-rail ;* the lower one, **5**, the *bottom-rail ;* **6**, the *middle* or *lock-rail ;* **7**, the *parting-rail.* See fig. 502.

**Door-roller.** A *Door-sheave*, which see.

**Door-sash.** A wooden frame, containing one or more panes of glass, placed in a door. In some cases one of these sashes is made to slide, so that it can be opened for ventilation. See **12** and **13**, fig. 502. See

    *Lower Door-sash.*      *Ventilating Door-sash.*
    *Upper Door-sash.*      *Ventilator-sash.*

**Door-sash Bolt.** A metal pin attached to a sliding-door sash to hold it any desired position. See **14**, fig. 502; fig. 505.

**Door-sash Plate.** A metal plate attached to a door-sash with suitable holes in it in which a *door-sash bolt* engages to hold the sash in any desired position. See **15**, figs. 502, and fig. 504.

**Door-shaft.** An iron shaft, which extends from the front to the rear platform of a street-car, for the purpose of enabling the driver to open the rear-door from the front platform.

**Door-shaft Crank.** An arm on the back end of a door-shaft which is connected with the back-door and forms a part of the mechanism by which the door of a street-car is opened by the driver.

**Door-shaft Crank-plate.** A slotted plate attached to a sliding-door of a street-car, to which a crank is connected for moving the door.

**Door-shaft Lever.** An arm on the front end of a door-shaft of a street-car, by which the driver operates a shaft which opens the back-door.

**Door-sheave.** A roller or wheel on which a sliding-door rolls. Such sheaves are sometimes placed at the bottom and sometimes at the top of the door. See **2**, figs. 397–399. See *Sliding-door Sheave.*

**Door-sheave Holder.** A frame or plate which holds the sheave or roller in its place, and by which it is attached to a door or other object. See **1**, figs. 397–399.

**Door-shoe.** A casting on the bottom of a sliding-door which slides on the door-track. See **70**, fig. 55.

**Door-sill.** A cross-piece attached to the floor on the under side of a door-opening. In car construction the term is usually applied to an iron plate used under passenger-car doors. See **64**, figs. 61, 62 ; **93**, figs. 750, 752.

**Door-slide.** A *Door-shoe,* which see.

**Door-stile.** One of the two upright pieces on the outer edges of a door-frame. See **150**, figs. 218, 222, 223, 230 ; **8**, fig. 502 ; **78**, fig. 753.

**Door-stop.** A peg or block against which a door strikes when opened. The stop is often provided with a rubber cushion, especially for swinging-doors. See fig. 506. See *Closed-door Stop. Open-door Stop.*

**Door-strap.** A leather strap or cord by which the back-door of a street-car is opened and shut by the driver in front.

**Door-strap Sheave.** A grooved wheel or pulley which is hung in a frame and forms a guide or carrier for a door-strap of a street-car.

**Door-track.** A metal bar or guide which supports a sliding-door, and on which it moves, or by which it is held in its place. See *Top Door-track. Bottom Door-track.*

**Door-track Bracket.** An iron or wooden block or support which is fastened to the side of a freight-car, and to which a door-track is attached or which holds a sliding-door in its place. See **67**, figs. 55, 59, 60, 63, 64, 69, 72.

**Door-way.** The passage or opening which is closed by a door.

**Door-window Mullion.** A middle upright bar in the sash or frame of a door-window. See **80**, fig. 753.

**Dope.** A term used to designate any mixed grease which is not fluid and is used for lubricating.

**Double-board Roof.** A roof made of two layers of boards, each of which extends from the comb of the roof to the eaves; the one layer being laid so as to break or cover the joints of that underneath. See fig. 68.

**Double Brace-pocket.** A casting which forms a socket for holding two braces or two braces and a post. See **41**, figs. 69, 71.

**Double Check-valve,** *for Westinghouse-brake.* A valve attached to the pipes underneath a car which is equipped with both the old and the automatic brake, so that either can be used. See fig. 735.

**Double-coil Nest-spring.** A spiral-spring with another smaller coil inside of it. See figs. 190, 212.

**Double-cone Lamp-globe.** A glass or porcelain lamp-globe, conical in form at the top and bottom, as shown in the engraving. See fig. 491.

**Double-deck Cattle-car.** A cattle-car with two floors, or stories, one above the other, for carrying small cattle—that is sheep, hogs, etc. See fig. 69.

**Double-deck Street-car.** A street-car with seats on top of the roof. See fig. 38.

**Double-door.** A door made in two parts. These are some-times fastened together by hinges, so as to fold back on each other, and sometimes each part is hinged to one of the door-posts. Such doors are used for mail, baggage, and postal cars. Sliding-doors are also sometimes made in two parts.

**Double Fire-door,** *for Spear Heater.* Two doors attached to the same frame to close the opening for the fire-door. The inside door is usually perforated to admit air and is intended to close the opening, so that in case of accident the fire would not fall out of the stove. See fig. 579.

**Double Iron-body-bolster.** A body-bolster composed of two iron trusses placed parallel to each other, and connected by iron plates or bars. See figs. 237, 238.

**Double-lens Tail or Signal-lamp.** A lamp, with two lenses on opposite sides, to be attached to the last car of a train so that the light through the one lens can be seen by the following trains, and that through the other by the locomotive runner of the train to which the lamp is attached. See fig. 496. In some lamps of this kind glass of different colors can be placed behind the lenses so as to change the color of the light.

**Double-lever Brake.** A brake which has two levers to a truck or a four-wheeled car, as shown in fig. 638. The object of using two levers is to equalize the pressure on the two brake-beams. In some cases such brakes are applied to but one of the trucks of a car, in other cases to both. See fig. 638.

**Double Pipe-strap and Back.** An iron band made with two bends for holding two pipes (as heater pipes) in their place. See fig. 615. See also *Single Pipe-strap.*

**Double-plate Wheel.** A cast-iron car-wheel, the rim and hub of which are united by two cast-iron plates or discs. See figs. 163, 164.

**Double Release-spring,** *for Westinghouse Car-brake.* A release-spring which consists of two coiled springs, one within the other.

**Double-washer.** A cast-iron washer made to take two rods or bolts. Also called a *twin-washer.* See fig. 789.

**Double Window-blind.** A window-blind made in two parts. It is made in this way so that, when raised up, it will occupy less room than if made in one piece. See **140,** figs. 215, 219, 222 ; **17, 18,** fig. 301.

**Double Window-blind Lift.** A metal finger-hold attached to the inner part of a blind, and which has a projection for raising the outer part. See fig. 325.

**Double Window-sash Spring.** A metal plate fastened at the centre to the edge of the stile of a window-blind to prevent it from rattling. See fig. 302.

**Draft-spring.** A *Draw-spring,* which see.

**Drain-cock of Engine,** *for Westinghouse-brake.* A faucet attached to the lower end of the steam-cylinder for draw-

ing off water which collects there. See **44,** fig. 665 ; fig. 740. See also *Reservoir Drain-cock.*

**Drain-cock of Triple-valve,** *for Westinghouse-brake.* A faucet attached to the lower end of the drain-cup for drawing off the water which collects in the latter. See **18,** fig. 703.

**Drain-cup,** *for Westinghouse Car-brake.* A globular receptacle or vessel attached underneath a triple-valve to collect water which may accumulate in the latter. See **10,** fig. 663; **3,** fig. 703.

**Draw-bar.** An open-mouthed bar at the end of a car to which the coupling-links are attached and from which the car is drawn. The draw-bars are usually provided with springs, to give elasticity to the connection between the cars, and arranged so as to resist both the tension and compression to which the draw-bar is subjected. See **23,** figs. 55–84 ; **29,** figs. 215–231 ; **1,** figs. 251–263 ; figs. 266–270. See

| | |
|---|---|
| *Bolt Draw-bar.* | *Potter Draw-bar.* |
| *Centre-draft Draw-bar.* | *Safford Draw-bar.* |
| *Height of Draw-bar.* | *Spring-pocket Draw-bar.* |
| *Open-mouth Draw-bar.* | *Three-link Draw-bar.* |

**Draw-bar Bolt.** A bolt which connects a draw-bar to a draw-spring and follower-plates. See **7,** figs. 252, 253, 255, 257, 266 ; **4,** fig. 267.

**Draw-bar Carry-iron.** A transverse iron bar bolted to the under side of the draw-timbers, and on which the draw-bar rests. It is often made of a ∪ shape, and the ends are bolted to the end-sills. See **9,** figs. 251–263.

**Draw-bar Chafing-plate,** *for Miller-coupler.* An iron plate framed into the platform-truss-beam above the draw-bar coupling-hook to protect it from abrasion by the latter. See figs. 48, 284.

**Draw-bar Coupling-hook.** A draw-bar made in the form of a hook for coupling cars together. This is the form of the Miller-coupler. See **11,** figs. 282–285 ; figs. 288, 289.

**Draw-bar Cross-timber,** *for Coal-car.* A transverse timber framed into the centre floor-timbers of a coal-car, and to which the ends of the draw-timbers are attached. Such timbers are used on four-wheeled cars which have no body-bolsters. See **138,** figs. 77, 78.

**Draw-bar Distance-piece.** A block or bar of iron or wood between the upper and lower plates of a wrought-iron draw-bar to stiffen it. In many cases, it serves as a thimble for the rivets which pass through the plates. See **4,** fig. 257 ; **2,** figs. 268, 270.

**Draw-bar Face-plate.** A wrought-iron plate attached to the outer end of a draw-bar, and which bears against a similar plate on the car next to it. When such a plate is made in one piece with the draw-bar, it is called a *draw-bar head.* See **2,** figs. 257, 259 ; **3,** fig. 268.

**Draw-bar Follower-plate.** An iron plate which bears against the end of a draw-spring. One plate of this kind bears against each end of the draw-springs. The tension and compression on the draw-bar is transmitted by the follower-plates to the draw-springs. See **14,** figs. 251–264. See *Auxiliary Draw-bar Follower-plate.*

**Draw-bar Friction-plate.** A cast-iron plate attached to the platform end-timber of street-cars, and through which the draw-bar passes. The plate protects the timber and dash-guard from the abrasion and wear of the draw-bar.

**Draw-bar Guides.** Wrought-iron bars which are fastened in pairs to lugs or *stops* bolted to the draw-timbers on each side of a draw-bar, forming guides in which the draw-bar follower-plates move. See **13,** figs. 251–264.

**Draw-bar Head.** The outer end of a solid draw-bar, which bears against a similar head on the adjoining car. When it is made in a separate piece from the draw-bar, it is called a *draw-bar face-plate.* See **3,** figs. 251–263, 266, 270.

**Draw-bar Jaw.** An iron strap which forms a guide, and also a stop, for the draw-bar followers or draw-spring plates. See **16,** figs. 251, 252, 255.

**Draw-bar Pocket.** A *Draw-spring Pocket,* which see.

**Draw-bar Sector.** A support which is fastened underneath the platform of a car for carrying a centre-draft draw-bar. It consists of an iron bar shaped like an arc of a circle. See **33**, figs. 231, 232.

**Draw-bar Side-Casting.** An iron casting of which a pair form guides for the draw-bar followers and hold them in their places. See fig. 265.

**Draw-bar Spring-pocket.** The space at the back end of a draw-bar which receives the draw-spring and follower-plates. See **1**, figs. 268, 270.

**Draw-bar Stem.** A *Draw-bar Bolt*, which see.

**Draw-bar Stirrup.** A *Draw-bar Carry-iron*, which see.

**Draw-bar Stop.** A casting which limits the movement of the draw-bar followers. These castings are bolted to the draw-bar timbers and form distance-pieces to which the draw-bar guides are bolted. See **17**, figs. 257–259, 261, 263.

**Draw-bar Yoke.** A *Draw-bar Carry-iron*, which see.

**Draw-clevis.** A wrought-iron bar with a forked end attached to the platform of a street-car and to which the horses are attached and by which the car is drawn. Two kinds of these are used, the one fastened to the platform so as to be immovable, whereas the other can slide lengthwise and its motion is resisted by a spring. The latter is called a *Spring Draw-clevis*, which see. Similar to a *Draw-hook*, which see.

**Drawer-pull.** A wooden or metal attachment to a drawer to take hold of in pulling it out. See fig. 431.

**Draw-gear.** A term used to designate the draw-bars, draw-timbers, buffing apparatus, and all their attachments—in short, the whole of the arrangements by which a car is drawn and which resists concussions. See figs. 251–292.

**Draw-gear Tie-rod.** A rod which connects an end-sill or platform end-timber with a body-bolster or draw-bar cross-timber to tie them together. See **139**, figs. 61–64, 74, 78.

**Draw-head.** A *Draw-bar Head*, which see. A draw-bar is sometimes called a *draw-head*.

**Draw-hook.** An iron hook attached to the end of a car, from which it is drawn and by which it is coupled to other cars. They are used chiefly on coal-cars and street-cars. See fig. 271; **106**, figs. 750, 751, 753. See also *Draw-bar Coupling-hook*.

**Draw-hook and Link.** A coupling-hook combined with several links, one of which is welded in a hole in the hook. They are used chiefly on coal-cars. See fig. 271.

**Drawing-room Car.** A passenger-car fitted up and furnished in a more luxurious manner than ordinary cars. Drawing-room cars are generally intended for day travel and are furnished with arm-chairs, sofas, carpets. etc., and an extra charge is usually made to passengers who travel in them. See fig. 2.

**Draw-off Cock,** *for Baker Heater.* A cock attached to the pipe *A*, fig. 581, for drawing off the water or emptying the pipes of a Baker heater. See fig. 619.

**Draw-rod.** A rod which unites two draw-bars, or the draw-gear at the opposite ends of a car, and which bears the strain or pull required to draw the train. See **4,** figs. 280, 281.

**Draw-spring.** A spring attached to a draw-bar to give the latter an elastic connection with the car. Such springs are usually so arranged as to resist either tension or compression on the draw-bar. See **24,** figs. 61–77, 78–82 ; **30,** figs. 215, 219, 229, 232 ; **5,** figs. 251–253, 257, 261. See *Auxiliary Buffer-spring.*

**Draw-spring Pocket.** A *Draw-bar Spring-pocket,* which see.

**Draw-spring Stop.** A metal sleeve or thimble in the centre of a spiral or volute draw-spring to resist the pressure to which the spring is subjected after the latter has been compressed a given distance. See **8,** fig. 257.

**Draw-timbers.** A pair of timbers attached below the frame at the end of a car, and which usually extends from the platform end-timber of passenger-cars, or the end-sill of freight-cars, to the bolster. The draw-bar attachments are bolted to the draw-timbers. In passenger-cars these timbers are usually the principal supports of the platform. On street-cars only one draw-timber is ordi-narily used, which is placed in the centre of the car, and to which the draw-bar is attached. See **26,** figs. 55–84, **31,** figs. 215–232 ; **10,** figs. 251–264 ; **100,** figs. 750, 751, 752.

**Draw-timber Guards.** Cast-iron lugs or wrought-iron straps or plates bolted to the sides of draw-timbers near their outer ends. They resist the lateral strains on the draw-bar, and protect the draw-timbers from abrasion. The carry-iron, which supports the outer end of a draw-bar, is sometimes bolted to the draw-timber guards. See **11,** figs. 252, 254, 258, 259, 260.

**Draw-timber Pocket.** A casting which is attached to the body-bolster or centre-sills of a car and which receives and holds the end of a draw-timber. See **18,** figs. 257–259.

**Draw-timber Tie-bar.** A transverse iron bar attached to the under sides of a pair of draw-timbers to tie them together. See **12,** figs. 251–255, 257–259.

**Drilling.** A term used in New Jersey to designate the act of moving cars from one track to another—as in making up or separating trains, and placing the cars on the tracks in the places where they are needed. See *Switching. Shunting. Regulating.*

**Drinking-cup.** A metal cup used for drinking water—or other liquids.

**Drip.** A receptacle to collect the waste or superfluous

liquid, as of a water-cooler. See *Urinal-drip.* *Water-drip.*

**Driving-wheel Brake,** *or* **Driver-brake.** A brake applied to the driving-wheels of a locomotive. See figs. 747–749.

**Drop,** *of Lamp.* "The drop of a centre lamp is its extreme length," measured from the ceiling to the lowest part of the lamp. See **9, 9,** fig. 470.

**Drop-bottom.** A door arranged at the bottom of a car for unloading it quickly by allowing the load or contents of the car to fall through the door-opening. See **123,** figs. 77–79.

**Drop-bottom Car.** A car so constructed that its contents can be readily unloaded from the bottom by means of drop-doors. See figs. 24, 25, 26, 27, 77.

**Drop-bottom Chain.** A chain which is wound on a shaft, and which holds up the drop-bottom of a coal-car. See **124,** figs. 77, 79.

**Drop-bottom Hinge.** A hinge which connects the drop-door or drop-bottom with the body of a coal-car. See **125,** fig. 77.

**Drop-door.** See *Drop-bottom.*

**Drop-door Beam,** *for Coal-car.* A piece of timber which extends transversely across the top of a coal-car, and which acts as a support for the winding-shaft and a tie for the sides of the car-body. See **126,** figs. 77, 79.

**Drop-letter-box Plate.** A metal plate for a letter-box, with a suitable opening in which letters are deposited, and a door or valve by which the opening is closed. See fig. 435.

**Drum.** 1. "A cylinder over which a belt or band passes.

2. "The barrel of a crane, windlass, winch, or capstan on which the rope or chain winds.

3. "A chamber of a cylindrical form used in heaters, stoves, and flues. It is hollow and thin, and generally forms a mere casing, but in some cases, as steam-drums, is adapted to stand considerable pressure."—*Knight.* See *Brake-shaft Drum. Circulating Drum.*

**Drum,** *for Creamer-brake.* A cast-iron case, with a ratchet attached, and which holds the involute spring used to apply a Creamer-brake. The spring is wound up in the drum, and is then held by a pawl acting on the ratchet on the drum. See **1,** fig. 646.

**Drum-cover,** *for Baker Car-heater.* A sheet-iron covering for the circulating drum on the outside of the car. See fig. 608.

**Drum-cover,** *for Creamer-brake.* A circular cast-iron lid for the drum with a ratchet on top, with which the jointed top-pawl engages. See **12,** figs. 646, 647.

**Drum-support,** *for Baker Car-heater.* A bracket attached to the roof of a car to hold the circulating drum of a Baker-heater. See fig. 603.

**Dual-burner.** A coal-oil lamp-burner with two wicks, by which a larger supply of oil can be fed to the flame than is possible with one wick only. See fig. 478.

**Dump-car.** A term used to designate both *Drop-bottom* and *Tip Cars*, which see.

**Dust-collar.** A grooved wrought-iron ring placed on a car-axle between the hub of the wheel and the journal to receive and hold a dust-guard. See **16**, fig. 151.

**Duster.** See *Feather-duster*.

**Dust-guard.** A thin piece of wood, leather, or other material inserted in a chamber at the back of a journal-box, and made to fit closely around the axle. Its use is to exclude dust and dirt from the back of the box and prevent the escape of oil and waste from it. Sometimes called *axle-packing* or *box-packing*. See **15**, figs. 138, 145, 146, 151.

**Dust-guard Bearing.** That portion of a car-axle between the journal and the wheel-seat on which the dust-guard bears. See **4**, fig. 143.

**Dust-guard Chamber.** The space in the back side of a journal-box occupied by the dust-guard. See **15**, figs. 138, 145, 146, 151.

**Dust Hand-hole.** An opening in a door-casing, under the seat of a street-car, to give access to the space into which the door slides for the purpose of removing dirt which accumulates there.

**Dust Hand-hole Door.** A gate or covering for a dust hand-hole.

# E

**Eames Vacuum Brake.** A system of continuous brakes, invented and patented by Mr. Fred. W. Eames, which is operated by exhausting the air from behind flexible india-rubber diaphragms attached to the trucks of each car. These diaphragms are connected to the brake-levers and the pressure of the air on the outside of the diaphragms is communicated to the levers, and from them to the brake-shoes. The rubber diaphragms cover the mouth of a large cast-iron shell or bowl, from which the air is exhausted by an ejector on the engine, which is connected with the shells by pipes and flexible hose between the cars. See figs. 653, 654.

**Eaves Fascia-board.** A projecting board on the outside of a passenger-car body, immediately under the eaves, and which forms an ornament or moulding in connection with the eaves-moulding. See **91**, figs. 55, 60, 63; **92**, figs. 219, 225, 226.

**Eaves-moulding.** A moulding attached to the outside of a car-body at the point where the roof joins the side of the car. See **90**, figs. 55, 59; **93**, figs. 215, 218, 219, 222, 225, 226; **48**, figs. 750, 752, 753. See *Clear-story Eaves-moulding*.

**Eccentric-lever,** *complete, for Westinghouse Driving-wheel Brake.* An arm consisting of a casting and screw or stud, one end of which is attached to a brake-head and the other connected with the piston-rod. The end or head of the casting is made of a cam-shaped or eccentric form and bears against another lever of the same kind, so that, when the two are raised upward, the brake shoes are forced against the driving-wheels. The stud or screw is intended to either lengthen or shorten the lever so as to adjust the pressure of the brake-shoes against the wheels when the shoes become worn. See **13,** fig. 747.

**Eccentric-lever Casting,** *for Westinghouse Driving-wheel Brake.* A casting which forms part of an eccentric-lever, and which has a cam-shaped or eccentric head, which bears against another corresponding casting opposite to it, both of which are connected to the brake piston-rod, so that, when the two are raised upward by the piston, the brake-shoes are forced against the driving-wheels. See **15,** fig. 747.

**Eccentric Lever-links,** *for Westinghouse Driving-wheel Brake.* Short iron bars by which an eccentric-lever is connected with a piston cross-head. See **28,** fig. 747.

**Eccentric-lever Nut,** *for Westinghouse Driving-wheel Brake.* A lock-nut which screws on an eccentric-lever stud, and which is intended to hold the latter and prevent it from unscrewing. See **18,** fig. 747.

**Eccentric-lever Stud,** *for Westinghouse Driving-wheel Brake.* A bolt with an eye at one end, which is attached to a brake-block, and a screw at the other, which is fastened to a casting, the two forming an eccentric-lever. See **19,** fig. 749.

**Eccentric Window-button.** A metal fastening for holding a hinged window or door shut. It consists of a round disc which is fastened by a screw which is not in the centre of the disc, but is eccentric to it. See fig. 768.

**Edge-rolled Spiral-spring.** A spiral-spring formed by rolling a flat bar of metal edgewise on a mandrel. See fig. 200.

**Egg-shaped Lamp-globe.** A lamp-globe resembling somewhat an egg in form. See fig. 489.

**Egg-shaped Stove.** A stove resembling an egg in form, for burning coal and for warming a car or other apartment. See fig. 543.

**Eight-wheeled Box-car.** A box-car having two trucks and eight wheels. See fig. 12.

**Eight-wheeled Gondola-car.** A gondola-car mounted on two trucks and eight wheels. See fig. 19.

**Eight-wheeled Hopper-bottom Coal-car.** A car with eight wheels and a bottom shaped somewhat like a mill-hopper, with a drop-door underneath for unloading or dumping the coal with which the car is loaded. See fig. 25 ; also *Coal Dump-car.*

**Ejector.** An appliance for operating a vacuum-brake by exhausting or "ejecting" air. It consists of a pipe, **1,** fig. 652, placed in the centre of a surrounding shell or casing, **2,** with an annular opening, **3,** between the pipe and the casing. When a current of steam is admitted at the lower end of **1,** and escapes at the upper end, the air in the casing at **4** is drawn out through the annular opening by the current of the escaping steam. The space, **4,** is connected by a pipe, **5,** with the appliances on the cars for operating the brakes. Suitable valves are also used in connection with the ejector to shut off and admit steam and air. See figs. 651, 652.

**Elastic-wheel.** A car-wheel in which some elastic material is interposed between the tire and the wheel-centre or hub to resist the concussions. Different substances are used, such as paper, wood, india-rubber, oakum, etc. See figs. 168, 169.

**Elbow.** A short **L**-shaped cast-iron tube for uniting the ends of two pipes, generally at right angles to each other. The pipes are screwed into the casting. See fig. 620.

**Elder-brake.** A brake for eight-wheeled cars, with a horizontal lever having a fixed fulcrum under the car-body, at its centre, and pulleys at each end, over which a chain passes, which is connected with the brake-levers of each truck. One lever on each truck also has a pulley or sheave at its end, over which a chain runs which is connected with the opposite lever, and also with the central lever. The latter is connected by rods and chains with brake-windlasses by which the brakes are applied at each end of the car. See fig. 645.

**Elliptic-spring.** A spring of elliptical form made of two sets of steel plates. Such springs are generally used for bolster-springs for passenger-cars. See figs. 185, 186. See *Combination Elliptic-spring.*

**Enclosed Step.** A step of a street-car which is covered or enclosed by a sheet-iron apron attached to a swinging door to prevent persons from riding on the step. See **3,** fig. 42.

**End.** See *Seat-end.*

**End Body-brace.** An inclined brace, or stick of timber, on the end-frame of a car-body, which acts as a brace. See **35,** figs. 58, 64, 84.

**End-body Brace-rod.** An inclined iron rod in the end-frame of a car-body which acts as a brace.

**End-carline.** A carline at the end of a car-body. See **54,** figs. 750, 752. See also *End-plate. Platform Roof-end Carline.*

**End-frame,** *of a Car-body.* The frame which forms the end of a car-body. It includes the posts, braces, end-rail, end-girth, etc.

**End-girth.** A girth in the end of a box-car. See **50**, figs. 55–72.

**End-girth Tie-rod.** A tie-rod extending across the end of a freight-car-body along the end-girth, and from one corner-post to the other, and intended to tie them together. See **51**, figs. 56, 58, 61, 64.

**End-hook.** See *Bell-cord End-hook.*

**End-panel.** A panel at the end and on the outside of a passenger or street car. See **70**, figs. 217, 223. See *Lower End-panel. Upper End-panel.*

**End-piece,** *of Truck-frame.* A transverse timber or bar of iron by which the ends of the two wheel-pieces of a truck-frame are connected together. See **17**, figs. 88–94 ; 115–125. See *Crooked End-piece. Inside End-piece. Outside End-piece.*

**End-plate.** A timber across the end and top of a car-body and which is fastened to the two side-plates. This piece is usually made of the proper form so as to serve the purpose of an end-carline. See **48**, figs. 55–72.

**End-play.** The movement, or space left for movement, of a part of machinery endwise, as of a shaft or axle. See *Lateral-play. Lateral-motion.*

**End-rafter.** This term is erroneously applied to the *End-carlines*, which see.

**End Roof-lights.** Small triangular-shaped glasses placed on each side of the end-ventilators of street-cars. See **62**, fig. 753.

**End Seat-panel.** A panel at the end of a street-car on the inside and at the end of a longitudinal or side seat. See **43**, fig. 752.

**End-sill.** The main outside transverse-timber of a car-body into which all the floor-timbers of box and passenger cars are framed. See **2**, figs. 55–84, 215–232 ; **9**, figs. 750–751.

**End-step,** *of Street-car.* A ledge, consisting usually of a wooden tread, supported on wrought-iron brackets, placed at the end and opposite, or under, the door of a street car-body, and used by persons in getting on or off the car. See **1**, fig. 41.

**End-timber.** See *Platform End-timber.*

**End-ventilator.** An aperture for the admission or escape of air at the end of a car, and usually placed over the windows. See also *Clear-story End-ventilator.* See **142**. fig. 218.

**End Window-panel.** A panel at the end and on the outside of a passenger-car alongside of the window. See **71**, fig. 217.

**Engine and Air-pump complete,** *for Westinghouse-brake.* A machine attached to a locomotive for compressing the air used to operate the brakes. It consists of a steam and an air cylinder, the pistons in which are connected to the same piston-rod, so that the air-piston is worked directly by the steam-piston. Suitable valves are provided for admitting and exhausting the steam and air to and from the cylinders. See figs. 664, 665.

**Equal-bar Nest-spring.** A nest-spring of any number of coils, each bar of which is of such a size that the resistance of the coil is proportioned to its diameter. See fig. 198.

**Equalizer.** An *Equalizing-bar*, which see.

**Equalizing-bar.** A wrought-iron bar which rests or bears on top of the journal-boxes, and extends from one to the other on the same side of a truck. The springs rest on the equalizing-bar between the two boxes. This bar is used to transfer part of the weight on one wheel to the other, and thus equalize it on both; hence its name. See **71**, figs. 115–129. Equalizing-bars are sometimes used to connect the ends of semi-elliptic springs, as shown in figs. 82, 127.

**Equalizing-bar Pedestal.** A casting which holds the centre of an equalizing-lever in its position. These are used on the Pennsylvania Railroad conductor's-cars. See **164**, fig. 82.

**Equalizing-bar Seat.** The surface on top of a journal-box on which an equalizing-bar rests. See **17**, figs. 138, 139.

**Equalizing-bar Spring.** A spring which rests on an equal-izing-bar and carries the weight of a car. Rubber, spiral, group-spiral, or volute springs are generally used for this purpose. See **79**, figs. 115–129.

**Equalizing-bar Spring-cap.** A casting on top of an equalizing-bar and which bears against the under side of a wheel-piece or truck-frame, and holds the equalizing-bar spring in its place. See **72**, figs. 115–129.

**Equalizing-bar Spring-seat.** A casting which is attached to the top of an equalizing-bar and on which its spring rests. See **73**, figs. 115–129.

**Equalizing Brake-lever.** A *Floating-lever*, which see.

**Equalizing-lever.** An *Equalizing-bar*, which see. A *floating-lever* is also called an equalizing-lever.

**Escutcheon.** A plate or guard for a key-hole of a lock. Similar plates for the holes through which the spindles to which the knobs or handles of a lock are attached are also called escutcheons. See figs. 534, 535. See *Seatlock Escutcheon. Door-latch Escutcheon.*

**Excursion Street-car.** A *Summer Street-car*, figs. 39, 40, which see. Also see *Suburban Excursion-car.*

**Exhaust-pipe of Engine,** *for Westinghouse-brake.* A pipe through which the exhaust steam is conveyed from the steam-cylinder of the engine and air-pump to the chimney. See **7, 7**, fig. 655 ; **46**, figs. 664, 665.

**Expander.** See *Brake-hose-coupling Packing-expander. Packing Expander. Piston-packing Expander.*

**Express-car.** A car for carrying light packages of freight for express companies. Such cars are usually run with passenger trains. See fig. 6. Also see *Combined Baggage and Express or Mail Car*, fig. 7. *Combined Passenger and Mail, Baggage, or Express Car*, fig. 8.

**Express Hand-car.** A hand-car with large wheels to run at a high speed, and used for carrying light packages, as newspapers or for similar service. See fig. 46.

**Extension.** See *Roof Running-board Extension*.

**External Cylinder-gauge.** A steel ring with a cylindrical hole which is very accurately made of a precise size, and used as a standard of measurement for the diameters of solid cylindrical objects.

**External Screw-gauge.** A steel ring with a screw-thread in the inside which is very accurately made of a precise size for measuring the diameters of male screws. See fig. 797.

**Eye.** " A small hole or aperture."—*Webster*. See

*Body Check-chain Eye.*          *Lamp-case Eye.*
*Berth-brace Eye.*          *Parallel Brake-hanger*
*Bull's-eye.*          *Eye.*
*Check-chain Eye.*          *Switching-eye.*
*Coupling-pin-chain Eye.*          *Truck Check-chain Eye.*

**Eye-bolt.** " A bolt having an eye or loop at one end for the reception of a ring, hook, or rope, as may be required."—*Knight*. See fig. 784. See

*Brake-beam Eye-bolt.*          *Lock Eye-bolt.*
*Brake Safety-chain Eye-*          *Lock-chain Eye-bolt.*
*bolt.*

**Eye-head Coupling-pin.** A coupling-pin with a hole or eye in its head. See fig. 275. See also *Solid-head Coupling-pin*.

## F

**Face.** See *Register-face*.

**Face of Rim,** *of Car-wheel*. The horizontal surface of the outside of the rim. See **24**, fig. 138.

**Face-plate.** A metal plate by which any object is covered, so as to protect it from wear or abrasion. A *journal-box cover* is sometimes called a face-plate. See

*Berth-latch Face-plate.*          *Dead-block Face-plate.*
*Buffer-block Face-plate.*          *Draw-bar Face-plate.*

**Facing.** " A covering in front, for ornament."—*Webster*. See *Clear-story Sill-facing*.

**Fancy-braided Bell-cord.** See *Bell-cord*.

**Fare-box Street-car.** A street-car in which the fare is collected in a box provided for the purpose, and under the observation of the driver. Such cars usually have an inclosed platform in front, so that access to the car can be had only from the rear. They are turned around at the end of each trip and are run without conductors. See fig. 37.

**Fare-wicket.** An opening in the main door of a street-car, through which the conductor collects fares from passengers on the platform without opening the main door. See **89**, fig. 753.

**Fare-wicket Door.** A cover or gate for a fare-wicket. See **89**, fig. 753.

**Fare-wicket Door-case.** A frame which incloses a fare-wicket and in which it slides. Such frames are made of either metal or wood. See **90**, fig. 753.

**Fascia-board.** See *Eaves Fascia-board. Inside-cornice Fascia-board. Inside-cornice Sub-fascia-board.*

**Fast Berth-hinge.** A berth-hinge, the two parts of which are fastened together and are not detachable. See *Berth-hinge. Loose Berth-hinge.* See fig. 351.

**Fast Coupling-link.** A coupling-link fastened to a draw-bar, so that it cannot be removed or lost. See **2**, figs. 267, 269.

**Fast Coupling-pin.** A coupling-pin fastened to a draw-bar so that it can be used for coupling and uncoupling, but cannot be removed from the bar. See **3**, fig. 267.

**Fastener.** That which fastens or holds any object, as a window, or a rope. See

    *Berth Safety-rope Fast-       Hat-cord End-fastener.*
      ener.             *Sash-fastener.*
           *Window-fastener.*

**Fast-joint Butt-hinge.** A butt-hinge, the two parts of which are so fastened together that they cannot be detached. See fig. 509. See *Loose-joint Butt-hinge. Loose-pin Butt-hinge.*

**Fast Lamp-globe.** A lamp-globe which is fastened to a lamp so that it cannot be detached.

**Faucet.** "A form of valve or cock in which a spigot or plug is made to open or close an aperture in a portion which forms a spout or pipe for the discharge or passage of a fluid."—*Knight.* See **3**, fig. 426; figs. 427–429. See

    *Alcove-faucet.*          *Telegraph-faucet.*
    *Lever-faucet.*          *Vertical Telegraph-faucet.*

**Faucet-alcove.** A *Water-alcove,* which see.

**Feather-duster.** A brush made of feathers used for dusting the inside of passenger cars. See fig. 449.

**Feed-door,** *for Baker Heater.* A door for closing the aperture in which the supply of fuel is fed to the fire. See fig. 594.

**Feed-door Handle,** *for Baker Heater.* A handle for opening and closing the feed-door. See fig. 595.

**Female Centre-plate.** The body and truck centre-plates are sometimes called male and female plates. See *Body Centre-plate. Truck Centre-plate.*

**Female-gauge.** An *External-gauge,* which see.

**Fender.** See *Door-fender.*

**Fender-board.** A board placed at the ends of passenger-car steps to prevent mud and dirt from being thrown on the steps by the wheels.

**Fender-guard.** An iron band attached to the outer edge of a fender-rail, extending around each corner of a street-car to the door-posts. See **22**, figs. 750–753.

**Fender-rail.** A longitudinal wooden rail on the outside of a street-car body between the belt-rail and the sill, and to which a fender-guard is attached to protect the panels from contact with the wheels of other vehicles. See **21**, figs. 750–753.

**Ferry Push-car.** A platform-car which is made very long and used for pushing or pulling other cars on or off a ferry-boat when the latter must be approached by an incline which is too steep for locomotives. The ferry-cars are used to connect those cars which are to be taken on or off the boat with the locomotive, so that the latter can push or pull the cars on the boat without running on the incline. See fig. 32.

**Filling-funnel,** *for Baker Car-heater.* A funnel attached to the combination-cock of a Baker heater for filling the circulating drum with water. See **28**, fig. 581; fig. 607.

**Fire-door,** *for Spear Heater.* The door through which the fuel is put into the stove. See **17**, figs. 550–553; figs. 567, 579. See *Double Fire-door*

**Fire-door-frame,** *for Spear Heater.* A rectangular cast-iron plate which is attached to the casing of the heater and incloses or surrounds the doors, and to which the latter is attached. See **18**, figs. 550–553; fig. 566.

**Fire-pot.** A cast-iron vessel or receptacle which holds the fuel or fire in a stove. See **12**, **12**, fig. 554; fig. 564; 4, fig. 581; fig. 585.

**Fire-proof Bottom,** *for Spear Heater.* A plate with circular corrugations, which is placed inside of the bottom-plate, on top of the floor, to protect it from the fire. See fig. 575.

**First-class Car.** A car used for carrying passengers who pay the regular rates of fare. The term is used to distinguish the passenger-car in ordinary use from those of an inferior grade for the accommodation of passengers who pay less than the regular fare, but does not include sleeping and drawing-room cars, in which an extra charge in addition to the ordinary fare is made. Fig. 4 represents a first-class car.

**Fittings.** *Furnishings,* which see.

**Fixed Brake-lever.** A brake-lever the upper end of which is fastened to a brake-lever stop.

**Fixed Freight-car-lock.** A lock which is attached to the side of a car. The bolt or hasp is fastened to the door.

**Flag-holder Plate,** *for Corner-post of Passenger-car.* A cast or malleable iron plate attached to the outside of a corner-post of a passenger-car to hold a socket for a signal-flag staff. See **161,** fig. 219.

**Flag-holder Socket,** *for Corner-post of Passenger-car.* A cast or malleable iron receptacle to receive and hold a signal-flag staff. It has a suitable lug cast on it which engages into a plate attached to the corner-post of a passenger car.

**Flag-holder,** *for Corner-post of Passenger-car.* A cast or malleable iron receptacle to receive and hold a signal-flag staff. It has a suitable lug cast on it, which engages into a plate attached to the corner-post of a passenger-car.

**Flange.** See *Wheel-flange.*

**Flanger.** See *Snow-flanger.*

**Flat-bar Spiral-spring.** A spiral-spring which is made by winding a flat bar of steel on a mandrel. See fig. 198.

**Flat-car.** A car, the body of which consists simply of a platform, which is not inclosed on the sides or top. See figs. 20, 21.

**Flat Coupling-pin.** A coupling-pin, the cross section of which is of an oblong form. See figs. 275, 276.

**Flax Bell-cord.** See *Bell-cord.*

**Floating Connection-rod.** In the Hodge-brake, a horizontal rod which connects the two floating-levers together. See **8,** fig. 642. In the Westinghouse-brake, a rod which connects a brake-cylinder-lever with a floating-lever. See **12,** fig. 661.

**Floating-lever.** One of two horizontal brake-levers which are used under the centre of a car-body, and form a part of the Hodge-brake. They are each connected at one end with one of the brake-levers on the truck, and at the other end with the brake-windlass. The centres of the floating-levers are connected together by a rod called a *floating connection-rod.* See **7,** fig. 642 ; **16,** fig. 661.

**Floor.** 1. "That part of a building or room on which we walk ; the bottom or lower part consisting, in modern houses, of boards, planks, or pavement.

2. "A platform of boards or planks laid on timbers, as in a bridge or car ; any similar platform."—*Webster.*

3. The boards which cover the floor-timbers of a car, and form the bottom on which passengers walk or freight is carried. In passenger-cars, the floor usually consists of two courses of boards. See **27,** figs. 55–84, 215–232 ; **12,** figs. 750–752. Also see

| | |
|---|---|
| *Inclined End-floor.* | *Main-floor.* |
| *Inclined Side-floor.* | *Platform-floor.* |
| *Intermediate Floor.* | *Upper-floor.* |

**Floor-beam.** A *Floor-timber,* which see.

**Floor-frame.** The main frame of a car-body underneath the floor, including the sills, floor-timbers, etc.

**Flooring.** A term used to designate the boards or lumber of which a floor is made.

**Floor-mat.** A texture or structure of hemp, cocoa-fibre,

rattan, india-rubber, wood, or other material, laid on the floor of a car for passengers to clean their boots and shoes on. Mats are placed on the floors of street-cars to take up the dirt and dust. See *Wood Floor-mat.*

**Floor-sill.** See *Sill.*

**Floor-timbers.** The main timbers in the frame of a car-body between the sills and underneath the floor, and on which the latter rests. See **3, 4,** figs. 55–84, 215–232 ; **10,** figs, 750–752. See

| | |
|---|---|
| *Centre Floor-timber.* | *Intermediate Floor-tim-* |
| *Diagonal Floor-timber.* | *ber.* |
| *Inclined Floor-timber.* | *Short Floor-timber.* |

*Transverse Floor-timber.*

**Floor-timber Braces.** Diagonal timbers let into the floor-timbers and sills under the floor to stiffen the floor-frame laterally. See **8,** fig. 83; **7,** fig. 220.

**Floor-timber Distance-block.** A short transverse piece of timber placed between adjoining floor-timbers and sills to stiffen them, the whole being fastened together with bolts. See **7,** figs. 78, 79, 81; **5,** fig. 220.

**Flush-bolt.** A bolt attached to a slide which is let into a door, sash, or window so as to be flush with its surface. See fig. 517, 537.

**Flush-bolt Keeper.** A plate which is attached to a door, sash, or window frame, and has a suitable hole, in which a flush-bolt engages. See fig. 51

**Flush-handle.** A handle for a lock or latch which is placed in a recess, as of a door, sash, or berth, and which does not project beyond the surface of the object to which it is attached. See figs. 530, 532.

**Flush Window-lift.** A metal plate with a recess, to take hold of, which is let into the sash so as to be flush with its surface. See fig. 318.

**Folding-side Gondola-car.** A gondola-car, the sides of which are attached with hinges, so that they can be folded up or down.

**Follower.** A *Follower-plate,* which see.

**Follower-bolt.** A *Piston Follower-bolt,* which see.

**Follower-plate.** See *Draw-bar Follower-plate. Auxiliary Draw-bar Follower-plate. Piston Follower-plate.*

**Foot-board.** See *Brake Foot-board.*

**Foot-board Bracket.** See *Brake Foot-board Bracket.*

**Foot-rest.** A horizontal wooden bar underneath a car-seat for the passengers who occupy the next seat to rest their feet on. See **172,** fig. 218; **8,** fig. 401. See *Movable Foot-rest. Side Foot-rest.*

**Foot-rest Carriers.** A pair of iron bars which are attached, one of them to the seat-stand and the other to the side of the car, and which carry or support a pair of movable foot-rests. The latter are fastened to the ends of of the carriers and can be tipped up or down by moving the carriers on their pivots. See **9,** fig. 400.

**Fount.** See *Lamp-fount.*

**Four-way-cock Plug,** *for Triple-valve of Westinghouse Car-brake.* A tapered conical spindle, with two passages in it which form a faucet for opening and closing communication between the brake-cylinder reservoir, brake-pipe, and triple-valve. See **17,** fig. 704.

**Four-wheeled Box-car.** A box-car carried on four wheels. See fig. 13.

**Four-wheeled Gondola-car.** A gondola-car mounted on four wheels. See fig. 23.

**Four-wheeled Hopper-bottom Coal-car.** A car with four wheels and a bottom shaped somewhat like a mill-hopper with a drop-door underneath for unloading or dumping the coal with which the car is loaded. See fig. 27. Also see *Coal Dump-car.*

**Frame.** See

| | |
|---|---|
| *Berth-spring Frame.* | *Match-striker Frame.* |
| *Continuous Truck-frame.* | *Mirror-frame.* |
| *Cushion-frame.* | *Name-panel Frame.* |
| *Diamond-truck Side-* | *Platform-hood Frame.* |
| *frame.* | *Register-frame.* |
| *Door-frame.* | *Side-frame.* |
| *End-frame.* | *Signal-bell Frame.* |
| *Fire-door Frame.* | *Truck-frame.* |
| *Floor-frame.* | *Truck Side-frame.* |

**Framed Spring-plank.** A spring-plank composed of several different pieces framed together. See fig. 134.

**Franklin Institute System of Screw-threads.** The Sellers system of screw-threads is often called the Franklin Institute system because the former was first proposed in a report to, and was recommended by, the Franklin Institute. See *Sellers System of Screw-threads.*

**Freight Barrow-truck.** A two-wheeled vehicle for moving freight by hand about a freight-house or station. See fig. 51. Sometimes called *freight-house truck.*

**Freight-car.** A general term used to designate all kinds of cars which carry goods, merchandise, produce, minerals, etc., to distinguish them from those which carry passengers. See figs. 12, 30.

**Freight-car Lock.** A lock for fastening the doors of freight-cars. See **79,** fig. 59. See *Fixed Freight-car Lock.*

**Freight-house Truck.** See *Freight Barrow-truck,* fig. 51, and *Freight Wagon-truck,* fig. 50.

**Freight-truck.** See *Freight Barrow - truck,* fig. 51. *Freight Wagon-truck,* fig. 50. *Push Baggage-car,* fig. 48.

**Freight Wagon-truck.** A four-wheeled vehicle for moving freight by hand about a railroad station or warehouse. See fig. 50.

**Fresnel Lantern.** A lamp inclosed in a cylindrical Fresnel lens. See fig. 499. See *Fresnel Lens.*

**Fresnel Lens.** A lens formed of concentive rings of glass or other transparent substances, one or both sides of which are bounded by spherical surfaces. The object of making a lens in this form is to reduce its thickness in the centre, and thus lessen the liability of having flaws and impurities in the glass, and also to reduce the absorption and aberration of the luminous rays which pass through the lens. Such lenses are also made of a hollow, cylindrical form and used to inclose signal-lamps. The outside of the glass is formed of successive rings, the external surfaces of which are bounded by spherical surfaces. See figs. 497, 498.

**Friction-block.** See *Swing-hanger Friction-block.*

**Friction-plate.** A metal plate attached to any object or surface to resist abrasion or friction. *Side-bearings* are sometimes called friction-plates. See *Chafing-plate. Draw-bar Friction-plate.*

**Friction-roller.** A wheel· or pulley interposed between a sliding object and the surface on which it slides to diminish the friction. See *Door Friction-roller. Sliding-door Friction-roller.*

**Frieze.** That portion of a passenger or street car-body on the outside, between the cornice or eaves of the roof and the tops of the windows. See *Letter-board.*

**Frieze-ventilator.** A ventilator placed in the frieze of a car. See **141**, fig. 215.

**Frieze Ventilator-plate.** A perforated metal plate placed on the outside of a frieze-ventilator to exclude rain and cinders from the car. See figs. 343, 344.

**Frieze Ventilator-register.** A register for a ventilator in the frieze or letter-board of a car. See fig. 346.

**Front.** See *Ash-pit Front. Alcove-front. Water-alcove Front.*

**Front Cylinder-head,** *for Westinghouse Car-brake.* A circular cast-iron plate or cover for the end of a cylinder opposite to the piston-rod. See **5**, figs. 729, 730. For convenience of designation, the end of the cylinder opposite to the piston-rod is called the front-end, and that adjoining the piston-rod, the back-end, as in locomotives.

**Front Cylinder-head,** *for Westinghouse Tender-brake.* Same as above for car-brake. See **5**, figs. 727, 728.

**Front Seat-bottom Rail.** A wooden strip at the front edge of a seat to which a wooden seat-bottom is attached. See **37**, figs. 750–752. See *Back Seat-bottom Rail.*

**Front Seat-rail.** A longitudinal strip of wood which extends along the front edge of ordinary passenger and street car-seats, and which supports the seat-bottom. See **36**, figs. 750, 752.

**Fulcrum.** "In mechanics, that by which a lever is sustained, or the point about which it moves."—*Webster.* See *Brake-lever Fulcrum.*

**Funnel.** "A vessel for conveying fluids into close vessels; a kind of inverted hollow cone with a pipe; a tunnel."—*Webster*. See *Filling-funnel*. *Poke-hole Funnel*.

**Furnishings.** This term is used to designate the smaller fixtures, hardware, etc., such as locks, latches, basket racks, seat-back arms, window-fastenings, hinges, etc., which are used in the inside of cars. See also *Car-furnishings*.

**Furring.** Pieces of wood placed in a wall or other position to nail something to as a panel or moulding. See *Window-panel Furring*. *Panel-furring*.

**Fusee.** The cone or conical part of a watch or clock, round which is wound the chain or cord. See *Berth-spring Fusee*.

# G

**Gagger.** A *Chaplet*, which see.

**Gain.** "In architecture, a beveling shoulder; a lapping of timbers, or the cut that is made for receiving a timber."—*Webster*. In car work the term generally means a notching of one piece of timber into another.

**Gasolier.** An ornamental arrangement of pipes and burners for lighting a railroad-car with gas. It is a chandelier for a railroad-car.

**Gas-burner.** "The jet-piece of a gas-lighting apparatus at which the gas issues and combustion takes place."—*Knight*. See *Bracket Gas-burner*.

**Gasket.** "A strip of leather, tow, or textile fabric, to form a packing or caulk a joint."—*Knight*. See *Journal-box-cover Gasket*.

**Gasket,** *for Top Steam-cylinder of Engine for Westinghouse-brake*. A piece of sheet copper, cut to the shape of the surfaces of contact of the steam-cylinder and its head, and placed between the two to make a steam-tight joint. See fig. 699.

**Gasket,** *for bottom of Air-cylinder for Westinghouse-brake*. Same as above for joint between the bottom of the air-cylinder and its head. See fig. 702.

**Gasket,** *for bottom of Steam-cylinder of Engine for Westinghouse-brake*. Same as above, for joint between the lower end of the steam-cylinder and centre-piece. See fig. 700.

**Gasket,** *for top of Air-cylinder for Westinghouse-brake*. Same as above, for joint between top of air-cylinder and centre piece. See fig. 701.

**Gate.** See *Platform-gate*.

**Gate,** *of a Casting-mould*. The opening in the mould through which the melted metal is poured. See *Ingate*.

**Gauge.** The distance between the heads of the rails of a railroad. The usual distance, 4 ft. 8½ or 9 in., is called the *standard-gauge*; if greater than this, a *broad-gauge* or *wide-gauge*; if smaller, a *narrow-gauge*.

Also a tool or instrument used as a standard of measurement. See

*Air-gauge.*
*Broad-gauge.*
*Cylindrical-gauge.*
*External Cylindrical-gauge.*
*External Screw-gauge.*
*Internal Cylindrical-gauge.*

*Narrow-gauge.*
*Pressure-gauge.*
*Screw-gauge.*
*Screw Pitch-gauge.*
*Screw-thread Gauge.*
*Standard-gauge.*
*Whitworth-gauge.*
*Wide-gauge.*

**Gauze.** See *Wire-gauze.*

**Gear.** Apparatus: In mechanics the term is used to designate a combination of appliances for effecting some result, as *valve-gear.* See *Draw-gear. Swing-motion Gear.*

**Gear-wheel,** *for Hand-car.* The larger cog-wheel of a hand-car which is attached to the crank-shaft and gears into a pinion on the axle of the car. See **5,** figs. 772–775.

**Gib,** *for Journal-bearings.* A *Journal-bearing Key,* which see.

**Girder.** "In architecture, the principal piece of timber in a floor. Its ends are usually framed into the summers, or breast-summers, and the joists are framed into it at one end. In buildings entirely of timber, the *girder* is fastened by tenons into the posts."—*Webster.*

"The term *girder* is restricted to beams subject to transverse strain, and exerting a vertical pressure merely on their points of support."—*Stoney.* The term in this country is often used synonymously with *truss.* Thus, engineers speak of a "Howe Truss," a "Pratt Truss," a "Warren Girder," and a "Lattice Girder." The term *truss* is never applied to a plate-girder, so that the distinction seems to be that a truss always consists of some system of open framing, whereas a girder may be either of open work or solid, as in a plate-girder.

**Girth.** A long horizontal piece of wood on the side of a box-car body fitted on the inside of the posts and braces so as to embrace them. In box-cars it is placed about half-way between the floor and the roof. See **49,** figs. 55–72. See also *End-girth.*

**Girth Tie-rod.** A horizontal rod extending from the door to the corner-post along the girth of a freight-car and intended to tie the two posts together.

**Gland.** A cover of a stuffing-box, as for a piston-rod etc. See *Piston-rod Packing-gland.*

**Glass.** See *Window-glass.*

**Glass-seal.** See *Lock-seal.*

**Globe.** See

*Double-cone Lamp-globe.*
*Egg-shaped Lamp-globe.*
*Fast Lamp-globe.*
*Lamp-globe.*

*Loose-globe.*
*Melon-shaped* **Lamp-***globe.*
*Pear-shaped Lamp-globe.*

**Globe-chimney.** A *Lamp-globe Chimney*, which see.

**Globe-holder.** Any contrivance for holding a globe on a lamp. Usually it consists of a metal ring, at the base of the globe, on which the latter rests, and to which it is fastened with springs, screws, or by the pressure of the globe-chimney on top when the latter is adjustable. See **7**, figs. 470, 475. See *Detachable Globe-holder.*

**Gondola-car.** A car with a platform-body which is inclosed with low side-boards. These side-boards are usually fixed, but are sometimes hinged so that they can be let down, and in some cases are removable. See figs. 19, 23. Also see *Folding-side Gondola-car. Eight-wheeled Gondola-car. Four-wheeled Gondola-car.*

**Gong.** A *Signal-bell*, which see.

**Graduating-spring,** *of Triple-valve for Westinghouse Car-brake.* A spiral-spring which acts against a collar on the graduating-stem to hold the latter against the triple-valve-piston when it is forced downward. See **8**, fig. 704; fig. 710.

**Graduating-stem,** *of Triple-valve for Westinghouse-brake.* A slender rod or pin which works in a hole drilled in the centre of the triple-valve-piston, and which, by the movement the latter, opens and closes communication from the chambers above and below the piston. See **7**, figs. 704, fig. 709.

**Grain-car.** A box-car, with tight inside doors, made for carrying grain.

**Grain-door.** A close-fitting movable door on the inside of a box-car by which the lower part of the door-opening is closed, when the car is loaded with grain, to prevent the latter from leaking out at the door-way. Such doors are usually made so that they can be thrown over on one side of the door-way and thus be out of the way when they are not used. A great variety of mechanical devices is used for accomplishing this purpose. See **62**, fig. 61.

**Grain-door Rod.** An iron rod attached to the door-posts on the inside of a box-car, and to which a grain-door is fastened or hinged. The door and rod are generally arranged so that the former can be moved to one side and out of the way when the car is not loaded with grain. See **63**, fig. 61.

**Grate.** A frame of iron bars for holding coals in a stove, fire-place, etc. See *Anti-clinker Grate. Safety-grate. Stove-grate.*

**Grate,** *for Baker Heater.* An iron casting with slots and bars on which the fire is made in a Baker heater. See **3**, figs. 581 ; fig. 584.

**Grate,** *for Spear Heater.* A circular cast-iron perforated plate on which the fire rests. Air is admitted to the fire through the openings. See **18**, fig. 554 ; figs. 570, 576.

**Grate-bar,** *for Spear Heater.* A cast-iron bar below the grate, and on which the latter rests. See **20**, figs. 554, fig. 571.

**Grated-door.** A door, consisting of a wooden frame with iron or wooden bars, used on cars for carrying live-stock. See fig. 55. Grated-doors are also shown in figs. 14, 15, 16.

**Grate-ring,** *for Spear Heater.* A cast-iron ring which surrounds the grate. See **19**, fig, 554; fig. 577.

**Grate-shaker.** An iron bar which can be attached to a grate to move it in shaking the fire. See fig. 600.

**Grating.** See *Window-grating.*

**Gravel-car.** A car for carrying gravel ; usually a *Tip-car,* which see.

**Grease-box.** A *Journal-box,* which see.

**Group-spring.** A spiral car-spring formed of a number of separate springs, united together so that they all act as one spring. When it consists of two, three, or four springs united it is called a *double,* or *two-group,* a *three-group, four-group spring,* etc. See figs. 211, 212.

**Guard.** See

    *Dash-guard.*         *Dust-guard.*
    *Door-guard.*         *Fender-guard.*
    *Draw-timber Guard.*    *Heat-guard.*
             *Window-guard.*

**Guard-band.** See *Door-guard Band.*

**Guard-pipe,** *for Creamer-brake.* A piece of ¾-in. gas-tubing attached to the hand-rail, and leading to the platform roof of a car to protect the wire connection of the brake. See **19**, fig. 646.

**Guide.** "That which leads or conducts."—*Webster.* See

    *Bell-cord Guide.*        *Brake-lever Guide.*
    *Bell-strap Guide.*       *Brake-rod Guide.*
    *Bell-strap Guide, with*   *Draw-bar Guide.*
     *Roller.*              *Journal-box Guide.*
         *Strap-hanger Guide.*

**Guide-bar.** See *Truck bolster Guide-bar.*

**Guide-block.** See *Truck-bolster Guide-block.*

**Guide-rail.** A *Door-track,* which see.

**Gum-spring.** A term used by Philadelphians to designate *India-rubber Car-springs,* which see.

**Gun-car.** See *Cannon-car.*

# H

**Hair.** See *Hard-hair. Curled-hair.*

**Half-elliptic Spring.** A spring composed of one set of plates in a form resembling the half of an ellipse. See figs. 82, 127 ; **2**, fig. 132 ; fig. 187.

**Half-elliptic Spring-bearing.** A cast or wrought iron plate on which the end of a half-elliptic spring rests. See **1**, fig. 132.

**Half-round-bar Spiral-spring.** A spiral spring made of a half-round bar of steel. See figs. 192, 193.

**Hammered Car-axle.** An axle made by forging under a hammer. Sometimes called *faggoted-axle.* Hammered axles are made either of slabs or bars of iron, which are piled together and then heated, welded, and forged into the form of the axle by hammering, usually under a steam hammer. The slabs are made by piling small pieces of scrap-iron, which are then heated and welded together by forging. The bars used for making such axles are sometimes made of rolled iron.

**Hand-car.** A small and light car arranged with cranks or levers and gearing so that it can be propelled by hand by persons riding on the car. Such cars are usually used for carrying workmen and tools. See *Crank Hand-car,* fig. 43; *Lever Hand-car,* fig. 44; *Inspection Hand-car,* fig. 45; *Express Hand-car,* fig. 46; *Three-wheeled Hand-car,* fig. 47.

**Hand-car Lever.** A pivoted iron bar which is connected with a crank of a hand-car and by which the car is propelled. The lever is worked by hand. See **19,** figs. 772, 773.

**Hand-car Truss-rod.** A transverse or longitudinal rod by which the floor-frame of a hand-car is trussed. See **26,** figs. 772–775.

**Hand-car Wheel.** A light wheel for hand-cars, with cast-iron rim and hub and wrought-iron spokes. See fig. 184.

**Hand-hole.** See *Dust Hand-hole. Fare-wicket.*

**Handle.** That part of any object, instrument, or device which is held in the hand when it is used. See

    *Ash-pit Door-handle.*        *Ladder-handle.*
    *Berth-latch Handle.*       *Lever-handle.*
    *Brake-shaft Crank-han-*    *Register-handle.*
      *dle.*                    *Saloon-handle.*
    *Corner-handle.*          *Sliding-door Handle.*
    *Corner-urinal Handle.*   *Side-urinal Handle.*
    *Door-handle.*           *Stove-pipe-damper Han-*
    *Feed-door Handle.*      *dle.*
    *Flush-handle.*          *Tank-valve-rod Handle.*
         *Urinal-handle.*

**Hand-rail.** A bar or rail to take hold of with the hand. See

    *Body Hand-rail.*       *Inside Hand-rail.*
    *Door Hand-rail.*       *Step Hand-rail.*

**Hand-rail,** *for Tank-car.* An iron pipe supported on posts on the outside of a tank-car for train-men to hold on in passing over the cars. See **121,** figs. 73–76.

**Hand-rail Bracket.** See *Inside Hand-rail Bracket.*

**Hand-rail Post,** *for Tank-car.* Vertical iron posts or stanchions attached to the outside of a tank-car, and which form a support for the hand-rail. See **122,** figs. 73–76.

**Hand-straps.** Straps made of leather, or other flexible material, and attached to the inside hand-rail for passengers to hold on by. They are generally made in the form of a double loop and are used chiefly in street-cars. See **96**, figs. 750, 753.

**Hand-wheel.** A *Brake-wheel*, which see.

**Hanger.** 1. "That by which a thing is suspended."—*Webster.*

2. "A means for supporting shafting of machinery."—*Knight.* See

| | |
|---|---|
| *Bell-cord Hanger.* | *Parallel Brake-hanger.* |
| *Bell-cord Fixed-hanger.* | *Rocker-bearing-timber* |
| *Bell-cord Strap-hanger.* | *Hanger.* |
| *Bell-cord Double-strap-* | *Safety-hanger.* |
| *hanger.* | *Spring-hanger.* |
| *Brake-hanger.* | *Step-hanger.* |
| *Door-hanger.* | *Strap-hanger.* |
| *Hat-cord Hanger.* | *Swing-hanger.* |
| *Link-hanger.* | *Swing-link Hanger.* |

**Hanger-link.** A *Swing-hanger*, which see.

**Hard-hair.** A quality of curled-hair which is very stiff or rigid. See *Curled-hair.*

**Hasp.** "A fastening clamp or bar fast at one end to an eye-bolt or staple, the other end passing over a staple, where it is secured by a pin, key, button, or padlock."—*Knight.* See *Door-hasp. Head-board Coupling-hasp.*

**Hat-cord End-fastener.** A metal plate, with a centre-hole and wedge-bushings, by which a hat-cord is fastened to the end of a car.

**Hat-cord Hanger.** A metal eye, or fastening, by which a hat-cord is attached to the ceiling of a car.

**Hat-cords.** Cords which are placed under the ceiling of a passenger-car and to which hats can be hung up by their rims. These are seldom used now.

**Hat-hook.** A metal hook for hanging hats on. See fig. 445.

**Hat-post.** An upright metal pin for hanging hats on. These are used chiefly in sleeping-cars. See **18**, figs. 296, 297; 2, fig. 371.

**Hat-post and Hook Combined.** A hat-post made in combination with a hook. The latter is used for hanging clothing or other light articles on. See fig. 447.

**Hat-rack.** A *Basket-rack*, which see.

**Hay-car.** A box-car for carrying baled hay. Such cars are usually made with larger bodies and doors than ordinary box freight-cars.

**Head.** See

| | |
|---|---|
| *Back Cylinder-head.* | *Dome-head.* |
| *Bottom Cylinder-head.* | *Draw-bar Head.* |
| *Brake head.* | *Front Cylinder-head.* |
| *Buffer-head.* | *Piston-head.* |
| *Cross-head.* | *Steam-piston Head.* |

*Tank-head.*     *Top Cylinder-head.*

**Head-board.** See *Berth Head-board.*

**Head-board Bolt.** A bolt for holding a head-board in its place. See fig. 367 ; 2, fig. 369.

**Head-board-bolt Bushing.** A socket for receiving a head-board bolt. See fig. 368.

**Head-board Coupling.** A metal hasp and keeper by which two parts of a head-board of a sleeping-car are connected together, or one part is fastened to the seat-back or side of the car. See figs. 365, 366.

**Head-board-coupling Hasp.** A hook which engages into a corresponding eye in a head-board-coupling keeper. See fig. 365.

**Head-board-coupling Keeper.** The portion of a head-board coupling which forms an eye for a corresponding catch. See fig. 366.

**Head-lining.** Painted cloth lining with which the ceilings of passenger-cars are covered. The painting on head-linings is intended to be of an ornamental character.

**Head-lining Nail.** A nail with a large button-shaped head especially made for fastening head-linings to the ceilings of cars. See fig. 448.

**Heater.** Any apparatus for warming a car, room, or building by convection; that is, by conveying hot water, steam, or warmed air into or through the apartments. The term generally refers to any arrangement for warm-ing apartments other than stoves, which heat by direct radiation. See *Baker Car-heater. Car-heater. Spear Anti-clinker Car-heater.*

**Heater-pipe Casing.** A wooden or iron covering over a heater-pipe in a passenger-car to prevent the feet of passengers from coming in contact with the hot pipes. The casing also forms a foot-rest. See **10,** fig. 401.

**Heat-guard.** A sheet-metal covering for the wood-work of a passenger-car, to protect it from the heat of a stove. Sometimes this covering is nailed to the side and ends of the car, and in other cases it is made to surround the stove. It is usually made of tin plates or zinc.

**Heat-guard,** *of Baker Car-heater.* A Russia-iron casing around the back of the upper part of a Baker heater to protect the wood-work of the car from the heat. See **11,** fig. 581; fig. 592.

**Height of Draw-bar.** This is the vertical distance measured from the centre of a draw-bar to the tops of the rails. At the meeting of the Master Car-builders' Association held at Richmond, Va., June 15, 1871, a resolution was unanimously adopted recommending that a height of *2 feet 9 inches* be adopted as a standard height for the draw-bars of all cars.

**Helper.** A term used to designate an assistant engine or horse to help trains or cars up grades.

**Helper-ring.** An iron ring fastened to the platform end-timber of a street-car and used to attach an extra horse to the car to pull up steep places.

**Hemp Bell-cord.** See *Bell-cord.*

**Hemp Floor-mat.** See *Floor-mat.*

**Hibbard-spring.** A spiral spring composed of several coils of steel of rectangular section. The coils are placed inside of each other and are made of different diameters and wound in opposite directions, or "right and left." The spring is named after the inventor. See fig. 199.

**Hinge.** "The hook or joint on which a door, gate, etc., turns."—*Webster.* See

| | |
|---|---|
| *Berth-hinge.* | *Loose-joint Butt-hinge.* |
| *Butt-hinge.* | *Loose-pin Butt-hinge.* |
| *Door-hinge.* | *Man-hole Hinge.* |
| *Drop-bottom Hinge.* | *Seat-hinge.* |
| *Fast Berth-hinge.* | *Sofa-hinge.* |
| *Fast-joint Butt-hinge.* | *Strap-hinge.* |
| *Loose Berth-hinge.* | *T-hinge.* |

**Hinge-**burner, *for Mineral-oil Lamp.* A burner of which the chimney-seat is hinged to the lamp-top so as to give access to the wick.

**Hodge-brake.** An arrangement invented by Nehemiah Hodge and patented by him in 1849, for operating the brakes on each truck of a car simultaneously, and equalizing the pressure on all the wheels. The brake may have either one or two levers, on each truck. Underneath the car-body are two levers called floating-levers, with movable fulcrums in their centres, which are connected together by a rod. One end of each of these levers is connected by a rod and chain to the brake-shaft, and the other end of the floating-lever is connected by a rod with the long arm of a brake-lever on a truck. See fig. 642.

**Holder.** "Something by which a thing is held."—*Webster.* See

| | |
|---|---|
| *Alcove Cup-holder.* | *Lamp-chimney Holder.* |
| *Basin-chain Holder.* | *Lamp-holder.* |
| *Berth Safety-rope Holder.* | *Mirror-sash Holder.* |
| *Brake-shaft Holder.* | *Side-lamp Holder.* |
| *Candle-holder.* | *Sliding-door Holder* |
| *Cup-holder.* | *Soap-holder.* |
| *Detachable-globe Holder.* | *Spring Window-holder.* |
| *Door-holder.* | *Ticket-holder.* |
| *Door-sheave Holder.* | *Tumbler-holder.* |
| *Globe-holder.* | *Window-curtain Holder.* |
| *Lamp-case Door-holder.* | *Window-sash Holder.* |
| | *Window-spring Holder.* |

**Hollow-spoke Wheel.** A cast-iron car-wheel made with hollow spokes. See figs. 166, 167.

**Hood.** See *Platform-hood. Ventilator-hood.* A *roof-apron* is sometimes called a hood.

**Hood,** *for Spear Heater.* A horizontal tube or covering

on the outside of a car, and on top of the cold-air pipe, so as to give the latter a **T** shape. The air is admitted to the pipe through the ends of the hood which are covered with wire netting or perforated plates so as to exclude cinders. The hood has a valve which is moved by the current of air produced by the motion of the car, so as to admit air which ever way the car runs. See **1, 1,** figs. 550, 551, 552.

**Hook.** See

Bell-cord End-hook.
Berth-curtain Hook.
Body Check-chain Hook.
Check-chain Hook.
Coat-and-hat Hook.
Coat-hook.
Coupling-hook.
Door-hook.
Door-latch Hook.
Draw-bar Coupling-hook.
Draw-hook.
Hat-post and Hook.
Lamp-case Hook.
Seal-hook.
Stake-hook.
Table-hook.
Table-leg Hook.
Tank-band Hook.
Tassel-hook.
Truck Check-chain hook.
Window-curtain Hook.

**Hopkins Journal-bearing.** See *Lead-lined Bearing.*

**Hopper.** See *Coal-hopper. Soil-hopper. Water-closet Hopper.*

**Hopper-bottom Coal-car.** A car with a bottom shaped somewhat like a mill-hopper, and with a drop-door underneath for unloading or dumping the coal with which the car is loaded. See figs. 24–27. See

Coal Dump-car.
Eight-wheeled Hopper-bottom Coal-car.
Four-wheeled Hopper-bottom Coal-car.
Hopper-bottom Gondola Coal-car.
Iron-hopper Coal-car.

**Hopper-bottom Gondola-car.** A Gondola-car made with a bottom shaped somewhat like a mill-hopper, and a drop-door underneath for unloading or dumping the coal, ore etc., with which the car is loaded, and which it is intended to carry. See fig. 24. Also see *Coal Dump-car.*

**Horizontal Brake-shaft.** A brake-shaft usually at the end of a car-body, whose position is horizontal instead of vertical. See **95**, figs. 55, 56, 69, 72.

**Horizontal Brake-shaft Chain.** A chain attached to a brake rod at the end of a car and running over a pulley to a horizontal shaft on which it is wound. See **104**, figs. 55, 56.

**Horizontal Telegraph-cock** or **Faucet.** See *Telegraph Faucet.*

**Horns.** See *Pedestal-horns.*

**Horse-car.** A box-car fitted up especially for carrying horses. See fig. 16. Street-cars drawn by horses are also sometimes called horse-cars. See *Street-car.*

**Hose.** Flexible tubing, made of leather, canvas, or india-rubber, for conveying water, air, or other fluids. See
  *Armored-hose.*                    *Coupling-hose.*
  *Brake-hose.*                      *Tender-hose.*

**Hose-couplings.** See *Brake-hose Couplings.*

**Hot-air Pipe,** *for Spear Heater.* A pipe by which the hot air is conducted from the heater and distributed through the car by registers at each seat. See **3,** figs. 550, 554.

**Hotel-car.** A sleeping car with a kitchen for cooking and arrangements for serving meals. See fig. 1. *Restaurant-cars* have kitchens, etc., but no sleeping-berths.

**House-car.** A *Box-car,* which see.

**Housing-box.** A *Journal-box,* which see.

**Hub-bolts.** Bolts by which the hub of a wheel is fastened to the wheel-plate. They are used with paper wheels. See **3,** figs. 176, 177.

**Hub of Wheel.** The central portion of a wheel into which the axle is fitted. The hub of a car-wheel is usually cylindrical in form, and projects beyond the discs or spokes of the wheel on each side. See **21,** fig. 138 ; figs. 154–184.

**Hydraulic-jack.** A tool or machine in which the power is exerted by means of the pressure of some liquid acting against a piston or plunger, for raising heavy weights, like a car. The pressure on the liquid is produced by a small pump worked by hand. See figs. 801, 802.

**Hydraulic-pressed Car-candles.** Candles made of paraffine which are subjected to hydraulic pressure.

# I

**Ice-car.** A car for transporting ice. Such cars are usually constructed with double roofs, floors, and sides, the space between which is filled with saw-dust or other non-conducting substance to prevent the ice from melting.

**Ice-pan.** A receptacle for carrying ice in refrigerator-cars.

**Inclined End-floor,** *of Coal-cars.* The sloping wooden floor at the end of a coal-car. See **134,** figs. 77–79.

**Inclined Floor-timbers,** *for Coal-car.* The wooden sills to which the inclined floor of a coal-car is nailed. See **153,** figs. 77, 79.

**Inclined-plane Car.** A car for carrying passengers which is drawn by a wire rope on a steep inclined-plane. The car is so arranged that the floor will be level when the wheels are on the incline. This is done by making the wheels at one end larger than at the other, or by raising up one end of the car-body higher than the other, when the car stands on a level track. See fig. 35.

**Inclined Side-floor,** *of Coal-cars.* The sloping wooden floor on the side of a coal-car. See **135,** figs. 78, 79.

**India-rubber Car-spring.** A spring consisting of a cylindrical block of india-rubber. Such springs are used both for carrying the weight of cars and for buffer and draw-springs. See fig. 214.

**India-rubber Floor-mat.** See *Floor-mat.*

**Ingate.** "The aperture in a casting-mould at which the melted metal enters."—*Knight.* Often called a *Gate,* which see.

**Inner Draw-bar Carry-iron,** *for Miller-coupler.* A **U**-shaped strap of wrought-iron bolted to the suspender-beam to support the draw-bar or draw-hook of a Miller-coupler. See **32,** figs. 282, 284.

**Inner-hung Brake.** When the brake-shoes and beams are attached to a truck, or four-wheeled car, *between* the wheels, it is called an *inner-hung brake.* When they are attached on the outside, it is an *outer-hung brake.* Figs. 100, 101, 639, 645 represent inner-hung brakes.

**Inscription-plate.** A metal plate with any kind of letter-ing or record on it. The cast-iron plate attached to the top of the platform end-timbers of the Miller-platform, with the dates of the patents on it. See **46,** figs. 283, 284, 285.

**Inside-casing.** *of Baker Heater.* Sheet-iron bent and riv-eted into the shape of a frustrum of a cone which forms the chamber for the fire in a Baker heater. See **5,** fig. 581 ; fig. 586.

**Inside-cornice.** A moulding on the inside of passenger-cars which fills the angle formed where the ceiling or roof joins the side of the car. See **94,** figs. 218, 225, 226; **36,** fig. 301.

**Inside-cornice Facia-board.** A projecting board on the inside of a passenger-car at the cornice, which forms a moulding or ornament under the cornice. See **95,** figs. 225, 226; **37,** fig. 301.

**Inside-cornice Sub-facia Board.** A projecting board under the inside-cornice facia-board. See **96,** figs. 225, 226; **38,** fig. 301.

**Inside End-piece,** *of Truck-frame.* The cross-piece at the end of a truck-frame which is next to the centre of the car.

**Inside Frieze-panel.** A panel on the inside of a street-car over a window. These panels are usually disfigured by advertisements and sometimes by very bad paintings. See **31,** fig. 750.

**Inside Hand-rail.** A rail, usually made of wood, attached to the rafters on the inside of passenger and street cars by metal brackets, and intended for passengers to hold fast to. In street-cars leather straps made in the form of loops are attached to these rails. See **94,** figs. 750, 752.

**Inside Hand-rail Bracket.** A metal knee or support which is fastened to the rafters of passenger and street cars and which forms a support for a hand-rail which is attached thereto. See **95**, figs. 750, 752; fig. 758.

**Inside-lining.** The boarding which is nailed to the insides of the posts of freight, baggage, and other cars. See **53**, figs. 61, 64, 82, 84; **97**, figs. 225, 226.

**Inside-lining Cap.** A *Girth*, which see.

**Inside-ring,** *for Spear Heater.* A perforated circular casting which is placed between the fire-pot and the casing of the heater. See **15**, fig. 554; fig. 560.

**Inside Top-plate,** *of Spear Heater.* A cast-iron plate, with a hole in the centre to which the smoke-pipe is attached, and which forms a cover for the fire-pot. See **11**, fig. 554; fig. 561.

**Inside Wheel-piece Plate.** An iron plate fastened to the inside of a wheel-piece to strengthen it. See **12**, figs. 128, 129.

**Inside Window-panel.** A panel inside of a passenger-car, between the windows. See **89**, figs. 215, 219, 226; **24**, fig. 298; **35**, figs. 300, 301.

**Inside Window-sill.** A horizontal piece of wood under the window, on the inside of a car. See **78**, figs. 225, 226; **5**, figs. 299, 301.

**Inside Window-stop.** A wooden strip attached to a window-post on the inside of a window-blind or an inner sash of a double window. It forms a groove in which the blind or window-sash slides. Sometimes the window-moulding forms a stop on the inside. See **86′**, fig. 225.

**Inspection-car.** A car used for inspecting the track of a railroad. One form is that of a gondola-car, which is inclosed and roofed over, but left open in front, and furnished with seats. In inspecting the track, it is pushed in front of a locomotive with the open end forward, from which the track is in full view of the occupants of the car. The term inspection-car is also used to designate a hand-car used for very much the same purpose. See *Inspection Hand-car,* fig. 45.

**Inspection Hand-car.** A hand-car which is usually provided with comfortable seats, and is used by officers in inspecting the track. See fig. 45.

**Intermediate-floor.** A floor consisting of boards placed between the sills and floor-timbers of passenger-cars and between the deafening or under floor and the upper or main floor. The purpose of the intermediate-floor is to exclude noise and stiffen the floor-timbers.

**Intermediate Floor-timbers.** The two main longitudinal timbers underneath the floor, which lie between the outside-sills and the centre floor-timbers. See **3**, fig. 55–84 : 216–231.

**Internal Cylindrical-gauge.** A solid steel cylinder which is very accurately made of a precise size and used as a standard of measurement of cylindrical holes.

**Internal Screw-gauge.** A solid steel cylinder with a

screw-thread on it, which is very accurately made of a precise size, for measuring the diameter of female screws. See fig. 798.

**Inverted Arch-bar.** A wrought-iron bar bent into somewhat the form of an inverted arch, and which forms the tension member of a truss of an iron side-frame of a truck. The ends of an inverted arch-bar rest on top of the journal-boxes and the arch-bar is on top of it. See **15,** figs. 95–112. See *Centre-bearing Inverted Arch-bar.*

**Inverted Body-queen-post.** A post in the side of a car-body which supports the body end-truss-rod. With the rod it forms a truss for holding up the end of the car-body. See **24,** figs. 750, 752.

**Inverted Body-truss-rod.** A truss-rod used to prevent the ends of a car-body from sagging. The rod is placed on the side of the car-body and rests on two queen-posts placed on top of the sill, and is attached to the latter at each end. See **23,** figs. 750, 752.

**Inverted Truss-rod Plate.** A wrought or cast iron bearing at the end of the sill of a street-car and through which the truss-rod passes and against which the nut on the rod bears. See **25,** fig. 750.

**Iron.** See

| | |
|---|---|
| *Carry-iron.* | *Knee-iron.* |
| *Cricket-iron.* | *Pull-iron.* |

| | |
|---|---|
| *Safety-beam Iron.* | *Truck-frame Knee-iron.* |
| *Step-iron.* | *Truss-rod Iron.* |

*Switching Iron.*

**Iron Body-bolster.** A body-bolster made of iron, usually in the form of a truss. See **12,** figs. 60–64; **10,** figs. 228–231; figs. 235–237, 240. See *Body-bolster Compression-bar. Body-bolster Tension-bar.*

**Iron-hopper Coal-car.** An iron car for carrying coal, the body of which is made somewhat of the form of a mill-hopper, and with a drop-door on the bottom for unloading the coal. See fig. 26.

**Iron-truck.** A car-truck of which the side-frames are made wholly of iron. These are often made of iron with wooden transoms and spring-planks, although iron transoms are now used in many cases. Figs. 95–114 are illustrations of different kinds of iron-trucks.

**Italian-hemp Bell-cord.** See *Bell-cord.*

# J

**Jack.** See

| | |
|---|---|
| *Hydraulic Jack.* | *Smoke-jack.* |
| *Lamp-jack.* | *Stove-pipe Jack.* |

*Water-closet Ventilating-jack.*

**Jamb.** See *Door-jamb.*

**Janney Car-coupler.** A draw-bar arranged to couple cars automatically, invented and patented by Mr. **Janney.**

The outer end of the draw-bar is made of a forked or **U** shape and to one arm an **L**-shaped knuckle or clutch is pivoted so that when the two draw-bars come together the two knuckles engage into each other A buffing or compressing device, consisting of two buffers, one on each side of the draw-bar, is also used in connection with the self-coupling apparatus described. See figs. 290–2.

**Jaw.** See *Draw-bar Jaw. Pedestal-jaw.*

**Jaw-bit.** A bar extending across the mouth of a jaw underneath a journal-box and bolted to the horns of the pedestal. See **77**, fig. 131 ; **5**, fig. 750.

**Jaw-spring.** A *Journal-spring,* which see.

**Joint-bolt.** A bolt used for fastening two timbers when the end of one joins the side of another. Such bolts have nuts which are let into the first timber and the bolt is inserted in a hole which is bored through both and screwed into the nut. See fig. 783.

**Joint-cover.** See *Window-moulding Joint-cover.*

**Jointed Side-pawl,** *for Creamer-brake.* A pawl which acts on a ratchet on the side of the drum to hold the latter when the spring is wound up by the brake-shaft. In applying the brake, this pawl is detached from the ratchet or drum which allows the spring to act on the brake-shaft and thus wind up the brake-chain. See **6**, figs. 646, 647.

**Jointed Top-pawl,** *for Creamer-brake.* A pawl with a knuckle-joint attached to the top arm which is keyed to the brake-shaft. The pawl acts on a ratchet on the drum-cover in winding up the brake-spring by the brake-shaft and wheel. See **5**, figs. 646, 647. The reserve power of the spring is communicated to the brake-shaft through this pawl.

**Journal.** The part of an axle or shaft on which the journal-bearing rests, or which rests on the journal-bearing, and is exposed to the friction caused by the revolution of the axle or of the journal. See **6**, fig. 143.

**Journal-bearing.** A block of metal, usually some kind of brass, in contact with a journal, and on which the latter turns. See **7**, fig. 138; fig. 141. In car construction the term journal-bearing usually means a *car-axle journal-bearing.* See

*Hopkins Journal-bearing.*

*Lead-lined Journal-bearing.*

*Master Car-builders' Standard Journal-bearing.*

*Stop-key Journal-bearing.*

*Stop Journal-bearing.*

**Journal-bearing Key.** A plate on top of a journal-bearing and which holds the latter in place. It is used so that the bearing can be readily removed from the box. Also called a *wedge, liner, slide, saddle, keeper,* etc. See **8**, figs. 138, 139 ; fig. 143. Also see *Master Car-builders' Standard Journal-bearing Key.*

**Journal-bearing Stop-key.** A journal-bearing key with a projection to which a stop-plate is attached that bears against the end of the axle to resist its lateral motion and wear. See **27,** figs. 146, 147 ; figs. 148–150.

**Journal-box.** A cast-iron box or case which incloses the journal of a car-axle and the journal-bearing and key, and which holds the oil and waste or packing for lubricating the journal. See **165,** figs. 77–84 ; **3,** figs. 88–127 ; **10,** figs. 138, 139 ; figs. 140–153 ; **4,** figs. 750, 753. Also see *Master Car-builders' Standard Journal-box.* A journal-box is also called an *axle-box, car-box, grease-box, housing-box, oil-box,* and *pedestal-box.* See *Top-reservoir Journal-box.*

**Journal-box Cover.** A door or lid covering an aperture on the outside of a journal-box, by means of which oil and packing are supplied and journal-bearings are inserted or removed. Such covers are usually made of cast-iron, sometimes of wood. See **4,** figs. 88–125 ; **11,** figs. 138, 153.

**Journal-box-cover Bolt.** A bolt used to fasten the cover to the box. Two of these are usually employed to each cover. Journal-box covers are, however, often held on by hinges and springs or some arrangement of lugs or grooved joints.

**Journal-box-cover Gasket.** A lining of canvas, india-rubber, leather, or other soft material which is interposed between the cover and the journal-box to make a tight joint.

**Journal-box-cover Hinge-pin.** A wrought-iron pin, by which a box-cover is connected to the box, and which forms part of the hinge. See **12,** figs. 138, 139.

**Journal-box-cover Spring.** A steel spring attached either to the box or cover for holding the latter open or shut. See **13,** figs. 138, 139.

**Journal-box Guides.** Iron bars or blocks placed one on each side of the journal-boxes of some iron-frame trucks in which journal-springs are used. These irons, while holding the box in place longitudinally and transversely, allow it to have a vertical motion between them. See **99,** fig. 127. When a pair of these guides are cast in one piece it is called a *Pedestal,* which see.

**Journal-brass.** A *Journal-bearing,* which see.

**Journal-packing.** Waste, wool, or other fibrous material saturated with oil or grease, with which a journal-box is filled to lubricate the journal. See **14,** figs. 138, 139. See *Side-journal Spring.*

**Journal-spring.** A spring which supports part of the weight of a car and is placed directly over the journal, and which usually rests on the journal-box under the truck-frame. Such springs are sometimes placed above the truck-frame and supported by straps, and the weight of the car is transmitted to the journal-box by a vertical pin or stirrup. See **78**, figs. 88–90, 105, 106 ; **2**, fig. 132.

# K

**Keeper.** " A ring, strap, pocket, or the like device for-detaining an object; as

1. " A jamb nut.

2. "The box on a door-jamb into which the bolt of a lock protrudes when shot.

3. " The latch of a hook, which prevents its accidental disengagement."—*Knight.* See

*Berth-latch Keeper.*

*Clear-story Window-latch Keeper.*

*Door-bolt Keeper.*

*Door-latch Keeper.*

*Door-lock Keeper.*

*Flush-bolt Keeper.*

*Head-board-coupling Keeper.*

*Sliding-door-latch Keeper.*

*Sofa-bolt Keeper.*

**Keg-shaped Spiral-spring.** A spring wound into a coil, the form of which resembles a keg or cask. This was patented by W. P. Hansell in 1876. See fig. 196.

**Key.** " In a *general sense*, a fastener ; that which fastens ; as a piece of wood in a frame of a building."—*Webster.* Hence, a pin inserted in a hole in a bolt, and used to secure the bolt or its nut.

" An instrument for opening or shutting a lock by pushing the bolt one way or the other."—*Webster.* See

*Brake-shoe Key.*

*Journal-bearing Key.*

*Journal-bearing Stop-key.*

*Seat-lock Key.*

*Master Car-builders' Standard Journal-bearing Key.*

*Master-key.*

*Stop-key.*

**Key-bolt.** A bolt perforated near the end to receive a key which takes the place of a nut. See fig. 782.

**Key-hole Plate.** An *Escutcheon*, which see.

**King-bolt.** A large bolt which passes through the bolster of a car-body and the centre of a truck, and which unites the one to the other so that the truck can turn about the bolt. Often called a *centre-pin.* See **18**, figs. 55–72; **16**, figs. 216, 219, 222, 229, 231 ; **9**, figs. 233, 235.

**King-bolt Plate.** A plate attached to the top of the floor of a car and which covers the head of the king-bolt. By removing the plate the king-bolt can be withdrawn. See **17**, figs. 216, 219, 220, 229, **10**, fig. 233.

**King-post.** A post or distance-piece between a truss-rod and the chord of a truss or a trussed beam. If one such piece is used in the centre of a rod or a pair of rods, it is called a king-post; if two, they are called *queen-posts.* In car construction they are made in two ways ; one adjustable, so that they may be lengthened or shortened, and the other without adjustment. See **5**, fig. 804. Also see

*Brake-beam King-post.*

*Cross-frame King-post.*

*Truck-bolster King-post.*     *Truck-frame King-post.*

**Knee.** See *Platform-hood Knee.*

**Knee-iron.** An **L**-shaped or angle-iron casting or forging which is fastened to the corner where two timbers are joined to strengthen the joint. See *Sill Knee-iron.* *Truck Knee-iron.*

**Knob.** See *Berth Safety-rope Knob.* *Door-knob.*

**Knob-escutcheon.** A *Door-latch Rose*, which see.

# L

**Ladder.** Bars of wood or iron attached to the side or end of a box-car so as to form steps by which persons may climb to and from the top of the car. See **59**, figs. 59, 60–63, 65.

**Ladder-handle.** A bent bar of iron fastened to the side, end, or top of a car for persons to take hold of in going up or down the ladder. See **60**, figs. 59, 60, 63, 65.

**Ladder-rod.** An iron *Ladder-round*, which see.

**Ladder-rounds.** Bars of wood or iron which form the steps of a ladder. See **2**, fig 14; **59**, figs. 59–65.

**Ladder-sides.** Vertical wooden pieces to which ladder-rounds are attached. See **1**, fig. 14.

**Lag-screw.** An iron bolt with a square or hexagonal head and with a wood screw-thread cut on it and intended to screw into wooden objects. Lag-screws are round under the head so that they can be turned after they enter the wood. See fig. 779.

**Lambrequin.** A cloth or drapery fastened over the upper part of a window. It covers the rod and rings or roller of the window curtains. See **28**, fig. 300.

**Lamp.** "A vessel for the combustion of liquid inflammable bodies for the purpose of producing light."— *Webster.* See

|  |  |
|---|---|
| *Adjustable-globe Lamp.* | *Mail-car Lamp.* |
| *Alcove-lamp.* | *Plastered-lamp.* |
| *Bull's-eye Lamp.* | *Post-office-car Lamp.* |
| *Candle-lamp.* | *Side-lamp.* |
| *Centre-lamp.* | *Signal-lamp.* |
| *Double-lens Tail-lamp.* | *Tail-lamp.* |
| *Loose-globe Lamp.* | *Train-signal Lamp.* |

**Lamp-alcove.** A metal casing or lining for a recess in the side of a car to contain a lamp. See *Alcove.* See fig. 492.

**Lamp-arms.** Rods by which a lamp is attached to the ceiling of a car. See **4**, figs. 470–472.

**Lamp-bottom.** The lower portion of a lamp which is removable, and which usually contains the wick, burner, and oil, or the candle, which is burned. See **20**, figs. 470, 472, 475, 476 ; figs. 483–485. See *Candle-lamp Bottom.*

**Lamp-bracket.** See *Side-lamp Bracket.*

**Lamp-burner.** That portion of a lamp by which the

opening on the top of the reservoir is closed, which holds the wick, and by which the latter is adjusted. See **8**, figs. 471–474 ; figs. 478–482.

**Lamp-canopy.** A *Smoke-bell*, which see.

**Lamp-case.** A box at the end of a street-car in which a lamp is placed. The case has a glazed door on the inside and usually colored glass on the outside for a signal or to designate the line to which the car belongs. See **74**, figs. 750, 752.

**Lamp-case Chimney.** A metal pipe through which the smoke and gases of a lamp escape from a lamp-case. See **76**, figs. 750, 753. This is very similar to a *Lamp-jack*, which see.

**Lamp-case Door.** A hinged sash which forms the front of a lamp-case facing the inside of the car. The sash is glazed with clear glass so as to allow the light of the lamp to illuminate the car. See **75**, fig. 752.

**Lamp-case Door-holder.** A hook or similar contrivance for holding a lamp-case door open. The latter is usually hinged on top so that the holder is attached to the ceiling of the car, so as to hold up the door. See fig. 769.

**Lamp-case Eye.** A metal catch or eye into which a lamp-case hook engages in order to hold the lamp-case door shut. See fig. 767.

**Lamp-case Hook.** A metal hook for fastening the lamp-case door or holding it shut. See fig. 767.

**Lamp-chimney.** A glass tube which incloses the flame of a lamp and which conducts away the smoke and gases. See **10**, figs. 471, 474.

**Lamp-chimney Bracket.** A projecting metal arm attached to the side of a car by one end and which has a chimney-holder at the other end by which a lamp-chimney is supported or held in its place on a lamp. See **12**, figs. 474, 475.

**Lamp-chimney Holder.** A short conical tube or ring made of sheet metal, the upper edge of which is cut or serrated or otherwise provided with projecting points, which act as springs and grasp a lamp-chimney so as to hold it in its place on the lamp. See **11**, figs. 472, 474.

**Lamp-chimney Reflector.** A bright or polished metal ring or plate which is placed near the top of a lamp-chimney to reflect the light downward. Usually it has a hole in the centre in which the chimney is inserted. See **15**, figs. 472, 474.

**Lamp-fount.** A sentimental term for a *Lamp-reservoir*, which see.

**Lamp-globe.** A glass or porcelain case or vessel inclosing or surrounding the flame of a lamp or candle, and intended to protect the latter from wind. Lamp-globes are usually globular in form but are often made of different shapes, as pear-shape, melon-shape, etc. See figs. 487–491. See

*Double-cone Lamp-globe.*      *Melon-shaped Lamp-*
*Egg-shaped Lamp-globe.*      *globe.*
     *Pear-shaped Lamp-globe.*

**Lamp-globe Chimney.** A metal tube attached to the top of a lamp-globe for conducting away the smoke. See **3**, figs. 470, 475.

**Lamp-holder.** See *Side-lamp Holder.*

**Lamp-jack.** A cap or covering over a lamp-vent on the outside of a car to exclude rain and prevent downward currents of air in the lamp. See **136**, fig. 218 ; **27**, figs. 296, 297. Also see *Lamp-case Chimney.*

**Lamp-reflector.** A polished surface placed either above or on the side of a lamp to reflect the light. See **14**, figs. 470, 493. See also *Alcove-lamp Reflector.*

**Lamp-reservoir.** The receptacle or vessel of a lamp, which holds the oil or other combustible liquid. See **6**, figs. 471, 474 ; 4:3, 484.

**Lamp-ring.** A metal ring at the base of a lamp, to which the lamp-bottom or reservoir and lamp-globe are attached. In centre-lamps the ring is supported by the lamp-arms. See **5**, figs. 470–472.

**Lamp-shade.** A conical-shaped reflector placed over a lamp to reflect the light downward, or hide it from the eyes of those near. See **2**, figs. 471, 494.

**Lamp-stay.** A horizontal bar of wood or metal by which a car-lamp is held so as to prevent it from swinging or shaking sideways. See **1**, fig. 470.

**Lamp-vent.** An opening, usually in the roof, through which the gases and smoke from a lamp escape from a car.

**Lantern.** A portable lamp, the flame or light in which is protected from wind and rain by glass, usually in the form of a globe. See figs. 500, 501. See

     *Conductor's-lantern.*      *Railroad-lantern.*
     *Fresnel-lantern.*      *Train-signal Lantern.*
     *Tri-colored Lantern.*

**Latch.** The primary sense of this word is—to catch, to close, stop, or make fast ; hence, an attachment to a door, window, etc., to hold it open or shut, is called a latch. The ordinary distinction between a latch and a lock is that a lock is opened with a separate key, whereas a latch has no separate key. See

     *Berth-latch.*      *Rim-latch.*
     *Clear-story Window-*      *Safety-grate Latch.*
     *latch.*      *Safety-strap Latch.*
     *Cupboard-latch.*      *Saloon Stop-latch.*
     *Door-latch.*      *Sliding-door Latch.*
     *Lift-latch.*      *Spring Door-latch.*
     *Night-latch.*      *Water-closet Latch.*
     *Window-latch.*

**Lateral-motion.** A movement sideways ; lateral-play ; end-play. The term is generally applied to the side or swing motion of a truck transversely to the track. See *Swing-motion.*

**Lateral-motion Spring.** A spring which acts between the end of a truck swing-bolster and the truck-frame to prevent the former from swinging too freely. Usually, such springs are of spiral form and are let into the end of the truck-bolster. See **40**, figs. 124, 126.

**Lateral-motion Spring-pin.** A pin in the centre of a spiral lateral-motion spring which holds the latter in its proper position. See **41**, fig. 126.

**Lateral-play.** The side-motion of any part of a car or machinery. The term is also used to designate the space left to permit of such side-motion ; as, the difference in length between a journal and its bearing, or the space left between a swing-bolster and a truck-frame to allow the bolster to swing sideways. See *Lateral-motion. End-play.*

**Lead-lined Journal-bearing.** A journal-bearing which has the surface which comes in contact with the axle covered with a thin layer of lead. The object in using a soft metal like lead is that it may fit itself to the journal as soon as the bearing is subjected to wear. Such bearings were patented by Mr. D. A. Hopkins, and are often called *Hopkins journal-bearings.*

**Lead-seal.** A lead disc made with two holes, which pass through the seal edgewise, in which the two ends of a piece of twisted wire are inserted. The lead is then pressed down on the wire with a seal press so that the wire cannot be withdrawn without defacing the seal. See figs. 539, 540.

**Leakage-valve,** *for Westinghouse Car-brake.* A small valve placed between the triple-valve and the brake-cylinder to prevent the leakage from the pipes from operating the triple-valve and thus applying the brakes. See **26**, fig. 663 ; figs. 705, 737.

**Leakage-valve Cap,** *for Westinghouse Car-brake.* A screw-plug which is screwed into the top of the chamber which contains the leakage-valve. See **13**, fig. 705.

**Leakage-valve Case,** *for Westinghouse Car-brake.* A small hollow metal cylinder, the inside of which forms a chamber which contains the leakage-valve plug. See **15**, fig. 705.

**Leakage-valve Plug,** *for Westinghouse Car-brake.* A cylindrical piece of metal which forms the moving part of a leakage-valve. See **14**, fig. 705.

**Leather.** See *Piston-packing Leather. Packing-leather. Piston-rod-packing Leather.*

**Leather Bell-cord.** See *Bell-cord.*

**Leather-seat.** A *Dust-guard Bearing,* which see.

**Ledge.** See *Window-ledge.*

**Left-chamber Cap,** *of Air-pump for Westinghouse-brake.*

A screw-plug which is screwed into the top of a discharge passage, over the lower discharge-valve, and which forms a cover to the passage. See **30**, fig. 665 ; fig. 692.

**Left-hand Brace-pocket.** A brace-pocket for a brace which inclines from the bottom toward the left, when a person on the outside is looking toward the car. If the brace inclines toward the right it is called a *right-hand pocket*. The same kind of pockets can be used at each end of the same brace. A right-hand pocket is shown at **40**, fig. 69. If the brace were on the other side of the post and inclined the opposite way the pocket would be left-hand.

**Left-hand Seat.** A car-seat with a stationary back in such a position that the seat-end is on the left side of a person sitting on the seat. In fig. 229, **123** is a right-hand seat, and **123′** a left-hand seat. In figs. 296–298, **26** is a right-hand, and **26′** a left-hand seat. See also figs. 406, 407.

**Left-hand Seat-end.** A seat-end which is on the left side of a person sitting in a seat which has a stationary or non-reversible back. See figs. 407, 409.

**Leg.** See *Seat-leg.*

**Lens.** See *Fresnel-lens.*

**Letter-board.** A horizontal board under the cornice on the outside of a passenger-car body, and extending its whole length, on which the name or initials of the company to which the car belongs, or other lettering, is usually painted. Also called a *frieze.* The term frieze, however, applies more properly to the *space* between the cornice and windows. See **91**, figs. 215, 219, 225, 226 ; **46**, figs. 750, 752, 753.

**Letter-box Plate.** See *Drop-letter-box Plate.*

**Lever.** " In mechanics, a bar of metal, wood, or other substance, turning on a support called a fulcrum."—*Webster.* See

| | |
|---|---|
| *Brake-lever.* | *Floating-lever.* |
| *Centre Brake-lever.* | *Hand-car Lever.* |
| *Cylinder-lever.* | *Release-lever.* |
| *Door-shaft Lever.* | *Roof-lever.* |
| *Eccentric-lever.* | *Tripping-lever.* |

*Uncoupling-lever.*

**Lever-casting.** See *Eccentric-lever Casting.*

**Lever-faucet.** A self-closing faucet which is shut by a spring and opened by the movement of a handle or lever. Also called *telegraph-faucet.* See fig. 428.

**Lever-frame,** *for Hand-car.* A wooden frame, shaped somewhat like a letter **A**, on top of a hand-car, which supports the lever-shaft and lever. See **17**, **18**, figs. 772–775.

**Lever-frame Cap,** *for Hand-car.* A short horizontal piece of timber, which forms the top member of a lever-frame of a hand-car, and to which the lever journal-bearings are fastened. See **18**, figs. 772–775.

**Lever-frame Post,** *for Hand-car.* An inclined wooden post which forms the upright member of a lever-frame of a hand-car. See **17**, figs. 772–775.

**Lever-frame Tie-rod,** *for Hand-car.* A vertical rod by which the lever-frame cap of a hand-car is bolted to the floor-frame of the car. See **25**, figs. 772, 773.

**Lever-guide.** See *Brake-lever Guide.*

**Lever Hand-car.** A hand-car which is worked by levers connected to cranks. These levers are sometimes placed horizontally, and sometimes they are vertical. See figs. 44, 46.

**Lever-handle,** *for Hand-car.* A cylindrical wooden bar attached to the levers of a hand-car to take hold of in working the levers and propelling the car. See **20**, figs. 772, 775.

**Lever-shaft,** *for Hand-car.* A short iron shaft to which the levers of a hand-car are attached and which forms a fulcrum on which they work. See **21**, figs. 772, 773.

**Lever-shaft Bearings,** *for Hand-car.* Cast-iron boxes or clamps by which the lever-shaft of a hand-car is held in its place and in which it works. See **22**, figs. 772–775.

**Lid.** See *Water-closet-seat Lid.*

**Lift.** A finger-hold attached to windows and window-blinds to take hold of in raising or lowering them. See

*Double Window-blind Lift.*
*Flush Window-lift.*
*Lower Window-blind Lift.*
*Single Window-blind Lift.*
*Upper Window-blind Lift.*
*Window Bar-lift.*
*Window-blind Lift.*
*Window Lift.*

**Lift-latch.** A lock, the latch of which is lifted by turning the knob instead of sliding it. See figs. 529, 530.

**Lift-latch Lock.** "A lock in which the latch is pivoted and lifted free of the keeper, passing through a notch in the box instead of being simply retracted."—*Knight.* Similar to figs. 529, 530.

**Light.** "A window; a place that admits light to enter; a pane of glass."—*Webster.* See *End Roof-light.*

**Lining.** See *Head-lining. Inside-lining.*

**Lining-strips.** Wooden or metal strips put on the inside of freight or baggage cars to protect the inside of the car from being injured by freight or baggage. See **54**, figs. 56, 58. Lining strips serve very much the same purpose as inside-lining.

**Link.** "A short connecting piece of circular or other equivalent shape; as one of the oval rings or divisions of a chain."—*Knight.*

A short bar with an eye at each end for connecting two things together or for supporting one from another. See

Brake-block Suspending-link.
Chain Coupling-link.
Coupling-link.
Crooked Coupling-link.

Draw-hook and Link.
Eccentric-lever Link.
Fast Coupling-link.
Hanger-link.
Triple Coupling-link.

**Link-hanger.** A *Swing-hanger*, which see.

**Lintel.** See *Door-lintel. Window-lintel.*

**Lock.** "In its primary sense, is anything that fastens, but we now appropriate the word to an instrument composed of springs, wards, and a bolt, used to fasten doors, chests, and the like. The bolt is moved by a key."—*Webster.* See

Barrel Seat-lock.
Berth-lock.
Car-door Lock.
Dead-lock.
Door-lock.
Freight-car Lock.
Fixed Freight-car Lock.
Lift-latch Lock.

Mortise-lock.
Padlock.
Rabbeted-lock.
Rim-lock.
Sash-lock.
Seal-lock.
Seat-lock.
Sliding-door Lock.

Spring Door-lock.

**Lock-chain.** A chain by which a padlock is fastened to a car. See **76**, fig. 59.

**Lock Eye-bolt.** An eye-bolt used instead of a staple for a lock.

**Lock-seal.** A piece of glass, lead, or paper, which forms a seal for a lock, so that the latter cannot be opened without its being known. The seal is so attached to the lock that the latter cannot be opened, or its bolt withdrawn, without defacing or destroying the seal.

**Lodging-car.** A passenger or box car fitted up with sleeping-accommodations for men at work on the line of a road.

**Long Brake-rod.** A rod on the Stevens-brake which connects two levers, one on each truck, together. See **12**, fig. 643.

**Long Seat-end.** A vertical frame of wood or iron which supports the end of the car-seat and also forms the arm or seat-end. See **3**, fig. 401. See also *Short Seat-end.*

**Long Brake-shaft.** A vertical brake-shaft which extends up above the top of a car and has the brake-wheel on the upper end, so that the brakes can be applied by a person on the roof of the car. See **94**, figs. 55, 84 ; **152**, figs. 215, 217, 219, 223.

**Longitudinal-seat.** A seat which extends lengthwise of a car. Such seats generally have their backs against the sides of the car. See **34**, figs. 750–752.

**Longitudinal-step.** A board which extends along the side of an open car, or a car with doors on the side. The board is used as a step in getting on or off the car, and also for passing from one end of the car to the other. Shown in figs. 39, 40.

**Longitudinal-step Bracket.** A bar of iron which is bent at right-angles and attached to the side of a car-body and supports a longitudinal-step. Shown in figs. 39, 40.

**Loose Berth-hinge.** A berth-hinge the two parts of which are detachable. See fig. 352. See *Berth-hinge. Fast Berth-hinge.*

**Loose-globe.** A lamp-globe which can be readily removed from a lamp. See fig. 475.

**Loose-globe Lamp.** A lamp or lantern in which the globe is attached to the frame by springs, screws, or catches, so that it can be easily removed. See fig. 473.

**Loose-joint Butt-hinge.** A butt-hinge the two parts of which are fastened together by a pin in such a way that they can be readily detached or so that a door can be lifted off its hinges when desired. See fig. 510. See also *Fast-joint Butt-hinge.*

**Loose-pin Butt-hinge.** A butt-hinge the two parts of which are fastened together by a pin which can be readily lifted out and the two parts thus be detached. See fig. 511.

**Loughridge Air-brake.** A system of continuous brakes, invented and patented by Mr. Wm. Loughridge, which is operated by compressed air. The air is compressed by an air-pump worked by an eccentric on one of the axles of the engine and is stored up in a tank on the engine or tender. When the brakes are applied, the compressed air is conveyed from the tank by pipes connected together between the cars by flexible hose to cylinders with pistons under each car, by means of which the pressure of the air is communicated to the brake-levers and thence to the brake-shoes.

**Lower Arch-bar.** See *Inverted Arch-bar.*

**Lower-berth.** The bed nearest the floor in a sleeping-car. See **1**, figs. 296–298. See *Berth.*

**Lower Brake-rod.** A rod which connects the two brake-beams or levers on the same truck. When one brake-lever only is used on each truck the rod is attached at one end to the lever and at the other end to the opposite brake-beam. When two levers are used, the rod is attached to each lever. See **97**, figs. 88–129 ; **5**, figs. 637–644 ; **14**, figs. 660, 661.

**Lower Brake-shaft-bearing.** An eye or support near the lower end of a vertical brake-shaft, on or against which the latter revolves, and which is thereby held in its place. The support for a brake-shaft at the lower end is called a *brake-shaft step.* A lower bearing is above the step. See **97**, figs. 60, 61, 63 ; **155**, figs. 215, 217 ; **124**, figs. 751, 753.

**Lower-cap,** *of Triple-valve for Westinghouse Car-brake.* A screw-plug which is screwed into the lower end of the main cap of a triple-valve. The lower-cap closes the chamber which contains the graduating-spring and forms a bearing for the latter. See **9**, figs. 704, 711.

**Lower-chord.** The lower outside member of a truss. See **14**, figs. 805, 807, 808, 809. (The distinction between a lower-chord and a truss-rod, in trusses like that represented in figs. 804, 806, is not very clear.)

**Lower Corner-plate.** A corner-plate attached to the outside of a car at the lower end of a corner-post, or to the outside and end sills where they join each other. See **57**, figs. 55, 59.

**Lower Discharge-valve,** *of Air-pump for Westinghouse-brake.* A puppet-valve at the bottom of the air-pump, through which the air below the piston escapes. See **33**, fig. 665 ; fig. 695.

**Lower Door-panel.** The panel next above the bottom-rail of a door. See **10**, fig. 502.

**Lower Door-sash.** The lower section or part of a door-sash which is made in two parts. See **13**, fig. 502.

**Lower End-panel.** The lowermost outside-panel on the end of a street-car. See **30**, fig. 753.

**Lower Outside-panel.** The lowermost panel in the outside of a street-car. It is usually made concave. See **28**, figs. 750, 752.

**Lower Seat-back Rail.** A horizontal wooden strip which forms the bottom rail of a seat-back. See **40**, figs. 750, 752. See *Upper Seat-back Rail.*

**Lower Steam-valve,** *for Engine of Westinghouse-brake.* A small piston by which steam is admitted to and exhausted from the lower end of the steam-cylinder of an engine for a Westinghouse-brake. See **14′**, figs. 665, 677.

**Lower Steam-valve Bushing,** *for Engine of Westinghouse-brake.* A ring or hollow metal cylinder in which the piston that forms the lower steam-valve works. See **18**, fig. 665 ; fig. 681.

**Lower Swing-hanger Pivot.** A pin, bolt, or bar, by which a spring-plank is attached to the lower end of a swing-hanger and on which it swings. See **48**, figs. 108, 127.

**Lower Wainscot-rail.** A longitudinal wooden bar or rail fastened to the posts on the inside of a passenger-car immediately above the truss-plank, and extending from one end of the car to the other. See **74**, figs. 225, 226 ; **2**, figs. 299–301.

**Lower Window-blind.** The lower section of a window-blind which is made in two parts. See **140**, figs. 215, 219, 222; **18**, fig. 301.

**Lower Window-blind Lift.** A metal catch or finger-hold attached to a lower window-blind for raising and lowering it. The lifts for lower blinds differ from those for a single-blind in having a lug or ledge which engages with the upper blind when the lower one is raised up half-way, and thus the upper one is raised with the lower one. See **26**, fig. 301 ; fig. 323.

**Lubricant.** A substance used for lubricating.

**Lubricator.** An instrument used for applying a lubricant. See *Automatic-lubricator*.

**Lug-bolt.** See *Strap-bolt*.

**L-window-button.** A catch shaped somewhat like a letter L, and attached to a window-post for holding up a window. See fig. 307.

# M

**Machine-bolt.** A bolt with a metal thread cut on it and with a square or hexagonal head. See figs. 776, 777.

**Mail-car.** A car for carrying mails. See fig. 6. Such cars are used only for carrying mail-bags and are not used for distributing mail-matter. Distributing mail-cars are called *Post-office Cars*, which see. See also *Combined Baggage and Express or Mail Car*.

**Mail-car Lamp.** See *Post-office-car Lamp*.

**Mail-catcher.** A contrivance consisting of a bent iron bar, attached to the door of a mail or post-office car, for taking up or "catching" mail-bags while the train is in motion. See figs. 5, 250.

**Main-cap of Triple-valve**, *for Westinghouse-brake*. A screw-plug which is screwed into the lower end of the cylinder or chamber which contains the triple-valve-piston. See **6**, fig. 704 ; fig. 708.

**Main-carline.** A carline which is made stronger than the ordinary carlines so as to support the roof of a freight-car and tie the two plates together. See **82**, figs. 61, 64.

**Main-rafter.** A *Main-carline*, which see.

**Main-reservoir**, *of Westinghouse-brake*. A cylindrical vessel or tank made of boiler-plate and usually carried on a locomotive to hold a supply of compressed-air for operating the brakes. See **1**, figs. 655–657.

**Male Centre-plate.** The body and truck centre-plates are sometimes called male and female. See *Body Centre-plate*. *Truck Centre-plate*.

**Malleable Brake-shoe.** A brake-shoe made of cast-iron and then annealed so as to give it some of the properties of wrought-iron.

**Man-hole.** An opening in a boiler or tank through which a man can creep to the inside. The tanks for tank-cars always have man-holes on top. See **110**, figs. 73, 76.

**Man-hole Cover.** A plate or lid to close a man-hole. See **111**, figs. 73–76.

**Man-hole Cover-chain.** A chain with which a man-hole cover is fastened to a tank to prevent it from falling off the tank when the man-hole is opened.

**Man-hole Hinge.** A hinge by which a man-hole cover is attached to a man-hole ring. See **113**, figs. 73, 74.

**Man-hole Ring.** A metal ring riveted around a man-hole, and which forms a seat for the cover. See **112**, figs. 73–76.

**Man-killers.** *Dead-blocks*, which see.

**Master Car-builders' Standard-axle.** This term is used to designate the form and dimensions for car-axles recommended by the Master Car-builders' Association in 1873. These are given in fig. 143.

**Master Car-builders' Standard Journal-bearing.** A form and size for journal-bearings recommended by the Master Car-builders' Association. Its dimensions are given in a lithograph published by that Association. See **7**, figs. 138, 139 ; fig. 141.

**Master Car-builders' Standard Journal-bearing Key.** A form and size for journal-bearing keys recommended by the Master Car-builders' Association. Its dimensions are given in a lithograph published by that Association. See **8**, figs. 138, 139 ; fig. 142.

**Master Car-builders' Standard Journal-box.** A form and size for journal-boxes recommended by the Master Car-Builders' Association. It is represented in a lithograph published by the Association. See **10, 10,** figs. 138, 139 ; fig. 140.

**Master Car-builders' Standard Pedestal.** A form and size for pedestals recommended by the Master Car-Builders' Association. Its dimensions are represented in a lithograph published by the Association. See **18**, figs. 138, 139.

**Master-key.** " A key which commands many locks of a certain set, the keys of which are not interchangeable among themselves. While neither one of a series of keys may suffice to open any lock, besides the one for which it is constructed, a master-key is one which may operate any one of the set."—*Knight*.

**Mat.** See *Floor-mat*. *Wooden Floor-mat*.

**Match-lighter.** A *Match-striker*, which see.

**Match-plate.** A *Match-striker*, which see.

**Match-striker.** A metal plate with a rough surface, or a piece of sand-paper, for rubbing matches on. See fig. 432.

**Match-striker Frame.** A metal frame for holding a piece of sand-paper on which matches are lighted. See fig. 433.

**Melon-shaped Lamp-globe.** A glass or porcelain globe shaped like a melon. See fig. 488.

**Member.** See *Compression-member*. *Tension-member*.

**Metal Screw-thread.** A form of screw-thread used when both the male and female screws are made of metal. Metal threads are made on the same size as the spaces between them, whereas the spaces between wood screw-threads are made wider than the projections. Metal threads are shown in figs. 776–778, 794–798. See also *Sellers System of Screw-threads*.

**Metal-seal.** See *Car-seal*. *Lead-seal*.

**Middle Corner-plate.** An outside corner-plate attached to a corner-post of a freight-car about half-way between its upper and lower ends. See **56**, figs. 55, 59.

**Middle Door-panel.** A panel near the middle of a door. See **11**, fig. 502.

**Middle Door-rail.** A horizontal piece or bar of wood intermediate between the top and bottom rails of a door. See **148**, figs. 218, 222, 223, 230 ; **6**, fig. 502 ; **81**, fig. 753.

**Middle of Axle.** The portion of a car-axle between the hubs of the wheels. **See 1**, fig. 143. See *Car-axle*.

**Middle Safety-beam.** A safety-beam which is intended to hold the centre-axle of a six-wheeled truck in case it should break. It is attached to the two transoms. See **52**, fig. 129.

**Middle-transoms,** *for Six-wheeled Trucks.* The two crosspieces of a six-wheeled truck-frame nearest its centre. These are sometimes made of iron to allow the two swinging spring-beams to be connected to each other by the bolster-bridge. See **21**, fig. 129.

**Milk-car.** A car for carrying milk in cans. Such cars are usually built with end-platforms, similar to baggage-cars, and are provided with the same kind of springs as passenger-cars. See fig. 17.

**Miller Car-coupler.** An arrangement for coupling cars automatically, used with the Miller platform It consists of two heavy iron hooks, which act as draw-bars and which are made to engage with each other by two springs when the cars come together. See figs. 282–289.

**Miller-platform.** A platform for passenger-cars designed and patented by Mr. E. Miller, and arranged so that the line of draft and the compressive strains on the car are in a direct line with the sills of the car. See figs. 282–289.

**Mine-car.** A small car used for carrying minerals in coal, iron, or other mines. Such cars usually have four wheels. See fig. 30.

**Mirror.** A looking-glass.

**Mirror-frame.** A frame for holding the glass of a mirror.

**Mirror-frame Spring.** See *Mirror-sash Holder*.

**Mirror-plate.** A looking-glass without a frame. When such glasses are used to form a panel in the side of a car they are generally set without a frame.

**Mirror-sash.** A frame of a mirror which covers a lamp-alcove in the side of a car. The frame is made to slide up and down like a window-sash. See fig. 375.

**Mirror-sash Holder.** A spring for holding up a mirror-frame when the latter is arranged as a sliding panel in the side of a car. See fig. 376.

**Monitor-top.** A *Clear-story*, which see.

**Mortise-lock.** " A lock adapted to be inserted into a mortise in the edge of a door, so as only to expose the selvage or edge-plate."—*Knight*. See fig. 525.

**Motion.** See *Lateral-motion.* *Swing-motion.*

**Mould.** See *Chill-mould.*

**Moulding.** " A mode of ornamentation by grooved or swelling bands or forms, following the line of the object."—*Knight.*

A strip of wood which forms an ornamental band, "following the line of the object," as of a cornice, a window, or door. See

| | |
|---|---|
| *Clear-story Eaves-mould-ing.* | *Seat-back Moulding.* |
| *Eaves-moulding.* | *Window Cove-moulding.* |
| | *Window-moulding.* |
| *Platform-hood Moulding.* | *Window-sill Moulding.* |

**Moulding-joint Cover.** A piece of wood, metal, or other material usually made in some ornamental design for covering the joints of two pieces of moulding. See *Window-moulding-joint Cover.*

**Movable Foot-rest.** Two horizontal wooden bars underneath a car-seat, and attached to two iron bars which are pivoted in the centre so that one of the former can be adjusted to a comfortable position for the passengers occupying the next seat, or be moved out of the way, if desired. See **8,** fig. 400.

**Muley-axle.** An axle without collars on the outer ends of the journals. See fig. 144.

**Mullion.** A slender bar between panes of glass or panel work. See

| | |
|---|---|
| *Door-mullion.* | *Window-blind Mullion.* |
| *Door-window Mullion.* | *Window-mullion.* |

**Muntin.** A corruption of the word *mullion.*

# N

**Nail.** " A small pointed piece of metal, usually with a head, to be driven into a board or other piece of timber, and serving to fasten it to other timber."—*Webster.* See *Clinch-nail.* *Head-lining Nail.*

**Name-panel.** A panel, usually of a circular or elliptical form, on the outside of a passenger-car body below the windows, on which the name or number of the car is usually painted. See **72,** fig. 219.

**Name-panel Frame.** A wooden moulding which incloses a panel on the centre and outside of a passenger-car body below the windows. The panel usually contains the number or name of the car, and is commonly of an oval or circular form. See **73,** fig. 219.

**Name-plate.** A metal plate with the name of a person or thing on it, as of the maker or patentee of a car or part of a car, the name of a railroad, etc. See *Door Name-plate.*

**Narrow-gauge.** The distance between the heads of the rails of a railroad when it is less than 4 ft. 8½ in. See *Gauge.*

**Narrow-tread Wheel.** A wheel with the ordinary width of tread, which is usually about 5 inches.

**Neck Door-bolt.** A door-bolt made with an off-set or bend as shown in fig. 515.

**Neck of Axle.** The portion of a car-axle just inside of the hub of the wheel See **2**, fig. 143.

**Needle-beam.** A *Cross-frame Tie-timber*, which see.

**Nest-spring.** A spiral spring with one or more coils of springs inside of it. See figs. 190, 193, 195, 198, 199. Also see

*Double-coil Nest-spring.*  *Quadruple-coil Nest-*
*Equal-bar Nest-spring.*  *spring.*
*Triple-coil Nest-spring.*

**Netting.** See *Basket-rack Netting.*

**Night-latch.** A spring door-lock which requires a key to be opened from the outside, but which can be opened from the inside without one. See fig. 527. Also called a *spring door-lock.*

**Nipple.** A short wrought-iron pipe with a screw-thread cut on the outside of each end. It is used for connecting pipe-fittings, such as couplings, tees, etc., of wrought-iron pipes together or with some other object, as a tank, a heater, etc. See fig. 622. See *Auxiliary-reservoir Nipple.* *Brake-hose Nipple.*

**Nosing,** *of a Lock.* A *Keeper*, which see.

**Nosing,** *of a stairs.* The part of a tread-board which projects beyond the riser. See **2**, fig. 244.

**Notice-plate.** A plate placed on a door or other part of a passenger-car with a notice of some kind to passengers inscribed thereon. See fig. 503.

**Nozzle.** See *Tank-nozzle.*

**Number.** See *Berth-number.*

**Nut.** "A small block of metal or wood containing a concave or female screw."—*Webster.* See **1**, figs. 776–778. See

*Eccentric-lever Nut.*  *Piston-rod Nut.*
*Packing-nut.*  *Piston-rod-packing Nut.*
*Release-rod Nut.*

# O

**Oil-box.** A *Journal-box*, which see.

**Oil-car.** A car made especially for the transportation of mineral oil. Some cars intended for this purpose are made with large tanks for receiving the oil in bulk ; others are made for carrying barrels of oil. See *Tank-car*, figs. 22, 73–76.

**Oil-cellar.** A cavity in the lower part of a journal-box for collecting the oil and dirt which runs off the axle at the dust-guard. See **28**, fig. 151. The oil-cellar is below the space occupied by the axle-packing.

**Oil-cup,** *for Air-cylinder of Westinghouse-brake.* A small metal cup attached to an air-pump to hold oil for lubricating an air-piston. See fig. 739.

**One-horse Street-car.** A street-car which is drawn by one horse. See fig. 41. See *Bob-tail Street-car.*

**Open-door Stop.** A block of iron or wood fastened to the side of a freight-car to prevent a sliding-door from sliding too far when it is opened. See **71**, figs. 55, 60, 69.

**Opener.** That which opens. See *Clear-story Window-opener. Ventilator-opener. Window-opener.*

**Open-mouth Draw-bar.** A draw-bar with a head which is open on the sides.

**Open Plate-wheel.** A light cast-iron single-plate wheel, for street-cars, with openings cast in the plate between the ribs, as shown in figs. 172 and 173.

**Open Return-bend.** A short cast-iron tube made of a **U**-shape for uniting two wrought-iron pipes. The pipes are screwed into the casting. It differs from a close return-bend in having the arms separated from each other, See fig. 618.

**Ore-car.** A car made especially for carrying iron or other ores. Ordinary gondola cars, which are sometimes lined with sheet-iron, and drop-bottom and tip cars are also used for this purpose.

**Ornament.** See *Corner-post Ornament.*

**Outer-hung Brake.** When the brake-shoes and beams are attached to the outside of the wheels of a truck or four-wheeled car it is called an *outer-hung* brake. When the shoes and beams are between the wheels it is an *inner-hung* brake. Figs. 637, 638, 640–644 represent outer-hung brakes.

**Outside Body-truss-rod.** When two or more truss-rods are used under each side of a car-body, those farthest from the centre are called *outside body-truss-rods.*

**Outside-casing,** *for Baker Car-heater.* The outside shell or covering for a Baker heater. It is made of Russia iron, and bent and riveted into the form of a frustrum of a cone. See **6,** figs. 581, 587.

**Outside End-piece,** *of Truck-frame.* The cross-piece of a wooden truck-frame next to the end of the car.

**Outside-panel.** A panel in the outside of a passenger or street-car under the windows. Those between the windows are called *outside window-panels.* See **67,** figs. 215, 219, 228 ; **27,** figs. 750, 752. Also see *Lower Outside-panel.*

**Outside Top-plate,** *for Spear Heater.* A cast-iron plate which forms the top of the outside casing of a Spear heater. See **10,** figs. 550–554 ; fig. 557.

**Outside-transoms,** *for Six-wheeled Truck.* The two transoms farthest from the centre of the truck, See **22,** fig. 129.

**Outside Wheel-piece Plate.** An iron plate fastened to the outside of a wheel-piece to strengthen it. See **11,** figs. 128, 129.

**Outside Window-panel.** A panel on the outside of a passenger-car between the windows. See **68,** figs. 215, 219, 226.

**Outside Window-sill.** A horizontal piece of wood or iron under a window on the outside of a car and on which the sash rests. See **77,** figs. 225, 226.

**Outside Window-stop.** A wooden strip attached to a window post on the outside of a window-sash to hold the latter in its place. See **84,** figs. 225; **51,** figs. 750, 752.

**Oval Coupling-pin.** A *Flat Coupling-pin*, which see.

**Over-hung Door.** A sliding-door which is hung from or supported on a rail above the door. The door in figs. 60 and 69 is over-hung. If the door is supported by a rail below it is called an *under-hung door.*

# P

**Packing.** *Journal-packing*, which see.

**Packing-expander.** A spring or other contrivance for spreading out the packing of a piston or valve so as to make them fit air-tight. See *Brake-hose-coupling Packing-expander.*

**Packing-gland.** See *Piston-rod Packing-gland.*

**Packing-leather.** A *dust-guard* is sometimes called a packing-leather. See *Piston-packing Leather. Piston-rod Packing-leather.*

**Packing-nut.** See *Piston-rod Packing-nut for Westinghouse-brake.*

**Packing-ring.** See *Piston-packing Ring. Rubber Packing-ring.*

**Packing-ring,** *of Clutch-coupling of Westinghouse-brake.* An india-rubber ring in a coupling-case which forms a seat for a coupling-valve, and also makes a tight joint between the two parts of the coupling. See **8,** figs. 715, 722.

**Packing-ring Washer,** *for Clutch-coupling of Westinghouse-brake.* A circular metal ring or washer which rests on the packing-ring of a clutch-coupling and which forms a bearing for the projections on the coupling-cap by which the packing-ring is held in place. See **7,** figs. 715, 721.

**Padlock.** A lock having a semi-circular link jointed at one end so that it can be opened, the other end of the link being fastened by a bolt. Such locks are used to secure a hasp or the like on a staple or similar device by passing the link through the staple. See fig. 536. See *Dead Padlock. Spring Padlock.*

**Pair of Trucks.** A *pair* of trucks means two truck-frames, each with two or more pairs of wheels, etc., complete for an entire car, and does not mean *one* truck-frame with wheels and axles for one end of a car only.

**Pair of Wheels.** This term is used to designate two car wheels fitted on one axle. Two pairs of wheels means two axles, with two wheels fitted to each of them.

**Palace-Car.** An extravagant term used to designate a car which is fitted up with more than the ordinary amount of ornament and elaborate finish and furniture. The term is applied to sleeping as well as day cars. See figs. 1, 2, 3.

**Pan.** See *Water Alcove-pan.* *Ice-pan.*

**Panel.** 1. A board inserted in the space left between the stiles and rails of a frame or between mouldings. Sometimes metal plates are used for this purpose.

2. The space between two vertical posts or braces and the two chords of a truss. The distance *a, b,* figs. 808, 809 is a panel. See

| | |
|---|---|
| *Clear-story End-panel.* | *Inside Frieze-panel.* |
| *Clear-story Side-panel.* | *Inside Window-panel.* |
| *Door-case Panel.* | *Lower End-panel.* |
| *Door-case Seat-panel.* | *Lower Outside-panel.* |
| *Door-case Top-panel.* | *Middle Door-panel.* |
| *Door-panel.* | *Name-panel.* |
| *End-panel.* | *Outside-panel.* |
| *End Seat-panel.* | *Outside Window-panel.* |
| *End Window-panel.* | *Twin Door-panels.* |

| | |
|---|---|
| *Upper Door-panel.* | *Ventilator-panel.* |
| *Upper End-panel.* | *Wainscot-panel.* |
| | *Window-panel.* |

**Panel-furring.** Horizontal bars or strips of wood between the posts of a passenger-car, and to which the outside panels are nailed. When a strip is made continuous and extends from one end of the car to the other, and is notched into the posts, it is called a *panel-rail.* See **59**, figs. 215, 218, 221, 226 ; **33**, fig. 752. See *Window-panel Furring.*

**Panel-frame.** See *Name-panel Frame.*

**Panel-lamp.** An *Alcove-lamp,* which see.

**Panel-rail.** A long wooden bar which extends the whole length of a passenger-car body on the outside, and is notched into the posts under the windows, and to which the panels are nailed. See **66**, figs 215, 218, 221, 225, 226.

**Panel-strip.** A narrow piece of wood or metal with which the joint between two panels, or a panel and a post, on the outside of a car, is covered. See **69**, figs. 215, 219, 228 ; **32**, fig. 750.

**Paper-wheel.** A car-wheel with a steel tire and a centre formed of compressed paper held between two plate-iron discs, as shown in fig. 176, which represents a section of a paper-wheel. The part **6, 6,** is made of compressed paper.

**Paragon Spiral-spring.** A spiral car-spring made of a

bar of metal whose section resembles a figure 8, which is wound on a mandrel edgewise to form the coil. See figs. 203, 204.

**Parallel Brake-hanger.** A bar or link attached to a brake-beam so as to cause the latter and the brake-head and shoe to maintain the same relative positions when the brakes are released. The object of this is to prevent the upper end of the brake-shoes from coming in contact with the wheel when the brakes are released. See **15**, figs. 629-631.

**Parallel Brake-hanger Carrier.** A bar which is attached to the truck-frame and has an eye or other device by means of which a parallel brake-hanger is suspended or attached to the truck-frame, See **16**, figs. 629, 630.

**Parallel Brake-hanger Eye.** A bar or bolt by which the lower end of a *parallel brake-hanger* is attached to a brake-beam. See **17**, figs. 629-631.

**Parting-rail.** A rail between the bottom and middle or middle and top rails of a door or partition. See **7**, fig. 502.

**Parting-strip.** A long thin piece of wood which acts as a distance-piece between two objects, as a window and a window-blind. See *Sash Parting-strip.*

**Passenger-car.** A railroad-car used for carrying passengers. Such cars are fitted with seats, windows, and other conveniences for the accommodation of passengers. See fig. 4.

**Passenger-car Truck.** A truck for carrying a passenger-car body. Such trucks are made so as to give the car an easy and agreeable motion. They have two sets of springs, one under the truck-bolster between the two truck-frames, and the others attached to the outside truck-frames, and have swing-motion bolsters. Figs. 115-129 are illustrations of different kinds of passenger-car trucks.

**Pawl.** "A pivoted bar adapted to fall into the notches or teeth of a wheel as it rotates in one direction, and to restrain it from back-motion. Used in windlasses, capstans, and similar machinery."—*Knight.* See

*Brake-pawl.* *Jointed Top-pawl.*
*Jointed Side-pawl.* *Side-pawl.*

**Pawl,** *for Ratchet-wheel of Winding-shaft.* A latch which secures the ratchet-wheel of a winding-shaft from turning. See **131**, fig. 77.

**Pear-shaped Lamp-globe.** A glass or porcelain lamp-globe shaped like a pear, See fig. 490.

**Pedestal.** A casting of somewhat the form of an inverted letter ∩ bolted to a truck-frame, and which holds the journal-box in its place and allows it to have a vertical movement. See **5**, figs. 88-94, 115-129; **18**, figs. 138, 139. See *Equalizing-bar Pedestal. Master Car-builders' Standard-pedestal.* The two projections of a pedestal are called *pedestal-horns,* and the space between them a jaw. In Great Britain, pedestals are called *horn-plates,* and are there made of wrought-iron.

**Pedestal-box.** A *Journal-box,* which see.

**Pedestal-brace.** A diagonal bar or rod bolted by one end to the lower end of a pedestal, and at the upper end to the truck-frame, its object being to hold or strengthen the pedestal. See **8,** figs. 77–79 ; figs. 118–125, 128, 129.

**Pedestal Brace-tie-bar.** An iron bar or rod bolted to the bottom of two or more pedestals on the same side of a truck, and extending upward from the end pedestals to the truck or car frame, and thus forming a brace. It is a *pedestal-brace* and a *pedestal tie-bar* combined in one piece. See **166,** fig. 77 ; **8′,** fig. 127.

**Pedestal-horns.** The projecting parts of a pedestal between which the journal-box works. See **100,** fig. 131 ; **19,** fig. 139.

**Pedestal-jaw.** The opening in a pedestal between the horns, which receives a journal-box. See **101,** fig. 131.

**Pedestal Stay-rod.** A transverse rod attached to the pedestal tie-bar on each side of a truck so as to prevent the lower ends of the pedestals from spreading apart. See **167,** figs. 77–84 ; **7,** figs. 122–126, 128, 129.

**Pedestal Tie-bar.** An iron bar or rod bolted to the bottom of two or more pedestals on the same side of a truck

or car, thus holding or tieing them together. See **163** fig. 82 ; **6,** figs. 88–137.

**Pedestal-timber.** A longitudinal timber sometimes used on four-wheeled cars, which is placed under the floor or alongside the sill and to which the pedestals are bolted. See **169,** figs. 82–84. This term is also used to designate the *Wheel-piece* of trucks, which see.

**Perforated Smoke-pipe Casing.** An outside pipe which incloses a smoke-pipe of a stove. The casing is perforated with holes through which the air circulates and thus comes in contact with the pipe. The casing also protects the wood-work of the car from the heat of the pipe. See **9,** fig. 553.

**Perforated-veneer Seat.** A seat made of several thin boards glued together, so that the grain of the various pieces runs in different directions and perforated with holes. See fig. 402.

**Piece.** See

    *Centre-piece.*         *End-piece.*
    *Distance-piece.*      *Wheel-piece.*

**Pillar.** 1. " A kind of irregular column.

    2. " A supporter ; that which sustains or upholds ; that on which some superstructure rests."—*Webster.* See *Transom-pillar.*

**Pin.** " A peg or bolt of wood or metal having many uses."—*Knight.* See

Brake-block Pin.
Centre-pin.
Coupling-pin.
Door-pin.
Eye-head Coupling-pin.
Fast Coupling-pin.
Flat Coupling-pin.
Journal-box-cover Hinge-pin.
Lateral-motion Spring-pin.
Solid-head Coupling-pin.

**Pinion,** for Hand-car. The smaller cog-wheel for a hand-car which is attached to the axle of the car, and into which the larger wheel on the crank-shaft gears. See **4,** figs. 772–774.

**Pipe.** "A tube for conveyance of water, air, or other fluids."—Knight. See

Brake-cylinder Pipe.
Brake-pipe.
Cold-air Pipe.
Conductors'-valve Discharge-pipe.
Conductors'-valve Pipe.
Discharge-pipe.
Exhaust-pipe.
Guard-pipe.
Hot-air Pipe.
Smoke-pipe.
Steam-pipe.
Stove-pipe.
Supply-pipe.
Triple-valve Branch-pipe.
Waste-pipe.
Water-drip Pipe.
Urinal-drip Pipe.

Urinal Ventilating-pipe.

**Pipe-coupling.** A short cast-iron tube with a thread cut on the inside at each end, and which is screwed on the ends of two pipes and used for uniting them together, or uniting one pipe with another object, as a cock or valve. In

some couplings the thread at one end is right hand and the other left hand, but generally they are both right-hand threads. See fig. 623. Also see Reducing Pipe-coupling.

**Pipe-reducer.** A Reducing Pipe-coupling, which see. See also Bushing for Pipes.

**Pipe Screw-threads.** Screw-threads used for connecting wrought-iron pipes together. Such screws are cut "tapered;" that is, the end of the pipe, or the inside of the coupling where the thread is cut, forms part of a cone, so that in screwing up the pipe a tight joint can be made. Pipe-threads are of a **V**-shape, sharp at the top and bottom, and their sides stand at an angle of 60° to each other. The following is the number of threads per inch for pipes of different sizes. The size given is the diameter of the inside of the pipe.

AMERICAN STANDARD SYSTEM OF PIPE-THREADS.

| Size of pipe. | No. of threads per in. | Size of pipe. | No. of threads per in. |
|---|---|---|---|
| ⅛ in. | 27 | 1 " | 11½ |
| ¼ " | 18 | 1¼ in. | 11½ |
| ⅜ " | 18 | 1½ " | 11½ |
| ½ " | 14 | 2 " | 11½ |
| ¾ " | 14 | 2½ to 8 in. | 8 |

**Pipe-stay,** for Creamer-brake. A cast-iron eye or plate

by which the guard-pipe is fastened to the hand-rail. See **16**, fig. 646.

**Pipe-strap.** An iron band for fastening a pipe against or to some other object. See *Single Pipe-strap*. *Double Pipe-strap*. See figs. 615, 616.

**Pipe-support,** *for Baker Heater*. A cast-iron stand screwed to the floor of a car, and with a receptacle at the top to receive and hold a pipe. See fig. 612.

**Pipe-turnbuckle.** A short tube with a right-hand screw on the inside at one end and a left-hand screw on the other end. The ends of two rods are screwed into the ends of the turnbuckle. Similar to fig. 791.

**Piston.** An arrangement consisting usually of a metal disc with packing, etc., made so as to fit air-tight and work back and forth in a cylinder. See **7 and 8**, fig. 665. The metal disc is called a *piston-head*. See

    *Air-piston.*                *Steam-piston.*
    *Reversing-piston.*         *Triple-valve Piston.*

**Piston,** *for Westinghouse Car-brake*. See **3**, fig. 730.

**Piston,** *for Westinghouse Driving-wheel Brake*. See **3,** fig. 749.

**Piston,** *for Westinghouse Tender-brake*. See **3**, fig. 728.

**Piston Follower-bolt.** A bolt used to fasten a piston follower-plate to a piston-head. See **11**, fig. 730.

**Piston Follower-bolt,** *for Westinghouse Car-brake*. See **11**, fig. 730.

**Piston Follower-bolt,** *for Westinghouse Driving-wheel Brake*. See **10**, fig. 749.

**Piston Follower-bolt,** *for Westinghouse Tender-brake*. See **9**, fig. 728.

**Piston Follower-plate.** A metal plate bolted to the front side of a piston to hold the packing in its place. See **8**, fig. 730.

**Piston Follower-plate,** *for Westinghouse Car-brake*. See **8**, fig. 730.

**Piston Follower-plate,** *for Westinghouse Driving-wheel Brake*. See **7,** fig. 749.

**Piston Follower-plate,** *for Westinghouse Tender-brake*. See **7**, fig. 728.

**Piston-head.** A metal disc attached to a piston-rod and which forms the main portion of a piston. See **3′**, fig. 730. See *Air Piston-head*. *Steam Piston-head*.

**Piston-head,** *for Lower Steam-valve for Engine of Westinghouse-brake*. See **14′**, fig. 677.

**Piston-head,** *for Upper Steam-valve for Engine of Westinghouse-brake*. See **14**, fig. 677.

**Piston-head,** *for Westinghouse Car-brake*. See **3′**, fig. 730.

**Piston-head,** *for Westinghouse Driving-wheel Brake*. See **3′**, fig. 749.

**Piston-head,** *for Westinghouse Tender-brake*. See **3′**, fig. 728.

**Piston-packing Expander.** A steel spring made of a rod

of round steel bent into a circular form and placed inside of the piston packing-leather so as to expand it and keep the piston tight. See **10**, fig. 730.

**Piston-packing Expander**, *for Westinghouse Car-brake.* See **10**, fig. 730.

**Piston-packing Expander**, *for Westinghouse Driving-wheel Brake.* See **9**, fig. 749.

**Piston-packing Expander**, *for Westinghouse Tender-brake.* See **10**, fig. 728.

**Piston Packing-leather**, *for Westinghouse Car-brake.* A circular piece or ring of leather which is pressed into the cylinder so that a section of one side of the ring is of an **L**-shape, and which is attached to and surrounds the piston and bears against the inside surface of the cylinder so as to make the former work air-tight in the latter. See **9**, fig. 730.

**Piston Packing-leather**, *for Westinghouse Driving-wheel brake.* See **8**, fig. 749.

**Piston Packing-leather**, *for Westinghouse Tender-brake.* See **8**, fig. 728.

**Piston Packing-ring.** A circular metal ring of rectangular section which is placed in grooves in the edge of a piston-head to make it work air-tight in its cylinder. The rings are cut in two diagonally at one point so that they may be sprung apart, or, if compressed, will spring open. See figs. 673, 678.

**Piston Packing-ring**, *for Air-piston of Westinghouse-brake.* See **9′**, figs. 665 ; fig. 673.

**Piston Packing-ring**, *for Lower Steam-valve for Engine of Westinghouse-brake.* See **16**, figs. 665, 677 ; fig. 679.

**Piston Packing-ring**, *for Piston of Triple-valve for Westinghouse-brake.* See **11**, fig. 704 ; fig. 713.

**Piston Packing-ring**, *for Reversing-piston of Engine for Westinghouse-brake.* See **21**, fig. 665, 683 ; fig. 684.

**Piston Packing-ring**, *for Steam-piston of Westinghouse-brake.* See **9**, fig. 665.

**Piston Packing-ring**, *for Upper Steam-valve for Engine of Westinghouse-brake.* See **15**, figs. 665, 677 ; fig. 678.

**Piston-rod**, *for Engine and Air-pump of Westinghouse-brake.* A rod to which the piston in the steam-cylinder and the piston in the air-cylinder of an engine and air-pump of a Westinghouse-brake are attached. The force exerted by the steam on the piston in the steam-cylinder is transmitted to the piston in the air-cylinder by the rod. See **7″**, figs. 665, 671.

**Piston-rod**, *for Westinghouse Car-brake.* A rod to which the piston of a car-brake cylinder is attached, and by which the power exerted against the piston is transmitted to the cylinder-levers. See **3″**, fig. 730.

**Piston-rod**, *for Westinghouse Driving-wheel Brake.* See **3″**, figs. 747, 749.

**Piston-rod,** *for Westinghouse Tender-brake.* See **3″,** fig. 728.

**Piston-rod Nut,** *for Air-pump of Westinghouse-brake.* A screw-nut on the lower end of the piston-rod and which holds the air-piston on the rod. See **25,** fig. 665.

**Piston-rod Packing-gland,** *for Engine and Air-Pump of Westinghouse-brake.* A metal ring which encircles the piston-rod, and which is forced into the stuffing-box and against the packing, which is thus compressed by the packing-nut, See **28,** fig. 665.

**Piston-rod Packing-leather,** *for Westinghouse Driving-wheel-brake.* A circular piece or ring of leather which is pressed or moulded so that a section of one side of the ring is of an **L**-shape, and which surrounds the piston-rod and is attached to the lower cylinder-head by a nut. The leather bears against the piston-rod and thus makes an air-tight joint through which the rod works. See **12,** fig. 749.

**Piston-rod Packing-nut,** *for Engine and Air-pump of Westinghouse-brake.* A nut which screws on the stuffing-box of the piston-rod and by which the packing is compressed around the piston-rod so as to make a steam-tight joint in which the rod works. See **27,** fig. 665; fig. 689.

**Piston-rod Packing-nut,** *for Westinghouse Driving-wheel Brake.* A nut which is used for holding the piston-rod packing-leather in its place, which thus makes an air-tight joint in which the piston-rod works. See **11,** figs. 747, 749.

**Piston-sleeve,** *for Westinghouse Tender-brake.* A hollow casting resembling a tube which is attached to the end of the piston-rod. See **6,** figs. 727, 728.

**Pit.** See *Ash-pit.*

**Pitching-roof.** A roof formed of one or more inclined plane surfaces. The term is used to distinguish a roof formed of plane surfaces from one formed of curved or arched surfaces. See figs. **63, 64, 65, 71, 72.**

**Pivot.** "A pin or short shaft on which anything turns."—*Webster.* See

*Clear-story Window-pivot.*
*Lower Swing-hanger Pivot.*
*Seat-back Arm-pivot.*
*Upper-berth-rest Pivot.*
*Ventilator-pivot.*
*Window-pivot.*
*Upper Swing-hanger Pivot.*

**Pivot-plate.** See *Seat-back-arm Pivot-plate.* *Window Pivot-plate.* *Ventilator Pivot-plate.*

**Plank.** "A broad piece of sawed timber, differing from a board only in being thicker. In America, broad pieces of sawed timber, which are not more than an inch or an inch and a quarter thick are called *boards;* like pieces from an inch and a half to three or four inches thick are called planks."—*Webster.* See

*Framed Spring-plank.*    *Swing Spring-plank.*
*Spring-plank.*    *Truss-plank.*

**Plank Car-roof.** A roof made of a single layer of planks which are tongued and grooved, and extend from the comb of the roof to the eaves. The joints of the planks are covered with sheet metal.

**Plastered-lamp.** A lamp with a fixed globe which is fastened to a lamp-frame with plaster of Paris.

**Plate.** 1. " A piece of metal, flat or extended in breadth.

2. " In architecture, the piece of timber which supports the ends of the rafters."—*Webster.*

3. In car-building, a horizontal piece of timber on top of the posts of a car-body, to which they are attached, and on which the roof carlines or rafters rest. See **46**, figs. 55–84 ; **93**, figs. 215, 218, 221, 222, 225, 226 ; **47**, figs. 750, 752. See

*Base-plate.*
*Berth-latch Face-plate.*
*Body-bolster Truss-plate.*
*Body Centre-plate.*
*Bogus-plate.*
*Bolster-plates.*
*Bottom Stove-plate.*
*Brake-block Suspending-*
    *plate.*
*Buffer-block Face-plate.*

*Buffer-plate.*
*Centre-plate.*
*Chafing-plate.*
*Clear-story Plate.*
*Corner-plate.*
*Coupling-pin Chafing-*
    *plate.*
*Coupling-pin Plate.*
*Dead-block Face-plate.*
*Door-sash Plate.*

*Door-shaft Crank-plate.*
*Draw-bar Chafing-plate.*
*Draw-bar Face-plate.*
*Draw-bar Follower-plate.*
*Draw-bar Friction-plate.*
*Drop-letter-box Plate.*
*End-plate.*
*Face-plate.*
*Flag-holder Plate.*
*Follower-plate.*
*Friction-plate.*
*Frieze-ventilator Plate.*
*Inscription-plate.*
*Inside Top-plate.*
*Inside Wheel-piece Plate.*
*Inverted Truss-rod-plate.*
*Key-hole Plate.*
*King-bolt Plate.*
*Letter-box Plate.*
*Lower Corner-plate.*
*Male Centre-plate.*
*Match-plate.*
*Mirror-plate.*
*Name-plate.*
*Notice-plate.*
*Outside Top-plate.*

*Outside Wheel-piece Plate.*
*Piston Follower-plate.*
*Pivot-plate.*
*Reversing-valve Plate.*
*Seat-back-arm Pivot-*
    *plate.*
*Seat-back-arm Plate.*
*Seat-leg Plate.*
*Sliding-door-latch Plate.*
*Stop-plate.*
*Striker-plate.*
*Suspending-plate.*
*Table-hook Plate.*
*Table-leg-hook Plate.*
*Threshold-plate.*
*Tie-plate.*
*Transom Chafing-plate.*
*Truck-bolster Chafing-*
    *plate.*
*Truck Centre-plate.*
*Uncoupling-lever Plate.*
*Uncoupling-lever Trun-*
    *nion-plate.*
*Upper Corner-plate.*
*Ventilator-pivot Plate.*
*Ventilator-plate.*

*Water-closet Door-plate*
*Wheel-piece Plate.*
*Wheel-plate.*

*Winding-shaft Plate.*
*Window-blind-bolt Plate.*
*Window-latch Plate.*

*Window-pivot Plate.*

**Plate-rod.** A horizontal metal rod which passes through two plates of a car-body to tie them together. See **47**, figs. 69, 71, 72.

**Plate-wheel.** A car-wheel of which the centre portion is formed of a disc or plate instead of spokes. See figs. 154–164, 170–181. See

*Combination Plate-wheel.*
*Double Plate-wheel.*

*Open Plate-wheel.*
*Single Plate-wheel.*

**Platform.** See *Car-platform.* *Miller-platform.*

**Platform End-timber.** A cross-timber at the outer end of a car-platform. See **38**, figs. 215–232 ; **103**, figs. 750–753.

**Platform-floor.** The floor at the end of a passenger or street car, outside of the car-body. This floor is supported by the platform-timbers and draw-timbers. See **34**, figs. 215–232 ; **104**, figs. 750–752.

**Platform-gate.** A gate used to close the entrance to a platform on passenger or street cars. It is closed to prevent people from getting on and off at that end. See **43**, fig. 228.

**Platform-hood.** A cover or canopy attached to the end of a car-body, and projecting over and covering the platform to protect passengers from rain or snow. They are made of either wood or sheet-iron. When it consists of an extension of the main roof of a car it is called a platform-roof ; but when it is a separate part, and fastened to the car-body, as is usually the case on street-cars, it is called a platform-hood. See **107**, figs. 219, 223 ; **115**, figs. 750, 753.

**Platform-hood Bow.** A bent wooden or iron bow which forms the outer edge of a platform-hood, and to which the platform-hood carlines are fastened. See **108**, figs. 219, 223 ; **116**, figs. 750, 753.

**Platform-hood Carlines.** Transverse-timbers which support the roof of a wooden platform-hood. See **117**, fig. 750.

**Platform-hood Frame.** An iron frame for supporting a hood which projects over the platform of a passenger-car.

**Platform-hood Knee.** An **L**-shaped piece of wrought-iron by which a platform-hood is fastened to the car-body. See **118**, figs. 750, 753.

**Platform-hood Moulding.** A small wooden moulding used to cover the nails with which the roofing canvas is fastened around the edge to the roof of a platform-hood. It corresponds with a roof-moulding. See **119**, figs. 750, 753.

**Platform-hood Post.** An upright iron bar or rod which is attached either to the platform or to the platform railing, and which supports a platform-hood. See **109**, figs. 219, 223, 228.

**Platform-post.** An upright iron post on the end platforms of cars to which the railing is attached. See **39**, figs. 215, 217, 219, 223, 228 ; **108**, figs. 750, 751, 753.

**Platform-rail.** A wrought-iron bar fastened to the tops of the platform-posts, the whole forming a railing on the end of a car-platform. On steam-cars an opening is generally left in the middle of the railing so as to allow persons to pass from one car to another. The railing is therefore made in two parts, and two platform rails are used. On street-cars no such passage-way is left, and the railing is therefore made continuous, and the rail is in one piece. The outside ends of the platform-rails of steam-cars are usually carried down to the end-timber, so as to form the outside post, but on street-cars they are not, but the outside end is attached to an ordinary post. See **41**, figs. 215, 217, 219, 223, 223 ; **110**, figs. 750, 751, 753.

**Platform-railing.** An inclosure consisting of iron posts and rails on the end of a platform of a car to prevent persons from falling off. See engravings of passenger and street cars, figs. 215–228 ; 750–753.

**Platform Railing-chain.** A chain connecting the two sections of the platform-rails of a passenger-car. The chain is intended to prevent passengers from falling off the platform. See **42**, figs. 217.

**Platform-roof.** That portion of a car-roof which projects over the platform. When this consists of an extension of the main roof of the car it is called a *platform-roof*, but when it is a separate canopy or cover fastened to the car-body, as is usually the case on street-cars, it is called a *platform-hood*. See **103**, figs. 215, 217, 228, 229.

**Platform-roof Carline.** A timber which forms part of a platform-roof, and which supports the roof-boards. See **104**, figs. 215, 229.

**Platform-roof End-carline.** The carline at the end of a roof which projects over the platform. See **105**, figs. 215, 229.

**Platform-sills.** Short longitudinal pieces of timber framed into or bolted to the end-sills and platform end-timbers of a passenger or street car to sustain the floor of the platform. See 37, figs. 215, 216, 217, 231.

**Platform-steps.** The stairs at each corner of a passenger-car which afford the means of ingress and egress. See **45**, figs. 215, 217, 219, 223. On street-cars, one step only is used, and it is usually made of plate-iron. See **114**, figs. 750–753.

**Platform Tie-rods.** Horizontal rods which pass through the platform end-timbers for the purpose of holding them and the other portions of the frame of the car securely together. See **162**, figs. 220, 223 ; **51**, figs. 282, 283, 285.

**Platform-timbers.** Pieces of timber attached to the bottom of a car-frame at each end outside of the draw-timber, and projecting beyond the end of the car, and which help to support the platform. They extend usually from the platform end-timbers to the bolster or, in street-cars, to one of the transverse floor-timbers. See **35**, figs. 215–231 ; **101**, figs. 751–753.

**Platform-timber Band.** A band made of plate-iron which covers and embraces the outer end of a platform end-timber of a street-car. See **105**, figs. 750–753.

**Platform-timber Clamp.** A **U**-shaped iron clamp or bolt with which a platform-timber is fastened to the end-sill of a car. See **36**, figs. 216, 229, 231, 232 ; **102**, figs. 750–753.

**Platform Trap-door.** A door which covers the space occupied by the steps, and thus extends the platform out to the side of the car. See **3**, fig. 244.

**Platform Truss-beam,** *for Miller-platform.* A short transverse piece of timber attached to the outer ends of the draw-timbers and which forms the bearing or abutment of the platform truss-rods. See **22**, figs. 282, 283, 284.

**Platform Truss-rod,** *for Miller-platform.* A rod which is fastened at one end to the body-bolster or centre-sills, then passes through or over the end-sill and from there

downward, and is fastened at the other end by a nut to the platform truss-beam. Its use is to support the platform and prevent it from sagging. See **23**, figs. 282–285.

**Play.** See *End-play. Lateral-play.*

**Plow.** See *Snow-plow.*

**Plug.** Besides its usual meaning, it designates a short solid metal cylinder, with a screw on the outside and a square or hexagonal end to take hold of with a wrench. It is screwed into the end of a pipe or hole in a plate, etc., to close the opening. See fig. 625. See *Basin-plug. Four-way-cock Plug. Leakage-valve Plug.*

**Plush.** " A species of shaggy cloth or stuff with a velvet nap on one side, composed regularly of a woof of a single thread and a double warp ; the one, wool of two threads twisted, the other of goat's or camel's hair. But some plushes are made wholly of worsted, others wholly of hair."—*Webster.* Plush is used in car-building chiefly as a covering for seats.

**Pocket.** This term is used to designate any object with a cavity or opening which forms a receptacle to hold anything in its place, as a

*Brace-pocket.*      *Left-hand Brace-pocket.*
*Corner-post Pocket.*      *Post-pocket.*
*Double Brace-pocket.*      *Right-hand Brace-pocket.*
*Draw-bar-spring Pocket.*      *Spring-pocket.*
*Draw-timber Pocket.*      *Stake-pocket.*

**Poke-hole Funnel.** A conical-shaped lining for an opening in a stove through which a poker is inserted to stir the fire. See fig. 578.

**Pole.** See *Ridge-pole.*

**Post.** A piece of timber or metal set upright and intended to support something else, as the *posts* of a house; the *posts* of a door; the *posts* of a gate; the *posts* of a fence; the *posts* of a bridge. See **12,** fig. 808. See

| | |
|---|---|
| *Body-post.* | *Lever-frame Post.* |
| *Body Queen-post.* | *Platform-hood Post.* |
| *Brake-beam King-post.* | *Platform-post.* |
| *Clear-story Post.* | *Queen-post.* |
| *Corner-post.* | *Sub-post.* |
| *Door-post.* | *Truck-bolster King-post.* |
| *Hand-rail Post.* | *Truck-frame King-post.* |
| *Hat-post.* | *Truck-frame Queen-post.* |

*Window-post.*

**Postal-car.** See *Post-office Car.*

**Post-bracket,** *for Creamer-brake.* A cast-iron ledge to which the cross-bar of a Creamer-brake is attached. Such brackets are made with bosses which embrace the end-posts, to which they are fastened by set-screws. See **3,** fig. 646.

**Post-office Car.** A car for carrying mail-matter, and fitted up with boxes and other conveniences for assorting and distributing the mails. See fig. 5.

**Post-office Car-lamp.** A lamp used in assorting letters and performing the other duties of the mail agents in post-office cars. See fig. 494.

**Post-pocket.** An iron casting which is attached to the outside of the sill of a car to receive and hold a post. Such pockets are more commonly used with cattle-cars, and are very similar to stake-pockets. Shown on the side of the car in fig. 24.

**Pot.** See *Fire-pot.*

**Potter Draw-bar.** A draw-bar made with a pair of ears on each side. To one pair of these a link is attached permanently, and to the other pair, and to the centre, other links can be coupled. The draw-bar was named after the inventor. See figs. 261–264, 269.

**Press.** See *Seat-press.*

**Press-beam.** A *Compression-beam,* which see.

**Pressure-gauge,** *for Baker Car-heater.* An ordinary steam-gauge attached to one of the pipes of a Baker heater to show the pressure in the inside of the pipes. See **30,** fig. 581, 609.

**Profile-carline.** A carline extending from one plate to the other and bent so as to conform to the shape or profile of the sides and roof of the clear-story. See fig. 247.

**Pull.** "A catch or lip upon a drawer, door, or window, by which it is pulled open."—*Knight.* See

*Clear-story Window-pull.*      *Door-pull.*

*Drawer-pull.*      *Window-blind Pull.*

**Pulley.** " A wheel with a grooved, flat, or slightly convex rim, adapted to receive a cord or band which runs over it. Its function is to transmit power or change the direction of motion."—*Knight.* See

     *Bell-cord Pulley.*      *Chain Pulley.*

     *Berth-chain Pulley.*      *Side-pulley.*

**Pull-iron.** A lug, socket, or eye-bolt attached to the end or side of a car, near the corner, for attaching a hook and chain by which the cars are pulled with horses or mules. Often a lug or socket is cast on the lower outside corner plate for this purpose. See **58**, figs. 69, 70, 71.

**Pull-ring.** A metal ring with a screw attached by which it is fastened to any object, as a sash, drawer, etc., to take hold of in opening it. See fig. 332. See *Clear-story Window-pull.*

**Pump.** See *Air-pump and Engine, complete. Car-pump. Wash-room Pump.*

**Punch.** See *Bell-punch.*

**Purlin.** A longitudinal piece of timber over the rafters, extending from one end of a car-roof to the other and to which the roof-boards are fastened. Sometimes called a *roof-strip.* See **83**, figs. 64, 70, 71, 72.

**Push Baggage-car.** A light car used at stations for moving baggage or freight from one train to another. It is moved or pushed by hand. Similar to fig. 48.

**Push-car.** A four-wheeled car used to carry materials and tools for workmen, and which is moved or pushed by hand. See fig. 48. Also see *Ferry Push-car.*

# Q

**Quadruple-coil Nest-spring.** A *Quadruple-coil Spiral-spring,* which see.

**Quadruple-coil Spiral-spring.** A spiral-spring composed of four coils of different diameters, the smallest ones being successively inside of the larger ones. See fig. 199.

**Quadruplet of Springs.** Four elliptic springs coupled together side by side so as to act as one spring. See **80**, figs. 122–124, 128, 129. Similar to fig. 186.

**Queen-post.** One or two vertical posts of a truss or truss-beam against which the diagonal members bear. When one post only is used, it is called a *King-post,* which see. Such posts are used for the truss-rods under car-bodies and trucks. See **6**, fig. 806. See *Body Queen-post. Inverted-body Queen-post Truck-frame Queen-post.*

**Queen-post Stay.** A rod or bar attached to a queen-post to prevent it from moving laterally. See *Body Queen-post Stay.*

**Quintuplet of Springs.** Five elliptic springs coupled

together side by side in a group so as to act as one spring. Similar to **80**, figs. 122–124, or fig. 186.

# R.

**Rabbet.** "A rectangular groove made longitudinally along the edge of one piece to receive the edge of another. It is common in paneling, and in door-frames for the door to shut into."—*Knight*. *Rabbet* is a corruption of the word *rebate*.

**Rabbeted-lock.** "A kind of lock whose face-plate is sunk within a rabbet cut in the edge of a door."—*Knight*. See fig. 524.

**Rack.** 1. "A frame for receiving various articles."—*Webster*.

2. "In *machinery*, a rectilineal sliding-piece, with teeth cut on its edge for working with a wheel."—*Brande*. See

Basket-rack.
Bible-rack.
Brush-and-comb Rack.
Card-rack.
Towel-rack.
Window-latch Rack.

**Radiator,** *to go under seats with Baker Car-heater.* A piece of iron pipe bent into a **U**-shape, which is laid under the seats of a car, and through which the hot water from a Baker heater circulates, and from which the warmth is radiated. Shown in fig. 580. See also fig. 610.

**Radiator-stand,** *for Baker Car-heater.* A support for the hot-water pipes of a Baker heater, by which the heat is distributed or radiated in a car. See figs. 611, 613, 614.

**Rafter.** A timber which supports the roof of a car, and which extends part way across the top, or from the plate to the ridge of the roof or to the base of the clear-story. When such timbers extend all the way across they are called *carlines*. See **101**, figs. 215, 218, 221, 222, 224, 229, 236. See *Main-rafter*.

**Rail.** "The horizontal part in any piece of framing or paneling."—*Webster*. See

Back-seat-bottom Rail.
Back Seat-rail.
Belt-rail.
Body Hand-rail.
Bottom-rail.
Clear-story Bottom-rail.
Door-case Intermediate-rail.
Door-case Top-rail.
Door-rail.
Fender-rail.
Front Seat-bottom Rail.
Front Seat-rail.

Guide-rail.
Hand-rail.
Inside Hand-rail.
Lower Seat-back Rail.
Lower Wainscot-rail.
Middle Door rail.
Panel-rail.
Parting-rail.
Platform-rail.
Sash-rail.
Seat-back Rail.
Seat-bottom Rail.
Seat-rail.

*Step Hand-rail.*
*Top Door-rail.*
*Top End-rail.*
*Top Side-rail.*
*Upper Belt-rail.*

*Upper Seat-back Rail.*
*Upper Wainscot-rail.*
*Wainscot-rail.*
*Window-blind Rail.*
*Window-rail.*

**Railing.** " A series of rails ; a fence."—*Webster.* See *Platform-railing. Step-railing.*

**Railing-chain.** See *Platform Railing-chain.*

**Railroad-car.** See *Car.*

**Railroad-lantern.** A lantern used by train-men and other employés of railroads, in the performance of their duties at night, to give light and signals. See fig. 500.

**Raised-roof.** A *Clear-story,* which see.

**Ratchet.** See *Bottom-ratchet. Uncoupling-lever Ratchet.*

**Ratchet-wheel.** See *Brake Ratchet-wheel. Winding-shaft Ratchet-wheel.*

**Rattan Car-seat.** A car-seat made of strips of rattan woven together. See fig. 403.

**Rattan Floor-mat.** A floor-mat made of rattan. See *Floor-mat.*

**Rebate.** " In architecture the groove or channel sunk on the edge of a piece of timber."—*Webster.* Sometimes written *Rabbet,* which see.

**Receiving-valves,** *of Air-pump for Westinghouse-brake.* Puppet valves, one of which is placed at the top and the other at the bottom of the air-pump cylinder, and which

admit the air into the cylinder. See **34,** fig. 665 ; fig. 696.

**Recording-bell.** A bell attached to a bell-punch or other instrument on which the conductor records the fares collected. The bell is intended to indicate or announce to the passengers that the conductor has recorded the fares received.

**Reducer.** A *Reducing Pipe-coupling,* which see. Also see *Bushing.*

**Reducing Pipe-coupling.** A pipe-coupling which is larger at one end than at the other for uniting two pipes of different diameters. Similar to fig. 623.

**Reducing Tee** *or* **T.** A **T**-shaped cast-iron tube for uniting one pipe at right angles with two others in the same line, and which are not all of the same size. See fig. 621.

**Reflector.** " A polished surface for reflecting light."—*Webster.* See *Lamp-reflector. Alcove-lamp Reflector. Lamp-chimney Reflector.*

**Refrigerator-car.** A car for carrying perishable articles, such as fruits, meat, etc., and constructed with compartments in which ice is carried to preserve the freight while in transit. Such cars are usually made with double floor, sides, and roof, so as to keep the ice from melting. See fig. 18.

**Register.** An aperture for the passage of air, provided

with suitable valves, doors, or sliding or revolving plates, by which the aperture is opened or closed. See fig. 346. See *Frieze-ventilator Register.* *Ventilator-register.*

**Register-face.** A grating with which the opening of a register is covered. It is usually made of some ornamental pattern. See **4**, fig. 346.

**Register-frame.** A metal frame or box which incloses or surrounds a register-opening. See **2**, fig. 346.

**Register-handle.** A metal arm, lever, or knob, attached to a register-valve, by which the valve is opened or closed. See **1**, fig. 346.

**Register-valve.** A slat or plate which is pivoted or hinged so that it can be used to open or close the aperture of a register. See **3**, fig. 346.

**Regulating.** The act of moving cars from one track to another as in making up or separating trains and placing the cars where they are needed. See also *Switching. Shunting. Drilling.*

**Release-lever,** *for Westinghouse Car-brake.* A bent lever, one end of which is attached to the cross-head, and the opposite end to a spiral-spring which is compressed when the piston is moved outward. By the action of the spring and the lever, the piston is forced inward and the brakes are released from the wheels when the compressed-air in the cylinder has been allowed to escape. See **5**, fig. 661 ; **12**, fig. 729.

**Release-lever Rod,** *for Westinghouse Car-brake.* A rod attached to the front cylinder-head and which forms a fulcrum for a release-rod. See **6**, fig. 661 ; **13**, fig. 729.

**Release-spring.** A spring usually attached to the end-piece of a truck for the purpose of throwing the brakes off or out of contact with the wheels. The name is also applied to any spring used to throw the brakes off from the wheels. See **91**, figs. 89, 115–129.

**Release-spring,** *for Westinghouse Car-brake.* A spiral-spring which acts against the end of a lever so as to move the brake-piston inward and thus release the brakes from the wheels after the compressed-air is allowed to escape from the cylinders. See **8**, fig. 661 ; **15**, fig. 729. See also *Double Release-spring.*

**Release-spring Bracket,** *for Westinghouse Car-brake.* An iron lug or ear bolted to a front cylinder-head and to which one end of a release-spring rod is attached. See **17**, fig. 729.

**Release-spring Nut,** *for Westinghouse Car-brake.* A nut which is screwed on a release-spring rod, and by which the pressure of the release-spring is adjusted. See **18**, fig. 729.

**Release-spring Rod,** *for Westinghouse Car-brake.* A rod attached at one end to the end of a release-lever, and which passes through the centre of a release-spring. The latter is attached to the rod by nuts and washers by which the pressure of the spring against the lever is adjusted. See **7**, fig. 661 ; **14**, fig. 729.

**Release-spring Washer,** *for Westinghouse Car-brake.* A washer on a release-spring rod against which the spring bears. See **16**, fig. 729.

**Reservoir.** A place or receptacle where anything is kept in store, as a tank or vessel. See *Auxiliary-reservoir for Westinghouse-brake. Main-reservoir. Lamp-reservoir.*

**Reservoir Drain-cock,** *for Westinghouse-brake.* A cock attached to the reservoir under the car or to the brake cylinder-head for exhausting the air from the reservoir of the automatic-brake to let off the brake if accidentally applied when disconnected from the engine. Similar to fig. 740.

**Reservoir Journal-box.** See *Top-reservoir Journal-box.*

**Rest.** That which supports something or on which it rests. See

|               |                  |
|---------------|------------------|
| Arm-rest.     | Side-rest.       |
| Berth-rest.   | Stake-rest.      |
| Sash-rest.    | Upper Berth-rest.|
| Side Foot-rest.| Window-blind Rest.|

*Window-sash Rest.*

**Restaurant-car.** A car provided with a kitchen and cooking appliances and arrangements for serving meals as in a restaurant. See fig. 3. *Hotel-cars* also have similar arrangements for serving meals, but they also have sleeping berths which restaurant-cars have not.

**Retaining-ring,** *for Wheel-tires.* A metal ring which is fastened to a wheel-centre and to the tire so as to hold the two together. Usually such rings have projections which fit into corresponding grooves, turned in the tire and in the wheel-centres, so as to hold the tire in its place in case it should break. See **1**, figs. 180, 181.

**Return-bend.** A short cast-iron tube made of a **U**-shape for uniting the ends of two wrought-iron pipes. See *Close Return-bend. Open Return-bend.*

**Reversible-seat.** A seat with a back which can be turned so as to face either way. See figs. 400–403. See *Car-seat.*

**Reversible Street-car.** A street-car with a body mounted on running-gear on which the body can be turned, or reversed, at the end of its route. See fig. 42.

**Reversing-cylinder,** *of Engine for Westinghouse-brake.* A small hollow metal cylinder placed in the steam-cylinder head and in which the reversing-piston works. See **19**, fig. 665 ; fig. 682.

**Reversing-cylinder Cap,** *of Engine for Westinghouse-brake.* A metal screw-plug which is screwed into the recess which receives the reversing-cylinder and holds the latter in its place. See **22**, fig. 665 ; fig. 685.

**Reversing-piston,** *of Engine for Westinghouse-brake.* A small piston placed above the steam-valves and which moves the latter in one direction. The excess of steam-pressure on the under side of the upper steam-valve, owing to its being larger than the lower one, moves them upward when the pressure on the reversing-piston is released. See 20, fig. 665 ; fig. 683.

**Reversing-valve**, *for Engine of Westinghouse-brake.* A slide-valve which works in a small cylinder in the steam-cylinder head, and which is operated by the piston. This valve controls the admission and exhaust of steam to and from the main steam-valves. See **13**, fig. 665 ; fig. 676.

**Reversing-valve Bushing**, *for Engine of Westinghouse-brake.* A hollow cylinder or tube in which the reversing-valve works and which forms a lining for the recess in the cylinder-head in which the valve is placed. See **23**, fig. 665 ; fig. 686.

**Reversing-valve Cap**, *for Engine of Westinghouse-brake.* A screw-plug which is screwed into the recess in which the reversing-valve works and which holds the reversing-valve bushing in its place. See **24**, fig. 665 ; fig. 687.

**Reversing-valve Plate**, *for Engine of Westinghouse-brake.* A plate attached to the top of a steam-piston and which moves the reversing-valve stem and valve. See **10**, fig. 665 ; fig. 674.

**Reversing-valve Stem**, *for Engine of Westinghouse-brake.* A rod attached at the upper end to the reversing-valve, and which extends downward into a hole bored into the piston-rod. The reversing-valve stem and valve are moved by the piston at each end of its stroke. The admission and exhaust of steam to and from the main steam-valve is thus changed at each end of the stroke of the piston, and by this means the main-valves are made to admit steam, alternately, above and below the steam-piston. See **12**, fig. 665 ; fig. 675.

**Revolving-chair.** A chair mounted on a stand so that it can turn on the latter. See fig. 404.

**Revolving-chair Stand.** A cast-iron post which supports a revolving-chair. The post is attached to a plate, fastened to the floor, in which it turns. See fig. 393.

**Revolving-chair-stand Base.** A cast-iron plate which is fastened to the floor of a car, and to which the chair-stand is attached, and on which it turns. See **1**, fig. 393.

**Revolving-chair-stand Socket.** A cast-iron post, with a cup-shaped receptacle, which holds the seat of a revolving-chair. See **2**, fig. 393.

**Rib.** See *Wheel-rib.*

**Ridge.** See *Roof-ridge.*

**Ridge-pole.** A longitudinal timber on top and in the centre of a roof, and on which the roof-boards rest. In some cases the rafters are framed into the ridge-pole. See **84**, figs. 61, 64, 69, 71.

**Right-and-left-screw Turnbuckle.** A turnbuckle shaped

somewhat like a link of a chain, with a right-hand screw at one end, and a left-hand screw at the other. See fig. 791.

**Right Chamber-cap,** *for Air-pump of Westinghouse-brake.* A screw-plug screwed into the top of the chamber, which receives the upper discharge-valve, and which forms a cover to the chamber and a stop for the valve. See **29,** fig. 665 ; fig. 691.

**Right-hand Brace-pocket.** A brace-pocket for a brace which inclines from the bottom toward the right when a person on the outside is looking toward the car. When the brace inclines toward the left, it is called a *left-hand pocket.* The same kind of pocket can be used at each end of the same brace. See **40,** fig. 69.

**Right-hand Seat.** A car-seat with a stationary back in such a position that the seat-end or arm is on the right-hand side of a person sitting on the seat. In fig. 229, **123** is a right-hand seat, and **123'** is a left-hand seat. In figs. 296–298, **26** is a right-hand seat, and **26'** left-hand. See also figs. 406, 407.

**Right-hand Seat-end.** A seat-end which is on the right-hand side of a person sitting in a seat which has a stationary or non-reversible back. See figs. 406, 408.

**Rigid-bolster Truck.** A car-truck with a bolster which has no lateral or swing motion. Figs. 88–107 represent rigid-bolster trucks.

**Rim-latch.** A latch which is attached to the outside of a door and is not let into it. See figs. 526–528.

**Rim-lock.** " A lock having an exterior metallic case which projects from the face of the door, differing thus from a mortise-lock."—*Knight.* See fig. 523.

**Rim of Wheel.** That portion of a car-wheel outside of the plate or spokes. When a separate tire is used, it is the portion of the wheel between the plate or spokes and the tire. See **23,** fig. 138. See *Face of Rim.*

**Ring.** See

| | |
|---|---|
| *Grate-ring.* | *Pull-ring.* |
| *Helper-ring.* | *Retaining-ring.* |
| *Inside-ring.* | *Rubber Packing-ring.* |
| *Lamp-ring.* | *Stove-pipe Ring.* |
| *Man-hole Ring.* | *Top-ring.* |
| *Packing-ring.* | *Ventilator-ring.* |

*Window-curtain Ring.*

**Ring,** *for Smoke-top of Baker Car-heater.* A cast-iron ring which is attached to a smoke-top to stiffen it, and also to hold the feed-door. See **18,** fig. 581 ; fig. 599.

**Riser.** See *Step-riser. Seat-riser.*

**Rivet.** " A pin of iron or other metal with a head drawn through a piece of timber or metal, and the point bent or spread and beat down fast to prevent it being drawn out, or a pin or bolt clinched at both ends."—*Webster.* See *Coupling-link Rivet.*

**Rocker,** *for Tip-car.* A curved or crescent-shaped casting on which the body of a tip-car rests, and on which it rolls or rocks when the body is tipped. See **155,** fig. 81.

**Rocker-bearing,** for *Tip-car.* A cast or wrought iron plate on which a rocker rests and rolls when the car-body is tipped. See **156,** fig. 81.

**Rocker-bearing Timber,** *for Tip-car.* A horizontal timber at the end of a tip-car on which the rocker-bearing rests and which supports the rocker and the body of the car. See **157,** fig. 81.

**Rocker-bearing-timber Hangers,** *for Tip-car.* Vertical timbers or iron bars framed and bolted to the end-piece of a tip-car frame and to which the rocker-bearing timbers are fastened. See **158,** fig. 81.

**Rocker Side-bearing.** A metal rocker which forms a side-bearing for a car. Such rockers are sometimes suspended like a pendulum and sometimes placed in a reverse position. See fig. 136.

**Rocker-timbers,** *for Tip-car.* Transverse timbers attached to the under side of the floor-timbers of a tip-car, and to which the rockers are attached. See **159,** fig. 81.

**Rocking-bar,** *for Grate of Baker Car-heater.* A horizontal bar which supports the grate, and on which the latter is attached by a pivot in the centre so that it can be turned and thus shake the fire. See **16,** fig. 581 ; fig. 597.

**Rock-plank.** A *Truss-plank,* which see.

**Rod.** In car-building this term generally means a slender bar of iron. It is also used to designate such a bar with a nut on each end in distinction from a bolt which has a head on one end and a nut on the other. See

*Basket-rack Rod.*
*Berth-curtain Rod.*
*Body-bolster Truss-rod.*
*Body Truss-rod.*
*Brace-rod.*
*Brace Straining-rod.*
*Brake-beam Truss-rod.*
*Brake-block Tie-rod.*
*Brake-rod.*
*Brake-shaft Connecting-rod.*
*Candle-rod.*
*Centre Body-truss-rod.*
*Connecting-rod.*
*Counter-brace Rod.*
*Cross-frame Truss-rod.*
*Cylinder-lever Tie-rod.*
*Draw-rod.*
*End Body-brace-rod.*
*End-girth Tie-rod.*
*Floating Connection-rod.*
*Girth Tie-rod.*

*Grain-door Rod.*
*Grate-rod.*
*Hand-car Truss-rod.*
*Inverted Body-truss-rod.*
*Lever-frame Tie-rod.*
*Long Brake-rod.*
*Lower Brake-rod.*
*Pedestal Stay-rod.*
*Piston-rod.*
*Plate-rod.*
*Platform Tie-rod.*
*Platform Truss-rod.*
*Release-lever Rod.*
*Release-spring Rod.*
*Safety-beam Tie-rod.*
*Safety-beam Truss-rod.*
*Secondary Brake-rod.*
*Side Body-brace-rod.*
*Sill Tie-rod.*
*Sill-and-Plate Rod.*
*Stay-rod.*
*Tank-valve Rod.*

*Tie-rod.*
*Towel-rod.*
*Transom Truss-rod.*
*Truck-bolster Truss-rod.*

*Truss-rod.*
*Wheel-piece Tie-rod.*
*Wheel-piece Truss-rod.*
*Window-curtain Rod.*

**Rolled-axle.** An axle made of rolled iron.

**Roller.** "That which rolls ; that which turns on its own axis ; particularly a cylinder of wood, stone, metal, etc." —*Webster.* See

*Door Friction-roller.*
*Friction-roller.*
*Side-bearing Roller.*

*Sliding-door Friction-roller.*
*Window-curtain Roller.*

**Roller Side-bearing.** A side-bearing with one or more rollers on which the car-body rests. The rollers are used so that the body will move freely on the bearings. See fig. 135.

**Roller Side-bearing Casting.** A casting for receiving or holding balls or rollers which form a side-bearing. See fig. 135.

**Roof.** "The cover or upper part of a house or other building, consisting of rafters covered with boards, shingles, or tiles, with a side or sides sloping from the ridge for the purpose of carrying off the water that falls in rain or snow."—*Webster.* See

*Arched-roof.*
*Car-roof.*

*Corrugated-metal Car-roof.*

*Platform-roof.*
*Raised-roof.*
*Tin Car-roof.*

*Double-board Car-roof.*
*Pitching-roof.*
*Plank Car-roof.*

*Winslow Car-roof.*

**Roof-apron.** A vertical or inclined metal or wooden screen attached to the end of a passenger-car roof to prevent cinders, rain, or snow from being driven on to the platform and into the door-way. See **106**, fig. 215.

**Roof-boards.** The boards which form a covering of a roof. See **86**, figs. 55-72 ; **102**, figs. 215-230 ; **55**, figs. 750, 752.

**Roof-braces.** Diagonal strips of wood or iron attached to the top of the rafters or carlines under the roof-covering to stiffen the roof. See **85**, fig. 70.

**Roof Corner-casting.** A cast-iron moulding for the corners of projecting-roofs which extend over the platforms of passenger-cars. They are made rights and lefts to be adapted to the two corners.

**Roofing-canvas.** A heavy duck for covering the outside of the roofs of cars.

**Roof-lever,** *for Creamer-brake.* A horizontal lever attached near the projecting roof of a car, and to which the branch line from the bell-cord is connected. It is also connected by a chain and rim with the tripping-lever. See **9**, fig. 648.

**Roof-light.** A *Clear-story Window,* which see. See also *End Roof-light.*

**Roof-ridge.** The intersection of the two plane surfaces forming a pitching-roof.

**Roof Running-board.** Boards placed over the ridge or centre of a freight-car roof, and extending the whole length of the car, and which is provided for train-men to walk or run on, in going from one end of a train to the other. See **87**, figs. 55, 56, 58, 59, 69, 71, 72.

**Roof Running-board Bracket.** An iron bracket attached to the end of a box-car and which supports a running-board extension. See **89**, figs. 60, 61, 63, 65.

**Roof Running-board Extension.** The part of a running-board on top of a box-car, which extends beyond the end of the car-body so as to bring the ends of the running-boards on adjoining cars nearer together to facilitate the passage of train-men from one car to another. See **88**, figs. 60–62.

**Roof-step.** A horizontal board on top of the roof of a freight-car and which extends from the running-board to near the side of the car above the ladder, its object being to assist persons in climbing to and from the top of a car, or to give a secure foothold for brakemen, and to protect the roof from wear by persons walking on it. See **92**, figs. 55, 56, 59.

**Roof-strap.** See *Diagonal Roof-strap.*

**Roof-strips.** A *Purlin,* which see.

**Rope.** " A large string or line composed of several strands twisted together."—*Webster.* See *Berth Safety-rope. Bell-rope. Berth-spring Rope.*

**Rose.** See *Door-latch Rose.*

**Round-bar Spiral-spring.** A spiral-spring made of one or more round bars of metal. See figs 189–191, 205–212.

**Rounds.** See *Ladder-rounds.*

**Rubber-centre Spiral-spring.** A spiral-spring with the space inside the coil filled with india-rubber. See figs. 205, 206.

**Rubber Packing-ring,** *of Triple-valve for Westinghouse Car-brake.* A circular india-rubber gasket which forms a seat for the triple-valve piston. See **10**, fig. 704 ; fig. 712.

**Rubber-seat,** *for Leakage-valve of Westinghouse-brake.* A circular ring of india-rubber, placed on the top of the leakage-valve case, and which forms a bearing for the leakage-valve. See **16**, fig. 705.

**Rubber-spring.** See *India-rubber Car-spring.*

**Rubber-tread,** *for Step.* An india-rubber covering fastened to a step of a car to prevent persons from slipping when ascending or descending the steps.

**Runners.** Apertures which connect the ingate of a mould for casting metals with the spaces made vacant by the withdrawal of the pattern.

**Running-board.** A plane surface made usually of boards for men to walk or run on. See *Roof Running-board.*

**Running-board,** *for Tank-car.* A horizontal iron plate on the side of the tank on which the train-men walk. See **119,** figs. 73–76.

**Running-board Brackets,** *for Tank-car.* Cast-iron brackets or knees which are attached to the main-sills of a tank-car, and project outward to support the running-board. See **120,** figs. 73, 74, 76.

## S

**Saddle.** "A seat or pad to be placed on the back of an animal to support the rider or the load."—*Knight.* Hence, a block or plate which acts as a bearing or support for a rod, beam, etc., in construction, is called a saddle. See *Body Truss-rod Saddle. Spring-saddle. Truss-rod Saddle.*

**Safety-beam.** A longitudinal timber in the frame of a truck attached to the end-piece and transom, and placed above the axles and between the wheels-pieces or truck side-frames. Iron safety-straps are attached to the beam and pass under the axles so as to hold them in position in case of a breakage of the latter or of the wheels. Such beams are placed on each side of the truck so as to hold both ends of the axle in case of a breakage. See **51,** figs. 91–94, 105–107, 115–129. See *Middle Safety-beam.*

**Safety-beam Block.** A block fastened to the under side of a safety-beam and to which a safety-strap is attached. It is put there to bring the safety-beam nearer to the axle, and is usually cut out so as to conform to the shape of the latter. See **53,** figs. 115–117.

**Safety-beam Iron.** A wrought-iron bar or casting bolted to the transom of a six-wheeled truck, and by which the middle safety-beam is attached to the transoms. See **60,** fig. 129.

**Safety-beam Tie-rod.** A rod which is placed alongside a safety-beam, parallel with it, and which passes through the end-piece and transom to tie them together. See **59,** figs. 115–117, 122–125, 128–129.

**Safety-beam Truss-rod.** A rod placed alongside or through a safety-beam, and extending from one end-piece of a truck to the other, and under the transoms so as to form a truss for the truck-frame. See **57,** figs. 93, 94.

**Safety-beam Truss-rod Bearings.** Cast or wrought iron pieces attached to the transoms of a truck, and against which a safety-beam truss-rod bears. See **58,** figs. 92, 94.

**Safety-bearing.** See *Axle Safety-bearing.*

**Safety-chain.** See *Brake Safety-chain.*

**Safety-coupling-chain.** A chain attached at one end to the platform of a car and hooked to the platform of an adjoining car or tender so as to prevent the train from being separated in case the coupling should be detached or broken. Usually two such chains are used between adjoining platforms. See **4**, fig. 244.

**Safety-grate**, *for Baker Heater*. A perforated-plate which is placed on top of the fire-pot over the fire to prevent the latter from falling out in case of an accident and the overturning of the car. See **9**, fig. 581 ; fig. 590.

**Safety-grate Latch**, *for Baker Heater*. A cast-iron fastening for holding a safety-grate in its place. See fig. 596.

**Safety-grate Spring**, *for Baker Heater*. A spring for holding the safety-grate in its place. See fig. 591.

**Safety-hanger.** See *Brake Safety-chain*. *Brake Safety-strap*. *Safety-hanger for Lower Brake-rod*.

**Safety-hanger**, *for Lower Brake-rod*. A metal loop or eye attached to a truck and through which the lower brake-rod passes. It is intended to prevent the brake-rod from falling on the track in case it or its connections should break.

**Safety-strap.** See *Axle Safety-strap*. *Brake Safety-strap*. *Spring-plank Safety-strap*.

**Safety-valve,** *for Baker Car-heater*. A valve formed of an india-rubber ball with which an opening on top of the circulating-drum is closed. When the pressure in the drum exceeds the elasticity of the rubber-ball, the latter

permits the steam or hot water to escape and thus relieve the former. See **26**, fig. 58 ; fig. 605.

**Safety-valve**, *for Westinghouse-brake*. A valve attached to the air-drum to prevent more than a certain pressure being carried in the former. See fig. 732.

**Safety-valve**, *for Westinghouse Driving-wheel Brake*. A valve attached to the pipe which connects the cylinder of the driving-wheel brake with the air-reservoir and which permits the air to escape, when its pressure exceeds a certain point, so as to prevent the slipping of the wheels. Similar to fig. 732.

**Safety-valve Ball**, *for Baker Car-heater*. An india-rubber ball with which an opening in the circulating-drum of a Baker heater is closed, and which, by its elasticity, prevents the water or steam in the drum from escaping until it exceeds a certain pressure. See fig. 606.

**Safford Draw-bar.** A draw-bar invented and patented by Mr. J. B. Safford, which consists of a peculiarly-shaped head, which has a recess or "cove" in the sides so as to give room for a man's hand in coupling cars. See fig. 266.

**Saloon.** 1. The main room in a compartment-car. 2. A polite term to designate a *Water-closet*, which see.

**Saloon-handle.** A *Urinal-handle*, which see.

**Saloon-plate.** See *Notice-plate*.

**Saloon Stop-latch.** A spring-latch with an attachment by which the latch can be fastened on the inside. Similar to figs. 527, 528.

**Sash.** The frame of a window or blind in which the glass or slats are set. See

| | |
|---|---|
| *Door-case Window-sash.* | *Swinging-sash.* |
| *Door-sash.* | *Upper Door-sash.* |
| *Lower Door-sash.* | *Ventilator-sash.* |
| *Mirror-sash.* | *Window-blind Sash.* |
| | *Window-sash.* |

**Sash-fastener.** A *Window-latch*, which see.

**Sash-holder.** See *Window-sash Holder. Spring Window-holder.*

**Sash-lift.** See *Window-lift. Window-blind Lift.*

**Sash-lock.** A *Window-latch*, which see.

**Sash-opener.** A *Ventilator-opener*, which see.

**Sash Parting-strip.** A strip of wood attached to the window-post of a passenger-car which acts as a distance-piece between two sashes and against which the latter slide. See **83,** figs. 225 ; **16,** figs. 299, 301 ; **68,** fig. 752.

**Sash-prop.** A *Window-button*, which see.

**Sash-rail.** A horizontal piece of the frame of a window or blind in which the glass or slats are set. See **12, 14,** figs. 299–301. See *Window-rail. Window-blind Rail.*

**Sash-rest.** See *Window-sash Rest.*

**Sash-spring.** See

| | |
|---|---|
| *Double Window-sash Spring.* | *Spiral Window-sash Spring.* |
| *Single Window-sash Spring.* | *Window-sash Spring.* |

**Sash-stiles.** The upright pieces which form the two sides of a sash. See **11, 13,** figs. 299–301. See *Window-stile. Window-blind Stile.*

**Sash-stop.** See *Window-sash Stop.*

**Sax-&-Kear Wheel.** A wheel with a steel tire which, in the manufacture, is heated very nearly to the melting point and is then put in a mould, and melted cast-iron is poured in, which is thus welded to the steel-tire and forms the centre of the wheel. See figs. 174, 175.

**Scraper.** See *Snow-scraper.*

**Screen,** *for Hood of Spear-heater.* A perforated plate or wire netting, with which the openings of the hood, through which the air is admitted to the heater, are covered. The object of the screen is to exclude cinders. See **7,** figs. 550–552. See also *Base-plate Screen.*

**Screw.** 1. " A cylinder surrounded by a spiral ridge or groove, every part of which forms an equal angle with the axis of the cylinder, so that if developed on a plane surface it would be an inclined plane. It is considered as one of the mechanical powers."—*Knight.*

2. " A grooved piece of iron used for fastening to-

gether pieces of wood or metal; usually called a wood-screw."—*Webster.* See *Lag-screw. Wood-screw.*

**Screw-burner.** A lamp-burner to which the chimney is fastened by a screw.

**Screw-gauges.** Instruments for measuring the diameter or size of screws. They are of two kinds: one, fig. 797, an external gauge for measuring male screws, and the other, fig. 798, an internal gauge for measuring female screws.

**Screw Pitch-gauge.** "A gauge for determining the number of threads to the inch on screws and taps. It consists of a number of toothed plates turning on a common pivot, so that the serrated edge of each may be applied to the screw until one is found which corresponds therewith. The figures stamped on the plate indicate the number of threads to the inch."—*Knight.* See fig. 800.

**Screw-thread.** The groove, or the material between the grooves, which is cut on the outside surface of a cylinder to form a male screw, or on the inside surface of a cylindrical hole to form a nut or female screw. See

*Franklin Institute Sys-
tem of Screw-threads.*
*Metal Screw-thread.*
*Pipe Screw-thread.*
*Sellers System of Screw-
threads.*

*Standard System of
Screw-threads.*
*United States Standard
System of Screw-
threads.*
**V**-*shaped Screw-thread.*

*Whitworth System of
Screw-threads.*

*Wood Screw-thread.*

**Screw-thread Gauge.** A steel plate with notches in the edge of the precise form of screw-threads. The gauge is used for giving the proper form to the edges of screw-cutting tools. That illustrated in fig 799 is adapted to the Sellers system, recommended by the Franklin Institute, and adopted by the Army and Navy departments of the United States, and by the Master Mechanics' and Master Car-builders' associations. See fig. 799. See *Sellers System of Screw-threads.*

**Screw-top.** See *Bell-cord-hanger Screw-top. Bell-cord Strap-hanger Screw-top.*

**Seal.** See *Car-seal. Glass-seal. Lead-seal. Lock-seal.*

**Seal-hook.** An iron hook which is inserted into the hasp of a freight-car door, and to which a seal wire and metal-seal are attached. See fig. 542.

**Seal-lock.** A lock in which a seal made of glass, paper, or other material is inserted in the lock in such a manner as to cover the bolt or the key-hole. The lock cannot be opened without breaking the seal.

**Seal-press.** A pair of levers arranged like a pair of pincers and with two dies with which lead car-seals are compressed on the wire to which they are attached. The two dies leave an impression on the lead so that if the seals are removed or defaced it can be known. See fig. 541.

**Seal-wires.** Several strands of fine wire which are twisted together like a rope, and by which leaden seals are attached to car-doors. See fig. 540.

**Seat.** 1. "That on which one sits."—*Webster.*

2. "The flat portion of a chair or sofa to support the person."—*Knight.*

3. In *Mechanics:* "The part on which another thing rests, as a valve-seat."—*Knight.* See

| | |
|---|---|
| *Axle-seat.* | *Perforated-veneer Seat.* |
| *Bolster-spring Seat.* | *Rattan Car-seat.* |
| *Cane-seat.* | *Reversible-seat.* |
| *Car-seat.* | *Right-hand Seat.* |
| *Corner-seat.* | *Rubber-seat.* |
| *Discharge-valve Seat.* | *Side-seat.* |
| *Equalizing-bar Seat.* | *Slat-seat.* |
| *Equalizing-bar Spring-* | *Spiral-spring Seat.* |
| *seat.* | *Spring-seat,* |
| *Leather-seat.* | *Tank-valve Seat.* |
| *Left-hand Seat.* | *Water-closet Seat.* |
| *Longitudinal-seat.* | *Wheel-seat.* |

**Seat,** *for Hand-car.* A horizontal board which is placed either lengthwise or crosswise on a hand-car for the occupants to sit on. See **12**, figs. 772–775.

**Seat-arm.** The portion of a seat-end which supports the arm of a person sitting in the seat. See **5**, figs. 400, 401.

**Seat-back.** That part of a seat which forms a support for the backs of passengers. In steam-cars, if the seats are placed crosswise the backs are usually made reversible so that passengers can sit facing the direction in which the train is moving, if the car is running either way. In some cases on steam-cars, and usually on street-cars, the seats are placed longitudinally with the backs against the side of the car. See **125**, figs. 215, 216, 218, 219, 220, 229, 230 ; **11**, figs. 400, 401. See *Slat Seat-back.*

**Seat-back Arm** An arm by which the back of a seat is attached to the seat-end or the side of the car. Such arms are usually attached to the frame, seat-ends, or side of the car by a pivot so that the back can be reversed. Sometimes called *striker-arm*, and also *back-arm*. See **13**, figs. 400, 401 ; fig. 415.

**Seat-back-arm Pivot.** A metal pivot by which a seat-back arm of a reversible-seat is attached to a seat-end or the side of a car. In some cases the pivot is made in one piece with a seat-back arm-plate. The latter then becomes a *Seat-back-arm Pivot-plate*, which see. See fig. 416.

**Seat-back-arm Pivot-plate.** A metal plate to which a seat-back-arm pivot is attached. The former is fastened to a seat-end and the latter holds the end of a seat-back arm. See fig. 418.

**Seat-back-arm Plate.** A plate fastened to a seat-end with a hole in the centre which receives and holds a seat-back-arm pivot. In some cases the pivot is made in one piece with the plate. The latter is then called a *Seat-back-arm Pivot-plate*, which see. See fig. 417.

**Seat-back-arm Washer.** A small washer for the head of a screw by which a seat-back arm is fastened to a seat-end. See **1**, fig. 415.

**Seat-back Band.** A wood or metal band or moulding which is fastened around the edge of a seat-back to give it a finish and protect it from wear. See **12**, figs. 400, 401.

**Seat-back Board.** A board which is placed between the two seat-back rails of a longitudinal seat, and which is usually made in the form of a raised panel so as to make a comfortable rest for the backs of passengers. See **42**, figs. 750, 752.

**Seat-back Curved-stop.** A seat-back stop of a curved form, resembling somewhat a letter **S**. See **14**, fig. 400 ; fig. 420.

**Seat-back Moulding.** A *Seat-back Band*, which see.

**Seat-back Rail.** A longitudinal wooden strip which forms a part of a seat-back. See *Upper Seat-back Rail. Lower Seat-back Rail.*

**Seat-back Round-stop.** A seat-back stop with a round flange by which it is fastened to the seat-end, and with a lug in the centre, on which the seat-back arm rests. See fig. 421.

**Seat-back Slats.** Narrow strips of wood which are used to form a seat-back. They are used chiefly for seats which are not upholstered.

**Seat-back Spring.** A spring placed in the upholstering in the back of a seat, and used to give elasticity to the back.

**Seat-back Stop.** A metal lug or bracket attached to a seat-end and sometimes to the side of the car and on which the seat-back arm rests. See **14**, figs. 400, 401 ; figs. 419–421.

**Seat-bottom.** The boards or floor in a seat-frame on which a cushion rests, or on which persons sit when no cushion is used. See **34**, figs. 750, 752.

**Seat-bottom Rail.** A wooden strip to which a wooden seat-bottom is attached. See *Back Seat-bottom Rail. Front Seat-bottom Rail.*

**Seat-bracket,** *for Hand-car.* A wrought-iron knee which forms a support for a seat of a hand-car. See **13**, figs. 772, 775.

**Seat-bracket Brace,** *for Hand-car.* A diagonal iron bar which braces a seat-bracket in a hand-car. See **14**, fig. 775.

**Seat-cushion.** A soft pad, or pillow on which passengers sit. Two kinds of cushions are used on cars : *Squab-cushions* and *Box-cushions*, which see.

**Seat-division.** A bar of wood or metal which is attached

to a car-seat to separate the space occupied by a passenger from that adjoining it. See **126**, figs. 229, 230.

**Seat-end.** A frame of wood or metal at the end of a car-seat which supports the arm of the occupant and to which the seat-back arm is attached. See **123**, figs. 215, 216, 218, 219, 220, 229 ; **2**, fig. 400 ; **3**, fig. 401. See also

*Aisle Seat-end.*     *Long Seat-end.*

*Corner-seat End.*    *Right-hand Seat-end.*

*Left-hand Seat-end.*    *Short Seat-end.*

*Wall Seat-end.*

**Seat-hinge.** A strap-hinge which is used in sleeping-cars to connect a seat with the seat-back. See also *Sofa-hinge.*

**Seat-leg.** A wooden post which supports a front seat-rail. These are not often used excepting for seats which extend longitudinally along the side of a car. See **35**, figs. 750, 752.

**Seat-leg Plate.** A metal plate with which the front of a seat-end or leg is covered to protect it from injury. See fig. 396.

**Seat-lock.** A lock for holding the back of a seat so that its position cannot be reversed. Such locks are attached either to the seat-end, seat-back arm, or the seat-back stop. See *Barrel Seat-lock.* See also **15**, fig. 401 ; figs. 419, 422.

**Seat-lock Bolt.** The latch of a seat-lock, which is moved in and out by a key to secure or release the seat-back. See **1**, figs. 419, 422.

**Seat-lock Escutcheon.** An escutcheon for the key-hole of a seat-lock attached to a wooden seat-end. See fig. 423.

**Seat-lock Key.** A key or instrument for shutting or opening a seat-lock by pushing the bolt one way or the other. See **2**, fig. 419.

**Seat-lock Spring.** The spring in a seat-lock which moves the bolt. See **2**, fig. 422.

**Seat-rail.** A wooden rail resting on and attached to the seat-end and to the side of the car, and which supports a seat-cushion or seat-bottom. See **1**, figs. 400, 401. See *Back Seat-rail.* *Front Seat-rail.*

**Seat-riser.** A vertical board or front of a seat, which incloses the space underneath, and which extends from the seat-rail to the floor. Such risers are seldom used with reversible-seats.

**Seat-slat.** A narrow strip of wood which forms part of a seat-bottom.

**Seat-spring.** A spiral or other metal spring used in a seat to give it elasticity. See figs. 411–413. See *Spiral Elliptic-seat-spring.*

**Seat-stand.** A support, usually made of cast-iron, on which the aisle-end of a seat rests. See **124**, figs. 215, 219 ; **6**, fig. 400. See also *Long Seat-end.*

**Secondary Brake-rod.** 1. A rod which connects one end of a floating-lever of a Hodge-brake with one of the brake-levers. See 6, fig. 642.

2. A rod which connects the centre brake-lever of a Tanner or Elder brake with one of the brake-levers on the truck. On a four-wheeled car it is the rod which connects the centre lever with one of the brake-beams. See **152**, fig. 80 ; **6**, figs. 640, 641, 644, 645 ; **132**, figs. 750, 751.

**Second-class Car.** A plainly-finished passenger-car, for carrying passengers who pay a lower rate of fare than first-class passengers do.

**Section.** See *Sleeping-car Section.*

**Sector.** In geometry : "A part of a circle included by an arc and the two radii drawn to its extremities."—*Davies.* Hence, any object whose shape is that of a part of a circle is called a sector. See *Clear-story Window-sector. Draw-bar Sector.*

**Self-acting Ventilator.** An *Automatic-ventilator*, which see.

**Self-closing Faucet** *or* **Cock.** A faucet which is provided with a spring by which it is closed when the plug, handle, or valve is released. See fig. 427.

**Sellers System of Screw-threads.** A system of screw-threads designed by William Sellers, of Philadelphia. The form of the threads is shown in fig. 796. The angle at which the sides of the thread stand to each other is 60 degrees, and the top and bottom of the threads are made flat. The proportions of the threads are determined by the following rule given by Mr. Sellers : "*Divide the pitch, or, what is the same thing, the sides of the thread, into eight equal parts ; take off one part from the top and fill in one part in the bottom of the thread ; then the flat top and bottom will equal one-eighth of the pitch, the wearing surface will be three-quarters of the pitch, and the diameter of screw at bottom of the thread will be expressed by the formula :*

$$D = \frac{1.299}{N,}$$

in which $D$ = diameter of the screw and $N$ = the number of threads per inch.

This system was recommended by a committee appointed by the Franklin Institute in 1864 ; was adopted as the standard by both the Army and Navy departments of the United States, and has been recommended by both the Master Car-builders' and the Master Mechanics' associations as the standard to be used in the construction of cars and locomotives. It is often called the *Franklin Institute Standard* and also the *United States Standard ;* but, as it was designed by Mr. Sellers, it should be known as the *Sellers System.* See fig. 796.

The following table gives the number of threads to the inch and the proportion of the threads of the Sellers system :

TABLE GIVING PROPORTIONS OF THE SELLERS SYSTEM OF SCREW-THREADS.

| Outside diameter of screw in inches | Number of threads per inch | Diameter of screw at the root of the thread in decimals of an inch | Width of top and bottom of thread in decimals of an inch | Outside diameter of screw in inches | Number of threads per inch | Diameter of screw at the root of the thread in decimals of an inch | Width of top and bottom of thread in decimals of an inch |
|---|---|---|---|---|---|---|---|
| ¼ | 20 | .185 | .0062 | 1 | 8 | .837 | .0156 |
| 5⁄16 | 18 | .240 | .0074 | 1⅛ | 7 | .940 | .0178 |
| ⅜ | 16 | .294 | .0078 | 1¼ | 7 | 1.065 | .0178 |
| 7⁄16 | 14 | .344 | .0089 | 1⅜ | 6 | 1.160 | .0208 |
| ½ | 13 | .400 | .0096 | 1½ | 6 | 1.284 | .0208 |
| 9⁄16 | 12 | .454 | .0104 | 1⅝ | 5½ | 1.389 | .0227 |
| ⅝ | 11 | .507 | .0113 | 1¾ | 5 | 1.491 | .0250 |
| ¾ | 10 | .620 | .0125 | 1⅞ | 5 | 1.616 | .0250 |
| ⅞ | 9 | .731 | .0138 | 2 | 4½ | 1.712 | .0277 |

**Set of Springs.** 1. A *set of springs* means all the springs for carrying the weight of one car. A *set of bolster-springs* consists of the springs which are placed between the truck-frames and carry the weight of the body only. A *set of equalizing-bar springs* means all the springs for a car on the equalizing-bars. A *set of wheel or journal springs* means all the springs which are placed directly over the journal-boxes of one car.

2. The amount of bend which is given to springs before they are loaded. See 2, figs. 185–187.

**Set of Wheels.** This term means a number of wheels sufficient for one car. A *set of wheels and axles* means the requisite number of wheels fitted to axles complete for one car.

**Sextuplet of Springs.** Six elliptic springs coupled together, side by side in a group, so as to act as one spring. Similar to **80**, figs. 122, 128.

**Shackle-bar.** A *Coupling-link*, which see.

**Shad-bellied Tank.** A *Telescopic-tank*, which see.

**Shade.** See *Lamp-shade*.

**Shaft.** "That part of a machine to which motion is communicated by torsion."—*Webster.* See

| | |
|---|---|
| *Brake-shaft.* | *Horizontal Brake-shaft.* |
| *Crank-shaft.* | *Lever-shaft.* |
| *Door-shaft.* | *Winding-shaft* |

**Shaker.** See *Grate-shaker*.

**Shank.** See *Buffer-shank*.

**Sheathing.** Boards which are tongued and grooved, and

with which the sides of cars are covered. See **52**, figs. 55-65, 82, 84.

**Sheave.** A wheel, roller, or pulley over which a cord or rope runs, or on which any object, as a door or window, rolls. See

|   |   |
|---|---|
| *Bell-cord Sheave.* | *Centre Brake-lever* |
| *Brake-lever Sheave.* | *Sheave.* |
| *Brake-shaft-chain* | *Door-sheave.* |
| *Sheave.* | *Door-strap Sheave.* |

*Sliding-door Sheave.*

**Shelf.** See *Spring-shelf.*

**Shell.** See *Berth-latch Shell.*

**Shoe.** A plate, block, or piece of any material on or against which an object moves, usually to prevent the latter from being worn. See *Brake-shoe. Door-shoe.*

**Short Floor-timber.** An auxiliary timber used in a car-floor, but not extending its whole length. See **5**, fig. 57.

**Short Seat-end.** A seat-end which does not extend below the seat or support it. See **2**, fig. 400. See *Long Seat-end.*

**Shot.** See *Cold-shot.*

**Shunting.** A term used in England to designate the act of moving cars from one track to another, as in making up or separating trains, and placing the cars on the tracks and in the places where they are needed. See *Switching. Drilling. Regulating.*

**Side.** See *Clear-story Side. Ladder-side. Truck-side.*

**Side-bearings.** Supports which are placed on each side of the centre-pins of a car, and intended to prevent too much rolling or rocking motion of the car-body. Usually there is a plate of iron or steel attached to the body-bolster on each side of the centre-pin which is called a *body side-bearing,* and a corresponding plate, block, or roller on the truck-bolster which is called the *Truck Side-bearing,* which see. Generally there is a little space left between the bearings on the body and those on the truck, so that the truck can turn freely on the centre-plate, although in some cases the weight of the car-body rests on the side-bearings instead of the centre-plates. See

|   |   |
|---|---|
| *Body Side-bearing.* | *Rocker Side-bearing.* |
| *Cup Side-bearing.* | *Roller Side-bearing.* |

*Truck Side-bearing.*

**Side-bearing Arch-bar.** A *Side-bearing Bridge,* which see.

**Side-bearing Bridge.** An iron bar, truss, or wooden beam which is attached to the spring-beams of a six-wheeled truck, and which supports the truck side-bearing. See **62**, figs. 129, 130.

**Side-bearing Roller.** A metal roller which forms a part of a truck side-bearing and on which a body side-bearing rests. These are not much used. See fig. 135.

**Side Body-brace.** An inclined beam or stick of timber in

the side-frame of a car-body, which acts as a brace. See **33**, figs. 56, 69, 77, 82 ; **51**, figs. 215, 229.

**Side Body-brace Rod.** An inclined iron rod in the side-frame of a car-body which acts as a brace. See **34**, fig. 61 ; **52**, fig. 221.

**Side-casting.** See *Draw-bar Side-casting.*

**Side Foot-rest.** A metal plate fastened to a truss-plank of a passenger-car, between the seats, for passengers to rest their feet on. Such plates are also used over heater-pipes as a guard to prevent the feet of passengers from coming in contact with the hot pipes. See **10**, fig. 401.

**Side-frame,** *of a Car-body.* The frame which forms the whole side of a car-body. It includes the posts, braces, plate, rail, girth, etc.

**Side-frame,** *of a Truck.* See *Truck Side-frame. Diamond-truck Side-frame.*

**Side Journal-spring.** A spiral or rubber spring which rests on a ledge on the side of a journal-box. These are used chiefly on street-cars, and in pairs, one spring being placed on each side of a box. See **6**, figs. 750, 752.

**Side-lamp.** A lamp attached to the side of a passenger-car. Such lamps are usually made with brackets by which they can be conveniently fastened. The term is used to distinguish side-lamps from centre-lamps which are suspended from the centre of the ceilings of cars. See figs. 474–476, 493.

**Side-lamp Braces.** Diagonal bars attached to a side-lamp and to the side of a car to help to support the lamp. See **18**, fig. 476.

**Side-lamp Bracket.** A metal bracket attached to the side or a partition of a passenger-car, and which supports a lamp. See **17**, fig. 477.

**Side-lamp Holder.** A metal ring or bowl-shaped receptacle usually attached to a bracket and used to hold a lamp. See **16**, fig. 477.

**Side-pawl,** *for Creamer-brake.* A pawl which acts on a ratchet underneath the drum, and which prevents the latter from reacting. See **10**, figs. 646, 647.

**Side-pulley.** A small wheel or pulley in a bell-cord guide, which is placed on the side of the bell-cord to guide it in an inclined direction. See **1**, figs. 459, 464. See *Bell-cord Guide with Side-pulley.*

**Side-rest,** *for Tip-car.* A block of wood or metal on top of the frame of a tip-car on which the body rests when it is tipped. See **160**, fig. 81.

**Side-seat.** A car-seat, the back of which is against the side of a car. See *Car-seat.*

**Side-step,** *for Street-car.* A ledge usually made of a wrought-iron plate and attached to the side of the platform of a street-car, and used as a step by persons in getting on or off the car.  See **114**, figs. 750–753.

**Side-stop,** *for Tip-car.* A cast-iron support attached to the wheel-piece of a tip-car, on which the body rests, and by which it is held in a horizontal position.  See **162**, fig. 81.

**Side-urinal.** A urinal constructed with one flat side so that it can conveniently be attached to a partition or side of a car.  See fig. 439.

**Side Urinal-handle.** A handle attached to the side of a water-closet.  See fig. 442.  See also *Corner Urinal-handle.  Urinal-handle.*

**Siding.** See *Sheathing.*

**Signal-bell.** A saucer-shaped bell attached to the platform hood of a street-car.  One of these is placed over each platform of the car, the front one being intended to signal to the driver and the rear one to the conductor. They are rung by a tongue or clapper, to which a strap is attached which extends from one platform to the other, so that the front bell can be rung from the back platform and the back bell from the front platform, or either bell can be rung from the inside of the car.  See **97**, fig. 750 ; **2**, fig. 766.  A similar bell used on locomotives is also called a signal-bell.

**Signal-bell Clapper.** A hammer attached to a signal-bell to strike and ring it.  See **1**, fig. 766.

**Signal-bell Frame.** A frame by which a street-car signal-bell is attached to the roof of the car.  See **3**, fig. 766.

**Signal-gong.** A *Signal-bell*, which see.

**Signal-lamp.** A lamp used for giving signals.  See *Double - lens Tail-lamp.   Tail - lamp.   Train Signal-lamp.*

**Signal-strap.** A *Bell-strap*, which see.

**Sill.** 1. " *Properly*, the basis or foundation of a thing ; *appropriately*, a piece of timber on which a building rests.  The lowest timber in any structure, as the sills of a house, of a bridge, of a loom, and the like.

2. "The timber or stone at the foot of a door ; the threshold.

3. "The timber or stone on which a window-frame stands, or the lowest piece in a window-frame."—*Webster.*

4. In *car-building*, the main outside longitudinal timber of a car-body, into which the body-posts of box and passenger cars are framed and on which the floor rests. See **1**, figs. 55–84, 215–231 ; **8**, figs. 750–752.  Also, see

*Clear-story End-sill.*      *End-sill.*
*Clear-story Sill.*      *Inside Window-sill.*
*Door-sill.*      *Platform sill.*
             *Window-sill.*

**Sill-and-plate Rod.** A vertical iron rod which passes through the sill and plate of a car-body frame and ties the two together. See **36,** figs. 61, 64, 69, 71, 72, 77 ; **54,** figs. 215, 216, 221.

**Sill Knee-iron.** An **L**-shaped or right-angled iron casting or forging bolted into the inside corner of a car-frame to strengthen it. See **9,** figs. 62, 64 ; **8,** fig. 220.

**Single-lever Brake.** A brake which has but one lever to a truck or four-wheeled car, as shown in fig. 637. In some cases, such brakes are applied to but one of the trucks of a car ; in other cases, to both. An objection to this form of brake is that the pressure is not equal on each brake-beam ; and, therefore, to overcome this difficulty, two levers are used, and the brake, as shown in fig. 638, is then called a *Double-lever Brake,* which see.

**Sill-step.** A bent bar of iron attached to the sill of a car, below the ladder, and which forms a step for getting to or from the ladder. See **30,** figs. 55–84.

**Sill-step Stay.** A diagonal iron rod or bar attached by one end to one of the floor-timbers and by the other to a sill-step to stiffen the latter. See **31,** figs. 73, 75, 82, 84.

**Sill Tie-rod.** A transverse tie-rod in the floor of a car for holding the sills together. See **10,** figs. 74. 76, 83 ; **9,** figs. 215–231; **11,** figs. 750, 751.

**Single Pipe-strap.** An iron band bent or formed in a **U**-shape to hold a pipe on a flat surface with screws inserted in ears or lugs on the strap. See fig. 616.

**Single-plate Wheel.** A cast-iron wheel with a centre made of a single plate of metal with ribs cast on the back. See figs. 154–158.

**Single-screw Turnbuckle.** A turnbuckle shaped like a link of a chain with a screw at one end and a swivel at the other. See fig. 790.

**Single Window-blind.** A blind which is made in one piece or section and large enough for one window.

**Single Window-blind Lift.** A metal finger-hold attached to the bottom rail of a single window-blind for raising and lowering it. It is the same as a window-lift but attached to a window-blind. See fig. 322. See *Double Window-blind Lift. Window-blind Lift.*

**Single Window-sash Spring.** A metal plate attached at one end to the edge of the stile of a window sash or blind to prevent it from rattling. See fig. 303.

**Sink.** See *Wash-stand Sink.*

**Skew-back.** A casting on the end of a truss or a trussed-beam, and to which a truss-rod is fastened. It is usually made in the form of a cap, and forms a bearing for the truss-rod nuts. See **7,** figs. 808, 809. See also *Truss-rod Washer.*

**Slab.** See *Wash-stand Slab.*

**Slat.** A narrow piece of board or timber. See *Seat-back Slat. Seat-slat. Window-blind Slat.*

**Slat Cattle-car.** A car for carrying cattle, the sides of which are inclosed with slats. See figs. 15, 69–72. See also *Box Cattle-car. Cattle-car.*

**Slat-seat.** A seat composed of narrow strips of wood. These are usually placed longitudinally on the seats with a space between them.

**Slat Seat-back.** A back of a seat made with narrow strips of wood.

**Sleeping-car.** A car provided with sleeping-berths or beds for the use of passengers at night. These berths are movable so that they can be changed to ordinary seats for use in the day-time, as shown in figs. 296, 297, 298. See fig. 1.

**Sleeping-car Section.** The space in a sleeping-car, which usually is occupied by two double-seats in day-time and by two berths or beds at night. In figs. 296, 297, two sections are shown, and in fig. 298, one.

**Sleeve.** See *Piston-sleeve. Stake-sleeve.*

**Sliding-door.** A door which is opened by sliding sideways instead of swinging on hinges. Such doors are shown in figs. 55, 60, 61, 69.

**Sliding-door Bracket.** A *Door-track Bracket*, which see.

**Sliding-door Friction-roller.** A small wheel attached to the top of a sliding-door to make it run easily. It does not carry the weight of the door, but its purpose is to reduce the friction of the top of the door in case it comes in contact with the door guides. See fig. 765.

**Sliding-door Handle.** A handle attached to a sliding-door and made of such a shape that the door can conveniently be moved by taking hold of the handle. See **6**, figs. 530, 532.

**Sliding-door Handle,** *for Street-cars.* A handle attached to a latch for opening and closing street-car doors. See **91**, fig. 753 ; fig. 759.

**Sliding-door Holder,** *for Street-cars.* A metal hook by which a sliding-door of a street-car is fastened on the inside. See fig. 762.

**Sliding-door-holder Catch.** A metal plate, eye, or keeper, which is attached to a door-post of a street-car, and into which a sliding-door holder engages so as to hold the door shut. See fig. 763.

**Sliding-door Latch.** A latch made with a hook instead of a bolt, for fastening sliding-doors. See figs. 530, 760.

**Sliding-door-latch Keeper.** A metal plate or hook attached to a door-post into or with which a sliding-door latch engages. See fig. 761.

**Sliding-door-latch Plates.** Metal plates, usually made of brass, which are placed on each side of a sliding-door, and which form bearings for the latch arbor. Used on street-cars. See **92**, fig. 753 ; **1**, fig. 759.

**Sliding-door Lock.** A lock made especially for fastening sliding-doors. Such locks usually have a hook which engages in a corresponding catch attached to the door-post.

The hook is secured in connection with the catch by means of a bolt which is operated by a key. See fig. 529.

**Sliding-door Sheave.** See *Door-sheave.*

**Sliding-door Track.** See *Door-track.*

**Slide-valve,** *for Triple-valve of Westinghouse Car-brake.* A small **D**-shaped valve, which forms a portion of the working parts of a triple-valve. See **12,** fig. 704 ; fig. 714.

**Smith Vacuum-brake.** A system of continuous brakes, invented and patented by Mr. J. Y. Smith, which is operated by exhausting the air from flexible india-rubber cylinders or bags, resembling the bellows of an accordion, which are placed under each car. One end or head of these cylinders is attached to the car-body and the other is connected by a rod to a system of brake-levers. When the air is exhausted from the cylinder the pressure of the air on the outside of the movable head is communicated to the brake-levers and thence to the brake-shoes. The air is exhausted by an ejector on the engine, which is connected with the india-rubber cylinders by pipes and flexible hose between the cars. See figs. 653, 654.

**Smoke-bell.** A cover or screen, which is made of glass, porcelain, or metal, shaped somewhat like a bell, and placed over a lamp to protect the ceiling of a car or room from the heat and smoke of the lamp. See **13,** figs. 471, 472.

**Smoke-jack.** See *Lamp-jack. Stove-pipe Jack.*

**Smoke-pipe,** *for Spear Heater.* The pipe by which the smoke is conducted from a Spear heater to the outside of the car. The stove-pipe of a Spear heater is called a smoke-pipe to distinguish it from the cold-air pipe. See **4,** figs. 550, 551, 563.

**Smoke-pipe Cap,** *for Spear Heater.* A covering on top of the smoke-pipe to exclude rain and wind. See **5,** figs. 550–553.

**Smoke-pipe Casing,** *for Spear Heater.* An outside pipe which incloses a smoke-pipe leaving a space between the two through which air is admitted from the top and descends and circulates around the smoke-pipe and the stove and is thus warmed. See **8,** fig. 552. See also *Perforated Smoke-pipe Casing.*

**Smoke-top,** *for Baker Car-heater.* The upper part of a Baker heater, which is made of Russia iron, and is of a conical form. See **12,** fig. 581 ; fig. 593.

**Snow-flanger.** A bar of iron or steel attached to a car or engine to scrape away snow and ice on the sides of the heads of the rails so as to make room for the flanges of the wheels.

**Snow-plow.** "A machine operated like a plow, but on a larger scale, for clearing away the snow from railroads." —*Webster.* The parts of a snow-plow corresponding with the plow-share and mould-board of an ordinary plow are mounted on running gear similar to that used for freight-cars. See fig. 34. Snow-plows are also attached to the cow-catchers of locomotives.

**Snow-scraper.** A plate or bar of iron or steel attached to an engine or car to scrape away the snow and ice from the rails. See *A*, fig. 33.

**Soap-dish.** A dish or receptacle for holding soap on a wash-stand. See fig. 387.

**Soap-holder.** A bracket with a receptacle attached for holding soap near a wash-stand. Such brackets are usually attached to a partition or the side of the car. See fig. 386.

**Socket.** "Any hollow thing or place which receives and holds something else."—*Webster.* See

> *Berth-curtain-rod Socket.*
> *Chair-leg Socket.*
> *Flag-holder Socket.*
> *Revolving-chair-stand Socket.*

**Socket-castor.** A castor attached to a metal socket which fits on the end of a chair, table, or sofa leg, etc. See fig. 390.

**Socket-washer.** A large washer with a cavity to receive the head or nut of a bolt or rod so that it will not project beyond the surface of the wood to which it is attached. Also called *cup-washer.* See fig. 788.

**Sofa-bolt.** A sliding bolt used for holding a sofa in a sleeping or drawing-room car in its place.

**Sofa-bolt Keeper.** A plate into which a sofa-bolt engages.

**Sofa-castor.** A castor intended for the leg of a sofa. See *Castor.* See fig. 391.

**Sofa-hinge.** A hinge by which the seat and back of a sofa are fastened together so that they can be changed from a sofa into a bed. See fig. 350. See *Seat-hinge.*

**Soffit-board.** A board which forms the under side or ceiling of some subordinate part or member of a building or a car, as of a staircase or cornice. See *Clear-story Soffit-board.*

**Soil-hopper.** A metal or porcelain hopper used in water-closets. See fig. 440.

**Solid-head Coupling-pin.** A coupling-pin, the head of which is made solid; that is, without a hole or opening in it. See *Eye-head Coupling-pin.* See fig. 274.

**Solid-leather Bell-cord.** See *Bell-cord.*

**Spear Anti-clinker Car-heaters.** Heaters or stoves manufactured by Mr. James Spear, of Philadelphia, for heating cars, and made with a sheet-iron outside casing which leaves an air-space between the stove and casing, into which a current of air is admitted, and is warmed by coming in contact with the stove, and then escapes into the car. Several different patterns of these heaters are made, designated by the manufacturers as patterns *A*, *B*, *C*, and *D*, and represented by figs. 550,

551, 552, 553. In fig 550, or pattern *A*, the cold air is admitted through a hood **1, 1,** on top of the car, and is carried down to the bottom of the stove by a pipe, **2, 2,** and then circulates around the pipe, as shown by the darts in the section, fig. 554, and enters the car through a hot-air pipe, **3**, figs. 550, 554, which extends the whole length of the car, with registers at each seat. In pattern *B*, fig. 551, the hot-air pipe is not used, the warmed air escaping directly into the car through openings in the base of the stove. In pattern *C*, fig. 552, an independent cold-air pipe is not used, but the smoke-pipe is inclosed in a casing, with a space between the two, through which the cold air descends and passes over the stove and escapes at the base, as shown by the darts. In pattern *D*, fig. 553, no hood is used on top of the car, but the cold air enters the air-space from the inside of the car at the base of the stove and escapes at the top, as shown by the darts.

The "anti-clinker" feature of these heaters consists in a peculiarly-arranged grate, shown in the section, fig, 554, with an annular opening between it and the base of the stove, through which the clinkers can be removed from the grate.

**Spear Stove.** See *Spear Anti-clinker Car-heater.*

**Spider.** See *Centre Brake-lever Spider.*

**Spindle.** See *Door-latch Spindle.*

**Spiral-elliptic Seat-spring.** A spring made of a thin band of steel and wound on a spiral-coil, the transverse section of which is elliptical. See fig. 413.

**Spiral Seat-spring.** A light spiral-spring made of wire for upholstering car-seats. See fig. 412.

**Spiral-spring.** A spring made of a metal rod or bar coiled in the form of the thread of a screw, so that it can be compressed or extended in the direction of the axis around which it is coiled. See figs. 189–212. See

*Compound Spiral-spring.*
*Cluster-spring.*
*Dinsmore Spiral-spring.*
*Double-coil Nest-spring.*
*Edge-rolled Spiral-spring.*
*Equal-bar Nest-spring.*
*Flat-bar Spiral-spring.*
*Group-spring.*
*Half-round-bar Spiral-spring.*
*Hibbard-spring.*
*Keg-shaped Spiral-spring.*
*Nest-spring.*
*Paragon Spiral-spring.*
*Quadruple-coil Spiral-spring.*
*Round-bar Spiral-spring.*
*Rubber-centre Spiral-spring.*
*Spiral-elliptic Seat-spring.*
*Spiral Seat-spring.*
*Spool-shaped Spiral-spring.*
*Square-bar Spiral-spring.*
*Triple-coil Nest-spring.*
*Wool-packed Spiral-spring.*

**Spiral-spring Cap.** A casting or plate which forms a

bearing for the top of a spiral-spring, and which also holds it in its place. See **4**, figs. 192, 193, 206, 208, 210, 212.

**Spiral-Spring Seat.** A casting or plate which forms a bearing for the bottom of a spiral-spring, and which also holds it in its place. See **3**, figs. 192, 193, 206, 208, 210, 211, 212.

**Spiral Window-sash Spring.** A spring made of iron bent into a spiral form and let into the edge of the stile of a window or blind sash to prevent it from rattling. See fig. 304.

**Spittoon.** A vessel to receive discharges of spittle and other abominations. See fig. 388.

**Splash-board.** A board attached in an inclined position on the inside of passenger-car steps. It serves very much the same purpose as the risers of steps, and prevents mud and dirt being thrown on the steps by the wheels and from the track. See **49**, figs. 219, 223.

**Splice.** "The union of ropes by interweaving the strands."—*Webster*. Hence, any appliance by which the ends of a rope, cord, beam, or bar are united. See *Bell-cord Splice*.

**Spoke.** "One of the radial arms which connect the hub with the rim of a wheel."—*Knight*.

**Spoke-wheel.** A wheel the rim or tire of which is connected with the hub by spokes instead of one or more plates. These spokes are sometimes made of solid cast-iron, in others they are cast hollow, and in still others are made of wrought-iron. See *Hollow-spoke Wheel. Hand-car Wheel. Wrought-iron Wheel.*

**Spool-shaped Spiral-spring.** A spring wound into a coil the form of which resembles a spool on which thread is wound. This form was patented by W. P. Hansell in 1874 and 1875. See fig. 197.

**Spring.** One or more elastic bodies used to resist sudden concussion, as the springs on which the weight of a car rests, or the buffer or seat springs. Springs are also used to produce motion in the reverse direction to that caused by a force applied in some other way, as the brake-springs and the spring of a door-latch. See

*Auxiliary Buffer-spring.*
*Berth-spring.*
*Body-spring.*
*Bolster-spring.*
*Brake-hose Coupling-*
    *valve Spring.*
*Brake-spring.*
*Buffer-spring.*
*Candle-spring.*
*Car-spring.*
*Cluster-spring.*

*Combination Elliptic-*
    *spring.*
*Compound Spiral-spring.*
*Couplet of Springs.*
*Coupling-spring.*
*Dinsmore Spiral-spring.*
*Double-coil Nest-spring.*
*Double Release-spring.*
*Double Window-sash*
    *Spring.*
*Door-latch Spring.*

Door-lock-bolt Spring.
Draft-spring.
Draw-spring.
Edge-rolled Spiral-
spring.
Elliptic-spring.
Equal-bar Nest-spring.
Equalizing-bar Spring.
Eureka Edge-rolled
Spiral-spring.
Flat-bar Spiral-spring.
Graduating-spring for
Triple-valve.
Group-spring.
Gum-spring.
Half Elliptic-spring.
Half-round-bar Spiral-
spring.
Hibbard-spring.
India-rubber Car-spring.
Journal-box-cover Spring.
Journal-spring.
Keg-shaped Spiral-spring.
Lateral-motion Spring.
Mirror-frame Spring.

Nest-spring.
Paragon Spiral-spring.
Quadruple-coil Spiral-
spring.
Quadruplet of Springs.
Quintuplet of Springs.
Release-spring.
Round-bar Spiral-spring.
Rubber-centre Spiral-
spring.
Safety-grate Spring.
Sash-spring.
Seat-back Spring.
Seat-lock Spring.
Seat-spring.
Set of Springs.
Sextuplet of Springs.
Side Journal-spring.
Single Window-sash
Spring.
Spiral-elliptic Seat-
spring.
Spiral Seat-spring.
Spiral-spring.
Spiral Window-sash
Spring.

Spool-shaped Spiral-
spring.
Square-bar Spiral-
spring.
Swing-bolster Spring.
Swing-motion Spring.
Triple-coil Nest-spring.
Triplet of Springs.

Volute-springs.
Vose Graduated-spring.
Window-blind Spring.
Wool-packed Spiral-
spring.
Window-latch Spring.
Window-sash Spring.

**Spring-band.** A wrought-iron strap which embraces the plates of an elliptic or semi-elliptic spring at the centre. See **1**, figs. 185–187.

**Spring-beam.** A transverse timber which rests on top of the body-springs of a six-wheeled truck. There are two such beams to each truck, on which the bolster-bridges which support the bolster rest. See **42**, figs. 129, 130.

**Spring-block.** A piece of wood used as a distance-piece above or below a spring. See **76**, figs. 121, 126.

**Spring-bracket.** See *Tender-spring Bracket for Westing-house-brake.*

**Spring-burner.** A lamp-burner to which the chimney is fastened by a spring. See fig. 482.

**Spring-cap.** A cup-shaped piece of cast or wrought iron for holding the top of a spring and against which the latter bears. See *Bolster-spring Cap. Equalizing-bar Spring-cap. Spiral-spring Cap.*

**Spring-case.** A cast-iron box made in two parts to hold

one or more spiral or india-rubber springs. See fig. 210. The upper portion, **4**, of the case is called a *Spring-cap* and the lower portion, **3**, a *Spring-seat*, which see.

**Spring Door-latch.** A latch for a door, the bolt of which is thrown into contact with a catch by a spring and is disengaged by a knob or handle. Such latches are not arranged so as to be fastened with a key. See fig. 526.

**Spring Door-lock.** A lock with a bolt which is moved by a spring so as to engage with its keeper, and which is disengaged from the outside with a key, but can be opened from the inside without one. Often called a *night-latch*. See fig. 527.

**Spring Draw-clevis.** A draw-clevis which can slide longitudinally and whose movement is resisted by a spring, so as to give it elasticity when subjected to tension. Used chiefly on street-cars. The term is used to distinguish such a draw-clevis from one which is attached rigidly to a car without a spring.

**Spring Draw-hook.** A draw-hook which can slide longitudinally, and whose movement is resisted by a spring, so as to give it elasticity when subjected to tension. Used chiefly on street-cars. The term is used to distinguish such a draw-hook from one which is attached rigidly, without a spring, to a car.

**Spring-hanger.** A bar or **U**-shaped iron strap which sustains the end of a semi-elliptic spring. See **170**, fig. 82 ; **102**, fig. 127.

**Spring-hanger Iron.** A bent bar of iron or knee fastened to a pedestal timber or wheel-piece, and to which the spring-hangers are attached. See **171**, fig. 82.

**Spring-padlock.** A padlock, the hasp of which is locked without a key when pressed into the lock.

**Spring-plank.** A transverse timber underneath a truck-bolster and on which the bolster-springs rest. See **43**, figs. 91–104, 108–129. Also see *Framed Spring-plank. Swing Spring-plank.*

**Spring-plank Bearing.** A casting on which a spring-plank rests, and which is supported by the lower swing-hanger pivot. See **44**, figs. 108–127.

**Spring-plank Safety-strap.** A **U**-shaped strap of iron attached to the transoms of a truck, and which embraces or passes under the spring-plank, so as to hold it up in case the swing-hangers or their attachments should break. See **45**, figs. 118–126.

**Spring-plank Timber.** A timber forming one of the sides of a framed spring-plank. See fig. 134.

**Spring-pocket.** See *Draw-bar Spring-pocket.*

**Spring-pocket Draw-bar.** A draw-bar with an opening or "pocket" at the back end in which the draw-spring is placed. See figs. 257–259, 268, 269, 270.

**Spring-saddle.** A ∩-shaped bar of wrought-iron, which

is placed on top of a journal-box and on which a spring rests. See **103**, fig. 127. On street-cars it has projecting ledges, thus ⌂, and the springs rest on the ledges on each side of the box. See **7**, fig. 750.

**Spring-seat.** A plate or cup-shaped piece of cast or wrought iron on which the bottom of a spring rests. See *Bolster-spring Seat. Equalizing-bar Spring-seat. Spiral-spring Seat.*

**Spring-shelf.** A ledge or bracket cast on the side of a journal-box of a street-car and on which a side journal-box spring rests.

**Spring-stud.** A round iron bar which rests on the top of the journal-box or spring-seat of street-cars and passes through the centre of a spiral or rubber spring. The upper end works in a guide and thus holds the spring in its place. A similar bar has been used on steam-cars for transmitting the weight from the spring to the journal-box.

**Spring Window-holder.** A metal spring which is attached to a window-post to hold up a window or window-blind. See fig. 305.

**Spring-yoke.** A *Spring-saddle*, which see.

**Sprue.** The piece of metal which fills the gate or channel through which the metal is poured in making a casting. This piece is broken off when the casting is cooled. The *gate* of a mould is often called a sprue.

**Sprue-hole.** A *gate* of a mould for casting metals.

**Squab-cushion.** A cushion formed of a bag or case stuffed with curled hair or other elastic material. Such cushions are not attached to the seat, but are loose, and laid on the seat-bottom.

**Square-bar Spiral-spring.** A spiral-spring made of a square bar of metal. See figs. 194, 195.

**Square Door-bolt.** A door-bolt made of a square bar of metal. See fig. 514.

**Square Neck-door-bolt.** A door-bolt made of a square bar of metal, and with an offset, or "neck," in the bar, as shown in fig. 515.

**Staff.** See *Brake-staff. Ventilator-staff.*

**Stake.** A stick of wood attached to the side or end of a platform-car to keep the material with which it is loaded from falling off. See **1, 1**, fig. 21.

**Stake-hook.** A hook on the side of a platform-car to hold a stake in an upright position. See **3**, fig. 21.

**Stake-pocket.** A cast-iron receptacle attached to the side or end of a platform or flat car to receive the end of a stake. See **1, 1**, figs. 19, 20, 86, 87.

**Stake-pocket U-bolt.** A U-bolt used for fastening stake-pockets to the sides of platform-cars. See **2**, fig. 86.

**Stake-rest.** A bracket or support on which a stake of a platform-car rests when it is turned down horizontally. See **2**, fig. 21.

**Stake-sleeve.** A casting with an opening to receive a stake, and a horn-shaped projection to hold the hinged side of a platform or gondola car. The sleeve is placed on the stake, as shown at **2**, fig. 87.

**Stanchion.** The primary meaning of this term is a prop or support. On shipboard it is used to designate a metal post hanger or support with an eye in one end which carries a rope, railing, etc. As applied to car and locomotive work it has a similar meaning, and is used to designate a metal post or hanger with an eye in one end, which holds a rod or other object, as a hand-rail or curtain-rod. The opposite end is usually fastened by a nut, or with a flange or lugs which form a part of the stanchion. See fig. 436. Also see *Window-curtain-rod Stanchion.*

**Stand.** "Something on which a thing rests or is laid."—*Webster.* See

   *Radiator-stand.*       *Seat-stand.*
   *Revolving-chair Stand.*    *Wash-bowl Stand.*
          *Water-cooler Stand.*

**Standard Car-axle.** See *Master Car-builders' Standard-axle.*

**Standard,** *for Cross-bar of Creamer-brake.* An upright brace fastened to the platform of a car and which supports one of the cross-bars. See **14**, fig. 646.

**Standard-gauge.** The usual distance between the rails of railroads in this country, which is 4 ft. 8½ in. See *Gauge.*

**Standard System of Screw-threads.** See *Sellers System of Screw-threads,* also called the *Franklin Institute System of Screw-threads, Pipe-threads,* and *United States Standard System of Screw-threads. Whitworth System of Screw-threads.*

**Staple.** A U-shaped piece of wrought-iron pointed at the ends to be driven into wood to hold a hasp, hook, pin, etc.

**Stay.** A beam, bar, rod, etc., by which two or more objects are connected together to prevent lateral deviation of one or both of them. See

   *Body Queen-post Stay.*     *Pipe-stay.*
   *Lamp-stay.*           *Sill-step Stay.*

**Stay-rod.** A rod which acts as a stay. See *Pedestal Stay-rod.*

**Steam-car.** A term used to designate cars drawn in trains by steam-power, to distinguish them from street-cars, which are usually drawn by animal power.

**Steam-cylinder,** *for Westinghouse-brake.* A hollow cast-iron cylinder which is accurately bored out on the inside to receive a piston which works the air-pump for a Westinghouse-brake. The cylinder has suitable passages cast with it for admitting and exhausting the steam. See **3**, figs. 655, 656, 664, 665 ; fig. 667.

**Steam-cylinder Head**, *for Westinghouse-brake*. A cast-iron cover for the top of the steam-cylinder of the engine used to work the air-pump of a Westinghouse-brake. See **2**, figs. 664, 665 ; fig. 666.

**Steam-pipe**, *for Engine of Westinghouse-brake*. A pipe for conveying steam from the boiler to the steam-cylinder of the engine and air-pump. See 6, fig. 655 ; 45, fig. 664, 665.

**Steam-piston**, *for Engine of Westinghouse-brake*. An arrangement of a cast-iron disc with packing-rings, etc., made so as to fit air-tight and work up and down in the steam-cylinder of an engine for a Westinghouse-brake. See **7′**, fig. 665 ; fig, 671. The cast-iron disc is called a *piston-head*.

**Steam Piston-head**, *for Engine of Westinghouse-brake*. A short cast-iron cylinder or disc with grooves turned in the edge to receive packing-rings, and which forms the main portion of the piston in a steam-cylinder. See **7′**, figs. 665, 671.

**Steam-valve**, *for Engine of Westinghouse-brake*. See *Upper and Lower Main Steam-valves*.

**Steam-valve Bushing**. See *Upper and Lower Steam-valve Bushing*.

**Steeled-wheel**. A wheel made of cast-iron to which a proportion of steel has been added. The process has been patented by Mr. W. G. Hamilton.

**Steel-tired Wheel**. A wheel with a steel tire. In some cases, the tire is welded to the body or centre of the wheel. which is made of cast iron. Usually, however, it is either bolted or shrunk on. Figs. 174–177 and 180–183 represent steel-tired wheels.

**Steel-wheel**. A wheel which is made wholly of steel. See figs. 178, 179.

**Stem**. See *Buffer-stem*. *Graduating-stem*. *Reversing-valve Stem*.

**Step**. 1. A ledge in stairs, or a round or rung in a ladder.

2. A foot-piece for ascending or descending to or from a car or other vehicle, or for standing in certain places or positions.

3. The bottom support on which the lower end of a timber or of an upright shaft or wheel rests. See

| | |
|---|---|
| *Box-steps.* | *Longitudinal-step.* |
| *Brake-shaft Step.* | *Platform-steps.* |
| *Brake-step.* | *Roof-step.* |
| *Enclosed-step.* | *Side-step.* |
| *End-step.* | *Sill-step.* |

*Tank-step.*

**Step Hand-rail**. One or two rails attached to the step of a street-car when no platform is used. The rails are attached at the lower ends to the step and extend up diagonally, and are fastened at their upper ends to the door-posts. See **2,** fig. 41.

**Step-hanger.** A wrought-iron rod or bar by which the steps are supported from the corner of a car and from the platform-timber. See **48,** figs. 215, 217, 219, 223.

**Step-iron.** A flat iron bar, which is bent so as to conform to the shape of the platform-steps and their risers and to which they are fastened. It is bolted at the upper end to the platform-timber. See **47,** figs. 215, 217, 219, 223.

**Step-railing.** An iron bar attached to posts on the back end of a street-car step, on which there is no platform, to assist passengers in getting on and off the car. It also prevents passengers from being thrown off the step if the car is started suddenly.

**Step-riser.** The vertical portion of a step in stairs. See **5,** fig. 244.

**Stevens Brake.** An arrangement of brake-levers invented by F. A. Stevens and patented in 1852. It consists of two levers on each truck, the short arms of which are connected together by a rod in the usual way, the long arm on one of these, on each truck, is connected by a rod and chain with the brake-shaft, and the long arms of the other two are connected together by a rod so that the brakes can be applied from either end of the car, and the pressure is equalized on all the wheels. See fig. 643.

**Stile.** An upright piece on the outer edge of framing or paneling, as of a door or sash. See

    *Door-stile.*              *Window-blind Stile.*
    *Sash-stile.*              *Window-stile.*

**Stirrup.** A kind of ring or bent bar of iron resembling somewhat the stirrup of a saddle. See *Draw-bar Stirrup.*

**Stirrup-block,** *for Miller-platform.* A block attached to one of the centre-sills next to the platform end-timber, to receive the bolts which hold the draw-bar stirrup. See **30,** figs. 282, 283.

**Stock-car.** A *Cattle-car,* which see.

**Stop.** That which prevents or limits the movement of any object. See

| | |
|---|---|
| *Brake-lever Stop.* | *Seat-back Curved-stop.* |
| *Blind-stop.* | *Seat-back Round-stop.* |
| *Centre-stop.* | *Seat-back Stop.* |
| *Closed-door Stop.* | *Ventilator-stop.* |
| *Door-stop.* | *Window-blind Stop.* |
| *Draw-bar Stop.* | *Window-latch Lower-* |
| *Draw-spring Stop.* |   *Stop.* |
| *Inside Window-stop.* | *Window-latch Stop.* |
| *Open-door Stop.* | *Window-latch Upper-* |
| *Outside Window-stop.* |   *Stop.* |
| *Sash-stop.* | *Window-stop.* |

**Stop,** *for Miller Coupling-hook.* A casting attached to the platform end-timbers of a car for the purpose of limiting the lateral movement of the hook on the adjoining car. See **13**, figs. 282, 284, 285.

**Stop-bolt.** See *Discharge-valve Stop-bolt.*

**Stop-brace,** *for Miller Coupling-hook.* An iron bar attached to the lower end of a stop, and extending backward and upward and fastened at the other end to one of the draw-timbers. See **14**, figs. 282–285.

**Stop-cock,** *for Brake-pipe of Westinghouse-brake.* A faucet attached to the brake-pipe of a Westinghouse automatic-brake so that the pipe can be closed if the brake-hose are uncoupled. In the latter case, if the compressed-air is allowed to escape from the brake-pipe, the brakes would be applied. The stop-cock is used to prevent the brakes from being applied in case a car is detached from the train. See **29**, fig. 661 ; fig. 733.

**Stop Journal-bearing.** A journal-bearing with a lug or projection which bears against the end of the axle to resist its lateral motion and wear. See fig. 145.

**Stop-key.** See *Journal-bearing Stop-key.*

**Stop-key Journal-bearing.** A journal-bearing which has a key to which a stop-plate is attached to resist the lateral motion and end-wear of the axle. See figs. 147–150.

**Stop-latch.** A spring door-latch with an attachment by which the latch can be fastened on one side. See figs. 527, 528. Also see *Saloon Stop-latch.*

**Stop-plate,** *for Journal.* A metal plate in the inside of a journal-box which forms an end-bearing for the axle and checks its end-motion. The plate is either held in position by flanges cast in the box, or is attached to the journal-bearing or its key. See **3**, figs. 146, 148, 149.

**Stop-wedge.** See *Journal-bearing Stop-key. Stop-key Journal-bearing.*

**Stove.** An apparatus made usually of iron variously constructed, in which a fire is made for warming a room, house, or car by direct radiation. See **128**, figs. 216, 220 ; figs. 543–548. When the warming is effected by convection, as with warm air, hot water, etc., the apparatus is called a *heater.* See

*Chilson Stove.*              *Egg-shaped Stove.*
*Cylindrical Stove.*          *Spear Stove.*
              *Winslow Car-stove.*

**Stove-pipe.** A tube, usually of sheet-iron, for conveying the smoke from a stove or heater and for creating a draft through the fire.

**Stove-pipe Damper.** A valve in the stove-pipe for regulating the draft of air through the fire.

**Stove-pipe Damper-handle.** A handle for moving a stove-pipe damper.

**Stove-pipe Jack.** A covering or bonnet for the aperture of a stove-pipe on the outside of a car. See **129**, fig. 218 ; **5**, figs. 550–553.

**Stove-pipe Ring.** A metal plate or ring attached to the ceiling of a passenger-car around the opening through which the stove-pipe passes from the inside to the outside of the car. It is used for ornament or "to make a finish" around the opening for the stove-pipe. See fig. 549.

**Stove-plate.** See *Bottom Stove-plate.*

**Stove-ring.** A *Stove-pipe Ring,* which see.

**Straight-tank,** *for Tank-car.* A cylindrical tank made with two rings or plates of metal placed alternately inside and outside of each other, as in fig. 73. See also *Telescope-tank.*

**Strainer.** See *Air-strainer.*

**Straining-rod.** See *Brace Straining-rod.*

**Strap.** A long narrow strip of leather, cloth, or metal. See

| | |
|---|---|
| *Axle Safety-strap.* | *Door-strap.* |
| *Bell-cord Strap.* | *Double Pipe-strap.* |
| *Bell-strap.* | *Hand-strap.* |
| *Brake Safety-strap.* | *Pipe-strap.* |
| *Dash-guard Strap.* | *Roof-strap.* |
| *Diagonal Roof-strap.* | *Safety-strap.* |

*Signal-strap.*

**Strap,** *for Drop-door Beam.* A wrought-iron band attached to the top of a drop-door beam and extending downward on the outside of the car to strengthen the connection of the beam with the sides of the car, and protect it from wear in loading the car. See **127**, figs. 77–79.

**Strap,** *or* **Lug-bolt.** A round bolt with a flat bar of iron welded to it, and usually with a hook on the end which serves the purpose of a head. Sometimes the flat bar has holes in it, by which it is attached to a piece of timber or other object by one or more separate bolts or screws. See fig. 780.

**Strap-hanger.** See *Bell-cord Double Strap-hanger. Bell-cord Strap-hanger.*

**Strap-hinge.** A door-hinge the two parts of which are made longer than those of a butt-hinge, and of a triangular shape. See fig. 512.

**Street-car.** A light car, usually with four wheels, constructed for carrying passengers on street-railroads and generally drawn by horses. See figs. 36–42. See

| | |
|---|---|
| *Double-deck Street-car.* | *One-horse Street-car.* |
| *Excursion Street-car.* | *Reversible Street-car.* |
| *Fare-box Street-car.* | *Summer Street-car.* |

*Top-seat Street-car.*

**Street-car Axle.** A light axle used under street-cars. See **2**, figs. 750–753.

**Street-car Wheel.** A light cast-iron, single-plate wheel made for street-cars. See figs. 170–173 ; **1**, figs. 750, 753. See also *Open-plate Wheel.*

**Striker.** See *Match-striker.*

**Striker-arm.** A *Seat-back Arm*, which see.

**Striker-plate.** A *keeper* for a door latch or lock. See *Keeper.* *Door-latch Keeper.*

**String-board.** A vertical board which supports the ends of passenger-car steps.

**Stringer.** In *Carpentry* : " A horizontal timber connecting posts in a frame, as a tie-timber of a truss-bridge ; a horizontal tie in a floor-framing."—*Knight.* This term is often applied to the *Floor-timbers*, which see.

**Strip.** See

    *Diagonal Roof-strip.*        *Parting-strip*
    *Lining-strip.*             *Roof-strip.*
    *Panel-strip.*           *Sash-parting Strip.*

**Strut.** An inclined bar, beam, or member of a frame. A truss or girder, etc., which is subjected to a strain of compression. A vertical strut in a truss, etc., is called a post ; **8, 9,** in figs. 805, 807, 809, are struts.

**Stud.** 1. In *Building* : " A small piece of timber or joist inserted in the sills and beams between the posts to support the beams or other main timbers. The boards on the outside and the laths on the inside of a building are also nailed to the studs."—*Webster.*

    2. In car construction, a short vertical wooden post placed between the window-posts in the sides or ends of passenger and street cars below the windows. They ex-

tend from the sills to the window-sills. See 60, figs. 215, 221 ; **16,** fig. 750.

    3. A standing bolt, pin, boss, or protuberance designed to hold an attached object in place. See

    *Brake-block Suspending-*    *Eccentric-lever Stud.*
      *stud.*                    *Spring-stud.*
           *Suspending-stud.*

**Stud,** *for Jointed Side-pawl of Creamer-brake.* A standing bolt attached to the cross-bars which acts as a pivot for the jointed side-pawl. See **13,** fig. 646.

**Suburban Excursion-car.** A car with open sides and ends, which may be closed with curtains or blinds, for carrying passengers on suburban steam-roads in summer. See fig. 9.

**Summer Street-car.** A street-car with open sides and ends, which may be closed with curtains. Such cars are used on street-railroads for summer travel. See figs. 39, 40.

**Summer Street-car Curtain.** A cloth, usually made of heavy canvas, to inclose open cars and exclude rain or sunshine. Shown in figs. 39, 40.

**Sun-burner,** *for Mineral-oil Lamp.* A lamp-burner which is provided with a chimney, which is wide at its base, and is held in its place by a thin circular metal plate, cut with indentations around its outer edge, which act as springs to hold the chimney in its place. See fig. 479.

**Supply-pipe,** *of Air-pump for Westinghouse-brake.* A pipe through which the air enters the air-pump. See **8, 8,** fig. 655 ; **47,** figs. 664, 665.

**Support.** "That which upholds, sustains, or keeps from from falling, as a prop, a pillar, a foundation of any kind."—*Webster.* See *Cylinder-lever Support. Drum-support. Pipe-support.*

**Suspender-beam,** *for Miller-platform.* A short transverse piece of timber framed into the draw-bar timbers underneath the end-sill of a car-body. See **29,** fig. 284.

**Suspending-link.** See *Brake - block Suspending - link. Swing-hanger.*

**Suspending-plate.** See *Brake-block Suspending-plate.*

**Suspending-stud.** See *Brake-block Suspending-stud.*

**Sweeper.** See *Sweeping-car.*

**Sweeping-car.** A car with rotary brooms for sweeping snow from a railroad track. The brooms are attached to a horizontal shaft which is connected by suitable gearing with the axles, and the brooms are thus made to revolve. See fig. 33.

**Swing-beam.** See *Swing-bolster. Swing Spring-plank.*

**Swing-bolster.** A truck bolster which bears on springs that are supported by a transverse timber called a spring-plank which is suspended by hangers or links, so that it can swing laterally to the truck. As the springs rest on this plank and they support the bolster, the latter can swing with the spring-plank. The object of providing this swinging motion to the bolster is to prevent, as much as possible, the lateral blows and shocks to which the truck is subjected from being communicated to the car-body, and, *vice-versa*, to prevent the momentum of the car-body from acting with its full force on the truck. See **30,** figs. 108–129.

**Swing-bolster Spring.** See *Lateral-motion Spring.*

**Swing-hangers.** Bars or links of iron which are attached at their upper ends to the transoms of a swing-motion truck, and by which the spring-plank is suspended to the lower ends so that it can swing laterally. They are made in different ways. Sometimes they consist of solid bars with an eye at each end ; in other cases, they are made like a link of a chain, and are then called *Swing Link-hangers,* which see. They are also made with a fork or clevis at one end and a boss at the other. See **46,** figs. 108–129.

**Swing-hanger Friction-block.** A casting, or bearing, on which the upper end of a swing link-hanger rests. See **50,** figs. 116, 117.

**Swing-hanger Pivot.** An iron pin, bolt, or bar, by which a swing-hanger is suspended, or which supports a spring-plank. See *Lower Swing-hanger Pivot. Upper Swing-hanger Pivot.*

**Swing-hanger Pivot-bearing.** An eye-bolt, iron plate,

or casting attached to a transom, on which the upper swing-hanger pivot rests, or by which it is attached to the transom. See **49**, figs. 108–129.

**Swing-hanger Shaft.** A *Swing-hanger Pivot*, which see.

**Swinging-sash.** A window or blind sash which is hung and swings on hinges. See *Door-case Sash*.

**Swing Link-hanger.** A swing-hanger made in the form of a link of a chain. See **46**, fig. 117 ; fig. 137.

**Swing-motion.** A term applied to an arrangement of hangers and other supports for the springs and truck-bolster which enables a car-body to swing laterally on the truck.

**Swing-motion Gear.** The combination of the bolster, spring-plank, swing-hangers, pivots, and pins by which a car-body is suspended on a truck and enabled to swing laterally.

**Swing-motion Spring.** A *Bolster-spring*, which see. See also *Lateral-motion Spring*.

**Swing-motion Truck.** A truck with a bolster and spring-plank suspended on swing-hangers so that they can swing laterally to the truck-frame. Figs. 108–129 are representations of *swing-motion trucks*.

**Swing Spring-plank.** A transverse timber underneath the bolster of a four-wheeled truck, and under the spring-beam of a six-wheeled truck, and on which the body-springs rest. A *swing spring-plank* differs from an or-dinary spring-plank from the fact of being supported by hangers or links so that it can swing laterally to the truck, while an ordinary spring-plank has no such movement. See **43**, figs. 108–129.

**Switching.** The act of moving cars from one track to another by means of switches, as in making up or sepa-rating trains, and placing the cars on the tracks and in the places where they are needed. See also *Drilling. Regulating. Shunting.*

**Switching-eye.** A cast-iron socket attached to the corner of a freight-car, to which the hook of a chain or a push-ing-bar can be attached, to move the car either by horses or by an engine on an adjoining track. Such eyes are often cast on a lower corner-plate, as shown in fig. 279. A *pull-iron* is sometimes called a switching-eye.

# T

**T,** *or* **Tee.** A **T**-shaped, cast-iron tube for uniting one pipe at right angles to two others in the same line. The pipes are screwed into the arms of the **T**. See fig. 621. Also see *Reducing-tee*.

**Table.** See *Water-table*.

**Table-hook.** A hook attached to a movable table for fastening it to the side of a car. Such tables are fur-nished in drawing-room, sleeping and smoking cars, for

**TAB**  161  **TAN**

the convenience of passengers. See **19**, fig. 298 ; fig. 394.

**Table-hook Plate.** An eye or plate on the side of a passenger-car to which a hook on a movable table is attached. See **20**, fig. 298 ; fig. 395.

**Table-leg Hook.** A metal hook which is attached to a diagonal support for a table, and which engages in a plate attached to the side of the car. See **40**, fig. 300. Similar to fig. 394.

**Table-leg-hook Plate.** A plate attached to the side of a car and which forms an eye or fastening in which a table-leg hook engages. See **41**, fig. 400. Similar to fig. 395.

**Tail-lamp.** A signal-lamp attached to the rear end of a train. See **141**, figs. 82, 83 ; figs. 495, 496. Also see *Double-lens Tail-lamp. Train Signal-lamp.*

**Tank.** A vessel or reservoir of considerable size to contain fluids. See.

    *Shad-bellied Tank.*      *Telescopic-tank.*
    *Straight-tank.*        *Water-tank.*

**Tank,** *for Tank-car.* A sheet or plate iron vessel, usually of cylindrical form, for carrying oil or other liquids on cars specially constructed for the purpose. See **106**, figs. 73–76. See also *Telescopic-tank. Straight-tank.*

**Tank-band.** A flat strip or bar of iron which passes over the top of a tank for a tank-car, and through the frame for holding the former to the latter. Sometimes these bands are fastened to a hook or eye attached to the top of the tank. See **107**, figs. 73–76.

**Tank-band Hook.** An iron hook riveted to the top of a tank for a tank-car, to which the tank-bands are fastened. The object in attaching the bands in this way is to prevent the tank from turning.

**Tank-car.** A car provided with one or more tanks for carrying oil or other liquids. Usually the tank is made of iron, and is cylindrical in form, as shown in figs. 22, 73–76.

**Tank-dome.** A cylindrical extension attached to the top of a tank for a tank-car. See **108**, figs 73–76.

**Tank-head.** An iron sheet or plate which forms the head or end of a tank. See **106′**, figs. 93–96.

**Tank-nozzle.** A short pipe which is attached to the under side of a tank for transporting oil or other liquids. The pipe is used to draw-off or empty the contents from the tank. See **115**, figs, 93, 96. It is usually cast in one piece with the *Tank-valve Seat*, which see.

**Tank-nozzle Cap.** A cover which is screwed on the outer end of a tank-nozzle to prevent the escape of the contents of the tank in case the valve should leak. See **118**, figs. 93, 96.

**Tank-nozzle-cap Chain.** A chain by which a tank-nozzle cap is fastened to the nozzle to prevent it from being lost.

**Tank-step,** *for Tank-car.* A metal shelf or bracket fastened to a tank of a tank-car, which forms a step to give access to the top of the tank or the top of the dome.

**Tank-valve.** A valve, attached to the bottom of a tank for transporting oil or other liquids, to draw off the contents of the tank. See **114,** figs. 73, 76.

**Tank-valve Cage.** A metal inclosure over the top of a tank-valve, and which forms a guide in which the valve works. See **116,** figs. 73, 76.

**Tank-valve Rod.** A rod for opening and closing a tank-valve and which extends from the valve to the top of the dome. See **117,** figs. 73, 76.

**Tank-valve-rod Handle.** A lever which can be attached or detached to or from the top of the valve-rod of a tank-car to turn it, and thus open or close the tank-valve.

**Tank-valve Seat.** A metal plate, with one opening in it, which is closed by the valve. It is riveted to the under side of the tank and has a nozzle attached to it to which suitable pipes are connected for conducting the oil or other liquid from the tank. See **115,** figs. 73, 76.

**Tanner-brake.** An arrangement of levers and rods for operating the brakes on both trucks at the same time, which is said to be the invention of Mr. Henry Tanner and which was patented by him in 1852. It is illustrated in fig. 644. It consists of a lever, **9,** having a fixed fulcrum in its centre attached to the body of the car. The ends of this lever are connected by rods and chains, **4, 4,** with the brake-shafts at the two ends of the car ; and at points intermediate between the ends and the fulcrum the lever is connected by rods, **6, 6,** with the brake-levers, **2, 2.** The centre-lever, **9,** can thus be operated and the brakes be applied to both trucks by the brake-shaft and wheel at either end of the car. A difficulty with this form of brake is, that unless the adjustment of the connecting-rods and brake-shoes is perfect the pressure of the brakes will not be alike on the two trucks.

**Tarpaulin.** A painted, oiled, or tarred cloth or canvas used on open cars to protect freight from the weather.

**Tassel.** See *Window-curtain Tassel.*

**Tassel-hook.** See *Window-curtain Holder.*

**Tee.** See **T.**

**Telegraph-cock,** *or* **Faucet.** A self-closing cock, the lever of which resembles the key of a telegraph instrument. See *Lever-faucet.* When these are arranged to attach to the side of a vessel they are called *horizontal telegraph-faucets,* as shown at fig. 428. When they are made, as shown at fig. 382, so as to attach to the top, they are called *vertical telegraph cocks* or *faucets.*

**Telescopic-tank,** *for Tank-car.* A cylindrical tank made with the rings or plates of metal in the centre on the outside, while those toward the ends are placed inside of those nearest the centre, analogous to the manner in which the tubes of a telescope slide into each other.

**Tender-hose,** *for Westinghouse-brake.* A hose which connects the brake-pipe on the tender with the engine, and which has no coupling, and is usually attached to the engine or tender by a union-joint. See **11,** figs. 655, 656 ; fig. 743.

**Tender-spring Bracket,** *for Westinghouse-brake.* A cast-iron bracket which is bolted to the tender-frame and which acts as a bearing for a release-spring. See fig. 744.

**Tension-bar.** A bar which is subjected to a strain of tension. See *Body-bolster Tension-bar.*

**Tension-member.** A rod, bar, or beam which is subjected to a tensile strain and forms a part of a frame, truss, beam, or girder. *Truss-rods, brace-rods,* etc., are tension members. See *Compression-member.*

**Thimble.** 1. A bushing.

2. A sleeve or tube through which a bolt passes, and which may act as a distance-piece. See

    *Axle Safety-bearing        Body-bolster Thimble.*
    *Thimble.                    Brake-shaft Thimble.*
                    *Buffer-thimble.*

**T-hinge.** A door-hinge, one part of which is made long and triangular-shaped, like a strap-hinge, and the other part like a butt-hinge, so that the shape of the whole resembles a letter **T.** See fig. 513.

**Thread.** See *Screw-thread.*

**Three-link Draw-bar.** A draw-bar to which three coupling-links may be attached. One of these is usually fastened to the draw-bar by a pin, riveted fast, so that the link cannot be detached. This is the same as a *Potter Draw-bar,* which see. See figs. 261–264, 269.

**Three-way Cock,** *for Westinghouse-brake.* A cock on the locomotive by which the runner either releases or admits the compressed-air from or to the brake-pipes, and thus either applies the brakes or takes them off, as required. See **10,** fig. 657 ; figs. 658, 659.

**Three-wheeled Hand-car.** A hand-car with two wheels arranged to run on one rail, somewhat like a velocipede, but with a third wheel running on the opposite rail to steady the vehicle. They are worked either with levers operated by the hands, or by treadles with the feet, or with both. See fig. 47.

**Threshold,** *or* **Threshold-plate.** A *Door-sill,* which see.

**Throttle-valve,** *for Westinghouse Engine and Pump.* An angle globe-valve, attached to the locomotive for admitting steam to and shutting it off from the engine, which works the air pump. See fig. 736.

**Ticket-holder.** A metal clip or spring attached to the side of a sleeping-car berth for holding the tickets of the occupants of the berth. See fig. 377.

**Tie.** " A beam or rod which secures parts together and is subjected to a tensile strain. It is the opposite of a strut or straining-piece, which acts to keep objects apart, and is subject to a compressing force."—*Knight*.

**Tie-bar.** A bar which acts as a tie. See *Draw-timber Tie-bar*. *Pedestal Tie-bar*. *Transom Tie-bar*.

**Tie-plate.** A *Main-carline*, which see.

**Tie-rod.** A rod which acts as a tie. See

| | |
|---|---|
| *Brake-block Tie-rod.* | *Lever-frame Tie-rod.* |
| *Cylinder-lever Tie-rod.* | *Platform Tie-rod.* |
| *End-girth Tie-rod.* | *Safety-beam Tie-rod.* |
| *Girth Tie-rod.* | *Sill Tie-rod.* |

*Wheel-piece Tie-rod.*

**Tie-timber.** See *Cross-frame Tie-timber*.

**Tightener.** See *Window-curtain-cord Tightener*.

**Timber.** A stick of wood of considerable size. See

| | |
|---|---|
| *Brake-hanger Timber.* | *Pedestal-timber.* |
| *Centre Floor-timber.* | *Platform End-timber.* |
| *Cross frame Tie-timber.* | *Platform-timber.* |
| *Diagonal Floor-timber.* | *Rocker-bearing Timber.* |
| *Draw-bar Cross-timber.* | *Rocker-timber.* |
| *Draw-timber.* | *Short Floor-timber.* |
| *Floor-timber.* | *Spring-plank Timber.* |
| *Intermediate Floor-timber.* | *Transverse Floor-timber.* |
| *Wheel-timber.* | |

**Tin Car-roof.** A roof consisting of a layer of boards which rest on the rafters and run lengthwise to the car and are covered with tin plates the edges of which are soldered together.

**Tip.** An ornamental knob or boss attached to the end of a rod. See *Basket-rack Tip*. *Berth Curtain-rod Tip*.

**Tip-car.** A car so constructed that its body can be tipped or inclined so as to allow its contents to slide out. Sometimes called *dump-car*. For *Four-wheeled Tip-car*, see fig. 29 ; for *Eight-wheeled Tip-car*, see fig. 28.

**Tip-car Door.** A door or gate on the side of a tip-car for unloading the contents of the car. See **154**, fig. 81.

**Tire.** A heavy hoop or band of iron forming the ring or periphery of a wheel to impart strength to it and to resist the wear on the rails. In this country car-wheels are generally cast in one piece without a separate tire, but within a few years steel-tired wheels have come into considerable use. See **5**, figs. 176–183.

**Tire-bolt.** A screw-bolt for holding a wheel-tire on a wheel-centre. When retaining rings are used the bolts pass through the rings and hold them and the centre and tire together. See **2**, figs. 176–183.

**Tool-car.** A box-car arranged for carrying all kinds of tools, ropes, etc., which are used, in case of accident to trains on the road, in replacing or removing the cars or engines on or from the track. Such cars are often used when any heavy objects are to be moved, as is necessary in erecting bridges, etc.

**Top.** See *Cast-iron Top. Smoke-top.*

**Top-arm,** *for Creamer-brake.* A cast-iron arm keyed to the brake-shaft, to which a pawl is attached which forms the connection between the drum and brake-shaft, and which acts on a ratchet on the drum-cover. By this means the involute spring is wound up by the action of the brake-shaft and wheel. See **4,** figs. 646, 647.

**Top-chord.** The upper outside member of a truss. See **13,** figs. 804, 806–810. (The distinction between a *top-chord* and *braces* or between a *top-chord* and a *truss-rod,* in trusses like those represented in figs. 805, 811, is not very clear.)

**Top Cylinder-head,** *for Westinghouse Driving-wheel Brake.* A circular cast-iron plate or cover for the upper end of a cylinder for a driving-wheel brake. See **5,** fig. 749.

**Top Door-rail.** The uppermost horizontal bar or piece of a door-frame. See **149,** figs. 218, 222, 223, 230 ; **4,** fig. 502 ; **82,** fig. 753.

**Top Door-track.** A metal bar or guide at the top of a door on which it slides or by which it is held in its place. See **65,** figs. 60, 63, 64, 69–72.

**Top End-rail,** *for Coal-car.* A horizontal stick of timber which forms the top of the end-frame of a coal-car. See **137,** figs. 77–79.

**Top-plate.** See *Outside Top-plate.*

**Top-reservoir Journal-box.** A journal-box having a res- ervoir for oil or grease above the journal, from which the oil flows to the journal. See fig. 153.

**Top-ring,** *for Base-plate of Spear-heater.* A cast-iron ring which rests on top of the base-plate, and to which the casing is attached. See **22,** figs. 550–554 ; fig. 562.

**Top-seat Street-car.** A *Double-deck Street-car,* which see. See fig. 38.

**Top Side-bearing.** A *Body Side-bearing,* which see.

**Top Side-rail,** *of Coal-car.* The horizontal piece of timber which forms the top of the side of a coal-car. See **136,** figs. 77–79.

**Towel-bracket.** A bracket for supporting a towel-roller. See **2,** fig. 380.

**Towel-rack.** One or more rods or arms arranged for hanging towels on.

**Towel-rod.** A rod for hanging towels on. See figs. 378, 379.

**Track.** A rail or bar which forms a path on which anything, as a door, runs. See *Bottom Door-track. Top Door-track.*

**Track-sweeper.** A *Sweeping-car,* which see.

**Train-car.** A *Conductor's-car,* which see.

**Train of Cars.** A number of cars coupled together.

**Train Signal-lamp.** A lamp attached to a car as a signal, usually to the last one on a train. See **141,** figs. 82, 83 ; figs. 495, 496. See *Double-lens Tail-lamp. Tail-lamp.*

**Train Signal-lantern.** A *lantern* used for giving signals at night either to or from trains. Ordinary railroad lanterns are often used for that purpose, but they sometimes have globes of colored glass. See *Tri-colored Lantern.*

**Transom.** One or two horizontal cross-beams which are attached to the side-frames of a truck and between which the swing-bolster is placed. The transoms are usually made of wood, but recently they have been made of iron. See **20**, figs. 108–127. See *Middle-transoms. Outside-transoms.*

**Transom Bearing-block.** A piece of wood or iron placed on top of a transom, under the attachment or bearing of a swing-hanger, to raise it up higher.

**Transom-casting.** A casting attached to a truck-frame and to which the end of one or both of the transoms are fastened. See **28**, figs. 108–114.

**Transom Chafing-plate.** A plate attached to the side of a transom to prevent the motion of the swing-hangers, springs, and swing-bolster from abrading the transoms. See **27**, figs. 115, 116–129.

**Transom-pillar.** A small casting placed under a transom and resting on the lower truss-bar of an iron truck. It acts as a distance-piece between the two. See **29**, figs. 112, 114.

**Transom Tie-bar.** A wrought-iron bar bolted to a pair of transoms to hold them together. It is sometimes placed above and sometimes below the transoms. See **23**, figs. 118–126.

**Transom Truss-block.** A bearing or distance-piece, made of wood or iron, underneath a truck-transom, and against which a transom truss-rod bears. See **25**, figs. 91–93, 118–121, 128, 129.

**Transom Truss-rods.** Rods which are attached at their ends to the wheel-pieces, and which extend across the truck and alongside the transoms and are inclined downward toward the centre so as to strengthen the transoms. Generally, two such rods are used with each truck. See **24**, figs. 91–93, 118–129.

**Transom Truss-rod Washer.** An iron bearing for a nut on the end of a transom truss-rod. See **26**, figs. 91–93, 115–129.

**Transverse Floor-timbers.** Timbers which extend across the car underneath the floor and on which the latter rests. See **11**, figs. 73–76 ; **10**, figs. 750–752.

**Tread.** 1. The part of a step on which the foot is placed.

2. The outer surface or part of a car-wheel which bears on the rails. See **25**, fig. 138 See *Rubber-tread.*

**Tread-board.** The horizontal part or board of a step on which the foot is placed. See **46**, figs. 215, 216, 217, 219, 220, 223.

**Triangular Washer.** An iron plate or block, the cross-section of which is of a triangular shape, and which forms a bearing for the nut or head of an inclined brace-rod. See fig. 787.

**Tri-colored Lantern.** A lantern with a cylindrical case and an opening on one side only. This case is inclosed by another, containing glasses of different colors, and which can be turned so as to bring either glass in front of the opening and thus change the color of the light.

**Trigger.** See *Window-latch Trigger.*

**Trimming-cap.** A *Seat-back-rail Cap,* which see.

**Tripping-lever,** *for Creamer-brake.* A small lever by which the side-pawl is disengaged from the spring-drum. See 7, figs. 646, 647.

**Triple-coil Nest-spring.** A spiral-spring with two other coils inside of it. One of the coils is inside of the other. See figs. 191, 198.

**Triple Coupling-link.** Three coupling links attached to each other like the links of a chain. Such couplings are used when the draw-bars differ considerably in height. See 1, fig. 271.

**Triplet of Springs.** Three elliptic springs fastened together side by side so as to act together. See 80, figs. 115, 118, 119, 129.

**Triple-valve,** *for Westinghouse Automatic-brake.* A small slide-valve which is operated by a piston, the two being contained in a suitable body or case and placed between the auxiliary-reservoir and the brake-cylinder of Westinghouse Automatic-brake, for admitting the air from the former to the latter when the brakes are to be applied, and for releasing it from the brake-cylinder when the brakes are to be taken off. See 9, fig. 663; figs. 703, 704.

**Triple-valve Branch-pipe,** *for Westinghouse Automatic-brake.* A short pipe by which the triple-valve is connected with the brake-pipe. See 24, figs. 661, 663.

**Triple-valve Case,** *for Westinghouse Brake.* A casting with suitable chambers and passages cast in it, and which contains the working parts of a triple-valve. It forms the main body of what is called the triple-valve. See 20, figs. 703, 704.

**Triple-valve Piston,** *for Westinghouse Car-brake.* A small piston which operates a slide-valve, the two together forming the working parts of a triple-valve. See 4, fig. 704; fig. 706.

**Truck.** "A small wheel; hence, *trucks,* a low carriage for carrying goods. stone, etc., either on common roads or on railroads. Indeed, this kind of carriage is often called *a truck,* in the singular."—*Webster.* The term is applied to different kinds of small vehicles used on and about railroads, sometimes in a confusing sense. See

    *Baggage Barrow-truck.*      *Baggage Wagon-truck.*

*Barrow-truck.*

*Car-truck.*

*Cleveland-truck.*

*Continuous-frame Truck.*

*Diamond-truck.*

*Freight Barrow-truck.*

*Freight Wagon-truck.*

*Iron-truck.*

*Pair of Trucks.*

*Passenger-car Truck.*

*Rigid-bolster Truck.*

*Swing-motion Truck.*

*Wagon-truck.*

*Warehouse-truck.*

*Whole-frame Truck.*

*Wooden-frame Truck.*

**Truck-bolster.** A cross timber or beam in the centre of a truck to which the lower centre-plate is fastened, and on which the car-body rests. The truck-bolster is connected to the body-bolster by a centre-pin which passes through it. See **30**, figs. 88–128. The truck-bolster for a six-wheeled truck consists of a frame formed of two timbers at each end, called *spring-beams,* which rest on the springs, and one in the centre, called a *truck centre-beam,* to which the truck centre-plate is attached. All three are united together by longitudinal iron bars or wooden beams. This is represented in fig. 130. See *Swing-bolster.*

**Truck-bolster Chafing-plate.** A plate attached to a swing-bolster to protect it from wear. See **36,** figs. 115, 116, 124, 128, 129.

**Truck-bolster Guide-bars.** Iron castings in the iron side-frame of a truck, between the arch-bars, which form a guide for the end of the bolster. See **37,** figs.

95–104. These are not used with trucks which have a swing-motion, and only with rigid-bolster trucks when the latter have bolster-springs.

**Truck-bolster Guide-block.** A cast-iron shoe attached to a truck-bolster, and which slides vertically between the bolster guide-bars. See **38,** figs. 95–103. They are not used on trucks which have a swing-motion, and only with rigid-bolster trucks which have bolster-springs.

**Truck-bolster King-post.** A short pillar at the centre of a truck-bolster against which the truss-rod bears. See **33,** fig. 106.

**Truck-bolster Truss-block.** A block of wood or iron underneath a truck-bolster which acts as a bearing or distance-piece for one or more truss-rods. See **32,** figs. 98–104.

**Truck-bolster Truss-rod.** A rod attached near the ends of a wooden truck-bolster, usually with nuts, and which extends lengthwise to it, and passes below the bolster at the centre, so as to form a truss. Generally, two or more such rods are used for each bolster and are intended to strengthen it. See **31,** figs. 88–107.

**Truck-bolster Truss-rod Bearing.** An iron bearing placed under a truck-bolster truss-rod to prevent it from crushing into the bolster or truss-block. See **34,** figs. 88–90, 96–104.

**Truck-bolster Truss-rod Washer.** An iron bearing for a

nut on the end of the truss-rod of a truck-bolster. See **35,** figs. 88–90, 97–107.

**Truck Centre-plate.** A metal plate in the centre of the top of a truck-bolster on which the body centre-plate rests and which bears the weight of the car-body. The king-bolt, or centre-pin, passes through both centre-plates. See **63,** figs. 89–129.

**Truck Check-chain Eye.** An eye-bolt, clevis, or other similar attachment for fastening a check-chain to the the truck. See **70,** fig. 122. See also *Body Check-chain Eye.*

**Truck Check-chain Hook.** An iron hook, or similar form of attachment by which check-chains are fastened to a car-body. See **69,** fig. 122.

**Truck End-piece.** See *End-piece of Truck-frame.*

**Truck-frame.** A structure composed of wooden beams or iron bars, to which the journal-boxes or pedestals, springs, and other portions of a car-truck are attached, and which forms the skeleton of a truck. Such frames are shown in figs. 88–137. See *Continuous Truck-frame. Truck Side-frame.*

**Truck-frame King-post.** An iron post which forms a distance-piece between an inverted arch-bar and the main bar of a continuous-frame truck. See **18,** figs 105, 106.

**Truck-frame Queen-posts.** Short iron columns between an upper arch-bar or wheel-piece and an inverted arch-

bar, which act as distance-pieces between these two members. See **39,** fig. 91.

**Truck Knee-iron.** An ∟-shaped or right-angle casting or forging bolted into the inside corner of a truck-frame to strengthen it. See **81,** fig. 119.

**Truck-side.** A *Truck Side-frame,* which see.

**Truck Side-bearing.** A plate, block, or roller, which is attached to the top of a truck-bolster, and on which a corresponding bearing fastened to the body-bolster rests. Their purpose is to prevent the car-body from having too much rocking or rolling motion. *Truck Side-bearings* are made of various forms, such as a plain metal plate, to protect a wooden bolster from wear, a cup-shaped casting to hold oil or grease and waste, and various forms of rollers, balls, rockers, studs, and the like. See **61,** figs. 88–129. See

   *Cup Side-bearing.*      *Roller Side-bearing.*
   *Rocker Side-bearing.*    *Side-bearing.*

**Truck Side-frame.** The longitudinal portion of a truck-frame, on the outside of the wheels, which extends from one axle to the other and to which the journal-boxes and bolsters or transoms are attached. Such frames are shown in figs. 88–137, 131, 133. See *Diamond-truck Side-frame.*

**Truss.** A frame to which rigidity is given by uniting the parts so that its figure shall be incapable of alteration by turning of the bars about their joints. The simplest form of truss is that in which a rod and post are put underneath a beam to strengthen it, as in fig. 804, or two beams are framed together in the form of a letter **A**, and tied together at their lower ends by a rod or another beam, as shown in fig. 805. These are called *king-post trusses*. Another form is that in which two posts are used, as shown by figs. 806, 807, which are called *queen-post trusses*. In order to prevent this form of truss from altering its shape when unequally loaded, counter-braces, **11** and **9**, are added. The extension of the principle of the truss represented by fig. 806, that is, by the addition of more posts, gives the well-known form of truss represented by fig. 808, in which all the braces are subjected to strains of tension and the posts to compression. This is known as the *Pratt* or *Whipple truss*. The extension of the principle represented in fig. 807 gives the well-known *Howe-truss*, fig. 809, in which the braces are subjected to strains of compression, and the vertical members to tension. As cars are not so unequally loaded as bridges, the trusses used in car-frames usually have braces which incline in one direction only, from the centre to the point of support, as shown in figs, 215, 221, 229.

**Truss-arch.** A timber or plank made in the form of an arch, and set edgewise in the side of a passenger-car frame to strengthen it. See fig. 246.

**Truss-beam.** See *Platform Truss-beam.*

**Truss-block.** A distance-piece, between a truss-rod and the compression member of a trussed beam, and which forms a bearing for both. See **4**, figs. 810, 811. See *Body-bolster Truss-block. Transom Truss-block. Truck-bolster Truss-block.*

**Trussed Brake-beam.** A brake-beam trussed with suitable rods to strengthen it. See **4**, figs. 629, 631.

**Truss-plank.** A wide piece of timber bolted to and usually locked into the posts of a passenger-car frame, and placed on the inside of the car and immediately above the sills. See **63**, figs. 215–226 ; **1**, fig. 300.

**Truss-plank Cap.** A strip of wood attached to the top of a truss-plank between the seat-frames. See **64**, figs. 225, 226.

**Truss-rod.** An inclined rod used in connection with a king or queen post truss, or trussed-beam, to resist the deflection of the beam. It is attached to the ends of the beam, and is supported in the middle by a king-post, truss-block, or two queen-posts between the beam and the rod, See **1**, figs. 804, 810, 811. See.

| | |
|---|---|
| *Body-bolster Truss-rod.* | *Hand-car Truss-rod.* |
| *Body Truss-rod.* | *Inverted Body-truss-rod.* |
| *Brake-beam Truss-rod.* | *Outside Body-truss-rod.* |
| *Centre Body-truss-rod.* | *Platform Truss-rod.* |
| *Cross-frame Truss-rod.* | *Safety-beam Truss-rod.* |

*Transom Truss-rod.          Truck-bolster Truss-rod.*
*Wheel-piece Truss-rod.*

**Truss-rod Bearing.** An iron plate or casting on top of a truss-rod in which a king or queen post or truss-block rests, and which forms a bearing on the truss-rod. A *truss-rod saddle* is underneath a truss-rod and forms a bearing for the latter. See **3,** figs. 804, 810, 811. See also *Body-bolster Truss-rod Bearing. Body Truss-rod Bearing. Truck-bolster Truss-rod Bearing.*

**Truss-rod Iron.** A piece or bar of iron, having a lug, eye, or knuckle, to which a body truss-rod is attached, and which is bolted to the under side of a sill opposite or below a body-bolster. See **24,** figs. 228, 229, 231.

**Truss-rod Saddle.** A wrought or cast iron bearing underneath a truss-rod, and on which the latter bears. A *truss-rod bearing* is on top of a truss-rod. See *Body Truss-rod Saddle.*

**Truss-rod Washer.** A large flat or beveled washer used under a nut on the end of a truss-rod. Sometimes called a skew-back. See **2,** figs. 804, 806, 810, 811. See *Body-bolster Truss-rod Washer. Truck-bolster Truss-rod Washer.*

**Tumbler.** 1. A drinking glass.

2. (*Foundry :*) A machine for cleaning castings, locomotive-tubes, etc. It consists of a case mounted on a shaft on which it is made to revolve. The articles inside of the case are cleaned by their attrition against each other and the case.

3. (*Locksmithing :*) " A latch engaging within a notch in a lock, bolt, or otherwise, opposing its motion until it is lifted or arranged by the key so as to remove the obstacle."—*Knight.*

**Tumbler-holder.** A bracket or stand for holding glass tumblers or drinking-cups.

**Turnbuckle.** A coupling with a right and left hand screw, or with a screw and swivel used for shortening or lengthening rods. The commonest form is that of a link with a swivel and screw. See **23,** figs. 215, 216, 219, 228, 229 ; **26,** fig. 750 ; figs. 790–791. See *Right and Left Screw Turnbuckle. Pipe Turnbuckle. Single-screw Turnbuckle.*

**Twin Door-panels.** A pair of panels side by side in a door. See **10,** fig. 502 ; fig. 753.

**Twin-washer.** *A Double-washer,* which see.

**Twin-window.** Two small and rather narrow windows placed side by side. See **138,** figs. 228, 229.

# U

**U-Bolt.** A double bolt made of a bar of iron, bent in the shape of the letter **U,** with a nut and screw on each end. See fig. 781. See *Brake-hanger Carrier. Stake-pocket* **U**-bolt.

**Uncoupling-chain.** A chain by which the uncoupling lever of a Miller-coupler is connected with the coupling-hook or draw-bar. See **16,** fig. 285.

**Uncoupling-lever,** *for Miller-coupler.* A lever attached to the platform of a car, and connected by a chain with a Miller coupling-hook or draw-bar to disengage or uncouple it from the one on the adjoining car. See **15,** fig. 285, 286.

**Uncoupling-lever Plate.** A plate attached to the top of the platform end-timber of a Miller-platform, and through which the uncoupling-lever works. See **18,** fig. 285, 286.

**Uncoupling-lever Ratchet.** A ratchet into which the uncoupling-lever of a Miller-coupler engages, and which holds the lever in any desired position. The ratchet is attached to the platform-railing See **17,** fig. 283.

**Uncoupling-lever Trunnion-plate.** A cast-iron box, or bearing, attached to the under side of a platform end-timber, and which holds the pin on which the uncoupling-lever works. See **21,** figs. 282, 285.

**Uncoupling-lever Wedge.** An iron wedge which is inserted in the opening in an uncoupling-lever plate to hold the lever in either one of its extreme positions. See **19,** fig. 285.

**Uncoupling-lever Wedge-chain.** A chain by which an uncoupling-lever wedge is fastened to the platform end-timber to prevent it from being lost. See **20,** fig. 285.

**Under-hung Door.** A sliding-door which is supported and slides on a rail below the door. The door in fig. 55 is under-hung.

**Union,** *for Engine and Pump of Westinghouse-brake.* A nut and thimble for connecting a pipe to the engine or pump. See **35, 36, 37,** figs. 664, 665, 697.

**Union-joint.** A means of uniting the ends of two pipes with a nut. The latter is attached to one pipe with a collar, and is screwed on the opposite pipe, or on a thimble attached to the pipe. See fig. 697. Often called simply a *union.*

**United States Standard System of Screw-threads.** This term is often used to designate the *Sellers System of Screw-threads,* which see.

**Upholstery.** In passenger-car construction, the cushions, curtains, carpets, beds, etc., and generally the material from which they are made.

**Upper Belt-rail.** A horizontal wooden bar attached to the posts on the outside and above the windows of passenger and street cars. See **82,** figs. 225, 226 ; **44,** figs. 750, 752.

**Upper-berth.** The top berth in a sleeping-car section. See **2,** figs. 296–298. See *Berth.*

**Upper-berth Rest.** A metal ledge, lug, or shelf, which

supports an upper-berth of a sleeping-car when it is lowered. See fig. 354.

**Upper-berth-rest Pivot.** A pivot or pin attached to a suitable plate which is fastened to an upper-berth. The pin engages in a hole in a *Berth-rest,* which see. See fig. 355.

**Upper Brake-shaft Bearing.** An eye or bearing by which the upper end of a brake-shaft is held in its place and in which it revolves. In passenger and street cars the bearing is usually attached to the hand-rail. On freight box-cars, when the brakes are operated from the top of the car, the bearing is attached to the end of the body near the top. See **96**, figs. 55–84 ; **156**, figs. 215, 217, 219, 223 ; **123**, figs. 750, 753.

**Upper-cap,** *of Triple-valve for Westinghouse Car-brake.* A screw-plug which is screwed into the top of the chamber of a triple-valve. See **5**, fig. 704 ; fig. 707.

**Upper Corner-plate.** An outside corner-plate attached to the corner of a car on the outside next to the eaves of the roof or to the top-rail. See **55**, figs. 55, 59, 60, 63, 65, 77, 79.

**Upper Discharge-valve,** *of Air-pump for Westinghouse-brake.* A puppet-valve at the top of the air-pump cylinder through which the air above the piston escapes. See **32**, fig. 665 ; fig. 694.

**Upper Door-sash.** The part of a double window-sash in a car-door which covers the upper part of the opening. This upper section is usually made movable, so that it can be lowered for ventilation. See **12**, fig. 502.

**Upper End-panel.** A panel on the outside and end of a street-car above the window. See **29**, fig. 753.

**Upper-floor,** *for Cattle-car.* A floor in cattle-cars for carrying small cattle, as sheep, hogs, etc., which forms a second story or upper deck in the car. See **28**, figs. 69–72.

**Upper Seat-back Rail.** A horizontal wooden bar which forms the top-rail of a seat-back. See *Lower Seat-back Rail.* See **41**, figs. 750, 752.

**Upper Steam-valve,** *for Engine of Westinghouse-brake.* A small piston by which steam is admitted to, and exhausted from, the upper end of the steam-cylinder of an engine for a Westinghouse-brake. See **14**, figs. 665, 677.

**Upper Steam-valve Bushing,** *for Engine of Westinghouse-brake.* A ring or hollow metal cylinder in which the piston, which forms the upper steam-valve works. See **17**, fig. 665 ; fig. 680.

**Upper Swing-hanger Pivot.** A pin, bolt, or bar, by which the upper end of a swing-hanger is attached to the transom, and on which it is suspended. See **47**, figs. 108–129. See also *Lower Swing-hanger Pivot.*

**Upper Wainscot-rail.** A longitudinal wooden bar or rail, fastened to the posts on the inside of a passenger-car, immediately under the window, and extending from one end of the car to the other.  See **75**, figs. 225, 226 ; **3**, figs. 299–300.

**Upper Window-blind.**  The part of a double blind which covers the upper part of a window.  See **17**, fig. 301.

**Upper Window-blind Lift.**  A metal catch, or finger-hold, attached to an upper window-blind for raising and lowering it.  It is distinguished from a *lower window-blind lift* in not having a lug or ledge, described in the definition of the latter term.  See **25**, fig. 301 ; fig. 324.

**Urinal.**  A metal or porcelain receptacle used in water-closets to receive urine, and from which it is conveyed below the car by a pipe leading through the floor.  See **132**, figs. 216, 220 ; figs. 438, 439.  See *Corner-urinal. Side-urinal.*

**Urinal-cover.**  A wooden or sheet-metal lid for inclosing a urinal.

**Urinal-drip.**  A pan under a urinal.

**Urinal Drip-pipe.**  A pipe by which the contents of a urinal-drip are conducted below the floor of a car.

**Urinal-handle.**  A handle in a water-closet, placed above the urinal to hold on to.  They are sometimes fastened in the corner of the water-closet and are then called *corner urinal-handles ;* and sometimes to the side, and are then called *Side Urinal-handles*, which see.  See figs. 442, 443.

**Urinal Ventilating-pipe.**  A pipe attached to a urinal, and communicating with the top of a car, to convey the foul air and vile smells from a urinal.

# V

**Vacuum-brake.**  A system of continuous-brakes which is operated by exhausting the air from some appliance under each car by which the pressure of the external air is transmitted to the brake levers and shoes.  An ejector on the engine is ordinarily used for exhausting the air and it is connected with the rest of the train by pipes and flexible hose between the cars.  See *Eames Vacuum-brake.  Smith Vacuum-brake.*

**Valve.**  A lid, cover, or plug for opening and closing an aperture or passage.  See

| | |
|---|---|
| *Brake-hose Coupling-valve.* | *Register-valve.* |
| *Check-valve.* | *Reversing-valve.* |
| *Conductor's-valve.* | *Safety-valve.* |
| *Coupling-valve.* | *Slide-valve of Triple-valve.* |
| *Discharge-valve.* | *Steam-valve.* |
| *Double Check-valve.* | *Tank-valve.* |
| *Leakage-valve.* | *Throttle-valve.* |
| *Lower Discharge-valve.* | *Triple-valve.* |
| *Lower Steam-valve.* | *Upper Discharge-valve.* |
| *Receiving-valve.* | *Upper Steam-valve.* |

*Ventilator-valve.*

**Valves,** *for Top-plate of Spear-heater.* Two semi-circular dampers by which the annular opening between the smoke-pipe and its casing of Spear's pattern *C* stove is opened and closed. See fig. 559.

**Valve-seat.** "The flat or conical surface on which a valve rests."—*Knight.* See *Discharge-valve Seat. Tank-valve Seat.*

**Valve-stem.** A rod attached to a valve, and by which the latter is moved. See *Reversing-valve Stem.*

**Veneer.** "A thin leaf of a superior wood for overlaying an inferior wood."—*Webster.* See *Ceiling-veneers.*

**Vent.** "A small aperture; a hole or passage for air or other fluid to escape."—*Webster.* See *Lamp-vent.*

**Ventilator.** A contrivance for admitting or exhausting air to or from a car or other apartment. See **116, 142, 143,** figs. 215, 218, 222, 224; fig. 348. See
*Automatic-ventilator. Clear-story Ventilator.*
*Clear-story End-ventilator. End-ventilator.*
*Clear-story Side-ventilator. Frieze-ventilator.*
*Self-acting Ventilator.*

**Ventilator-deflector.** A metal plate or board placed in such a position at a ventilator-opening that it will cause a current of air to flow into or out of the car when the latter is in motion. See **1,** figs. 347, 348.

**Ventilator-door.** A door for closing the aperture of a ven-tilator through which the air passes. See fig. 345. See *Ventilator-valve.*

**Ventilator-hood.** A shield over the outside of a ventilator to prevent the entrance of sparks, cinders, rain, or snow. It is sometimes intended to direct the current of air either into or out of the car. See also *Clear-story End-ventilator Hood.*

**Ventilator-opener.** A lever, shaft, or other device for opening and closing ventilator-sashes or panels in a clear-story. It is the same as fig. 333.

**Ventilator-panel.** A panel in the frame of a valve or door for closing the aperture of a ventilator. See **116,** figs, 218, 224.

**Ventilator-pivot.** A pin on which a ventilator door or sash is swung or hinged. It is the same as a *Clear-story Window-pivot,* fig. 327.

**Ventilator Pivot-plate.** A metal plate which forms a socket in which a ventilator-pivot works. It is the same as a *Window-latch Plate,* figs. 314, 315.

**Ventilator-plate.** See *Frieze-ventilator Plates.*

**Ventilator-register.** A metal plate or frame attached to a ventilator opening, and provided with slats which are arranged so as to turn, and thus either open or close the ventilator opening. See fig. 346.

**Ventilator-ring.** A metal ring attached to the ceiling of a car around the opening for a ventilator in the roof to make a finish to the opening. These are seldom used now. See fig. 342.

**Ventilator-sash.** The rails and stiles which form the outside portion of a ventilator, valve, door, or window, and into which the panel or glass is fitted. See **116**, figs. 215–224.

**Ventilator-staff.** A stick or rod of wood or metal used to reach the fastenings of ventilators to open or close them. See fig. 348½.

**Ventilator-stop.** A small metal bracket on which a ventilator-sash rests when open. Same as fig. 771.

**Ventilator-valve.** A door for opening or closing the aperture of a ventilator. Such doors are usually made to turn on pivots at or near their centres. See **116**, figs. 215–224.

**Vertical Telegraph Cock,** *or* **Faucet.** A telegraph cock or faucet made of an upright form so as to attach to the top of a horizontal surface, as the top of a wash-stand. See fig. 382. See *Telegraph-faucet*.

**Volute-spring.** A spring made of a flat bar of steel coiled with a kind of scroll resembling the volutes used as an ornament in the capitals of ancient Roman and Grecian architecture. The coil is made in a conical form so that the spring can be compressed in the direction of the axis around which it is coiled. See fig. 213.

**Vose Graduated-spring.** A round-bar single-coil spiral-spring, with two conical india-rubber springs on the inside, one attached to the spring-seat and the other to the spring-cap. When the spiral spring is extended, there is some space between the two rubber springs. The weight is first supported by the spiral-spring until this is compressed far enough to bring the two rubber-springs in contact, when they support part of the load. See fig. 208.

**V-shaped Screw-thread.** A term used to designate a thread which is of a **V**-shape, and made with a sharp edge at the top and a sharp groove at the root, as shown in fig. 794, and which differs in that respect from the Sellers system, which is flat at the top and at the root, and from the Whitworth system, which is rounded at those points, as shown in figs. 795, 796.

**V Window-button.** A catch, with a **V**-shaped notch in the end, which is fastened to a window-post for holding up a window. See fig. 306.

# W

**Wagon-truck.** A four-wheeled vehicle for moving baggage or freight about a station or warehouse. See fig. 49. See *Baggage Wagon-truck*, fig. 52. *Freight Wagon-truck*, fig. 50.

**Wainscot-panel.** A board which forms a panel under the

windows and between the two wainscot-rails. See **76**, figs. 215, 225, 226 ; **4**, figs. 299–301.

**Wainscot-rails.** Longitudinal wooden bars or rails fastened to the posts on the inside of a passenger-car below the windows and extending from one end of the car to the other. See *Lower Wainscot Rail. Upper Wainscot-rail.*

**Wall Seat-end.** The seat-end next the wall or side of a car. See **4**, figs. 400, 401.

**Warehouse-truck.** A small vehicle which is used for moving freight about a warehouse. See

   *Baggage Barrow-truck.*     *Freight Barrow-truck.*
   *Baggage Wagon-truck.*     *Freight Wagon-truck.*
                *Wagon-truck.*

**Wash-bowl.** A hollow vessel or dish to hold water for washing—and for various other uses. A basin. Wash-bowls are used in sleeping and drawing-room cars, and generally form a part of a fixed wash-stand.

**Wash-bowl Pipe.** A pipe connected to a fixed wash-bowl for carrying off the waste water. The pipe is closed by a basin-plug. See **4**, fig. 424.

**Wash-bowl Stand.** A support for a wash-bowl.

**Washburn-wheel.** A cast-iron car-wheel, designed and patented by Nathan Washburn in 1850. It consists of two plates, which extend from the hub to about half the distance between it and the rim. There they unite into one plate which extends to the rim. The plates are all curved so as to contract when the wheels are cooled without danger of fracturing the wheel. The single plate and the rim are united together and strengthened by curved ribs cast on the inside of the wheel. See figs. 161, 162.

**Washer.** 1. An annular plate of metal or other material which is placed under the head of a bolt or under a nut to give it a secure bearing. See fig. 785.

2. A brush for washing objects, as windows or cars. See

   *Base-washer.*     *Double-washer.*
   *Bell-cord-guide Washer.*     *Packing-ring Washer.*
   *Beveled-washer.*     *Release-spring Washer.*
   *Body-bolster Truss-rod*     *Seat-back-arm Washer.*
    *Washer.*     *Socket-washer.*
   *Brace-rod Washer.*     *Transom Truss-rod*
   *Buffer-spring Washer.*      *Washer.*
   *Buffer-stem Washer.*     *Triangular-washer.*
   *Car-washer.*     *Truck-bolster Truss-rod*
   *Cross-frame Truss-rod*      *Washer.*
    *Washer.*     *Truss-rod Washer.*
           *Twin-washer.*

**Wash-room Pump.** A pump used in the wash-room of a car for pumping water up from a tank into a basin or wash-bowl. See fig. 381.

**Wash-stand Sink.** A cast-iron plate with one or more bowls made in one piece and lined with porcelain and used for the top of a wash-stand. See **3,** fig. 424.

**Wash-stand Slab.** A stone slab which forms the top for a wash-stand.

**Water-alcove.** A recess in the side of a partition of a passenger-car to receive the faucet of a water-cooler or water-pipe and drinking-cup. The term is generally used to designate a metal casing or lining with which the recess is covered. See **134,** figs. 219, 220 ; fig. 426.

**Water-alcove Front.** A metal guard usually made of some ornamental design which incloses the bottom of a water-alcove to prevent the drinking-cup from falling off. See **1,** fig. 426.

**Water-alcove Pan.** The bottom of a water-alcove. See **2,** fig. 426.

**Water-closet.** A retiring room furnished with a urinal and soil-hopper. Sometimes politely called a *saloon.* See **130,** figs. 216, 218, 219, 220.

**Water-closet Door-plate.** A metal plate attached to a water-closet door to designate the place to which the door leads. See also fig. 441.

**Water-closet Handle.** See *Urinal-handle.*

**Water-closet Hopper.** See *Soil-hopper.*

**Water-closet Latch.** A latch for water-closet doors which consists of a spring-bolt, usually with a stop on the inside which locks the bolt fast, or with a separate bolt for fastening the door from the inside. See fig. 526.

**Water-closet Seat.** A wooden seat with a hole in it over a soil-hopper. See **131,** figs. 216, 220.

**Water-closet Seat-lid.** A wooden cover for the hole in a water-closet seat.

**Water-closet Ventilating-jack.** A cap or covering on the top of a ventilating-pipe for a water-closet. See fig. 437.

**Water-cooler.** A tank or vessel for carrying drinking water which is usually cooled with ice. The sides are generally made double, and the space between is filled with some non-conducting substance to keep the ice from melting and keep the water cool. See **133,** fig. 216. **1,** fig. 424.

**Water-cooler Stand.** A table, shelf, or support for a water-cooler. See **3,** fig. 424.

**Water-drip.** A pan or receptacle to receive the waste water from a water-cooler.

**Water-drip Pipe.** A pipe connected with a water-drip for conveying away the waste water from a water-cooler.

**Water-table.** A *Window-ledge,* which see.

**Water-tank.** A vessel or reservoir for holding water. Those used on cars generally carry water for drinking or washing, and are usually made of sheet-iron.

**Webbing.** A strong fabric, from one to four inches wide,

made of hemp or other material which is not liable to stretch. It is used for supporting the seat-cushions.

**Wedge.** A *Journal-bearing Key*, which see. See *Stop-wedge. Uncoupling-lever Wedge.*

**Wedge-chain.** A chain by which an uncoupling-lever wedge is attached to the platform of a car. See **20,** fig. 285.

**Westinghouse Air-brake.** A system of continuous brakes invented and patented by Mr. George Westinghouse, Jr., which is operated by compressed-air. The air is compressed by a steam-pump on the engine and is stored up in a tank on the engine or tender. When the brakes are applied the compressed-air is conveyed from the tank by pipes connected together between the cars by flexible hose to cylinders with pistons under each car, by means of which the pressure of the air is communicated to the brake-levers, and thence to the brake-shoes. This was the first form of brake invented by Mr. Westinghouse ; a later and improved form is the *Westinghouse Automatic Air-brake*, which see.

**Westinghouse Automatic Air-brake.** A system of continuous brakes, invented and patented by Mr. George Westinghouse, Jr., which is operated by compressed-air. The air is compressed by a steam-pump on the engine, and is stored up in a tank on the engine and in other tanks under the tender and under each car, which are con-nected with the steam or air-pump by pipes and flexible hose between the cars. When the brakes are to be applied, compressed-air is admitted from the tank on the engine to an ingeniously contrived valve called a *triple-valve* under each car, which releases the compressed-air, stored up in the tank under that car, and admits it to a cylinder provided with a piston which is connected with a system of brake-levers, and the pressure of the air is thus transmitted to the brake-shoes. In this brake, the air for operating the brakes on each car is stored up in a tank on that car, whereas in other systems of air-brakes the compressed-air to operate the pistons under each car must all flow from the tank on the engine, and in vacuum-brakes the air from the appliances on the car used to operate the brakes must flow forward to the engine, before the brakes can be applied. This consumes an appreciable amount of time, whereas the application of the automatic-brake is almost instantaneous. The triple-valve is so arranged, too, that the brakes can be applied from each car by pulling a cord, and they will also be applied to the rear part of a train in case it should break in two parts, if one or more cars should be separated from the rest of the train. See figs. 655–745.

**Wheel.** A circular frame or solid piece of wood or metal which revolves on an axis. See

    *Brake-wheel.*            *Brake Ratchet-wheel.*

*Broad-tread Wheel.*
*Car-wheel.*
*Combination Plate-wheel.*
*Combination-wheel.*
*Compromise-wheel.*
*Double-plate Wheel.*
*Elastic-wheel.*
*Gear-wheel.*
*Hand-car Wheel.*
*Hand-wheel.*
*Hollow-spoke Wheel,*
*Narrow-tread Wheel.*
*Open-plate Wheel.*
*Pair of Wheels.*

*Paper-wheel.*
*Plate-wheel.*
*Ratchet-wheel.*
*Sax & Kear Wheel.*
*Set of Wheels.*
*Single-plate Wheel.*
*Spoke-wheel.*
*Steeled-wheel.*
*Steel-tired Wheel.*
*Steel-wheel.*
*Street-car Wheel.*
*Washburn-wheel.*
*Winding-shaft Ratchet-*
    *wheel.*

*Wrought-iron Wheel.*

**Wheel-box.** A covering for that part of the wheel of a street-car which projects through the floor. The sides of the box are usually made of wood and the top of sheet-iron, but they are sometimes made entirely of wood or metal. See **13**, figs. 750, 752.

**Wheel-box Button.** A stick of wood attached by a bolt to the top of a wheel-box of a street-car so that it can be turned, somewhat like a door-button, to hold the wheel-box in its place. See **14**, figs. 750, 752.

**Wheel-centre.** The portion of a car-wheel inside of the tire. The term is used to designate the central part of wheels which have separate tires, and is seldom applied to wheels which are made solid or in one piece. See **4**, figs. 180–183.

**Wheel-flange.** A projecting edge or rim on the periphery of a car-wheel for keeping it on the rail. See **26**, fig. 138.

**Wheel-piece.** A stick of timber in a wooden-frame truck, which forms the side of the frame and to which the pedestals are attached. See **10**, figs. 88–94, 115–129, 131.

**Wheel-piece Plate.** An iron plate riveted to the inside or outside of a wheel-piece of a truck to strengthen it. See **11, 12**, figs, 128, 129. According to its position, it is called the *Inside* or the *Outside Wheel-piece Plate*, which see.

**Wheel-piece Tie-rod.** A rod which is placed on the inside and lengthwise along a wheel-piece and which ties the two end-pieces together. It is almost the same as a wheel-piece truss-rod. The latter is depressed at the middle so as to act as a truss-rod, while a tie-rod is straight from one end of a truck to the other.

**Wheel-piece Truss-rod.** A rod which extends lengthwise to a wheel-piece and is inclined downward toward its centre so as to strengthen it. It differs from a tie-rod in being depressed at the middle so as to form a truss, while the tie-rod runs straight from one end of the truck to the other. See **13**, figs. 118–126.

**Wheel-plate.** That part of a plate car-wheel which connects the rim and the hub. It occupies the place and fulfills the same purpose as the spokes do in an open or spoke wheel. See **22**, fig. 138.

**Wheel-ribs.** Projections cast usually on the inner side of plate car-wheels to strengthen them. They are placed in a radial position and are often curved so as to permit the wheel to contract when it cools. Shown in figs. 155, 158, 162, 170.

**Wheel-seat.** The part of an axle which is inserted in the hub of a wheel. See **3**, fig. 138, 143.

**Wheel-timber.** A *Wheel-piece*, which see.

**Wheel-tread.** The outer surface or part of a car-wheel which bears on the rails. See **25**, fig. 138.

**Whitworth-Gauges.** See *Cylindrical-gauges.*

**Whitworth System of Screw-threads.** A system of screw-threads designed by Sir Joseph Whitworth, of England, and which is almost universally used in that country. It differs from the Sellers system in that the sides of the threads stand at an angle of 55 degrees instead of 60 degrees, and the tops of the threads and the spaces between them at the root are rounded, as shown in fig. 795, instead of being flat, as in the Sellers system. The number of threads per inch in the two systems is as follows :

| Diameter of screw | No. of threads per in | Diameter of screw | No. of threads per in | Diameter of screw | No. of threads per in | Diameter of screw | No. of threads per in |
|---|---|---|---|---|---|---|---|
| 1/4 | 20 | 1/2 | 12 | 1 | 8 | 1 5/8 | 5 |
| 5/16 | 18 | 5/8 | 11 | 1 1/8 | 7 | 1 3/4 | 5 |
| 3/8 | 16 | 3/4 | 10 | 1 1/4 | 7 | 1 7/8 | 4 1/2 |
| 7/16 | 14 | 7/8 | 9 | 1 3/8 | 6 | 2 | 4 1/2 |
| | | | | 1 1/2 | 6 | | |

The Whitworth system is used to a limited extent in this country.

**Whole-frame Truck.** A *Continuous-frame Truck*, which see.

**Wicket.** See *Fare-wicket.*

**Wide-gauge.** The distance between the heads of the rails of a railroad when it is greater than 4 ft. 8½ in. See *Gauge.*

**Winding-shaft,** *for Drop-doors of Coal-cars, etc.* A shaft extending crosswise on a car, and on which the chains for closing the drop-doors are wound. See **129**, figs. 77, 79.

**Winding-shaft Plate.** A plate on the side of a drop-bottom coal-car which forms a bearing for the winding-shaft. See **133**, figs. 77–79.

**Winding-shaft Ratchet-wheel.** A notched wheel attached to a winding-shaft, with which a pawl engages and thus prevents the shaft from turning. See **130**, figs. 77, 79.

**Windlass.** See *Brake-windlass.*

**Window.** "An opening in the wall of a building or car for the admission of light and of air when necessary. This opening has a frame on the sides, in which are set movable sashes containing panes of glass."—*Webster.* See **137**, figs. 215–217, 219, 223, 228–230 ; **6**, figs. 299–301 ; **64**, figs. 750, 552, 753. See also *Clear-story Window. Twin-window.*

**Window Bar-lift.** A short horizontal metal bar attached to a heavy sash with two flanged studs or stanchions. They are generally used for the large sashes of sleeping and drawing-room cars. See fig. 319.

**Window-blind.** A wooden screen composed of a frame and slats placed in the window to exclude sunshine. Such blinds are made in one or more sections or parts. See also **140**, figs. 215, 219, 222 ; **17, 18**, fig. 301 ; **69**, fig. 750. See

| | |
|---|---|
| *Double Window-blind.* | *Single Window-blind.* |
| *Lower Window-blind.* | *Upper Window-blind.* |

**Window-blind Bolt.** A bolt used for holding a window-blind in any desired position. See fig. 320.

**Window-blind-bolt Bushing.** A bushing for lining a hole into which a blind-bolt slides. They are also used for sash-bolts. Same as *Window-latch Bushing,* fig. 310.

**Window-blind-bolt Plate.** A plate attached to the post or moulding of a car-window and in which a window-blind bolt engages. Same as *Window-latch Plate,* figs. 314, 315.

**Window-blind Lift.** A metal hook or catch fastened to a blind to take hold of in raising or lowering a window-blind. They are usually attached to the bottom rails of steam-car blinds, which are raised above the window. Street-car blinds are lowered below the window, and therefore the lift is attached to the top rail of the blind. Also called *window-blind pull.* See **25, 26**, fig. 301 ; figs. 321–324 ; **73**, fig. 750. See

| | |
|---|---|
| *Double Window-blind Lift.* | *Single Window-blind Lift.* |
| *Lower Window-blind Lift.* | *Upper Window-blind Lift.* |

**Window-blind Mullion.** An upright bar in the centre of a window-blind sash. See **15**, fig. 301 ; **72**, fig. 750.

**Window-blind Pull.** A *Window-blind Lift,* which see.

**Window-blind Rail.** A horizontal piece or bar of a window-blind sash. See **14**, fig. 301 ; **71**, fig. 750.

**Window-blind Rest.** 1. A wooden strip placed in the

groove in which a window-blind slides and on which it rests when down.

2. A horizontal strip of wood, used on street-cars, which extends from one body-post to another and on which the blind rests when it is lowered. See **49**, fig. 752.

**Window-blind Sash.** The frame in which the slats of a window-blind are set or held. See **86**, figs. 215, 219, 222, 225 ; **13, 14**, fig. 301 ; **70, 71**, fig. 750.

**Window-blind Slat.** One of a number of thin strips of wood which are set in the frame of a window-blind in an inclined position, but with some space between them, so as to exclude the sunshine, but to permit the air to circulate freely in warm weather. See **17, 18**, fig. 301 ; **69**, fig. 750.

**Window-blind Spring.** The same as a *Window-sash Spring*, which see.

**Window-blind Stile.** An upright piece or bar which forms part of a window-blind sash. See **13**, fig. 301 ; **70**, fig. 750.

**Window-blind Stop.** An *Inside Window-stop*, which see.

**Window-button.** A small piece of metal swiveled by a screw, and which supports a window when it is up and holds it open. See figs. 306, 307. See **L** *Window-button.* **V** *Window-button.*

**Window-casing.** A frame which incloses or surrounds a window. See **7**, figs. 299, 301. Often called an *Inside Window-stop*.

**Window-cornice.** An ornamental projecting structure usually made of wood and placed over a window on the inside. It is used for decoration only. See **34**, fig. 300.

**Window Cove-moulding.** A small concave moulding around the sides and top of a window on the inside of a passenger-car. See **87**, fig. 225.

**Window-curtain.** A cloth or some kind of textile material hung over a window to exclude sunshine, and which can be either raised, lowered, spread, or drawn aside at pleasure. See **23**. fig. 298 ; **27**, figs. 299, 300.

**Window-curtain Bar.** An iron bar attached to the lower edge of a rolling window-curtain as a weight to hold the curtain down.

**Window-curtain Cord.** A piece of twine attached to a window-curtain roller for rolling up or raising the curtain.

**Window-curtain-cord Tightener.** An adjustable metal fixture attached to the side of a window for keeping the window-curtain cord taut. See fig. 339.

**Window-curtain Holder.** A metal hook fastened to the window-post on the side of a window for holding a curtain when it is drawn aside. See **29**, figs. 299, 300 ; fig. 340.

**Window-curtain Hook.** A metal hook attached to a window curtain, and by which the latter is hung from a rod over the window.

**Window-curtain Leather.** A strip of leather sewed to the lower edge of a rolling window-curtain, partly for ornament, and to take hold of in moving the curtain, and to protect its lower edge from wear. See **28,** figs. 296, 298.

**Window-curtain Pulley.** A small grooved wheel, which is attached to a window-curtain roller, and on which a cord runs to turn the roller and thus raise or lower the curtain. See fig. 336.

**Window-curtain Rings.** Rings made of metal, wood, india-rubber, or other material, which are attached to a curtain and by which it is hung from a rod over the window so that it can be drawn or withdrawn over or from the window. See **32,** fig. 299 ; fig. 335.

**Window-curtain Rod.** A rod placed over a window and to which a window-curtain is hung. See **30,** fig. 299 ; fig. 334.

**Window-curtain-rod Bracket.** An angular knee or stay usually made of metal and attached to the side or over a window and which forms a support for a window-curtain roller. See fig. 338.

**Window-curtain-rod Stanchion.** A metal eye, bolt, or post, attached to the side of a passenger-car and which holds a window-curtain rod in its place. See **31,** fig. 299 ; **1,** fig. 334.

**Window-curtain Roller.** A wooden or metal cylinder placed over a window and on which a curtain is rolled. The curtains in figs. 298 and 300 are hung on rollers.

**Window-curtain Roller-bearing.** A small metal eye screwed fast to the side of a window to hold the pin or journal of a window-curtain roller, and in which the latter turns. See fig. 337.

**Window-curtain Tassel.** An ornamental bunch of strings attached to a window-curtain and used to take hold of in pulling the curtain down. See **33,** fig. 300.

**Window-fastener.** A *Window-latch,* which see.

**Window-glass.** Panes of glass used for windows. See **6,** figs. 299–301.

**Window-grating.** A wrought or cast iron partition made of bars, or in other form placed on the outside of the windows of passenger-cars to prevent passengers from being injured by putting their heads or arms outside.

**Window-guards.** Small metal rods, usually made of iron, placed in front of the end windows of passenger and street cars to protect the glass from being broken. See **77,** fig. 753.

**Window-holder.** See *Spring Window-holder. Window-button. Window-latch.*

**Window-latch.** A spring-bolt which is attached to a window-sash or a window-blind and provided with a suitable thumb lever so that the bolt can be withdrawn with the finger and thumb of one hand. Such latches are used for holding car-window sashes up in any desired position, and also to fasten them down when the window is closed. See **22**, figs. 298–301 ; figs. 308, 309. See *Clear-story Window-latch.*

[A variety of terms are used to designate this part of a car. In most of the trade catalogues it is called a *sash-lock,* but Webster says the word lock is " now appropriated to an instrument composed of a spring, wards, and a bolt of iron or steel, used to fasten doors, chests, and the like. *The bolt is moved by a key.*" Knight says a lock is "a device having a bolt *moved by a key,* and serving to secure a door, lid, or other object." The device used for fastening car-windows is therefore not properly a lock, because it has no key. Of the word latch Webster says : "The primary sense of the root is, to catch, to close, stop, or make fast." Therefore *Window-latch* was the term adopted to designate this device.]

**Window-latch Bolt.** A metal pin in a window-latch, which holds the sash in any desired position. See **1**, figs. 308, 309.

**Window-latch Bushing.** A metal ring or thimble let into a parting-strip to receive the bolt of a window-latch. It acts as a *Window-latch Stop,* which see. See fig. 310.

**Window-latch Lower-stop.** A stop attached to a window-post, near the bottom of a window, into which the window-lock bolt engages to hold the window down, and prevent it from being opened from the outside. See **24**, fig. 301 ; fig. 312. See *Window-latch Stop.*

**Window-latch Plate.** A metal plate attached to a window-post, and with a suitable hole in it, in which a window-latch bolt engages. See figs. 314, 315.

**Window-latch Rack.** A piece of metal attached to the side of a window with notches on one side, shaped like saw-teeth, against which the blind or sash-bolts catch. The notches are intended to hold the blind or window at any desired height. See fig. 313.

**Window-latch Spring.** A spring, usually of spiral form, and made of wire, attached to a window-latch bolt to move it out, so as to engage with the stop or plate when the window is in the desired position. See **2**, fig. 309.

**Window-latch Stop.** A metal lug or plate attached to the window-post, parting-strip, or mouldings, and with which the bolt of a window-latch engages to keep the window up or down. See **23, 24,** fig. 301; figs. 311, 312. See *Window-latch Lower-stop. Window-latch Upper-stop. Window-latch Bushing.*

**Window-latch Trigger.** A thumb-piece or handle with which a window-latch bolt is withdrawn from its stop or keeper. See **3**, figs. 308, 309.

**Window-latch Upper-stop.** A stop above the one which holds the window down. See **23**, fig. 301 ; fig. 311. See *Window-latch Stop.*

**Window-ledge.** A projecting moulding outside of a car which extends from one end of it to the other above the windows, and intended to shed the rain. It is used chiefly on street-cars. See **45**, figs. 750, 752, 753.

**Window-lift.** A metal finger-hold or leather strap attached to the bottom rail of a window-sash for raising and lowering it. Leather straps are seldom used excepting on street-cars. See **21**, figs. 298–301 ; figs. 316–319 ; **67**, figs. 750, 752. See *Flush Window-lift. Window Bar-lift.*

**Window-lintel.** A horizontal piece of wood on the outside of a passenger-car between the posts and over the window-openings. See **90**, figs. 215, 221, 224.

**Window-moulding.** A strip of wood, usually of an ornamental shape, around or on each side of a window, which generally covers the joint between the panel and post on the inside of passenger-cars, and which sometimes forms a groove on the post in which a window or window-blind slides. See **88**, fig. 225 ; **8**, figs. 299–301 ; **52**, figs. 750, 752. See *Inside Window-stop.*

**Window-moulding Base.** An ornament made of wood, metal, or other material which is attached to the lower end of a window-moulding. See **10**, fig. 301.

**Window-moulding Joint-cover.** A piece of metal, wood, or other material, used for covering the joints of window-mouldings when two pieces join each other. See **9**. fig. 301 ; fig. 341.

**Window-mullion.** An upright piece or bar in the middle of a window-sash. Similar to **146′**, fig. 218.

**Window-opener.** A contrivance, as a lever or rod, for opening a window. It is used chiefly for the windows in the clear-story of a car which are out of reach. See *Clear-story Window-opener.*

**Window-panel.** See *End Window-panel. Inside Window-panel. Outside Window-panel.*

**Window-panel Furring.** Horizontal distance-pieces of wood placed between the window-posts and to which the paneling is fastened. See **59**, figs. 215, 218, 221, 226.

**Window-pivot.** A metal pin or pivot attached to a sash and on which the latter turns. See *Clear-story Window-pivot,* fig. 327.

**Window-pivot Bushing.** A ring or lining for the hole in a clear-story window-post, in which a window-pivot works. Same as fig. 310. See *Clear-story Window-pivot Bushing.*

**Window-pivot Plate.** A plate attached to a window-post or frame, with a hole or eye in which a window-pivot works. Sometimes they are provided with springs so as to prevent the sash from rattling. See fig. 331. See also *Clear-story Window-pivot Plate.*

**Window-post.** A post at the side of a window-opening against which the sash and blind slide, and which forms part of the frame of the side of a car-body. See **58**, figs. 215, 216, 218, 221, 226, 229, 230 ; **15**, figs. 750–752.

**Window-rail.** A horizontal piece or bar of a window-sash. See **12**, figs. 299–301 ; **65**, figs. 750, 752, 753.

**Window-sash.** A frame which holds the window-glass. See **85**, figs. 215, 219, 225, 226, 228, 229 ; **11, 12,** figs. 299–301 , **65, 66,** figs. 750, 752, 753. See *Door-case Window-sash.*

**Window-sash Holder.** See *Window-latch. Spring Window-holder.*

**Window-sash Lift.** A *Window-lift*, which see.

**Window-sash Rest.** A strip of wood used on street-cars, and which extends from one body-post to another, and on which the sash rests when it is lowered. See **50**, fig. 752.

**Window-sash Spring.** A metal spring attached to the edge of the stile of a window or blind sash to prevent it from rattling. These are made of various forms, some of them consist of a metal plate, like that shown in fig. 303, attached to the window-sash at one end, which is called a *single window-sash spring* ; others like that shown in fig. 302, which is a metal plate fastened in its centre to the sash, and is called a *double window-sash spring.* Still others are of a spiral form, and are let into the sash, as shown by fig. 304, and are called *spiral window-sash springs.*

**Window-shade.** A term used to designate a window-curtain, which is rolled on a roller above the window, in distinction from one which is drawn aside. See **23**, figs. 296, 298 ; **27′,** fig. 300.

**Window-sill.** A horizontal piece under a window, on which a window or blind sash rests when down. Window-sills are made of wood and also of cast-iron. See *Inside Window-sill. Outside Window-sill.*

**Window-sill Cap.** A thin board attached to the top of an inside window-sill. See **79**, figs. 225, 226.

**Window-sill Moulding.** A small wooden moulding under an inside window-sill. See **80**, figs. 225, 226.

**Window-spring.** See *Window-sash Spring. Spring Window-holder.*

**Window-stile.** An upright piece or bar of a window-sash. See **11**, figs. 299–301 ; **66**, figs. 750, 752.

**Window-stop.** See *Outside Window-stop. Inside Window-stop.*

**Winslow Car-roof.** A car-roof, patented by A. P. Winslow, which consists of metal plates which extend crosswise to the car. They are made with corrugations and are let into grooves in the rafters. The latter are covered with strips of sheet-iron and the whole with a layer of transverse boards, which are fastened to longitudinal purlins attached to the rafters or carlines. See fig. 66.

**Winslow Car-stove.** A stove which was invented and patented by Mr. A. P. Winslow, of Cleveland. It has a reservoir in the base for water, which is intended to put out the fire in case the car is overturned.  See figs. 547, 548.

**Wire.**  See *Seal-wires*.

**Wire-covered Bell-cord.**  See *Bell-cord*.

**Wire-gauze,** *for Ventilator.*  A fine netting made of wire with which the outside of ventilator openings are covered to prevent the admission of dust into the cars.

**Wood.**  See *Dead-wood*.

**Wooden-frame Truck.**  A car-truck, of which the wheel-pieces and end-pieces are made of wood.  Figs. 88–94, 115–126, 128, 129 are illustrations of *wooden-frame trucks*.

**Wooden Floor-mat.**  A sort of grating made of strips of wood, with distance-pieces and spaces between, and bolted together.  They are placed on the floors of horse-cars so that the feet of passengers will not come in contact with the dirt and moisture on the floor.

**Wood-screw.**  A small cylindrical bar of iron with a wood screw-thread cut on it and with a slotted head so that it can be turned with a screw-driver, and used for fastening any object, as a hinge or a lock, etc., to wood.

**Wood Screw-thread.**  A form of screw-thread used for male screws which are intended to screw into wooden objects.  It differs from a metal thread in having the spaces between the projections wider than the latter.  This kind of thread is shown in fig. 779.

**Wool-packed Spiral-spring.**  A spiral-spring the centre of which is packed with wool.  See fig. 209.

**Worm.**  See *Brake-chain Worm*.

**Wrecking-car.**  See *Tool-car.  Derrick-car.*

**Wrench,** *for Packing-nuts of Westinghouse-brake.*  A wrench for screwing up the piston-rod packing-nuts.  See fig. 745.

**Wrench,** *for Discharge-valve Seats of Westinghouse-brake.*  A wrench for screwing and unscrewing the discharge-valve seats.  See fig. 746.

**Wrought-iron Wheel.**  A car-wheel with a steel tire and with a wrought-iron centre.  Such wheels are made either with spokes or with solid plates.  See figs. 182, 183.

# Y

**Yoke.**  See *Spring-yoke*.

# ENGRAVINGS.

[*See the Directions and Index to Engravings, following the Preface.*]

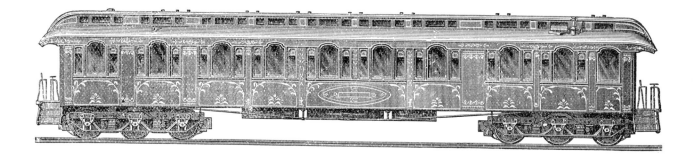

*Fig.* 1.

SLEEPING AND HOTEL CAR.

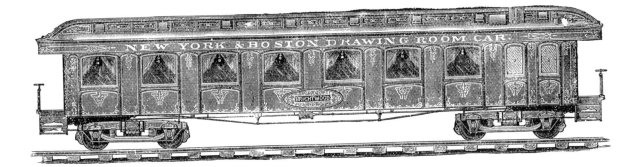

Fig. 2.

DRAWING-ROOM CAR.

*Fig. 3.*

RESTAURANT CAR.

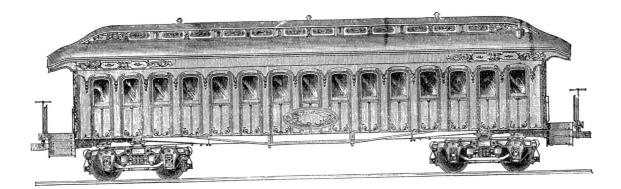

*Fig. 4.*

PASSENGER CAR OR COACH.

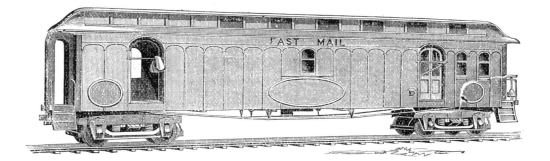

*Fig.* 5.

Post-office Car.

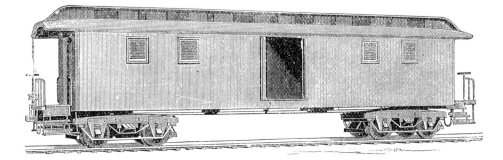

*Fig.* 6.

EXPRESS, MAIL OR BAGGAGE CAR.

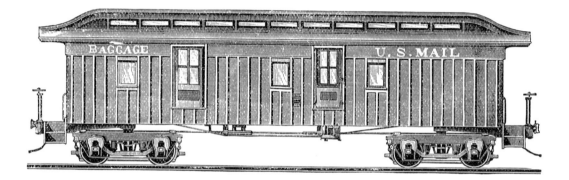

*Fig. 7.*

Combined Baggage and Express or Mail Car.

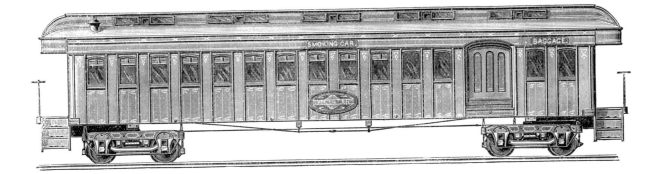

*Fig.* 8.

COMBINED PASSENGER AND MAIL, BAGGAGE, OR EXPRESS CAR.

*Fig. 9.*

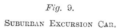

Suburban Excursion Car.

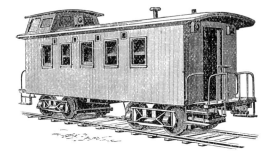

*Fig.* 10.

EIGHT-WHEELED CONDUCTOR'S OR CABOOSE CAR.

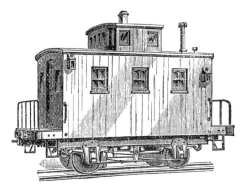

*Fig.* 11.

FOUR-WHEELED CONDUCTOR'S OR CABOOSE CAR.

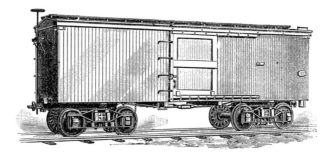

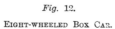

Fig. 12.

EIGHT-WHEELED BOX CAR.

Fig. 13.

FOUR-WHEELED BOX CAR.

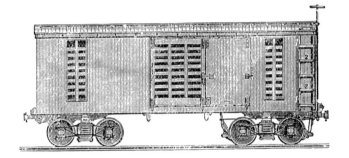

*Fig.* 14.

COMBINED BOX AND CATTLE CAR.

1. *Ladder-sides.*
2. *Ladder-rounds.*

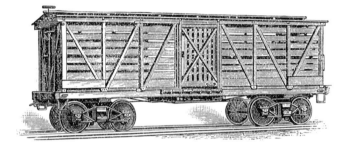

*Fig.* 15.

CATTLE CAR.

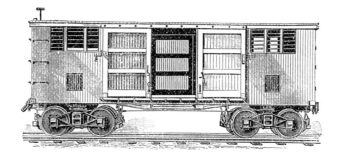

*Fig.* 16.

HORSE CAR.

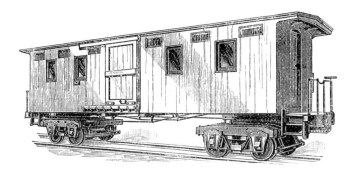

*Fig. 17.*

MILK CAR.

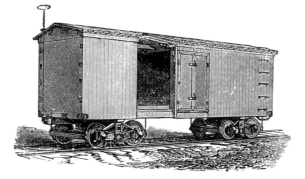

*Fig.* 18.

REFRIGERATOR CAR.

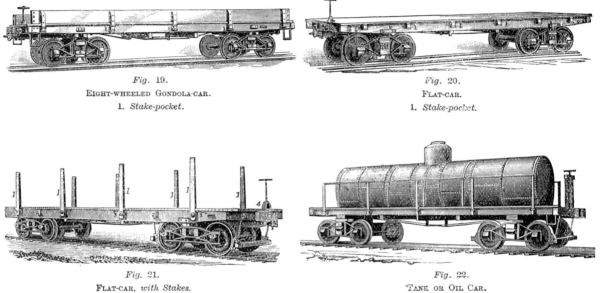

*Fig. 19.*

EIGHT-WHEELED GONDOLA-CAR.

1. *Stake-pocket.*

*Fig. 20.*

FLAT-CAR.

1. *Stake-pocket.*

*Fig. 21.*

FLAT-CAR, *with Stakes.*

1. *Stake.*   2. *Stake-rest.*   3. *Stake-hook.*

*Fig. 22.*

TANK OR OIL CAR.

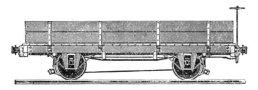

*Fig.* 23.

FOUR-WHEELED GONDOLA-CAR.

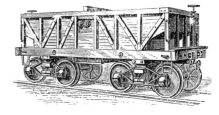

*Fig.* 25.

EIGHT-WHEELED HOPPER-BOTTOM COAL-CAR.

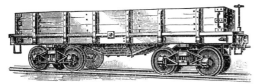

*Fig.* 24.

HOPPER-BOTTOM GONDOLA-CAR.

*Fig.* 26.

IRON-HOPPER COAL-CAR.

*Fig* 27.
FOUR-WHEELED HOPPER-BOTTOM COAL-CAR.

*Fig.* 29.
FOUR-WHEELED TIP-CAR.

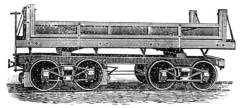

*Fig.* 28.
EIGHT WHEELED TIP-CAR.

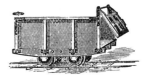

*Fig.* 30.
MINE-CAR.

*Fig. 31.*

DERRICK-CAR.

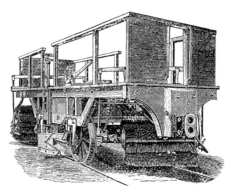

*Fig. 33.*

SWEEPING-CAR.

*A. Snow-scraper.*

*Fig. 32.*

FERRY PUSH-CAR.

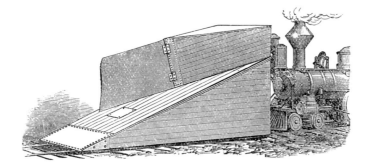

*Fig.* 34.

Snow-plow.

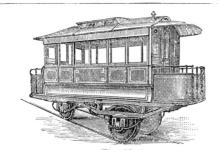

*Fig. 35.*

INCLINED-PLANE CAR.

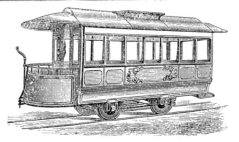

*Fig. 37.*

FARE-BOX STREET-CAR.

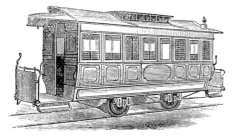

*Fig. 36.*

TWO-HORSE STREET-CAR,
*With two platforms.*

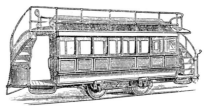

*Fig. 38.*

DOUBLE-DECK OR TOP-SEAT STREET-CAR.

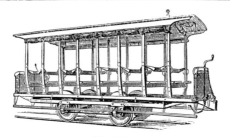

*Fig.* 39.
SUMMER STREET-CAR,
*With seats facing one way.*

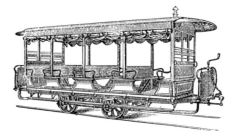

*Fig.* 40.
SUMMER STREET-CAR,
*With seats vis-à-vis.*

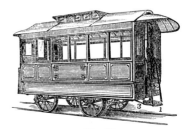

*Fig.* 41.
ONE-HORSE OR BOB-TAIL STREET-CAR.
1. *End-step.*    2. *Step Hand-rail.*    3. *Step-iron.*

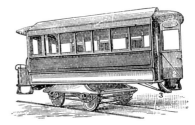

*Fig.* 42.
REVERSIBLE STREET-CAR.
1. *Door-apron.*    2. *Door Hand-rail.*    3. *Step-iron.*

Fig. 43.

CRANK HAND-CAR.

Fig. 44.

LEVER HAND-CAR.

Fig. 45.

INSPECTION HAND-CAR.

Fig. 46.

EXPRESS HAND-CAR.

Fig. 47.

THREE-WHEELED HAND-CAR

Fig. 48.

PUSH-CAR.

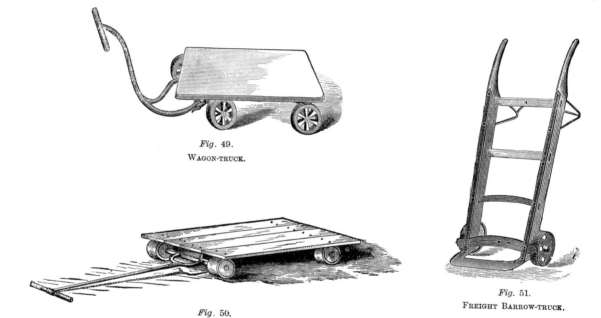

*Fig.* 49.

WAGON-TRUCK.

*Fig.* 50.

FREIGHT WAGON-TRUCK.

*Fig.* 51.

FREIGHT BARROW-TRUCK.

*Fig. 52.*
BAGGAGE WAGON-TRUCK.

*Fig. 53.*
BAGGAGE BARROW-TRUCK,

*Fig. 54.*
BAGGAGE BARROW-TRUCK,

# FREIGHT-CAR BODIES.

LIST OF NAMES OF THE PARTS OF FREIGHT-CAR BODIES WHICH ARE DESIGNATED BY THE NUMBERS IN FIGS. 55–84.

1 *Sill.*
2 *End-sill.*
3. *Intermediate Floor-timbers.*
4. *Centre Floor-timbers.*
5 *Short Floor-timber.*
6 *Brake-hanger Timber.*
7. *Floor-timber Distance-block.*
8. *Floor-timber Braces.*
9 *Sill Knee-iron.*
10 *Sill Tie-rod.*
11. *Transverse Floor-timbers.*
12. *Body-bolster.*
13. *Body-bolster Truss-rod.*
14. *Body-bolster Truss-rod Washer.*

15. *Body-bolster Truss-block.*
16. *Body Side-bearing.*
17. *Body Centre-plate.*
18. *King-bolt.*
19. *Body Truss-rod.*
20. *Body Truss-rod Saddle.*
21. *Body Truss-rod Bearing.*
22. *Cross-frame Tie-timber.*
23. *Draw-bar.*
24. *Draw-spring.*
25. *Auxiliary Buffer-spring.*
26. *Draw-timbers.*
27. *Floor.*
28. *Upper-floor.*

29. *Buffer-block.*
30. *Sill-step.*
31. *Sill-step Stay.*
32. *Dead-blocks.*
32'. *Buffer-beam.*
33. *Side Body-brace.*
34. *Side Body-brace Rod.*
35. *End Body-brace.*
36. *Sill-and-Plate Rod.*
37. *Body-counter-brace.*
38. *Brace-rod Washer.*
39. *Brace-pocket.*
40. *Right-hand Brace-pocket.*
41. *Double Brace-pocket.*
42. *Body-post.*
43. *Corner-post.*
44. *Door-post.*
45. *Corner-post Pocket.*

46. *Plate.*
47. *Plate-rod*
48. *End-plate.*
49. *Girth.*
50. *End-girth.*
51. *End-girth Tie-rod.*
52. *Sheathing.*
53. *Inside-lining.*
54. *Lining-strips.*
55. *Upper Corner-plate.*
56. *Middle Corner-plate.*
57. *Lower Corner-plate.*
58. *Pull-iron.*
59. *Ladder-rounds.*
60. *Ladder-handle.*
61. *Grated-door.*
62. *Grain-door.*
63. *Grain-door Rod.*
64. *Door-sill.*

65. *Top Door-track.*
66. *Bottom Door-track.*
67. *Door-track Bracket.*
68. *Door-hanger.*
69. *Door-brace.*
70. *Door-shoe.*
71. *Open-door Stop.*
72. *Closed-door Stop.*
73. *Door-hasp.*
74. *Door-pin.*
75. *Door-pin Chain.*
76. *Lock-chain.*
77. *Door-guards.*
78. *Door-handle.*
79. *Freight-car Lock.*
80. *Card-rack.*
81. *Carline, or Carling.*
82. *Main-carline.*
83. *Purlin.*
84. *Ridge-pole.*
85. *Roof-braces.*
86. *Roof-boards.*
87. *Roof Running-board.*
88. *Roof Running-board Extension.*
89. *Roof Running-board Bracket.*
90. *Eaves-moulding.*
91. *Eaves Fascia-board.*
92. *Roof-step.*
93. *Brake-wheel.*
94. *Brake-shaft.*
95. *Horizontal Brake-shaft.*
96. *Upper Brake-shaft Bearing.*
97. *Lower Brake-shaft Bearing.*
98. *Brake-shaft Step.*
99. *Brake-shaft Bracket.*
100. *Brake-step.*
101. *Brake step Bracket.*
102. *Corner-handle.*
103. *Brake Ratchet-wheel.*
103'. *Brake-pawl.*
104. *Horizontal Brake-shaft Chain.*
105. *Brake-shaft-chain Sheave.*
106. *Tank, for Tank-car.*
106'. *Tank-head.*
107. *Tank-band.*
108. *Tank-dome.*
109. *Dome-head.*
110. *Man-hole.*
111. *Man-hole Cover.*
112. *Man-hole Ring.*
113. *Man-hole Hinge.*
114. *Tank-valve.*
115. *Tank-valve Seat, or Tank-nozzle.*
116. *Tank-valve Cage.*
117. *Tank-valve Rod.*
118. *Tank-nozzle Cap.*
119. *Running-board.*
120. *Running-board. Brackets.*
121. *Hand-rail.*
122. *Hand-rail Post.*
123. *Drop-bottom.*
124. *Drop-bottom Chain.*
125. *Drop-bottom Hinge.*
126. *Drop-door Beam.*
127. *Strap, for Drop-door Beam.*
128. *Eye-bolt.*
129. *Winding-shaft.*
130. *Winding-shaft Ratchet-wheel.*
131. *Pawl, for Winding-shaft Ratchet-wheel.*
132. *Dog, for Pawl of Winding-shaft Ratchet-wheel.*
133. *Winding-shaft Plate.*
134. *Inclined End-floor.*
135. *Inclined Side-flooring.*
136. *Top Side-rail.*
137. *Top End-rail.*
138. *Draw-bar Cross-timber.*
139. *Draw-gear Tie-rod.*
140. *Coupling-pin.*
141. *Train Signal-lamp.*
142. *Brake-head.*
143. *Brake-beam.*
144. *Brake-hanger.*
145. *Brake-lever.*
146. *Brake-lever Fulcrum.*
147. *Brake-lever Guide.*
148. *Brake-lever Bracket.*

# Freight-car Bodies.

149. Brake-lever-bracket Brace.
150. Brake-shaft Chain.
151. Brake-shaft Connecting-rod.
152. Secondary Brake-rod.
152' Lower Brake-rod.
153. Inclined Floor-timbers.

154. Tip-car Door.
155. Rocker.
156. Rocker-bearing.
157. Rocker-bearing Timber.
158. Rocker-bearing-timber Hanger.
159. Rocker-timber.
160. Side-rest.
161. Centre-stop.

162. Side-stop.
163. Corner-post Brace.
164. Equalizing-bar Pedestal.
165. Journal-box.
166. Pedestal Brace-tie-bar.
167. Pedestal Stay-rod.

168. Pedestal Tie-bar.
169. Pedestal-timber.
170. Spring-hanger.
171. Spring-hanger Iron.
172. Pedestal.
173. Draw-bar Friction-plate.
174. Clear-story.

For list of names of the parts designated by the numbers in the engraving, see page 216.

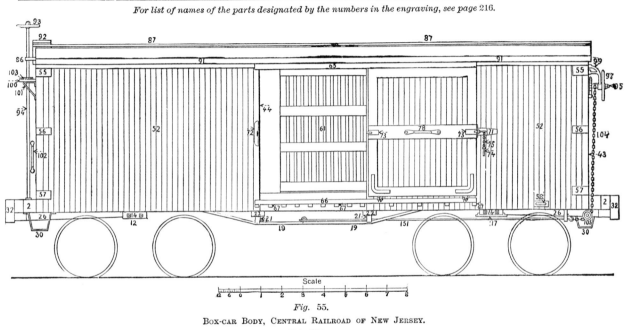

Scale

*Fig. 55.*

BOX-CAR BODY, CENTRAL RAILROAD OF NEW JERSEY.

*Side View.*

*For list of names of the parts designated by the numbers in the engraving, see page 216.*

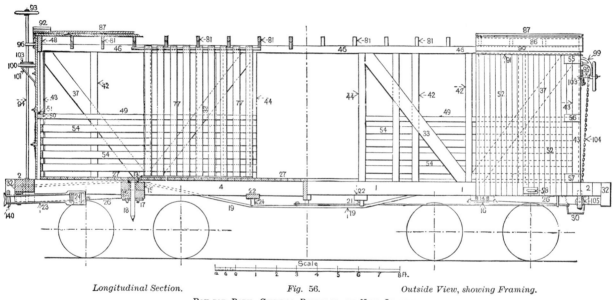

*Longitudinal Section.*       **Fig. 56.**       *Outside View, showing Framing.*

Box-car Body, Central Railroad of New Jersey.

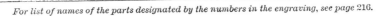

*For list of names of the parts designated by the numbers in the engraving, see page 216.*

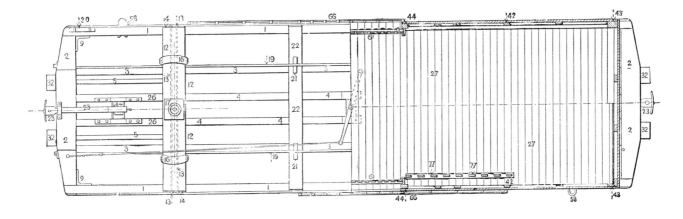

*Half Plan, showing Framing.*          Fig. 57.          *Half Plan, showing Floor.*

BOX-CAR BODY, CENTRAL RAILROAD OF NEW JERSEY.

*For list of names of the parts designated by the numbers in the engravings, see page 216.*

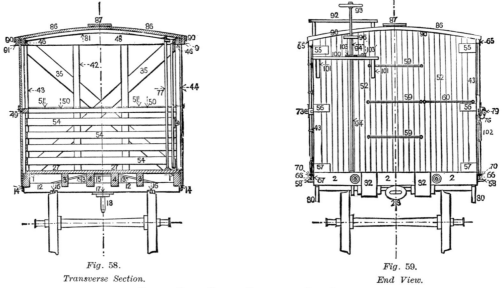

*Fig. 58.*

*Transverse Section.*

*Fig. 59.*

*End View.*

Box-car Body, Central Railroad of New Jersey.

*For list of names of the parts designated by the numbers in the engraving, see page 216.*

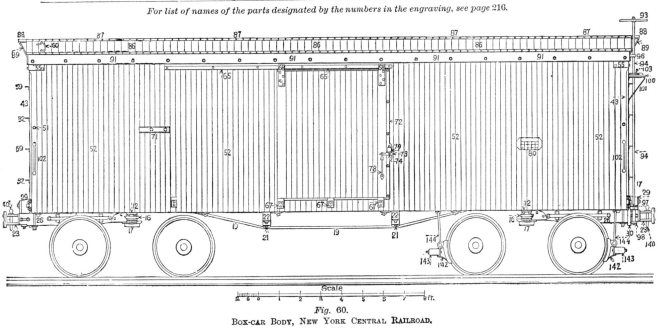

Scale

*Fig.* 60.
BOX-CAR BODY, NEW YORK CENTRAL RAILROAD,
*Side View.*

*For list of names of the parts designated by the numbers in the engraving, see page 216.*

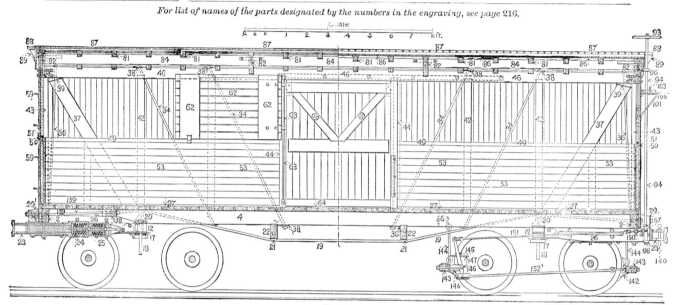

*Fig.* 61.

BOX-CAR BODY, NEW YORK CENTRAL RAILROAD.

*Longitudinal Section.*

For list of names of the parts designated by the numbers in the engraving, see page 216.

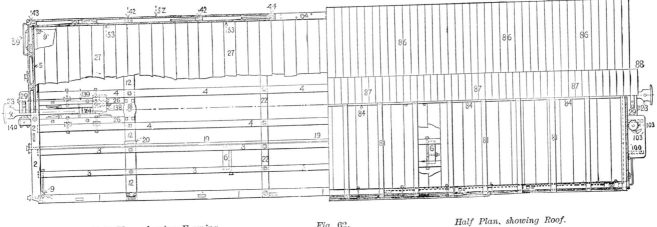

*Half Plan, showing Framing.*     *Fig. 62.*     *Half Plan, showing Roof.*

Box-car Body, New York Central Railroad.

*For list of names of the parts designated by the numbers in the engraving, see page 216.*

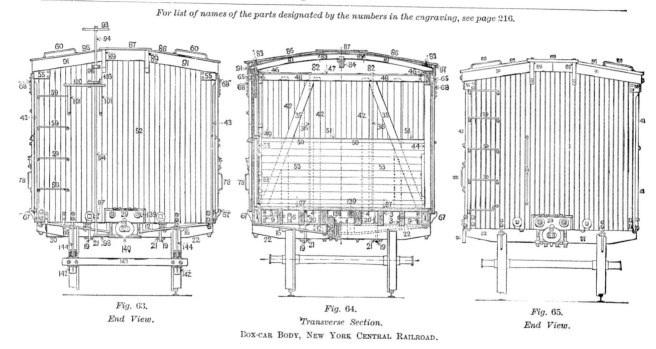

Fig. 63.

End View.

Fig. 64.

*Transverse Section.*

Fig. 65.

End View.

BOX-CAR BODY, NEW YORK CENTRAL RAILROAD.

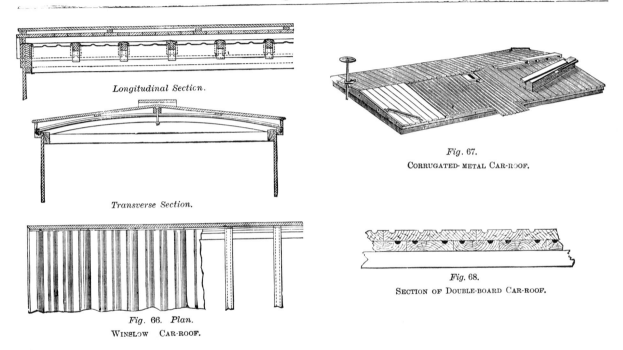

*Longitudinal Section.*

*Transverse Section.*

*Fig.* 66. *Plan.*

WINSLOW CAR-ROOF.

*Fig.* 67.

CORRUGATED- METAL CAR-ROOF.

*Fig.* 68.

SECTION OF DOUBLE-BOARD CAR-ROOF.

# *Freight-car Bodies.*

*For list of names of the parts designated by the numbers in the engraving, see page 216.*

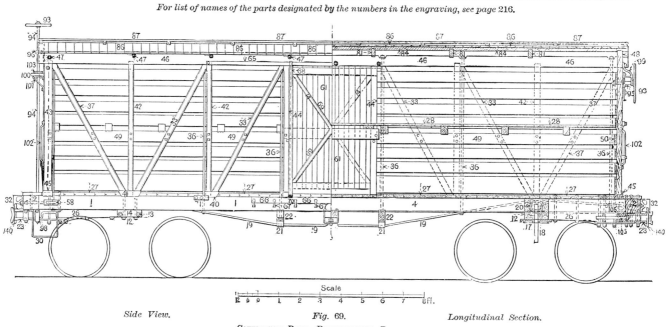

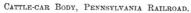

Scale

*Side View.* **Fig. 69.** *Longitudinal Section.*

CATTLE-CAR BODY, PENNSYLVANIA RAILROAD.

*For list of names of the parts designated by the numbers in the engraving, see page 216.*

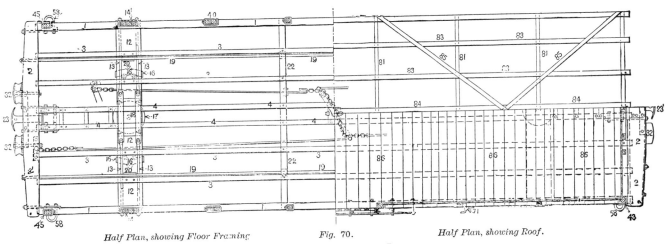

*Half Plan, showing Floor Framing.*     Fig. 70.     *Half Plan, showing Roof.*

CATTLE CAR BODY, PENNSYLVANIA RAILROAD.

*For list of names of the parts designated by the numbers in the engravings, see page 216.*

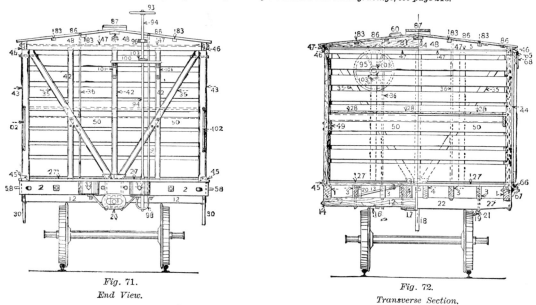

Fig. 71.
End View.

Fig. 72.
Transverse Section.

CATTLE-CAR BODY, PENNSYLVANIA RAILROAD.

For list of names of the parts designated by the numbers in the engraving, see page 216.

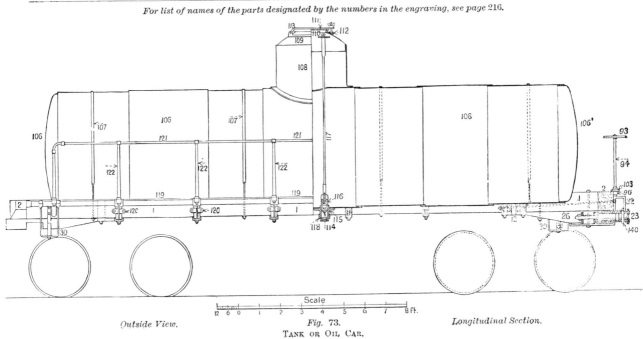

Scale

12  6  0    1    2    3    4    5    6    7    8 ft.

*Outside View.*                *Fig. 73.*                *Longitudinal Section.*

TANK OR OIL CAR.

*For list of names of the parts designated by the numbers in the engraving, see page 216.*

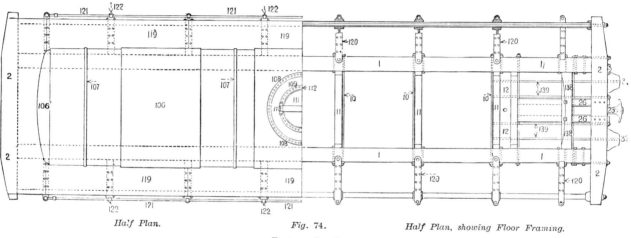

*Half Plan.*                    *Fig. 74.*            *Half Plan, showing Floor Framing.*

TANK OR OIL CAR.

*For list of names of the parts designated by the numbers in the engravings, see page 216.*

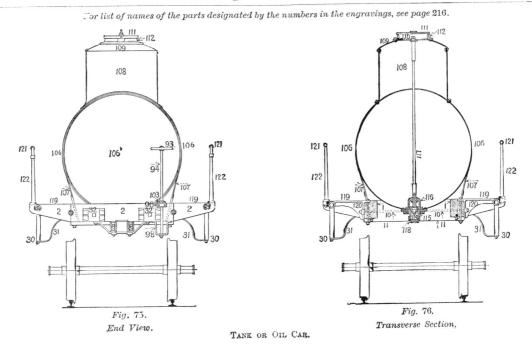

Fig. 75.

End View.

TANK OR OIL CAR.

Fig. 76.

Transverse Section,

*For list of names of the parts designated by* the numbers in the engraving, see page 216.

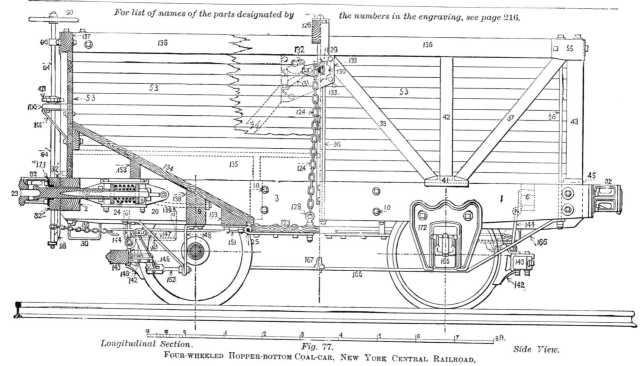

*Longitudinal Section.* 　　　　　　　*Fig. 77.* 　　　　　　*Side View.*

FOUR-WHEELED HOPPER-BOTTOM COAL-CAR, NEW YORK CENTRAL RAILROAD,

*For list of names of the parts designated by the numbers in the engraving, see page 216.*

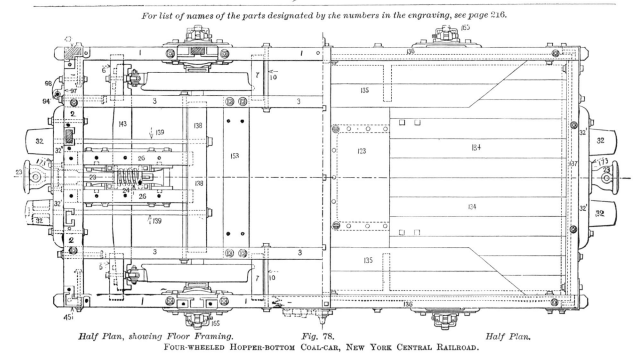

*Half Plan, showing Floor Framing.*     Fig. 78.     *Half Plan.*

FOUR-WHEELED HOPPER-BOTTOM COAL-CAR, NEW YORK CENTRAL RAILROAD.

*For list of names of the parts designated by the numbers in the engravings, see page 216.*

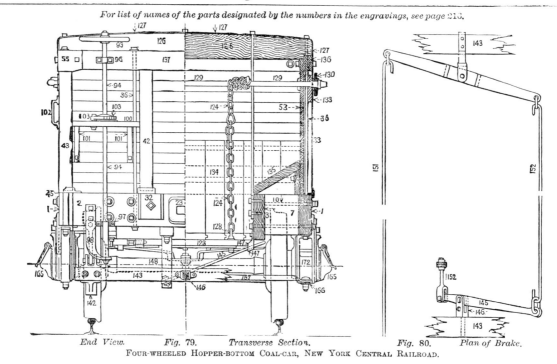

End View.     *Fig. 79.*     Transverse Section.     *Fig. 80.*     Plan of Brake.

FOUR-WHEELED HOPPER-BOTTOM COAL-CAR, NEW YORK CENTRAL RAILROAD.

*For list of names of the parts designated by the numbers in the engraving, see page 216.*

*Fig.* 81. Tip-car.

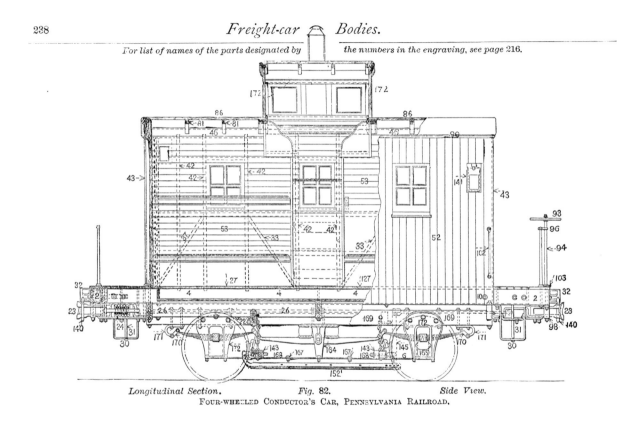

*For list of names of the parts designated by the numbers in the engraving, see page 216.*

Longitudinal Section.      Fig. 82.      Side View.

FOUR-WHEELED CONDUCTOR'S CAR, PENNSYLVANIA RAILROAD.

*For list of names of the parts designated by the numbers in the engraving, see page 216.*

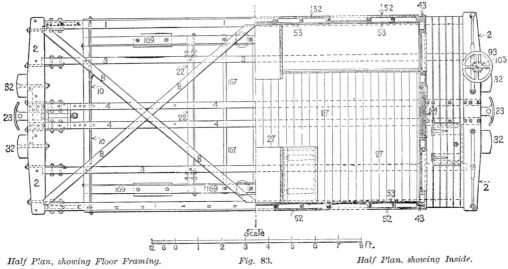

*Half Plan, showing Floor Framing.*     *Fig. 83.*     *Half Plan, showing Inside.*

FOUR-WHEELED CONDUCTOR'S CAR, PENNSYLVANIA RAILROAD.

*For list of names of the parts designated by the numbers in the engravings, see page 216.*

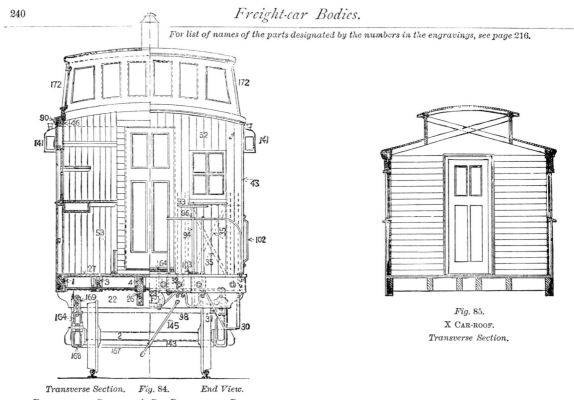

*Transverse Section.*    *Fig. 84.*        *End View.*

FOUR-WHEELED CONDUCTOR'S CAR, PENNSYLVANIA RAILROAD.

*Fig. 85.*

X CAR-ROOF.

*Transverse Section.*

*Fig.* 86.

STAKE-POCKET.

1. *Stake-pocket.*
2. *Stake pocket U-bolt.*

*Fig.* 87.

STAKE-SLEEVE.

1. *Stake-pocket.*
2. *Stake-sleeve.*

# CAR TRUCKS.

**52.** *Middle Safety-beam.*
**53.** *Safety-beam Block.*
**54.** *Axle Safety-bearing.*
**55.** *Axle Safety-strap.*
**56.** *Axle Safety-bearing Thimbles.*
**57.** *Safety-beam Truss-rod.*
**58.** *Safety-beam Truss-rod Bearing.*
**59.** *Safety-beam Tie-rod.*
**60.** *Safety-beam Iron.*
**61.** *Truck Side-bearing.*
**62.** *Side-bearing Bridge.*
**63.** *Truck Centre-plate.*
**64.** *Centre-plate Block.*
**65.** *Centre-bearing Beam.*

**66.** *Centre-bearing Arch-bar.*
**67.** *Centre-bearing Inverted Arch-bar.*
**68.** *Check-chain.*
**69.** *Truck Check-chain Hook.*
**70.** *Truck Check-chain Eye.*
**71.** *Equalizing-bar.*
**72.** *Equalizing-bar Spring-cap.*
**73.** *Equalizing-bar Spring-seat.*
**74.** *Bolster Spring-seat.*
**75.** *Bolster Spring-cap.*
**76.** *Spring-block.*

**77.** *Jaw-bit.*
**78.** *Journal-spring.*
**79.** *Equalizing-bar Spring.*
**80.** *Bolster-spring.*
**81.** *Truck-frame Knee-iron.*
**82.** *Brake-block.*
**83.** *Brake-head.*
**84.** *Brake-beam.*
**85.** *Brake Eye-bolt.*
**86.** *Brake-hanger.*
**87.** *Brake-hanger Carrier.*
**88.** *Brake Safety-chain.*
**89.** *Brake Safety-chain Eye-bolt.*
**90.** *Brake Safety-strap.*

**91.** *Release-spring.*
**92.** *Brake-lever.*
**93.** *Brake-lever Fulcrum.*
**94.** *Brake-lever Guide.*
**95.** *Brake-lever Stop.*
**96.** *Brake-lever Sheave.*
**97.** *Lower Brake-rod.*
**98.** *Brake-shoe.*
**99.** *Journal-box Guides*
**100.** *Pedestal-horns.*
**101.** *Pedestal-jaw.*
**102.** *Spring-hanger.*
**103.** *Spring-saddle.*
**104.** *King-bolt.*
**105.** *Journal-bearing.*
**106.** *Journal-bearing Key*

*For list of names of the parts designated by the numbers in the engraving, see page 242.*

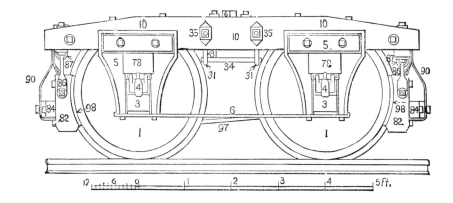

*Fig.* 88.
WOODEN FREIGHT-CAR TRUCK, NEW YORK & HARLEM RAILROAD.
*Side View.*

For list of names of the parts designated by the numbers in the engraving, see page 242.

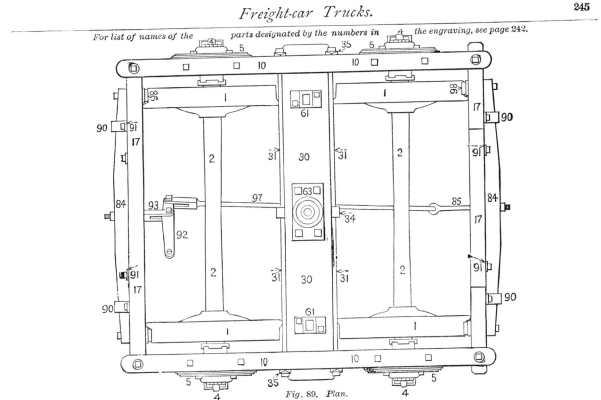

*Fig.* 89. *Plan.*

WOODEN FREIGHT-CAR TRUCK, NEW YORK & HARLEM RAILROAD.

*For list of names of the parts designated by the numbers in the engraving, see page 242.*

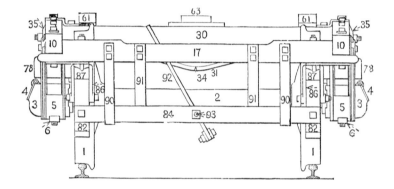

Fig. 90.

WOODEN FREIGHT-CAR TRUCK, NEW YORK & HARLEM RAILROAD.

*End View.*

*For list of names of the parts designated by the numbers in the engravings, see page 242.*

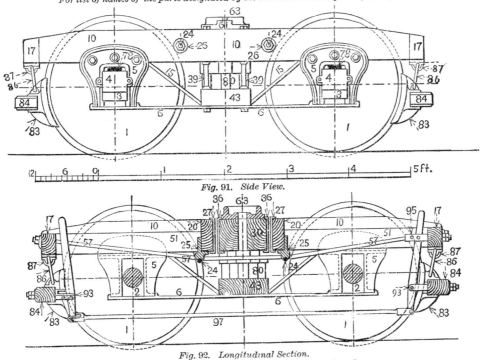

*Fig.* 91. *Side View.*

*Fig.* 92. *Longitudinal Section.*

WOODEN FREIGHT-CAR TRUCK, CENTRAL RAILROAD OF NEW JERSEY.

*For list of names of the parts designated by the numbers in the engraving, see page 242.*

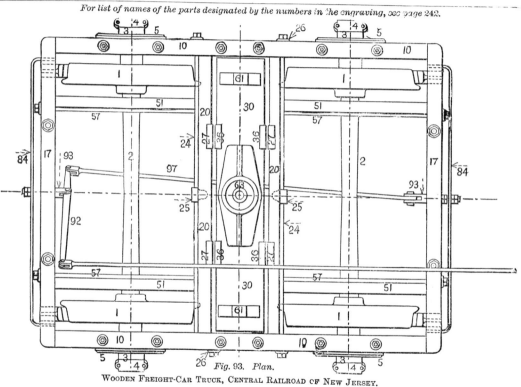

Fig. 93. Plan.

WOODEN FREIGHT-CAR TRUCK, CENTRAL RAILROAD OF NEW JERSEY.

*For list of names of the parts designated by the numbers in the engraving, see page 242.*

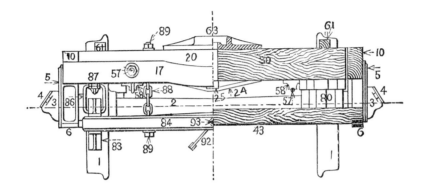

*End View.* *Fig.* 94. *Transverse Section.*

WOODEN FREIGHT-CAR TRUCK, CENTRAL RAILROAD OF NEW JERSEY.

*For list of names of the parts designated by the numbers in the engravings, see page 242.*

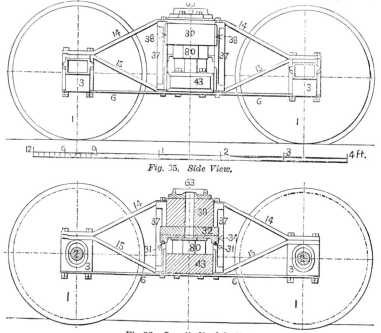

Fig. 95. *Side View.*

Fig. 96. *Longitudinal Section.*
DIAMOND-TRUCK, CENTRAL RAILROAD OF NEW JERSEY.

*For list of names of the parts designated by the numbers in the engraving, see page 242.*

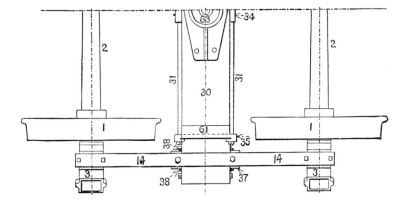

*Fig. 97.*
DIAMOND-TRUCK, CENTRAL RAILROAD OF NEW JERSEY.
*Half Plan.*

*For list of names of the parts designated by the numbers in the engravings, see page 242.*

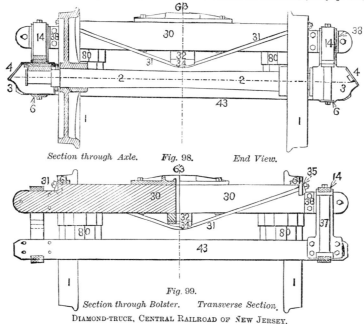

Section through Axle.     Fig. 98.     End View.

Fig. 99.

Section through Bolster.     Transverse Section.

DIAMOND-TRUCK, CENTRAL RAILROAD OF NEW JERSEY.

*For list of names of the parts designated by the numbers in the engravings, see page 242*

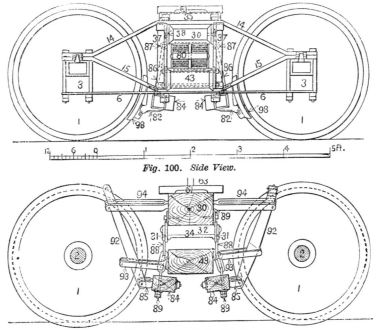

*Fig.* 100. *Side View.*

*Fig.* 101. *Longitudinal Section.*
DIAMOND-TRUCK, PENNSYLVANIA RAILROAD.

*For list of names of the parts designated by the numbers in the engraving, see page 242.*

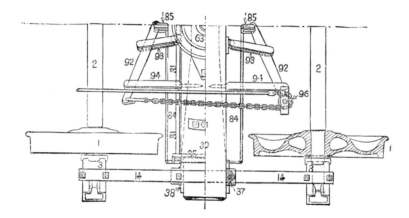

Fig. 102.

DIAMOND-TRUCK, PENNSYLVANIA RAILROAD.

*Half Plan.*

For list of names of the parts designated by the numbers in the engravings, see page 242.

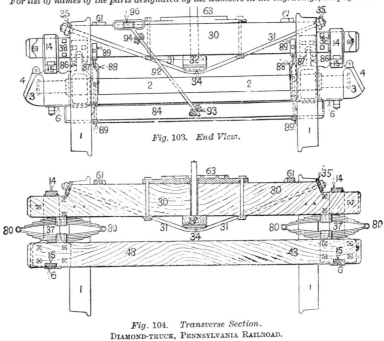

Fig. 103.   End View.

Fig. 104.   Transverse Section.
DIAMOND-TRUCK, PENNSYLVANIA RAILROAD.

*For list of names of the parts designated by the numbers in the engravings, see page 242.*

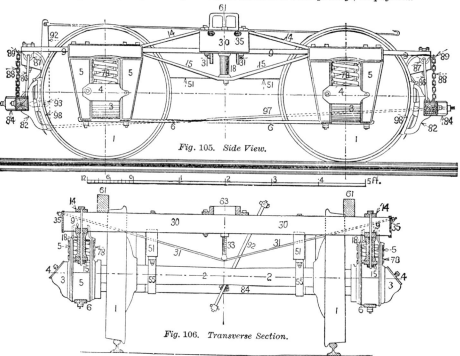

Fig. 105. *Side View.*

Fig. 106. *Transverse Section.*

CONTINUOUS-FRAME TRUCK, BOSTON & ALBANY RAILROAD.

*For list of names of the parts designated by the numbers in the engraving, see page 24?.*

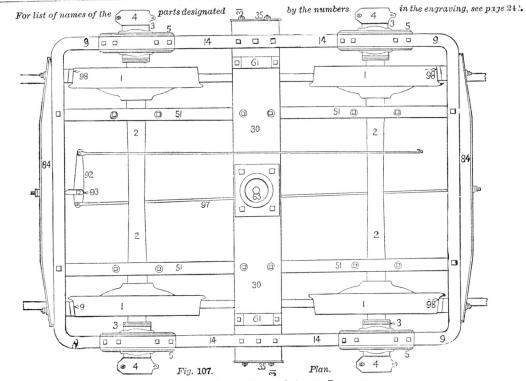

*Fig. 107.* Plan.

CONTINUOUS-FRAME TRUCK, BOSTON & ALBANY RAILROAD.

For list of names of the parts designated by the numbers in the engravings, see page 242.

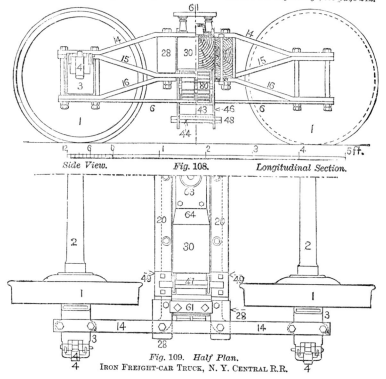

Side View.          Fig. 108.          Longitudinal Section.

Fig. 109.   Half Plan.
IRON FREIGHT-CAR TRUCK, N. Y. CENTRAL R.R.

*For list of names of the parts designated by the numbers in the engravings, see page 242.*

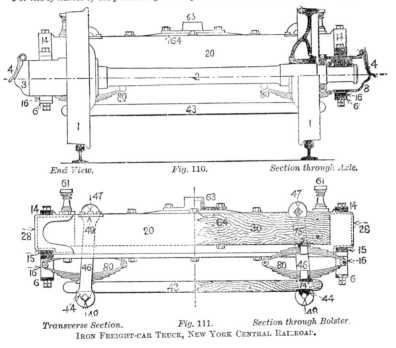

End View.  Fig. 110.  Section through Axle.

Transverse Section.  Fig. 111.  Section through Bolster.

IRON FREIGHT-CAR TRUCK, NEW YORK CENTRAL RAILROAD.

*For list of names of the parts designated by the numbers in the engravings, see page 242.*

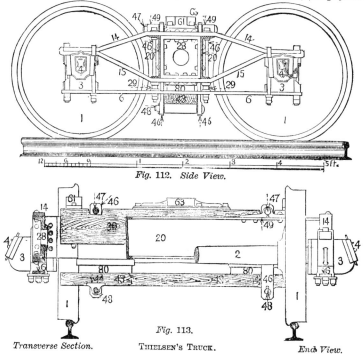

*Fig. 112. Side View.*

*Transverse Section.*       *Fig. 113.*       *End View.*

THIELSEN'S TRUCK.

For list of names of the parts designated by the numbers in the engraving, see page 242.

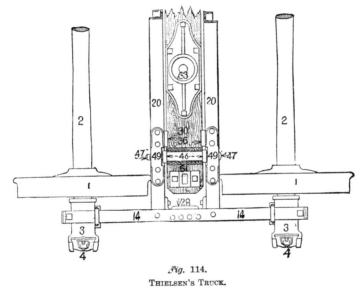

*Fig.* 114.

THIELSEN'S TRUCK.

*Half Plan.*

*For list of names of the parts designated by the numbers in the engraving, see page 242.*

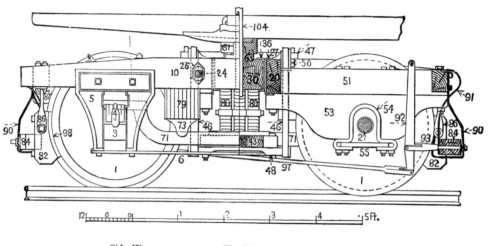

*Side View.*            Fig. 115.            *Longitudinal Section.*

PASSENGER-CAR TRUCK, NEW YORK & HARLEM RAILROAD.

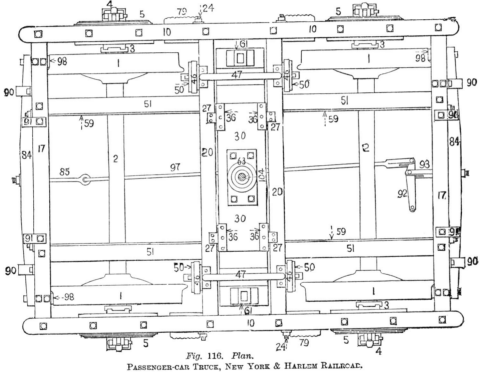

*Fig. 116. Plan.*

PASSENGER-CAR TRUCK, NEW YORK & HARLEM RAILROAD.

For list of names of the parts designated by the numbers in the engraving see page 242.

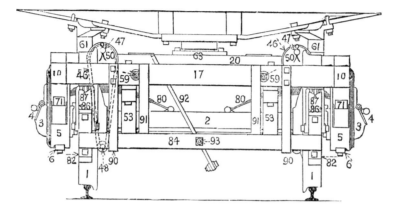

*Fig. 117.*

PASSENGER-CAR TRUCK, NEW YORK & HARLEM RAILROAD.

*End View.*

*For list of names of the parts designated by the numbers in the engraving, see page 242.*

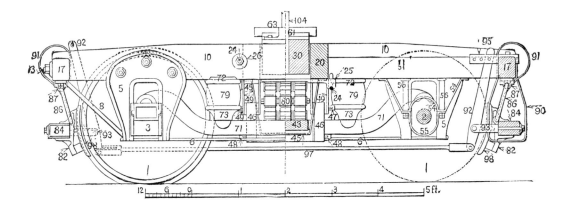

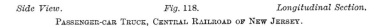

*Side View.*     *Fig.* 118.     *Longitudinal Section.*

PASSENGER-CAR TRUCK, CENTRAL RAILROAD OF NEW JERSEY.

For list of names of the parts designated by *the numbers in the engraving, see page 241.*

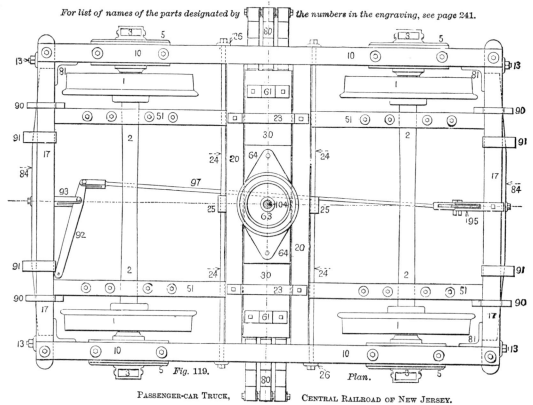

Fig. 119.

PASSENGER-CAR TRUCK, CENTRAL RAILROAD OF NEW JERSEY.

Plan.

*For list of names of the parts designated by the numbers in the engravings, see page 242.*

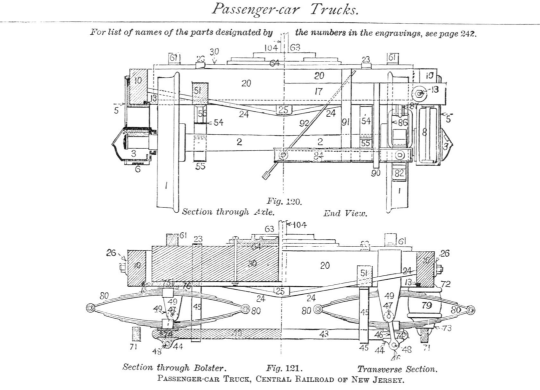

Fig. 120.

*Section through Axle.* *End View.*

*Section through Bolster.* Fig. 121. *Transverse Section.*

PASSENGER-CAR TRUCK, CENTRAL RAILROAD OF NEW JERSEY.

*For list of names of the parts designated by the numbers in the engraving, see page 242.*

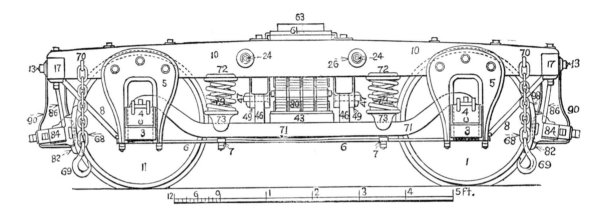

*Fig.* 122.

PASSENGER-CAR TRUCK, PENNSYLVANIA RAILROAD.

*Side View.*

*For list of names of the parts designated by the numbers in the engraving, see page 242.*

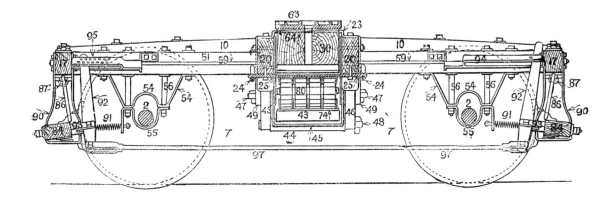

*Fig. 123.*

PASSENGER-CAR TRUCK, PENNSYLVANIA RAILROAD.
*Longitudinal Section.*

*For list of names of the parts designated by* *the numbers in the engraving, see page 242.*

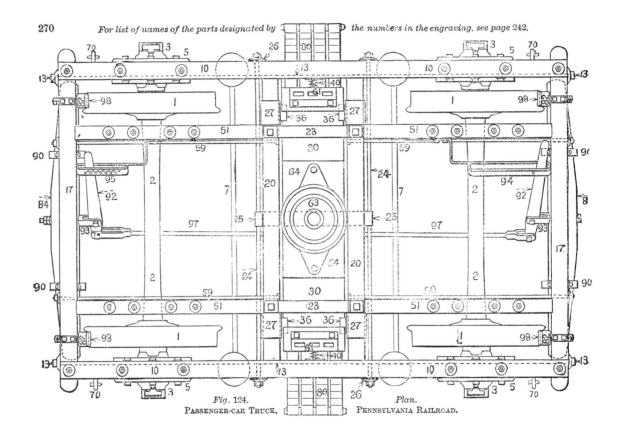

*Fig.* 124.

PASSENGER-CAR TRUCK,     Plan.

PENNSYLVANIA RAILROAD.

*For list of names of* 61 *the parts designated by* 63 *the numbers in the* 61 *engravings, see page 242.*

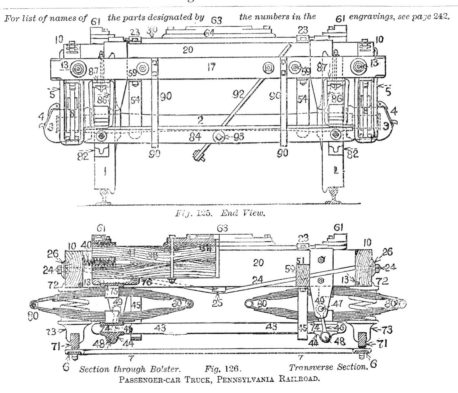

*Fig. 125. End View.*

*Section through Bolster.*    *Fig. 126.*    *Transverse Section.*

PASSENGER-CAR TRUCK, PENNSYLVANIA RAILROAD.

*For list of names of the parts designated by the numbers in the engraving, see page 242.*

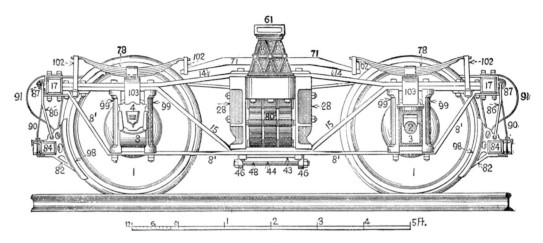

*Fig.* 127.

ALLEN IRON PASSENGER-CAR TRUCK, CHICAGO, BURLINGTON & QUINCY RAILROAD.

*Side View.*

For list of names of the parts designated by the numbers in the engraving, see page 242.

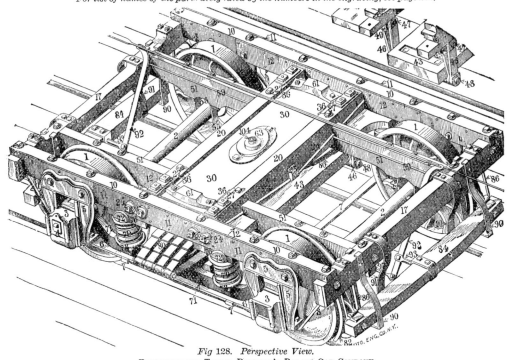

*Fig* 128. *Perspective View.*
PASSENGER-CAR TRUCK, PULLMAN'S PALACE CAR COMPANY.

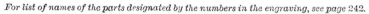

*For list of names of the parts designated by the numbers in the engraving, see page 242.*

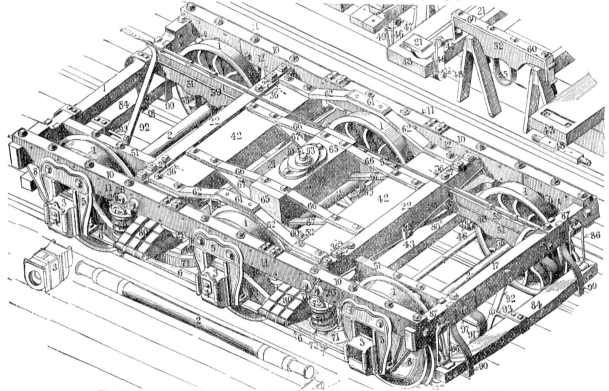

*Fig.* 129. Six-wheeled Passenger-car Truck, Pullman's Palace Car Company. *Perspective View.*

*For list of names of the parts designated by the numbers in the engraving, see page 242.*

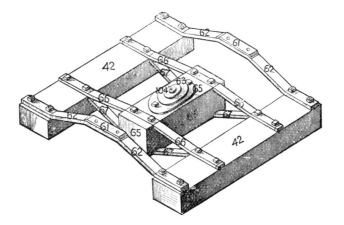

*Fig.* 130.

BOLSTER FOR SIX-WHEELED TRUCK.

*Perspective View.*

For list of names of the parts designated by the numbers in fig. 131, see page 242.

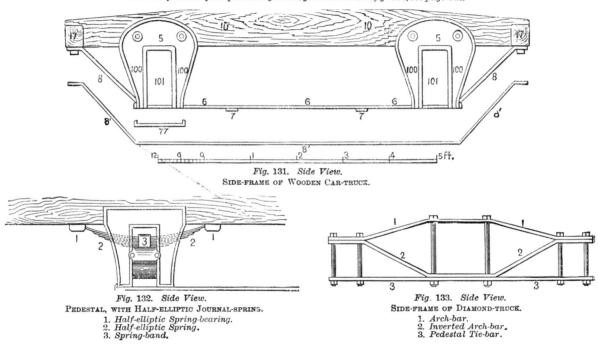

*Fig. 131. Side View.*
SIDE-FRAME OF WOODEN CAR-TRUCK.

*Fig. 132. Side View.*
PEDESTAL, WITH HALF-ELLIPTIC JOURNAL-SPRING.
1. *Half-elliptic Spring-bearing.*
2. *Half-elliptic Spring.*
3. *Spring-band.*

*Fig. 133. Side View.*
SIDE-FRAME OF DIAMOND-TRUCK.
1. *Arch-bar.*
2. *Inverted Arch-bar.*
3. *Pedestal Tie-bar.*

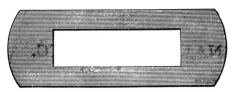

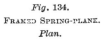

*Fig.* 134.

FRAMED SPRING-PLANE.

*Plan.*

*Fig.* 136.

ROCKER SIDE-BEARING.

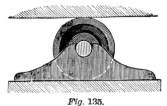

*Fig.* 135.

ROLLER SIDE-BEARING.

*Side View.*

*Fig.* 137.

OPEN SWING-HANGER, OR SWING LINK-HANGER.

# WHEELS, AXLES, JOURNAL-BOXES, ETC.

List of Names of the Parts of Wheels, Axles, Journal-boxes, etc., which are Designated by the Letters and Numbers in Figs. 138–153.

**A.** *Centre, of Axle.*
**B.** *Neck, of Axle.*
**C.** *Wheel-seat.*
**D.** *Dust-guard Bearing.*
**E.** *Journal.*
**F.** *Axle-collar.*
**3.** *Stop-plate.*
**7.** *Journal-bearing.*
**8.** *Journal-bearing Key.*

**9.** *Stop-key Journal-bearing.*
**10.** *Journal-box.*
**11.** *Journal-box Cover.*
**12.** *Journal-box-cover Hinge-pin.*
**13.** *Journal-box-cover Spring.*
**14.** *Journal-packing.*

**15.** *Dust-guard and Dust-guard Chamber.*
**16.** *Dust-collar.*
**17.** *Equalizing-bar Seat.*
**18.** *Pedestal.*
**19.** *Pedestal-horns.*
**20.** *Pedestal-jaw.*
**21.** *Hub, of Wheel.*
**22.** *Wheel-plate.*

**23.** *Rim, of Wheel.*
**24.** *Face, of Rim.*
**25.** *Tread of Wheel, or Wheel-tread.*
**26.** *Wheel-flange.*
**27.** *Journal-bearing Stop-key.*
**28.** *Oil-cellar.*
**29.** *Stop Journal-bearing.*

For list of names of the parts designated by the numbers in the engravings, see page 278.

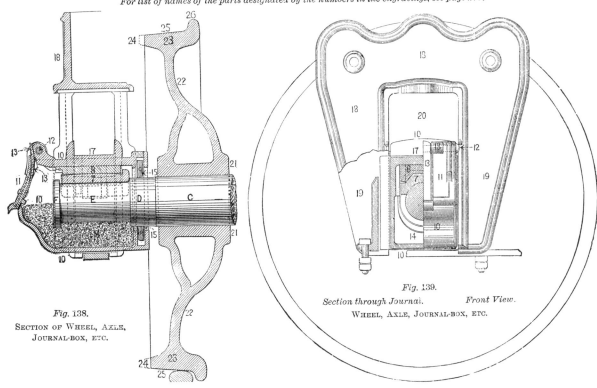

*Fig. 138.*

SECTION OF WHEEL, AXLE,
JOURNAL-BOX, ETC.

*Fig. 139.*

*Section through Journal.* Front View.

WHEEL, AXLE, JOURNAL-BOX, ETC.

Fig. 140.
JOURNAL-BOX.
*Perspective View.*

Fig. 142.
JOURNAL-BEARING KEY.

Fig. 141.
JOURNAL-BEARING.

"*The engraving herewith of the Standard Car and Tender Axle, recommended by the Master Car-Builders' and Master Mechanics' associations, at their conventions, held in 1879, is hereby approved.*"

*Committee of Master Car-Builders' Association.*

F. D. ADAMS, Boston & Albany Railroad.
M. N. FORNEY, *Railroad Gazette.*
JOHN KIRBY, Lake Shore & Mich. South. Ry.
S. A. DAVIS, Boston, Lowell & Nashua Railroad.

H. W. COOPER, Ind., Bloomington & West. Ry.
J. M. BOON, Pittsburgh. Fort Wayne & Chicago Ry.
W. S. HUDSON, Rogers Locomotive Works.
M. N. FORNEY, *Railroad Gazette.*

*Committee of Master Mechanics' Association.*

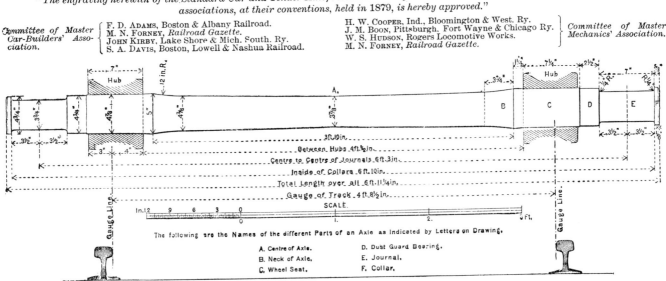

The following are the Names of the different Parts of an Axle as indicated by Letters on Drawing.

A. Centre of Axle.
B. Neck of Axle.
C. Wheel Seat.

D. Dust Guard Bearing.
E. Journal.
F. Collar.

*The engraving represents the* **dimensions of the axle when finished.** *Weight, finished, 347 lbs.*

Fig. 143.

MASTER CAR-BUILDERS' STANDARD AXLE.

*For list of names of the parts designated by the letters and numbers in the engravings, see page 278.*

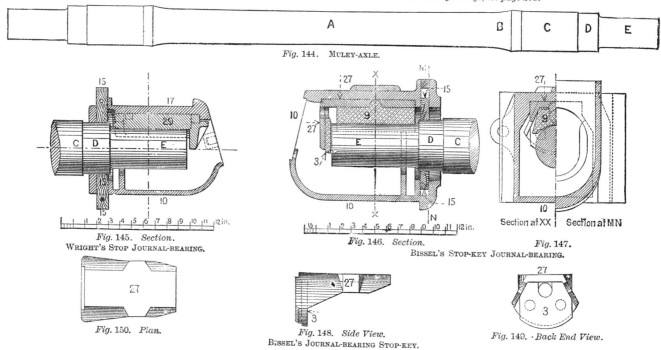

Fig. 144.   MULEY-AXLE.

Fig. 145.   *Section.*
WRIGHT'S STOP JOURNAL-BEARING.

Fig. 146.   *Section.*

Fig. 147.
BISSEL'S STOP-KEY JOURNAL-BEARING.

Section at XX    Section at MN

Fig. 150.   *Plan.*

Fig. 148.   *Side View.*
BISSEL'S JOURNAL-BEARING STOP-KEY.

Fig. 149.  *Back End View.*

*For list of names of the parts designated by the numbers in the engravings, see page 278.*

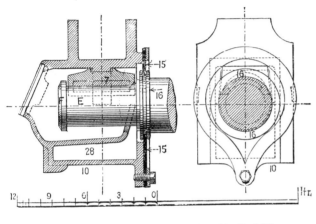

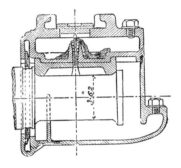

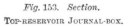

*Fig.* 151. *Section.*　　　　*Fig.* 152. *Back View.*

TIM'S JOURNAL-BOX.

*Fig.* 153. *Section.*

TOP-RESERVOIR JOURNAL-BOX.

*Fig. 154.*
*Front View.*

*Fig. 155.*
*Back View.*

*Fig. 156.*

SINGLE-PLATE WHEEL.

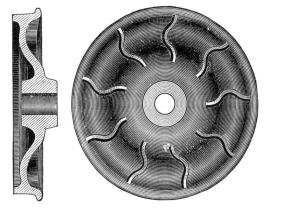

*Fig.* 157.      *Fig.* 158.

Section.      *Back View.*

SINGLE-PLATE WHEEL.

*Fig.* 159.

Section.

" COMBINATION " PLATE-WHEEL.

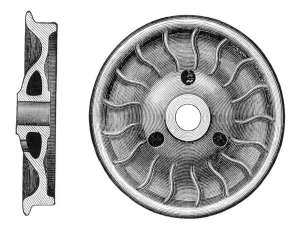

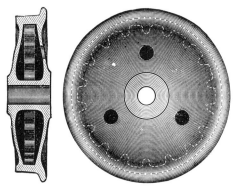

*Fig.* 161.                          *Fig.* 162.                          *Fig.* 163                          *Fig.* 164.
Section.                            *Back View.*                         Section.                           *Back View.*

"WASHBURN"-WHEEL.                                                    DOUBLE-PLATE WHEEL.

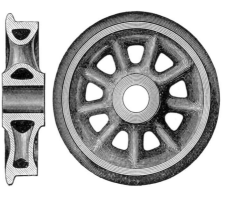

*Fig.* 165.           *Fig.* 166.          *Fig.* 167.

*Front View.*        *Section.*         *Front View.*

SPOKE-WHEEL.         HOLLOW-SPOKE WHEEL.

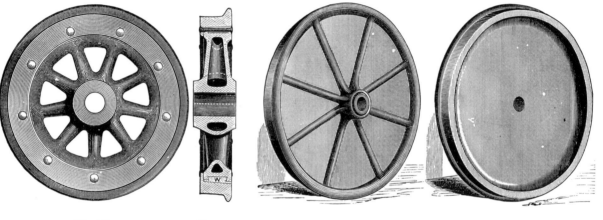

Fig. 168.　　　　　　Fig. 169.　　　　　　Fig. 170.　　　　　　　　　Fig. 171.

Front View.　　　　　Section.　　　　　Back View.　　　　　　　Front View.

ELASTIC-WHEEL.　　　　　　　　　　SINGLE-PLATE WHEEL FOR STREET-CARS.

Fig. 172.
Back View.

Fig. 173.
Front View.

OPEN PLATE-WHEEL, FOR STREET-CARS.

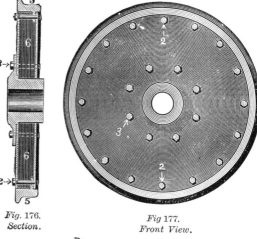

*Fig. 174.*
Section.

*Fig. 175.*
*Front View,*

*Fig. 176.*
Section.

*Fig 177.*
*Front View.*

SAX & KEAR WHEEL.

PAPER-WHEEL.
2. *Tire-bolt.*
3. *Hub-bolt.*
5. *Tire.*
6. *Compressed-paper.*

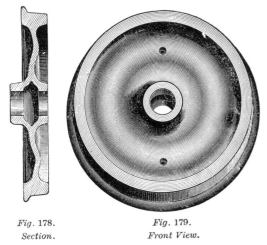

*Fig.* 178.
*Section.*

*Fig.* 179.
*Front View.*

SOLID STEEL-WHEEL.

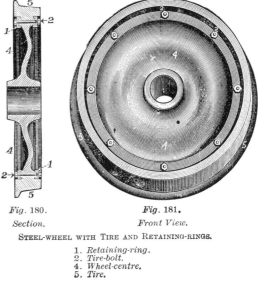

*Fig.* 180.
*Section.*

*Fig.* 181.
*Front View.*

STEEL-WHEEL WITH TIRE AND RETAINING-RINGS.

1. *Retaining-ring.*
2. *Tire-bolt.*
4. *Wheel-centre.*
5. *Tire.*

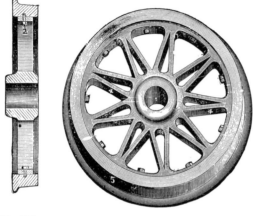

Fig. 182.
Section.

Fig. 183.
*Front View.*

Fig. 184.
HAND-CAR WHEEL.

WROUGHT-IRON WHEEL WITH TIRE.

2. *Tire-bolt.*
4. *Wheel-centre.*
5. *Tire.*

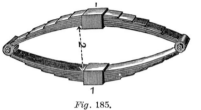

Fig. 185.

ELLIPTIC-SPRING.

Fig. 187.

HALF ELLIPTIC-SPRING.

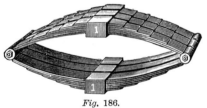

Fig. 186.

TRIPLET OF ELLIPTIC-SPRINGS.

Fig. 188.

COMBINATION ELLIPTIC-SPRING.

1. *Spring-band.*
2. *Set of Spring.*

Fig. 189.
ROUND-BAR SPIRAL
SINGLE-COIL SPRING.

Fig. 190.
ROUND-BAR SPIRAL
DOUBLE-COIL NEST-SPRING.

Fig. 191.
ROUND-BAR SPIRAL
TRIPLE-COIL NEST-SPRING.

Fig. 192.

Fig. 193. *Section.*
HALF-ROUND-BAR SPIRAL
DOUBLE-COIL NEST-SPRING.

*Fig.* 194.

SQUARE-BAR SPIRAL
SINGLE-COIL SPRING.

*Fig.* 195.

SQUARE-BAR SPIRAL
TRIPLE-COIL NEST-SPRING.

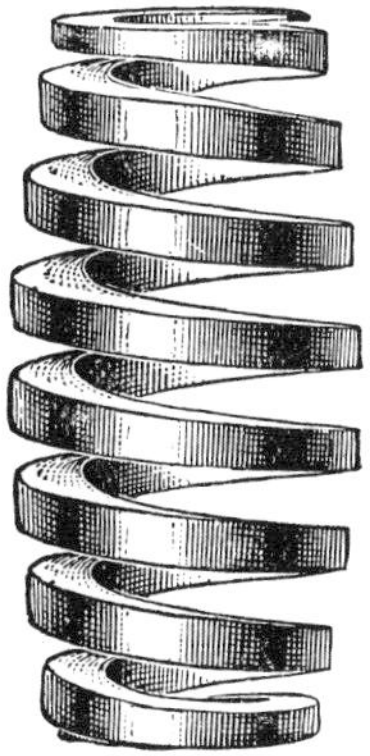

*Fig.* 196.

KEG-SHAPED SPIRAL-SPRING.

*Fig.* 197.

SPOOL-SHAPED SPIRAL-SPRING.

*Fig.* 198.

FLAT-BAR OR EQUAL-BAR
SPIRAL TRIPLE-COIL NEST-SPRING.

*Fig.* 199.

"HIBBARD" OR FLAT-BAR
SPIRAL QUADRUPLE-COIL NEST-SPRING.

*Fig.* 200.

EDGE-ROLLED SPIRAL-SPRING.

Fig. 201.

"Dinsmore" Spiral-
spring.

Fig. 202.

Section of "Dinsmore"
Spiral-spring.

Fig. 203.

"Paragon" Spiral-spring.

Fig. 204.

Section of Bar of
"Paragon" Spiral-spring.

Fig. 205.

Small Rubber-
centre Spiral-
spring.

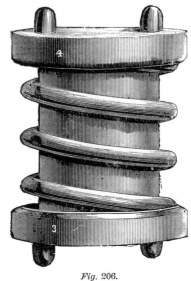

Fig. 206.

Rubber-centre Spiral-spring.

3. *Spring-seat.*
4. *Spring-cap.*

*Fig.* 207.

COMPOUND SPIRAL-SPRING.

*Fig.* 208.

"VOSE" GRADUATED SPIRAL-
SPRING.

3. *Spring-seat*.   4. *Spring-cap*.

*Fig.* 09.

EIGHT-GROUP WOOL-PACKED SPIRAL-SPRING.

*Fig.* 210.

OUTSIDE-VIEW OF SPRING-CASE FOR EIGHT-
GROUP WOOL-PACKED SPIRAL-SPRING.

*Fig.* 211.

TWO-GROUP SPIRAL-SPRING.

*Fig.* 212.

SIX-GROUP DOUBLE-COIL SPIRAL-SPRING.

3. *Spring-seat.*
4. *Spring-cap.*

*Fig.* 213.

VOLUTE SPRING.

*Fig.* 214.

INDIA-RUBBER SPRING.

# PASSENGER-CAR BODIES.

LIST OF NAMES OF THE PARTS OF PASSENGER-CAR BODIES WHICH ARE DESIGNATED BY THE NUMBERS IN FIGS. 215–232.

1. *Sill.*
2. *End-sill.*
3. *Intermediate Floor-timbers.*
4. *Centre Floor-timbers.*
5. *Floor-timber Distance-block.*
6. *Bridging.*
7. *Floor-timber Braces.*
8. *Sill Knee-iron.*
9. *Sill Tie-rod.*
10. *Body-bolster.*
11. *Body-bolster Truss-rod.*
12. *Body-bolster Truss-rod Washer.*
13. *Body-bolster Truss-block.*
14. *Body Side-bearings.*
15. *Body Centre-plate.*
16. *King-bolt.*
17. *King-bolt Plate.*
18. *Check-chain.*
19. *Body-check-chain Eye.*
20. *Body Truss-rod.*
21. *Body Truss-rod Saddle.*
22. *Body Queen-post.*
23. *Turnbuckle.*
24. *Truss-rod Iron.*
26. *Cross-frame Tie-timber.*
27. *Main-floor, or Car-floor.*
28. *Deafening-ceiling.*
29. *Draw-bar.*
30. *Draw-spring.*
31. *Draw-timbers.*
32. *Centre-draft Draw-bar.*
33. *Draw-bar Sector.*
34. *Car-platform, Platform-floor.*
35. *Platform-timbers.*
36. *Platform-timber Clamps.*
37. *Platform-sills.*
38. *Platform End-timber.*
39. *Platform-post.*
40. *Base-washer, for Platform-post.*
41. *Platform-rail.*
42. *Platform-railing Chain.*
43. *Platform-gate.*
44. *Body Hand-rail.*
45. *Platform-steps.*
46. *Tread-board.*
47. *Step-iron.*
48. *Step-hanger.*
49. *Splash-board.*
51. *Side Body-brace.*
52. *Side Body-brace-rod.*
53. *Brace Straining-rod.*
54. *Sill and Plate Rod.*
55. *Body-counterbrace.*
56. *Body-counterbrace-rod.*
57. *Brace-rod Washer.*
58. *Window-post.*
59. *Window-panel Furring.*
60. *Stud.*
61. *Corner-post.*
62. *Door-post.*

63. *Truss-plank.*
64. *Truss-plank Cap.*
65. *Belt-rail.*
66. *Panel-rail.*
67. *Outside-panel.*
68. *Outside Window-panel.*
69. *Panel-strips.*
70. *End-panel.*
71. *End Window-panel.*
72. *Name-panel.*
73. *Name-panel Frame.*
74. *Lower Wainscot-rail.*
75. *Upper Wainscot-rail.*
76. *Wainscot-panel.*
77. *Outside Window-sill.*
78. *Inside Window-sill.*
79. *Window-sill Cap.*
80. *Window-sill Moulding.*
81. *Belt-rail Cap.*
82. *Upper Belt-rail.*
83. *Sash Parting-strip.*
84. *Outside Window-stop.*
85. *Window-sash.*
86. *Window-blind Sash.*

86'. *Inside Window-stop* or *Window-casing.*
87. *Window Cove-moulding*
88. *Window-moulding.*
89. *Inside Window-panel.*
90. *Window-lintel.*
91. *Letter-board.*
92. *Eaves Fascia-board.*
93. *Eaves-moulding.*
94. *Inside-cornice.*
95. *Inside-cornice Fascia-board.*
96. *Inside-cornice Sub-fascia-board.*
97. *Inside-lining.*
98. *Plate.*
99. *Door-lintel.*
100. *Carline,* or *Compound-carline.*
101. *Rafter.*
102. *Roof-boards.*
103. *Platform-roof.*
104. *Platform-roof Carline.*
105. *Platform-roof End-carline.*

106. *Roof-apron.*
107. *Platform-hood.*
108. *Platform-hood Bow.*
109. *Platform-hood Post.*
110. *Clear-story.*
111. *Clear-story Sill.*
112. *Clear-story Bottom-rail.*
113. *Clear-story End-sill.*
114. *Clear-story Sill-facing.*
115. *Clear-story Post.*
116. *Clear-story End-panel,* or *Ventilator.*
117. *Clear-story Plate.*
118. *Clear-story Carline.*
119. *Clear-story Eaves-moulding.*
120. *Clear-story Inside-cornice.*
121. *Clear-story Soffit-board.*
122. *Car-seat.*
123. *Seat-end,* or *Aisle Seat-end.*
124. *Seat-stand.*

125. *Seat-back.*
126. *Seat-division.*
127. *Foot-rest.*
128. *Stove.*
129. *Stove-pipe Jack.*
130. *Water-closet.*
131. *Water-closet Seat.*
132. *Urinal.*
133. *Water-cooler.*
134. *Water-alcove.*
135. *Centre-lamp.*
136. *Lamp-jack.*
137. *Window.*
138. *Twin-window.*
139. *Small-window.*
140. *Window-blind.*
141. *Frieze-ventilator.*
142. *End-ventilator.*
143. *Clear-story Side-ventilator.*
144. *Clear-story Window.*
145. *Basket-rack.*
146. *Door-mullion.*
147. *Bottom-rail,* of **Door.**
148. *Middle Door-rail.*

**149.** *Top-rail,* of *Door.*
**150.** *Door-stile.*
**151.** *Door-panel.*
**152.** *Brake-shaft.*

**153.** *Brake-shaft Step.*
**155.** *Lower Brake-shaft Bearing.*

**156.** *Upper Brake-shaft Bearing.*
**157.** *Brake-wheel.*
**158.** *Brake Ratchet-wheel.*

**159.** *Brake-pawl.*
**160.** *Brake-chain Worm.*
**161.** *Flag-holder Plate.*
**162.** *Platform Tie-rod.*

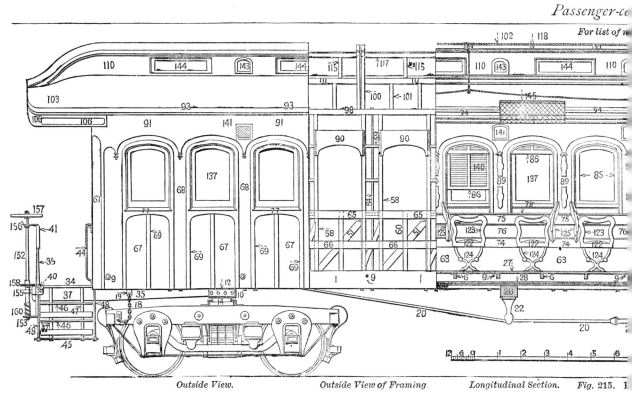

Outside View.          Outside View of Framing.          *Longitudinal Section.*     Fig. 215.

*the parts designated by the numbers in the engraving, see page 301.*

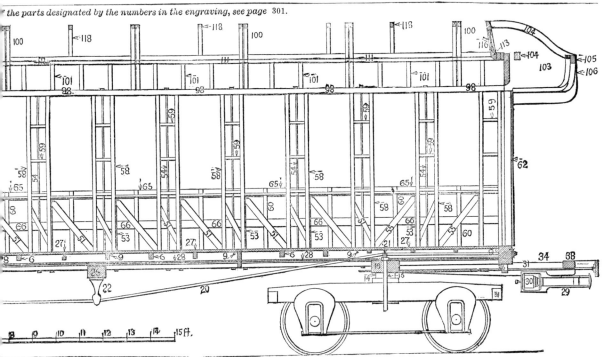

NGER-CAR BODY, CENTRAL RAILROAD OF NEW JERSEY.          *Longitudinal Section showing Framing.*

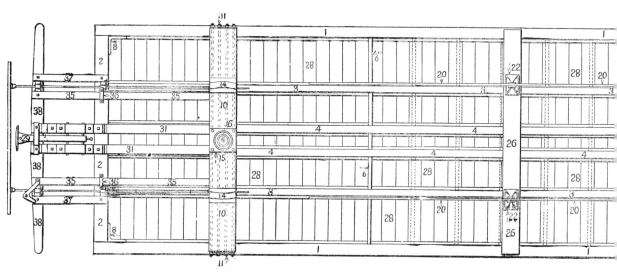

*Inverted Plan.*

*numbers in the engraving, see page* 301.

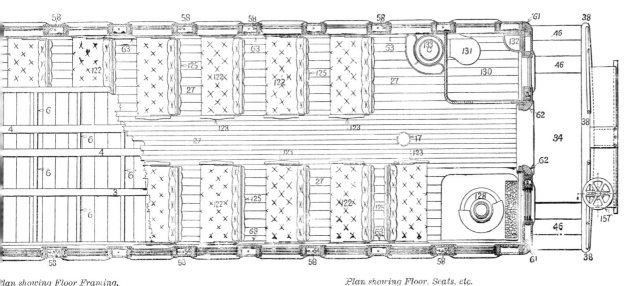

*Plan showing Floor Framing.*

6.

L. RAILROAD OF NEW JERSEY.

*Plan showing Floor, Seats, etc.*

For list of names of the parts designated by the numbers in the engravings, see page 301.

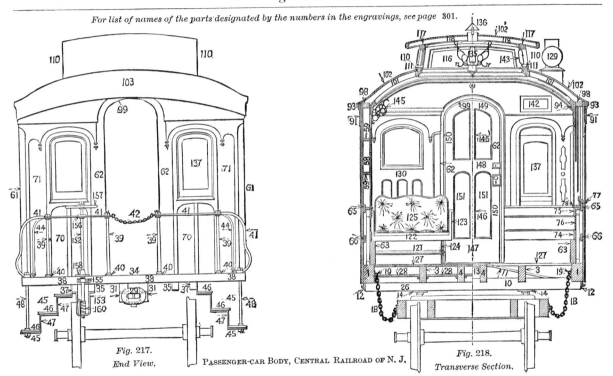

Fig. 217.
End View.

PASSENGER-CAR BODY, CENTRAL RAILROAD OF N. J.

Fig. 218.
Transverse Section.

*For list of names of the parts designated by the numbers in the engraving, see page 30*

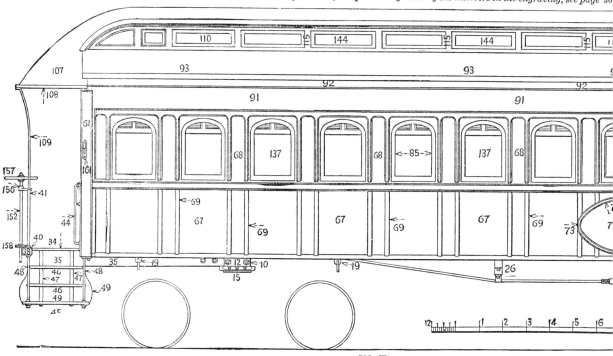

*Side View.* Fig. 219. Passenger-C.

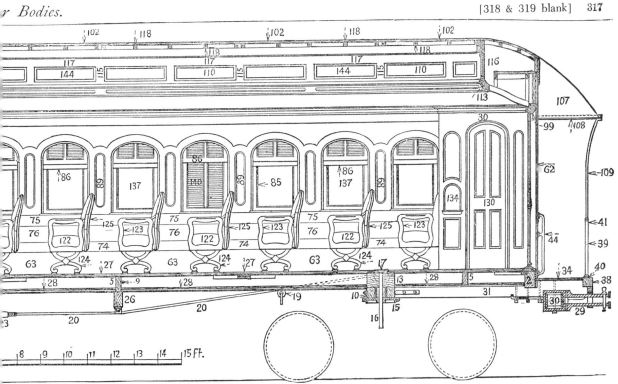

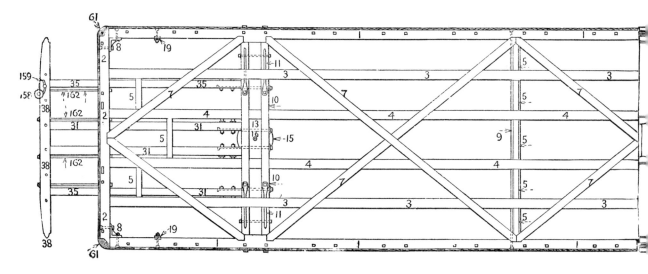

*Half Plan, showing Floor Framing.*

**Fig. 220**

PASSENGER-CAR BODY

*he numbers in the engraving, see page* 301.

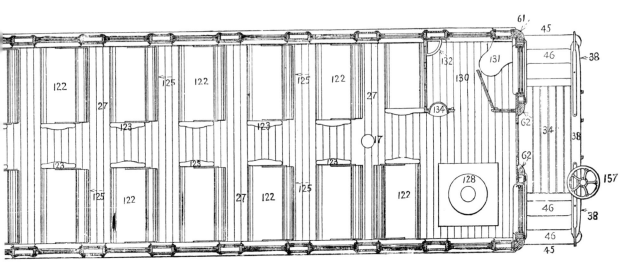

*Half Plan, showing Floor, Seats,* **etc.**

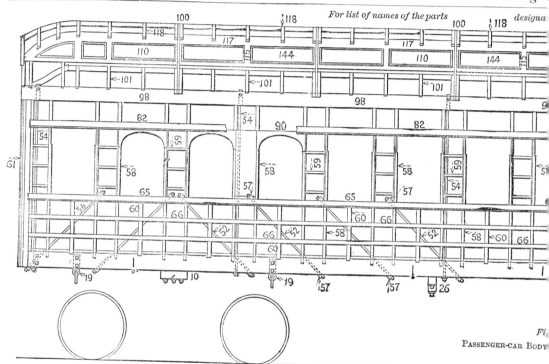

*Fi*

PASSENGER-CAR BODY

*Side View, showing Framing.*

the numbers in the    *engraving, see page* 301.

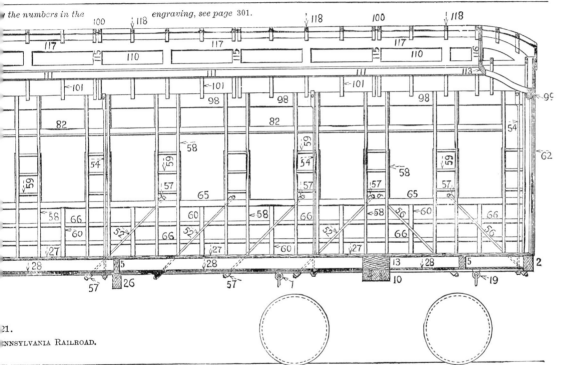

*Longitudinal Section, showing Framing.*

21.

ENNSYLVANIA RAILROAD.

For list of names of the parts designated by the numbers in the engravings, see page 301.

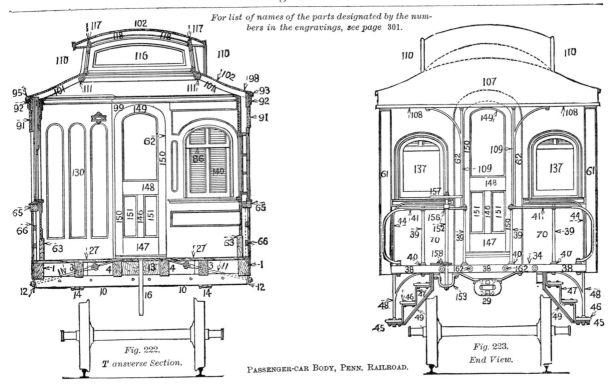

Fig. 222.
*T* ansverse Section.

PASSENGER-CAR BODY, PENN. RAILROAD.

Fig. 223.
End View.

*For list of names of the parts   designated by the numbers in the engraving, see page  301.*

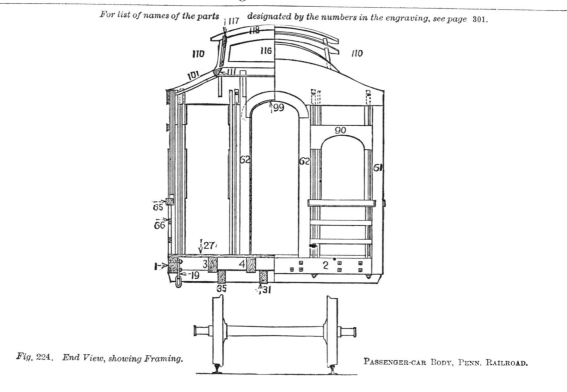

Fig. 224.  *End View, showing Framing.*          PASSENGER-CAR BODY, PENN. RAILROAD.

*For list of names of the parts designated by the numbers in the engravings, see page 301.*

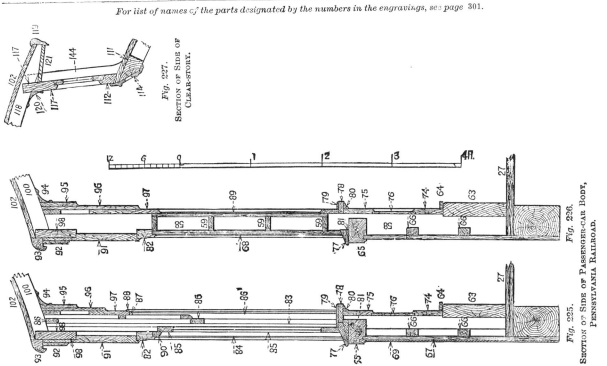

Fig. 227.
SECTION OF SIDE OF CLEAR-STORY.

Fig. 226.
Fig. 225.
SECTION OF SIDE OF PASSENGER-CAR BODY, PENNSYLVANIA RAILROAD.

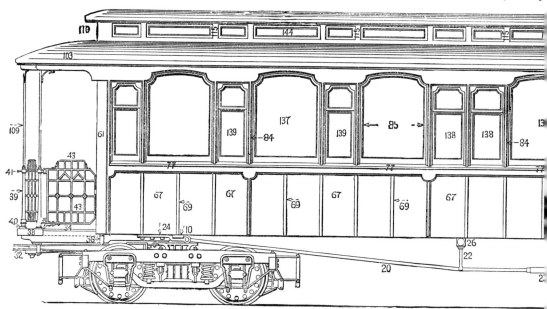

*Fig. 228.* PASSENGER-CAR, METROPOLITAN

*Side View*

*e numbers in the engraving, see page* 301.

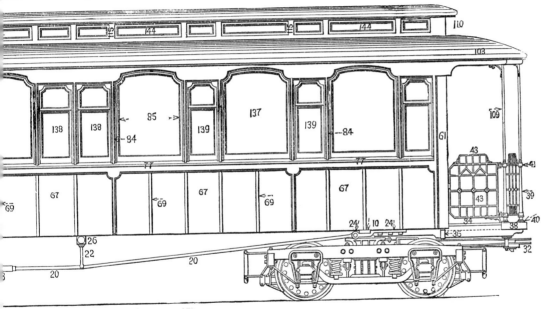

ELEVATED RAILROAD OF NEW YORK.

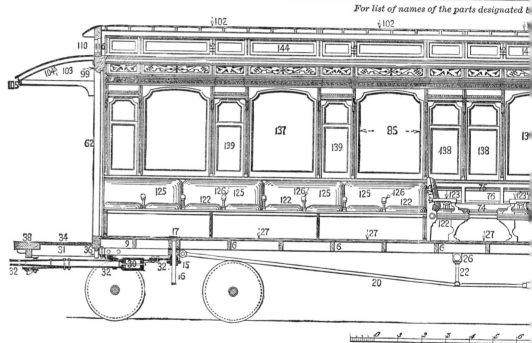

*Longitudinal Section.*

*e numbers in the engraving, see page* 301.

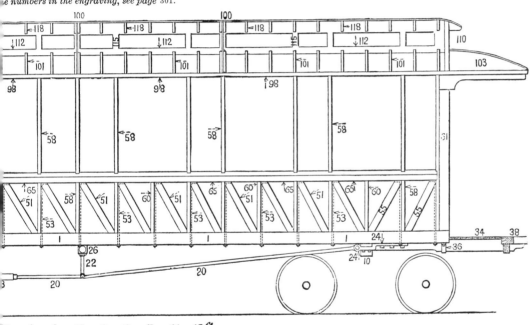

29.

ELEVATED RAILROAD OF NEW YORK.     *Side View, showing Framing.*

*For list of names of the parts designated by the numbers in the engraving, see page 301.*

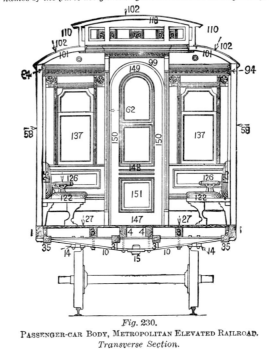

*Fig. 230.*

PASSENGER-CAR BODY, METROPOLITAN ELEVATED RAILROAD.

*Transverse Section.*

*For list of names of the parts designated by the numbers in the engraving, see page 301.*

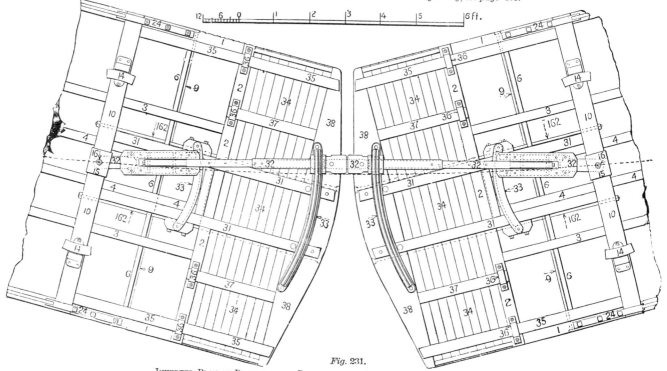

Fig. 231.

INVERTED PLAN OF DRAW-GEAR OF PASSENGER-CAR, METROPOLITAN ELEVATED RAILROAD.

*For list of names of the parts designated by the numbers in the engraving, see page* 301.

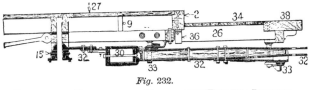

*Fig. 232.*

DRAW-BAR OF PASSENGER-CAR, METROPOLITAN ELEVATED RAILROAD.

*Longitudinal Section.*

# BOLSTERS, ETC.

LIST OF NAMES OF THE PARTS OF BOLSTERS, ETC., WHICH ARE DESIGNATED BY THE LETTERS AND NUMBERS IN FIGS. 233–239.

**1′.** *Body-bolster.*
**1.** *Body-bolster Compression-bar.*
**2.** *Body-bolster Tension-bar.*
**3.** *Body-bolster Thimble.*
**4.** *Body-bolster Truss-block.*
**5.** *Body-bolster Truss-rod Bearing.*
**6.** *Body-bolster Truss-rod.*
**7.** *Body-bolster Truss-rod Washer.*
**8.** *Body Centre-plate.*
**9.** *King-bolt.*
**10.** *King-bolt Plate.*
**11.** *Body Side-bearing.*
**12.** *Truck Side-bearing.*
**13.** *Truck-bolster.*
**14.** *Truck Centre-plate.*
**15.** *Centre-plate Block.*

*For list of names of the parts designated by the numbers in the engravings, see page 341.*

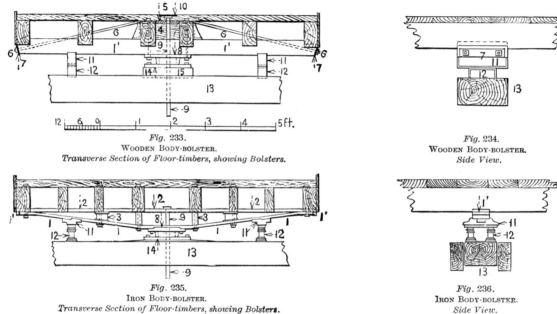

Fig. 233.
WOODEN BODY-BOLSTER.
*Transverse Section of Floor-timbers, showing Bolsters.*

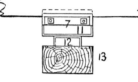

Fig. 234.
WOODEN BODY-BOLSTER.
*Side View.*

Fig. 235.
IRON BODY-BOLSTER.
*Transverse Section of Floor-timbers, showing Bolsters.*

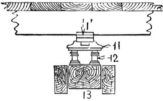

Fig. 236.
IRON BODY-BOLSTER.
*Side View.*

*For list of names of the parts designated by the numbers in the engravings, see page 341.*

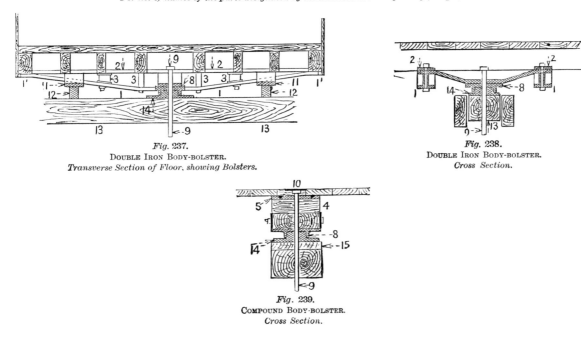

*Fig. 237.*
DOUBLE IRON BODY-BOLSTER.
*Transverse Section of Floor, showing Bolsters.*

*Fig. 238.*
DOUBLE IRON BODY-BOLSTER.
*Cross Section.*

*Fig. 239.*
COMPOUND BODY-BOLSTER.
*Cross Section.*

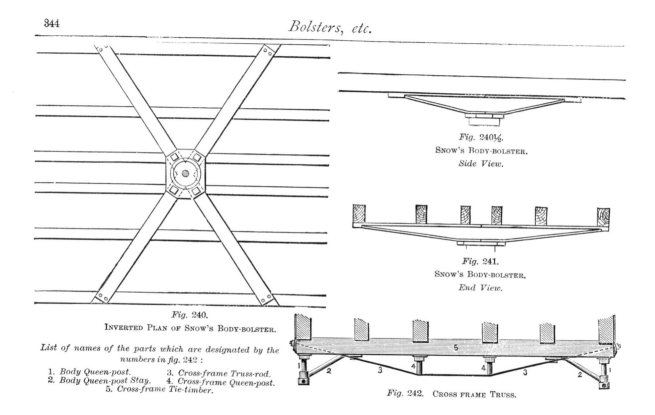

*Fig. 240.*

INVERTED PLAN OF SNOW'S BODY-BOLSTER.

*List of names of the parts which are designated by the*
*numbers in fig. 242 :*

1. *Body Queen-post.*        3. *Cross-frame Truss-rod.*
2. *Body Queen-post Stay.*   4. *Cross-frame Queen-post.*
          5. *Cross-frame Tie-timber.*

*Fig. 240½.*

SNOW'S BODY-BOLSTER.

*Side View.*

*Fig. 241.*

SNOW'S BODY-BOLSTER.

*End View.*

*Fig. 242.*   CROSS FRAME TRUSS.

# PASSENGER-CAR STEPS.

List of Names of the Parts of Passenger-car Steps, Platform etc., Designated by the Numbers in Fig. 44:

1. *Brake-chain Worm.*
2. *Nosing, Stairs.*
3. *Platform Trap-door.*
4. *Safety Coupling-chain.*
5. *Step-riser.*
6. *Tread-board.*
7. *String-board.*
8. *Brake-shaft.*
9. *Brake Ratchet-wheel.*
10. *Brake-pawl.*

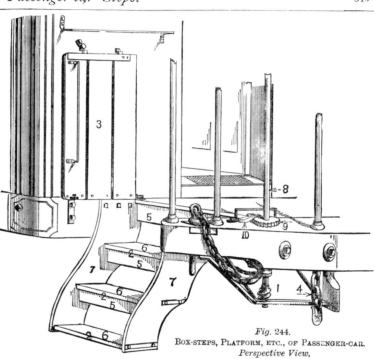

Fig. 244.
Box-steps, Platform, etc., of Passenger-car.
*Perspective View.*

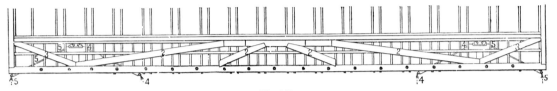

Fig. 245.

*Side View* of PORTION OF THE SIDE-FRAME OF A PASSENGER-CAR, SHOWING—1, *Compression-beam* ; 2, *Compression-beam Brace;* 3, *Counter brace* ; 4, *Body Brace-rod ;* 5, *Body Counter-brace Rod.*

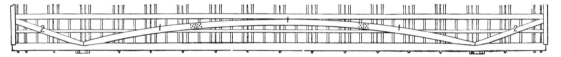

Fig. 246.

*Side View* of PORTION OF THE SIDE-FRAME OF A PASSENGER-CAR, SHOWING—1, *Truss-arch ;* 2, *Body Counter-brace.*

Fig. 247.

PROFILE-CARLINE.

Fig. 248.

SECTION OF COMPOUND-CARLINE.

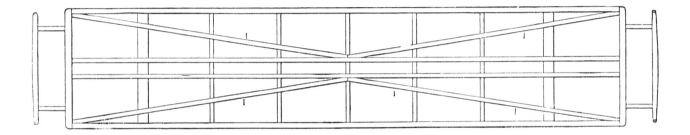

*Fig.* 249.
*Plan of* FLOOR-FRAMING, SHOWING—1, *Diagonal Floor-timber.*

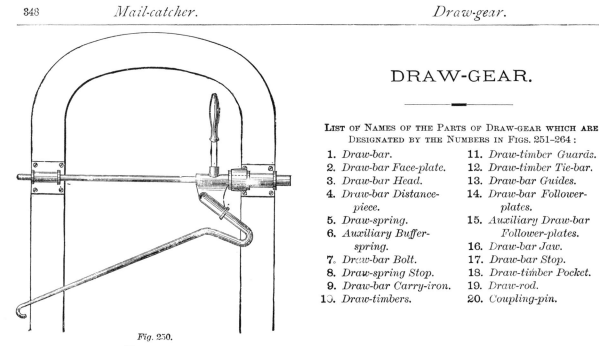

*Fig.* 250.

MAIL-CATCHER.

# DRAW-GEAR.

List of Names of the Parts of Draw-gear which are Designated by the Numbers in Figs. 251–264:

1. *Draw-bar.*
2. *Draw-bar Face-plate.*
3. *Draw-bar Head.*
4. *Draw-bar Distance-piece.*
5. *Draw-spring.*
6. *Auxiliary Buffer-spring.*
7. *Draw-bar Bolt.*
8. *Draw-spring Stop.*
9. *Draw-bar Carry-iron.*
10. *Draw-timbers.*
11. *Draw-timber Guards.*
12. *Draw-timber Tie-bar.*
13. *Draw-bar Guides.*
14. *Draw-bar Follower-plates.*
15. *Auxiliary Draw-bar Follower-plates.*
16. *Draw-bar Jaw.*
17. *Draw-bar Stop.*
18. *Draw-timber Pocket.*
19. *Draw-rod.*
20. *Coupling-pin.*

For list of names of the parts designated by the numbers in the engravings, see page 348.

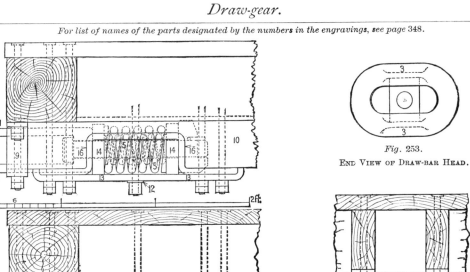

*Fig.* 251.
Side View.

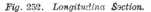

*Fig.* 252. *Longitudinal Section.* DRAW-GEAR FOR FREIGHT-CARS, PENNSYLVANIA RAILROAD.

*Fig.* 253.

END VIEW OF DRAW-BAR HEAD.

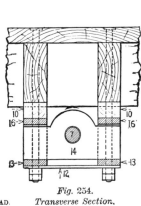

*Fig.* 254.
Transverse Section.

*For list of names of the parts designated by the numbers in the engravings, see page 348.*

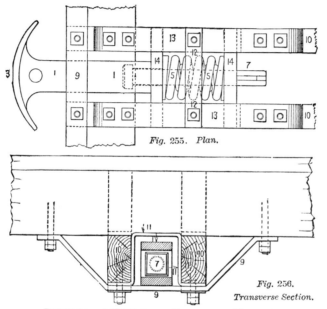

Fig. 255. Plan.

Fig. 256.
*Transverse Section.*

DRAW-GEAR FOR FREIGHT-CARS, PENNSYLVANIA RAILROAD.

For list of names of the parts designated by the numbers in the engravings, see page 348.

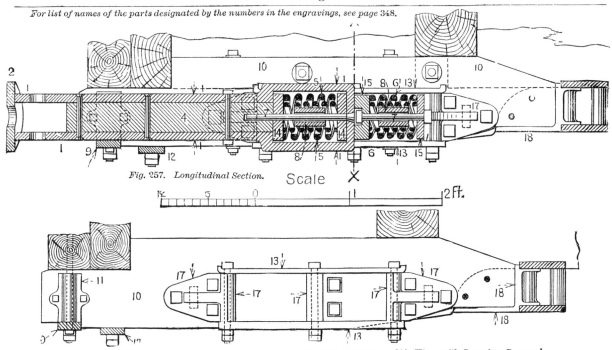

*Fig.* 257. *Longitudinal Section.*

Scale

*Fig.* 258. Draw-gear for Freight-cars, New York Central Railroad. *Side View, with Draw-bar Removed.*

*For list of names of the parts designated by the numbers in the engravings, see page 348.*

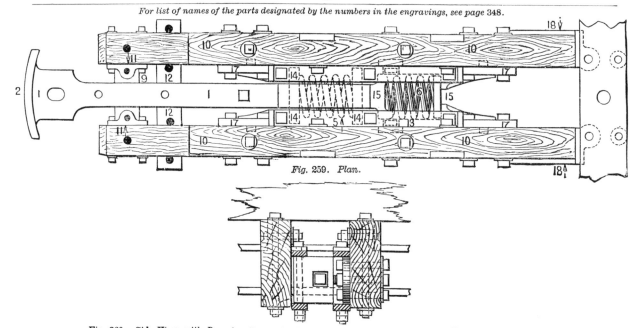

Fig. 259. *Plan.*

Fig. 260. *Side View, with Draw-bar Removed.* Draw-gear for Freight-cars, New York Central Railroad.

*For list of names of the parts designated by the numbers in the engravings, see page 348.*

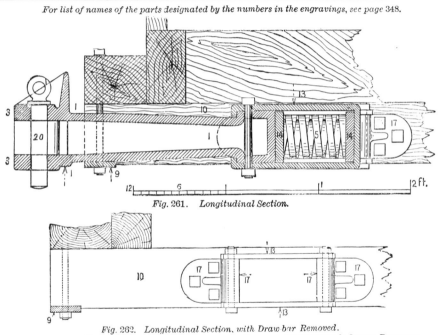

Fig. 261. *Longitudinal Section.*

Fig. 262. *Longitudinal Section, with Draw bar Removed.*

DRAW-GEAR, WITH POTTER DRAW-BAR, FOR FREIGHT-CARS, CHICAGO, BURLINGTON & QUINCY RAILROAD.

*Draw-gear.*

*For list of names of the parts designated by the numbers in the engravings, see page 348.*

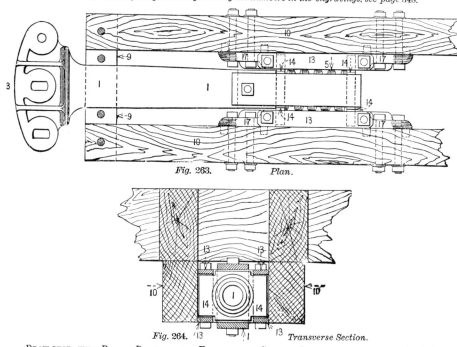

*Fig. 263.*     Plan.

*Fig. 264.*     *Transverse Section.*

DRAW-GEAR, WITH POTTER DRAW-BAR, FOR FREIGHT-CARS, CHICAGO, BURLINGTON & QUINCY RAILROAD.

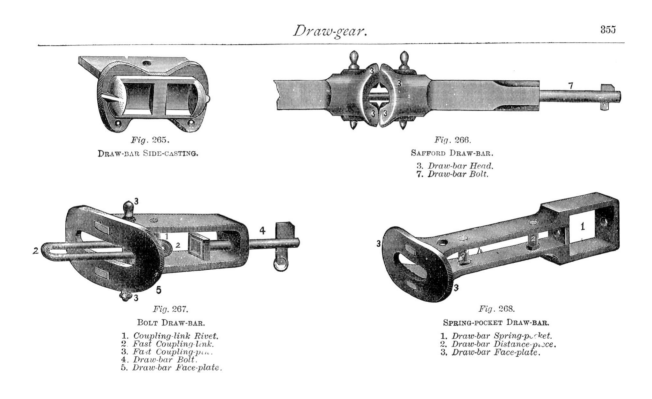

*Fig.* 265.

DRAW-BAR SIDE-CASTING.

*Fig.* 266.

SAFFORD DRAW-BAR.

3. *Draw-bar Head.*
7. *Draw-bar Bolt.*

*Fig.* 267.

BOLT DRAW-BAR.

1. *Coupling-link Rivet.*
2. *Fast Coupling-link.*
3. *Fast Coupling-pin.*
4. *Draw-bar Bolt.*
5. *Draw-bar Face-plate.*

*Fig.* 268.

SPRING-POCKET DRAW-BAR.

1. *Draw-bar Spring-pocket.*
2. *Draw-bar Distance-piece.*
3. *Draw-bar Face-plate.*

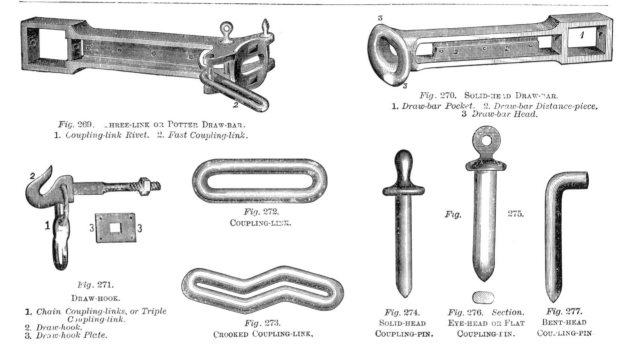

Fig. 269. THREE-LINK OR POTTER DRAW-BAR.
1. *Coupling-link Rivet.* 2. *Fast Coupling-link.*

Fig. 270. SOLID-HEAD DRAW-BAR.
1. *Draw-bar Pocket.* 2. *Draw-bar Distance-piece.*
3 *Draw-bar Head.*

Fig. 271.
DRAW-HOOK.
1. *Chain Coupling-links, or Triple Coupling-link.*
2. *Draw-hook.*
3. *Draw-hook Plate.*

Fig. 272.
COUPLING-LINK.

Fig. 273.
CROOKED COUPLING-LINK,

Fig. 274.
SOLID-HEAD COUPLING-PIN.

Fig. 275.

Fig. 276. *Section.*
EYE-HEAD OR FLAT COUPLING-PIN.

Fig. 277.
BENT-HEAD COUPLING-PIN

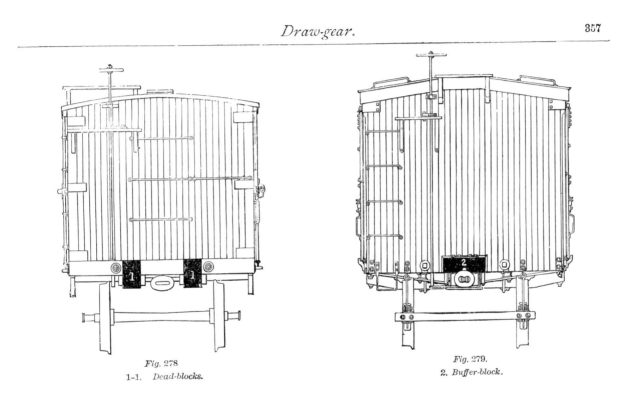

*Fig. 278*

1-1.  *Dead-blocks.*

*Fig. 279.*

2.  *Buffer-block.*

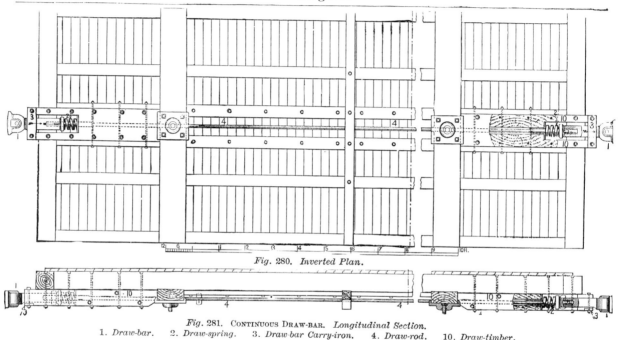

*Fig.* 280. *Inverted Plan.*

*Fig.* 281. Continuous Draw-bar. *Longitudinal Section.*

1. *Draw-bar.*     2. *Draw-spring.*     3. *Draw-bar Carry-iron.*     4. *Draw-rod.*     10. *Draw-timber.*

# MILLER-PLATFORM.

*For list of names of the parts designated by the numbers in the engravings, see page 359.*

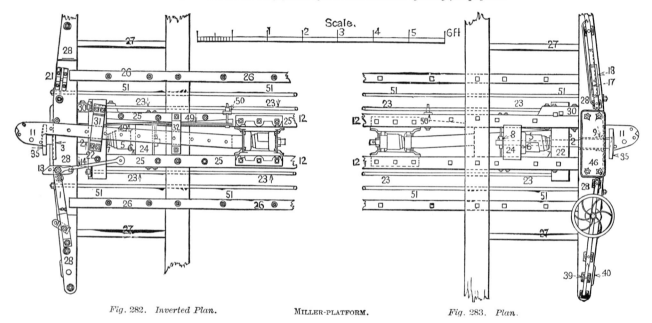

Fig. 282. *Inverted Plan.*

**MILLER-PLATFORM.**

Fig. 283. *Plan.*

*For list of names of the parts designated by the numbers in the engravings, see page 359.*

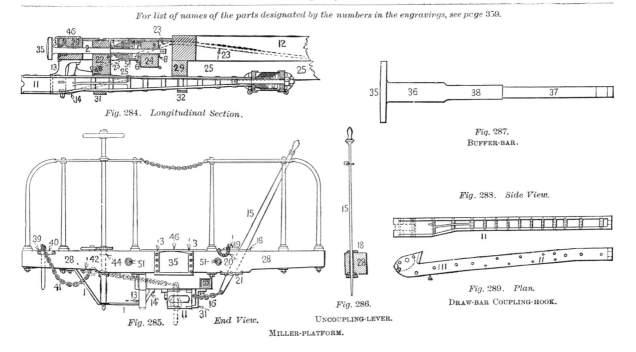

Fig. 284. *Longitudinal Section.*

Fig. 287.
BUFFER-BAR.

Fig. 288. *Side View.*

Fig. 289. *Plan.*
DRAW-BAR COUPLING-HOOK.

Fig. 285.   *End View.*
MILLER-PLATFORM.

Fig. 286.
UNCOUPLING-LEVER.

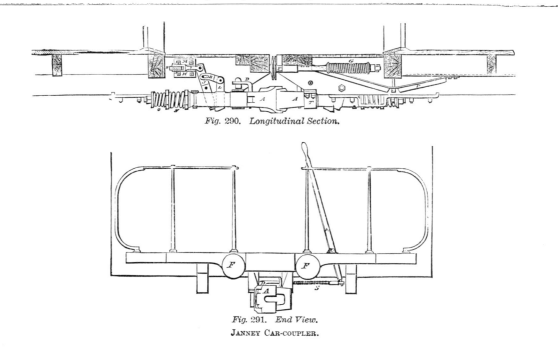

Fig. 290.  Longitudinal Section.

Fig. 291.  End View.

JANNEY CAR-COUPLER.

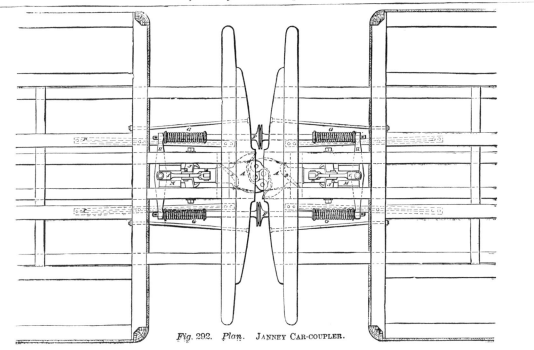

*Fig. 292. Plan.* JANNEY CAR-COUPLER.

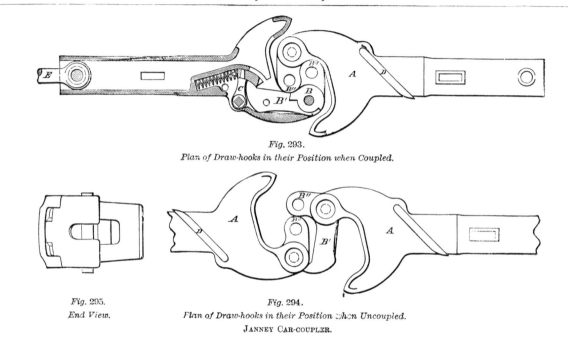

Fig. 293.

*Plan of Draw-hooks in their Position when Coupled.*

Fig. 295.
End View.

Fig. 294.

*Plan of Draw-hooks in their Position when Uncoupled.*

JANNEY CAR-COUPLER.

For list of names of the parts designated by the numbers in the engraving, see page 366.

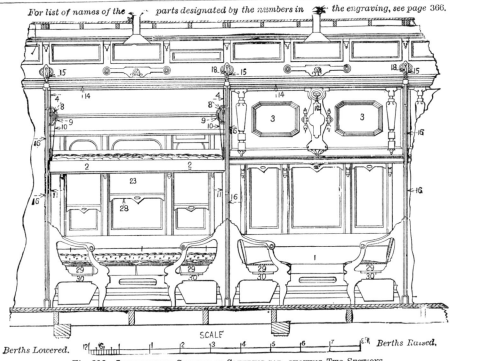

Berths Lowered.    SCALE    Berths Raised.

Fig. 296. LONGITUDINAL SECTION OF SLEEPING-CAR, SHOWING TWO SECTIONS.

# SLEEPING-CARS.

LIST OF NAMES OF THE PARTS OF SLEEPING-CARS WHICH ARE
DESIGNATED BY THE NUMBERS IN FIGS. 296–298 :

 1. Lower-berth.
 2. Upper-berth.
 3. Upper-berth, folded-up.
 4. Berth-brace.
 5. Berth-brace Eye.
 6. Berth-chain.
 7. Berth-chain Pulley.
 8. Berth-spring.
 9. Berth-spring Frame.
10. Berth-spring Rope.
11. Berth Safety-rope.
12'. Berth-latch.
12. Berth-latch Handle.
13. Berth-curtain.
14. Berth-curtain Rod.
15. Berth-curtain-rod
      Bracket.
16. Berth Head-board.
17. Head-board Bolt.
18. Hat-post.
19. Table-hook.
20. Table-hook Plate.
21. Window-lift.
22. Window-latch.
23. Window-curtain or
      Window-shade.
24. Inside Window-panel.
25. Ticket-holder.
26. Arm-rest.
27. Lamp-jack,
28. Window-curtain
      Leather.
29. Seat.
30. Right-hand Seat-end.
30'. Left-hand Seat-end.

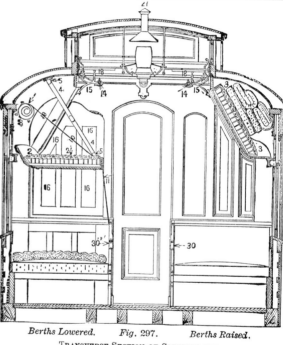

Berths Lowered.      Fig. 297.      Berths Raised.
TRANSVERSE SECTION OF SLEEPING-CAR,

For list of names of the parts designated by the numbers in the engraving, see page 366.

*Fig.* 298. PERSPECTIVE VIEW OF SECTION OF SLEEPING-CAR.

# CAR-WINDOWS.

List of Names of the Parts of Car-windows which are designated by the numbers in Figs. 299–301 :

1. Truss-plank.
2. Lower Wainscot-rail.
3. Upper Wainscot-rail.
4. Wainscot-panel.
5. Inside Window-sill.
6. Window, or Window-glass.
7. Window-casing, or In-side Window-stop.
8. Window-moulding.
9. Window-moulding-joint Cover.
10. Window-moulding Base.
11. Window-stile.
12. Window-rail.
13. Window-blind Stile.
14. Window-blind Rail.
15. Window-blind Mull-ion.
16. Sash Parting-strip.
17. Upper Window-blind, and Window-blind Slat.
18. Lower Window-blind.
19. Window-blind Stop.
21. Window-lift.
22. Window-latch.
23. Window-latch Upper-stop.
24. Window-latch Lower-stop.
25. Upper Window-blind Lift.
26. Lower Window-blind Lift.
27. Window-curtain.
27'. Window-curtain, or Window-shade.
28. Lambrequin.
29. Window-curtain Holder.
30. Window-curtain Rod.
31. Window-curtain-rod Stanchion.
32. Window-curtain Rings.
33. Window-curtain Tas-sel.
34. Window-cornice.
35. Inside Window-panel.
36. Inside-cornice.
37. Inside-cornice Fascia-board.
38. Inside-cornice Sub-fascia-board.
39. Arm-rest.
40. Table-leg Hook.
41. Table-leg-hook Plate.

*For list of names of the parts designated by the numbers in the engravings, see page 368.*

Fig. 299. Perspective View of Sleeping-car Window.

Fig. 300. Perspective View of Drawing-room-car Window.

*For list of names of the parts designated by the numbers in the engraving, see page 368.*

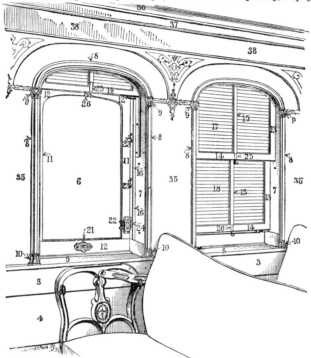

*Fig.* 301. Perspective View of Passenger-car Windows.

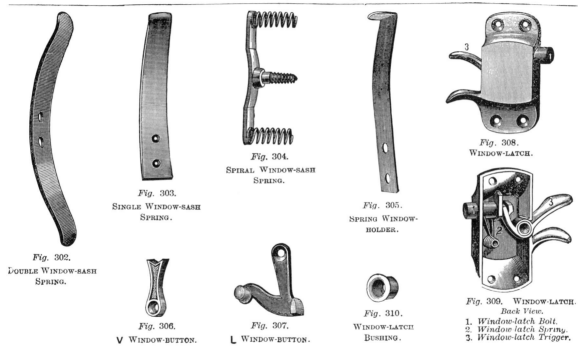

*Fig.* 302.
DOUBLE WINDOW-SASH
SPRING.

*Fig.* 303.
SINGLE WINDOW-SASH
SPRING.

*Fig.* 304.
SPIRAL WINDOW-SASH
SPRING.

*Fig.* 305.
SPRING WINDOW-
HOLDER.

*Fig.* 308.
WINDOW-LATCH.

*Fig.* 306.
V WINDOW-BUTTON.

*Fig.* 307.
L WINDOW-BUTTON.

*Fig.* 310.
WINDOW-LATCH
BUSHING.

*Fig.* 309.   WINDOW-LATCH.
*Back View.*
1. *Window-latch Bolt.*
2. *Window-latch Spring.*
3. *Window-latch Trigger.*

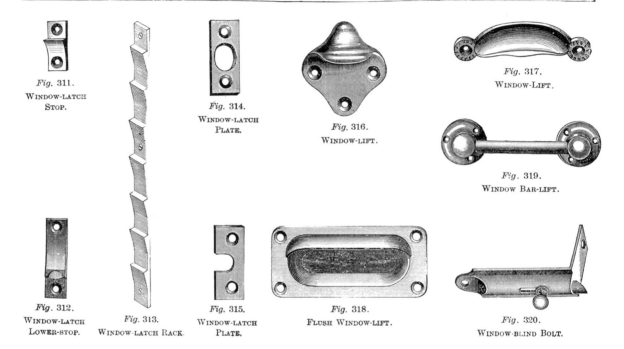

Fig. 311.
WINDOW-LATCH
STOP.

Fig. 314.
WINDOW-LATCH
PLATE.

Fig. 316.
WINDOW-LIFT.

Fig. 317.
WINDOW-LIFT.

Fig. 319.
WINDOW BAR-LIFT.

Fig. 312.
WINDOW-LATCH
LOWER-STOP.

Fig. 313.
WINDOW-LATCH RACK.

Fig. 315.
WINDOW-LATCH
PLATE.

Fig. 318.
FLUSH WINDOW-LIFT.

Fig. 320.
WINDOW-BLIND BOLT.

*Fig.* 321.

SINGLE WINDOW-BLIND LIFT.

*Fig.* 322.

SINGLE WINDOW-BLIND
LIFT.

*Fig.* 323.

LOWER WINDOW-BLIND
LIFT.

*Fig.* 324.

UPPER WINDOW-BLIND
LIFT.

*Fig.* 325.

DOUBLE WINDOW-BLIND LIFT

*Fig.* 331.

CLEAR-STORY WINDOW-LATCH KEEPER.

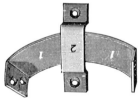

*Fig.* 326.

CLEAR-STORY WINDOW-SECTOR
AND CLAMP.

**1.** *Sector.*　　2. *Clamp.*

*Fig.* 327.

CLEAR-STORY WINDOW-PIVOT.

*Fig.* 329.

WINDOW-PIVOT
PLATE.

*Fig.* 328.

WINDOW-PIVOT.

*Fig.* 330.

CLEAR-STORY WINDOW-LATCH.

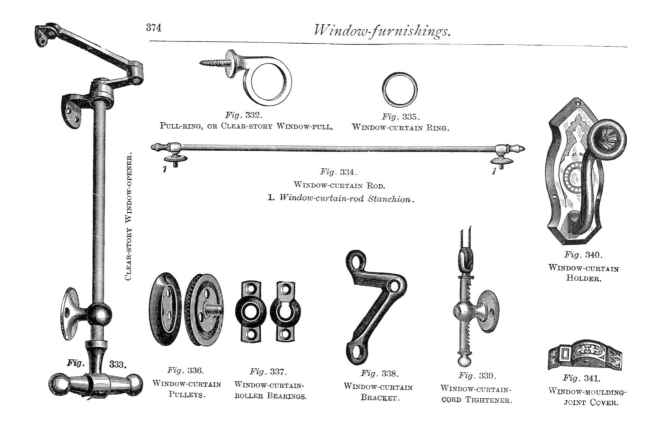

CLEAR-STORY WINDOW-OPENER.

*Fig.* 333.

*Fig.* 332.
PULL-RING, OR CLEAR-STORY WINDOW-PULL.

*Fig.* 335.
WINDOW-CURTAIN RING.

*Fig.* 334.
WINDOW-CURTAIN ROD.
1. *Window-curtain-rod Stanchion.*

*Fig.* 336.
WINDOW-CURTAIN
PULLEYS.

*Fig.* 337.
WINDOW-CURTAIN-
ROLLER BEARINGS.

*Fig.* 338.
WINDOW-CURTAIN
BRACKET.

*Fig.* 339.
WINDOW-CURTAIN-
CORD TIGHTENER.

*Fig.* 340.
WINDOW-CURTAIN
HOLDER.

*Fig.* 341.
WINDOW-MOULDING-
JOINT COVER.

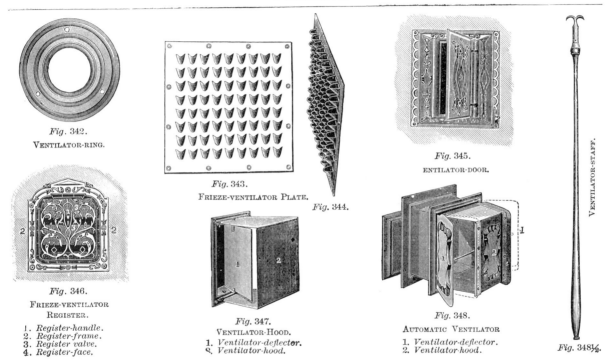

Fig. 342.
VENTILATOR-RING.

Fig. 343.
FRIEZE-VENTILATOR PLATE.

Fig. 344.

Fig. 345.
ENTILATOR-DOOR.

Fig. 346.
FRIEZE-VENTILATOR
REGISTER.

1. *Register-handle.*
2. *Register-frame.*
3. *Register valve.*
4. *Register-face.*

Fig. 347.
VENTILATOR-HOOD.
1. *Ventilator-deflector.*
2. *Ventilator-hood.*

Fig. 348.
AUTOMATIC VENTILATOR
1. *Ventilator-deflector.*
2. *Ventilator-hood.*

VENTILATOR-STAFF.

Fig. 348½.

*Fig.* 349.

SEAT-HINGE.

*Fig.* 351.

FAST BERTH-HINGE.

*Fig* 355.

UPPER-BERTH-REST PIVOT.

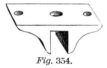

*Fig.* 354.

UPPER-BERTH REST.

*Fig.* 350.

SOFA-HINGE.

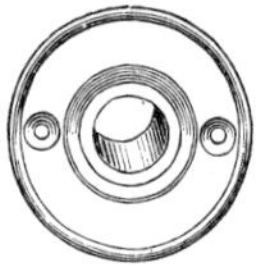

*Fig.* 353.

LOOSE BERTH-HINGE BUSHING.

*Fig.* 352.

LOOSE BERTH-HINGE.

*Fig.* 356.

UPPER-BERTH BRACKET.

**Fig. 357.**
BERTH-LATCH HANDLE.
1. *Berth-latch Face-plate.*

**Fig. 358.**
BERTH-LATCH BOLT.

**Fig. 359.**
BERTH-LATCH KEEPER.

**Fig. 360.**
BERTH-NUMBER.

**Fig. 361. BERTH-SPRING.**
1. *Berth-spring Frame.*
2. *Berth-spring Fusee.*
3. *Berth-spring Rope.*

**Fig. 362.**
BERTH-SPRING.
*Back View.*

**Fig. 363.**
BERTH SAFETY-ROPE
FASTENER.

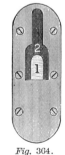

**Fig. 364.**
BERTH SAFETY-ROPE
HOLDER.

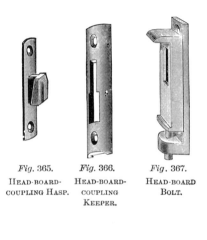

Fig. 368.
HEAD-BOARD BUSHINGS.

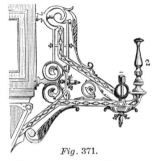

Fig. 371.
BERTH-CURTAIN-ROD BRACKET.
1. *Berth-curtain-rod Coupling.*
2. *Hat-post.*

*Fig.* 365.
HEAD-BOARD-
COUPLING HASP.

*Fig.* 366.
HEAD-BOARD-
COUPLING
KEEPER.

*Fig.* 367.
HEAD-BOARD
BOLT.

*Fig.* 372.
BERTH-CURTAIN-ROD TIP.

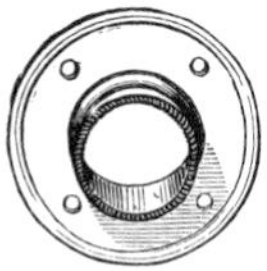

*Fig.* 369.
HEAD-BOARD BOLT.

*Fig.* 373.
BERTH-CURTAIN-ROD BUSHING,
OR SOCKET.

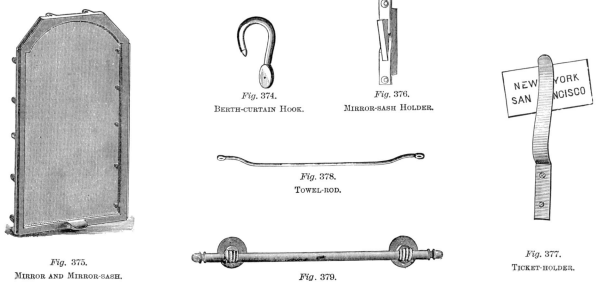

*Fig.* 374.

BERTH-CURTAIN HOOK.

*Fig.* 376.

MIRROR-SASH HOLDER.

*Fig.* 378.

TOWEL-ROD.

*Fig.* 375.

MIRROR AND MIRROR-SASH.

*Fig.* 379.

TOWEL-ROD.

*Fig.* 377.

TICKET-HOLDER.

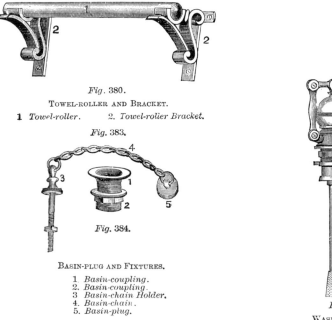

*Fig.* 380.

TOWEL-ROLLER AND BRACKET.

**1** *Towel-roller.*     2. *Towel-roller Bracket.*

*Fig.* 383.

*Fig.* 384.

BASIN-PLUG AND FIXTURES.

     1. *Basin-coupling.*
     2. *Basin-coupling.*
     3. *Basin-chain Holder.*
     4. *Basin-chain.*
     5. *Basin-plug.*

*Fig.* 381.

WASH-ROOM PUMP.

*Fig.* 382.

VERTICAL-TELEGRAPH, OR
LEVER-FAUCET OR COCK.

*Fig.* 385.

BRUSH AND COMB RACK.

Fig. 386.

SOAP-HOLDER.

Fig. 387.

SOAP-DISH.

Fig. 388.

SPITTOON.

Fig. 389.

CUSPADOR.

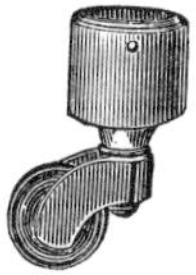

Fig. 390.

CHAIR OR
SOCKET CASTER.

Fig. 391.

SOFA-CASTER.

Fig. 392.

CHAIR-LEG
SOCKET.

Fig. 393.

REVOLVING-CHAIR STAND.

1. *Revolving-chair-stand Base.*
2. *Revolving-chair-stand Socket*

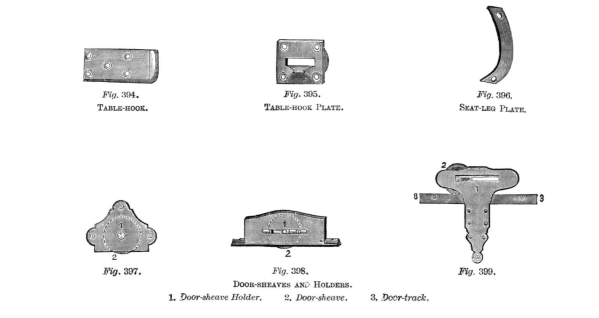

Fig. 394.

TABLE-HOOK.

Fig. 395.

TABLE-HOOK PLATE.

Fig. 396.

SEAT-LEG PLATE.

Fig. 397.

Fig. 398.

DOOR-SHEAVES AND HOLDERS.

1. Door-sheave Holder.    2. Door-sheave.    3. Door-track.

Fig. 399.

# CAR-SEATS.

List of Names of the Parts of Car-seats which are designated by the numbers in Figs. 400 and 401 :

1. *Seat-rail.*
2. *Seat-end, Aisle Seat-end, or Short Seat-end.*
3. *Seat-end, Long Seat-end, or Iron Seat-end.*
4. *Wall Seat-end.*
5. *Seat-arm.*
6. *Seat-stand.*
7. *Foot-rest.*
8. *Movable Foot-rest.*
9. *Foot-rest Carrier.*
10. *Heater-pipe Casing, or Side Foot-rest.*
11. *Seat-back.*
12. *Seat-back Band.*
13. *Seat-back Arm.*
14. *Seat-back Stop.*
15. *Seat-lock.*
16. *Arm-cap.*
17. *Cushion-frame.*
18. *Seat-spring.*

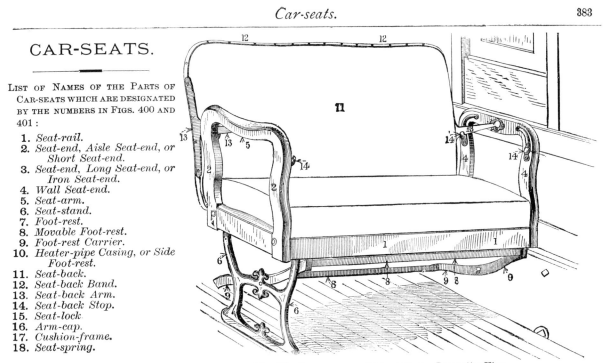

*Fig.* 400. Car-seat, with Wooden Ends. *Perspective View.*

*For list of names of the parts designated by the numbers in the engraving, see page 383.*

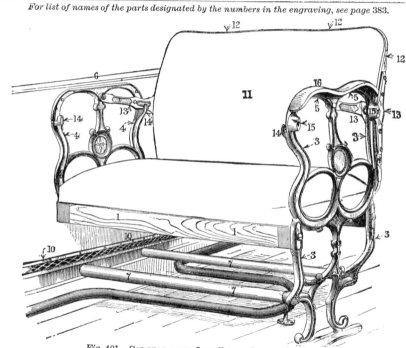

*Fig.* 401. Car-seat, with Iron Ends. *Perspective View.*

*For list of names of the parts designated by the numbers in the engravings, see page 383.*

*Fig.* 402. PERFORATED-VENEER CAR-SEAT.

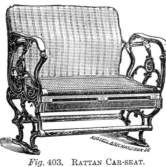

*Fig.* 403. RATTAN CAR-SEAT.

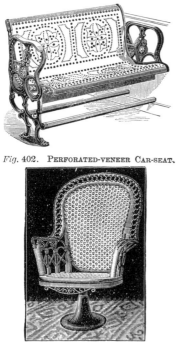

*Fig.* 404. CANE-SEAT REVOLVING-CHAIR.

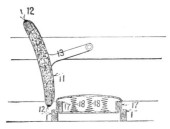

*Fig.* 405. SECTION OF CAR-SEAT AND BACK.

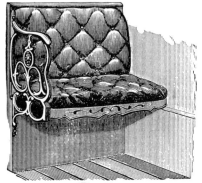

*Fig. 406.*

RIGHT-HAND CORNER-SEAT.

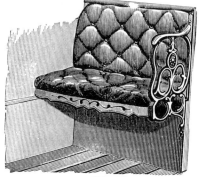

*Fig. 407.*

LEFT-HAND CORNER-SEAT.

*Fig. 410.*

ARM-CAP.

*Fig. 408.*

RIGHT-HAND SEAT END.

*Fig. 409.*

LEFT-HAND SEAT-END.

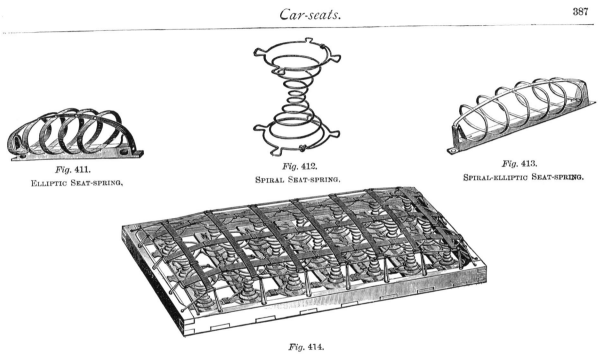

*Fig.* 411.

ELLIPTIC SEAT-SPRING,

*Fig.* 412.

SPIRAL SEAT-SPRING.

*Fig.* 413.

SPIRAL-ELLIPTIC SEAT-SPRING.

*Fig.* 414.

CUSHION-FRAME AND SEAT-SPRINGS.

*Fig.* 415.

SEAT-BACK ARM.

1. *Seat-back-arm Washer.*

*Fig.* 416.

SEAT-BACK ARM-PIVOT.

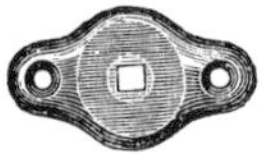

*Fig.* 417.

SEAT-BACK-ARM PLATE.

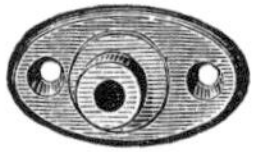

*Fig.* 418.

SEAT-BACK-ARM PIVOT-PLATE.

*Fig.* 419.

SEAT-BACK STOP.

1. *Seat-lock Bolt.*
2. *Seat-lock Key*

*Fig.* 420.

SEAT-BACK CURVED-STOP,

*Fig.* 421.

SEAT-BACK ROUND-STOP

*Fig.* 422.

BARREL SEAT-LOCK.

1. *Seat-lock Bolt.*
2. *Seat-lock Spring.*

*Fig.* 423.

SEAT-LOCK ESCUTCHEON.

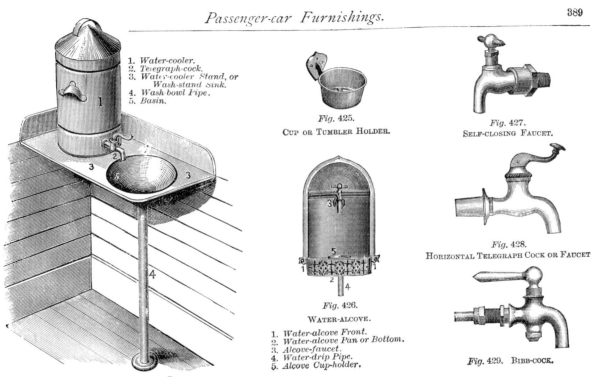

1. *Water-cooler.*
2. *Telegraph-cock.*
3. *Water-cooler Stand, or Wash-stand Sink.*
4. *Wash-bowl Pipe.*
5. *Basin.*

*Fig.* 424. WATER-COOLER AND BASIN.

*Fig.* 425.

CUP OR TUMBLER HOLDER.

*Fig.* 426.

WATER-ALCOVE.

1. *Water-alcove Front.*
2. *Water-alcove Pan or Bottom.*
3. *Alcove-faucet.*
4. *Water-drip Pipe.*
5. *Alcove Cup-holder.*

*Fig.* 427.

SELF-CLOSING FAUCET.

*Fig.* 428.

HORIZONTAL TELEGRAPH COCK OR FAUCET

*Fig.* 429.  BIBB-COCK.

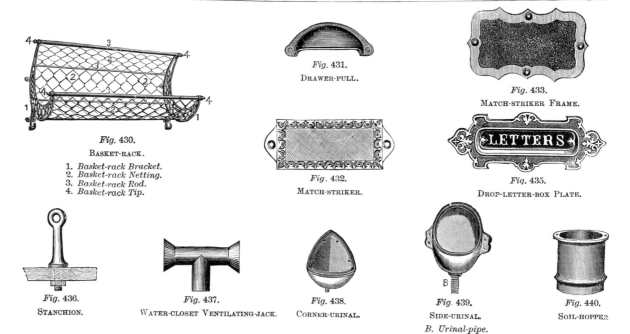

Fig. 430.

BASKET-RACK.

1. *Basket-rack Bracket.*
2. *Basket-rack Netting.*
3. *Basket-rack Rod.*
4. *Basket-rack Tip.*

Fig. 431.

DRAWER-PULL.

Fig. 432.

MATCH-STRIKER.

Fig. 433.

MATCH-STRIKER FRAME.

LETTERS

Fig. 435.

DROP-LETTER-BOX PLATE.

Fig. 436.

STANCHION.

Fig. 437.

WATER-CLOSET VENTILATING-JACK.

Fig. 438.

CORNER-URINAL.

Fig. 439.

SIDE-URINAL.

B. *Urinal-pipe.*

Fig. 440.

SOIL-HOPPER.

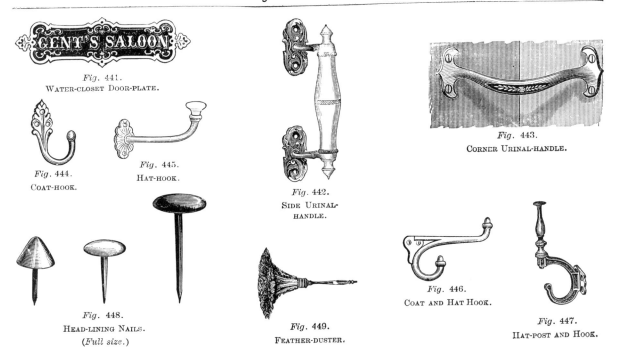

**GENT'S SALOON**

*Fig.* 441.
WATER-CLOSET DOOR-PLATE.

*Fig.* 444.
COAT-HOOK.

*Fig.* 445.
HAT-HOOK.

*Fig.* 442.
SIDE URINAL-
HANDLE.

*Fig.* 443.
CORNER URINAL-HANDLE.

*Fig.* 448.
HEAD-LINING NAILS.
(*Full size.*)

*Fig.* 449.
FEATHER-DUSTER.

*Fig.* 446.
COAT AND HAT HOOK.

*Fig.* 447.
HAT-POST AND HOOK.

LIST OF NAMES OF PARTS OF BELL-CORD FIXTURES WHICH
ARE DESIGNATED BY THE NUMBERS IN FIGS. 450–465.

1. *Bell-cord Pulley.*
2. *Bell-cord Strap.*
3. *Bell-cord Strap-hanger Bracket.*
4. *Bell-cord Guide.*

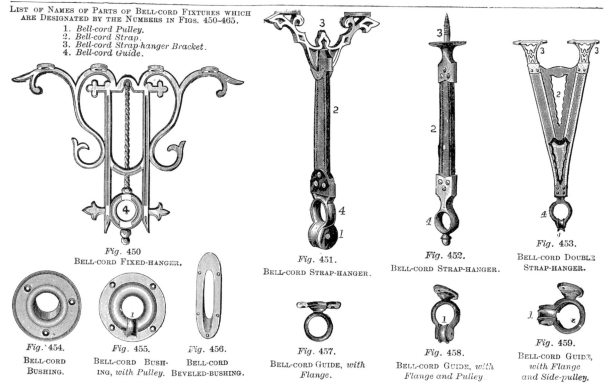

*Fig. 450*
BELL-CORD FIXED-HANGER.

*Fig. 451.*
BELL-CORD STRAP-HANGER.

*Fig. 452.*
BELL-CORD STRAP-HANGER.

*Fig. 453.*
BELL-CORD DOUBLE
STRAP-HANGER.

*Fig.* 454.
BELL-CORD
BUSHING.

*Fig.* 455.
BELL-CORD BUSH-
ING, *with Pulley.*

*Fig.* 456.
BELL-CORD
BEVELED-BUSHING.

*Fig.* 457.
BELL-CORD GUIDE, *with
Flange.*

*Fig.* 458.
BELL-CORD GUIDE, *with
Flange and Pulley.*

*Fig.* 459.
BELL-CORD GUIDE,
*with Flange
and Side-pulley.*

*For list of names of the parts designated by the numbers in the engravings, see page 392.*

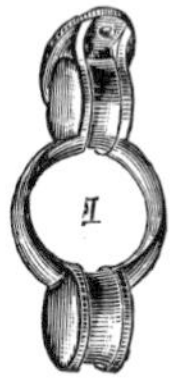

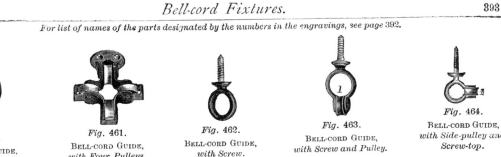

Fig. 460.
BELL-CORD GUIDE,
*with Two Pulleys.*

Fig. 461.
BELL-CORD GUIDE,
*with Four Pulleys.*

Fig. 462.
BELL-CORD GUIDE,
*with Screw.*

Fig. 463.
BELL-CORD GUIDE,
*with Screw and Pulley.*

Fig. 464.
BELL-CORD GUIDE,
*with Side-pulley and
Screw-top.*

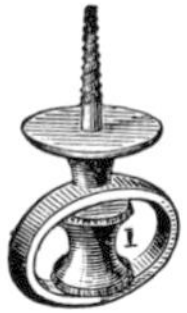

Fig. 465.
BELL-CORD GUIDE,
*with Centre-pulley.*

Fig. 466.
BELL-CORD-GUIDE WASHER.

Fig. 467.
BELL-CORD COUPLING.

Fig. 468.
BELL-CORD SPLICE.

Fig. 469.
BELL-CORD END-HOOK.

# LAMPS.

LIST OF NAMES OF THE PARTS OF LAMPS, ETC., WHICH ARE DESIGNATED BY THE NUMBERS IN FIGS. 470–496.

1. *Lamp-stay.*
2. *Lamp-shade.*
3. *Lamp-globe Chimney.*
4. *Lamp-arms.*
5. *Lamp-ring,*
6. *Lamp-reservo˙*
7. *Globe-holder.*

8. *Lamp-burner.*
9-9. *Drop of Lamp.*
10. *Lamp-chimney.*
11. *Lamp-chimney Holder.*
12. *Lamp-chimney Bracket.*
13. *Smoke-bell.*
4. *Lamp-reflector.*

15. *Lamp-chimney Reflector.*
16. *Side-lamp Holder.*
17. *Side-lamp Bracket.*
18. *Side-lamp Braces.*
20. *Lamp-bottom.*
21. *Candle-holder Cap.*

22. *Candle-holder Cup.*
23. *Candle-rods.*
24. *Candle-spring.*
25. *Alcove-lamp Reflector.*
26. *Bull's-eye.*
27. *Alcove-lamp.*

*For list of names of the parts designated by the numbers in the engravings, see page 394.*

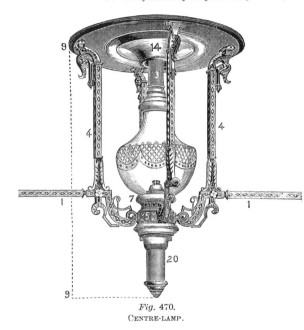

Fig. 470.
CENTRE-LAMP.

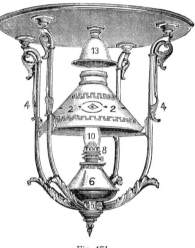

Fig. 471.
CENTRE-LAMP.

*For list of names of the parts designated by the numbers in the engravings, see page 394.*

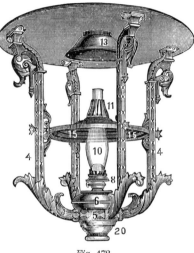

Fig. 473.
(*See fig. 475.*)

3

Fig. 472.

CENTRE LAMP,

Fig. 474.

SIDE-LAMP.

Fig. 475.

SIDE-LAMP,

*with Adjustable or Loose Globe,*

For list of names of the parts designated by the numbers in the engravings, see page 394.

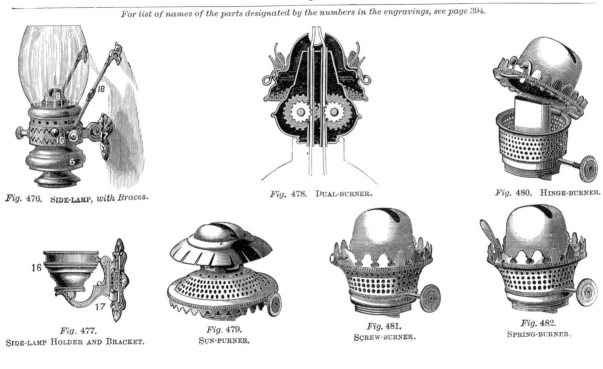

Fig. 476.  SIDE-LAMP, *with Braces.*

Fig. 478.  DUAL-BURNER.

Fig. 480.  HINGE-BURNER.

Fig. 477.
SIDE-LAMP HOLDER AND BRACKET.

Fig. 479.
SUN-BURNER,

Fig. 481.
SCREW-BURNER.

Fig. 482.
SPRING-BURNER,

*For list of names of the parts designated by the numbers in the engravings, see page 394.*

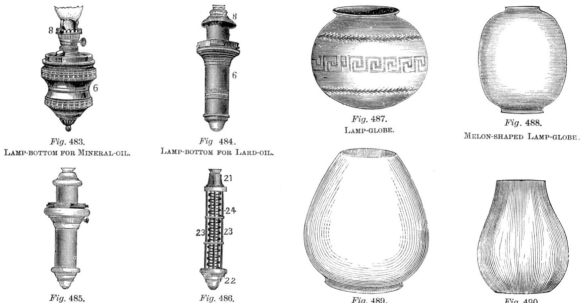

Fig. 483.
LAMP-BOTTOM FOR MINERAL-OIL.

Fig. 484.
LAMP-BOTTOM FOR LARD-OIL.

Fig. 487.
LAMP-GLOBE.

Fig. 488.
MELON-SHAPED LAMP-GLOBE.

Fig. 485.
LAMP-BOTTOM FOR CANDLES.

Fig. 486.
CANDLE-HOLDER.

Fig. 489.
EGG-SHAPED LAMP-GLOBE.

Fig. 490.
PEAR-SHAPED LAMP-GLOBE.

*For list of names of the parts designated by the numbers in the engravings, see page 394.*

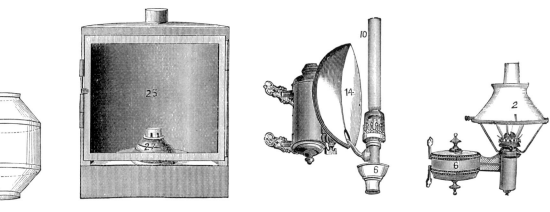

Fig. 491.
DOUBLE-CONE-SHAPED
LAMP-GLOBE.

Fig. 492.
LAMP-ALCOVE AND LAMP.

Fig. 493.
MAIL-CAR LAMP.

Fig. 494.
POST-OFFICE-CAR LAMP.

*For list of names of the parts designated by the numbers in the engravings, see page 394.*

Fig. 495.

TRAIN-SIGNAL, TAIL, OR BULL'S-EYE LAMP.

Fig. 496.

DOUBLE-LENS, TAIL, BULL'S-EYE, OR SIGNAL LAMP.

Fig. 497.   Fig. 498.

Front View.   Section.

FRESNEL-LENS.

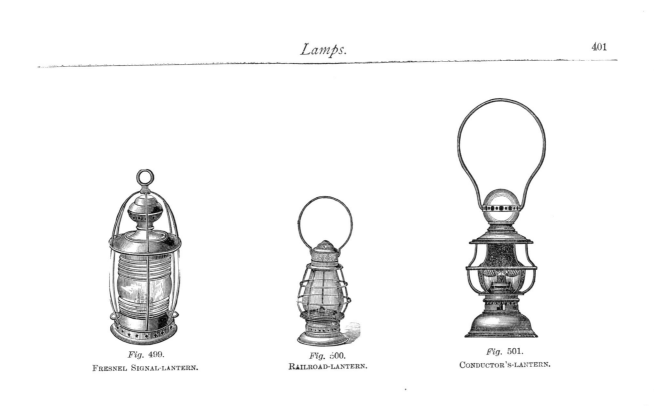

*Fig.* 499.
FRESNEL SIGNAL-LANTERN.

*Fig.* 500.
RAILROAD-LANTERN.

*Fig.* 501.
CONDUCTOR'S-LANTERN.

# DOORS AND DOOR-FUR-NISHINGS.

LIST OF NAMES OF THE PARTS OF DOORS, ETC., WHICH ARE
DESIGNATED BY THE NUMBERS IN FIG. 502 :

1. *Door-post or Jamb.*
2. *Door-mullion.*
3. *Door Name-plate.*
4. *Top Door-rail.*
5. *Bottom Door-rail.*
6. *Middle or Lock Door-rail.*
7. *Parting Door-rail.*
8. *Door-stile.*
10. *Lower or Twin Door-panels.*
11. *Middle Door-panel.*
12. *Upper Door-sash.*
13. *Lower Door-sash.*
14. *Door-sash Bolt.*
15. *Door-sash Plate.*
16. *Door-hinge.*
17. *Door-knob.*
18. *Door-lintel.*
19. *Door-lock.*
20. *Door-lock Keeper.*

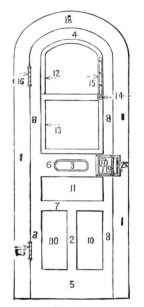

*Fig.* 502.

PASSENGER-CAR DOOR.

*Fig.* 504.
DOOR-SASH PLATE.

*Fig.* 503.
NOTICE-PLATE.

*Fig* 505.
DOOR-SASH BOLT.

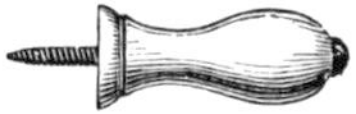

*Fig.* 506.
DOOR-STOP.

*Fig.* 507.
DOOR-HOLDER.

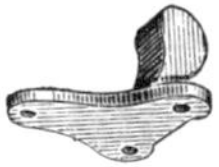

*Fig.* 508.
DOOR-HOLDER CATCH.

*Fig.* 512.
STRAP-HINGE.

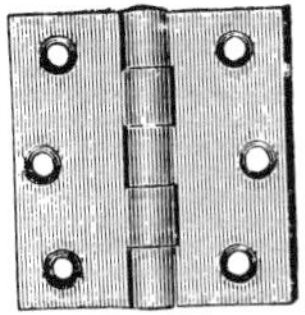

*Fig.* 509.
FAST-JOINT BUTT-
HINGE.

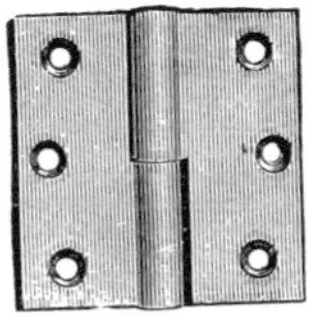

*Fig.* 510.
LOOSE-JOINT BUTT-
HINGE

*Fig.* 511.
LOOSE-PIN BUTT-
HINGE.

*Fig.* 513.
T-HINGE.

*Fig.* 514.

SQUARE DOOR-BOLT.

*Fig.* 515.

SQUARE-NECK-DOOR-BOLT.

*Fig.* 516.

BARREL DOOR-BOLT.

**1.** *Door-bolt Keeper.*

*Fig* 517.

FLUSH DOOR-BOLT.

*Fig.* 518.

DOOR-BUTTON.

*Fig.* 519.

DOOR-BUTTON AND PLATE.

*Fig.* 520.

DOOR-PULL.

*Fig.* 521.

DOOR-PULL.

# LOCKS.

LIST OF NAMES OF THE PARTS OF LOCKS WHICH ARE DESIGNATED BY THE NUMBERS IN FIGS. 522–531.

**1.** *Door-latch Bolt.*    **4.** *Door-latch Rose.*    **7.** *Door-lock Bolt.*    **9.** *Door-latch Keeper.*

**2.** *Door-latch Hook.*    **5.** *Door-knob.*    **8.** *Door-lock Keeper.*    **10.** *Door-latch Spindle.*

**3.** *Door-latch-hook Keeper.*    **6.** *Sliding-door Handle.*

*Fig. 522.*
CAR-DOOR LOCK.

*Fig. 523.*
RIM-LOCK OR DEAD-LOCK.

*Fig. 524.*
RABBETED-LOCK.

*Fig. 525.*
MORTISE-LOCK.

*Fig. 526.*
WATER-CLOSET LATCH.

*Fig. 527.*
SPRING DOOR-LATCH, OR NIGHT-
LATCH.

*Fig. 528.*
BAGGAGE-CAR DOOR-LOCK.

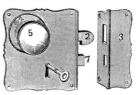

*Fig. 529.*
SLIDING-DOOR LOCK.

*For list of names of the parts designated by the numbers in the engravings, see page 405.*

*Fig.* 530.
SLIDING-DOOR LATCH.

*Fig.* 531.
DOOR-SPINDLE AND KNOBS.

*Fig.* 532.
FLUSH DOOR-HANDLE.
(*Same as fig.* 357.)

*Fig.* 533.
DOOR-LATCH ROSE AND
ESCUTCHEON.

*Fig.* 534.   *Fig.* 535.
ESCUTCHEONS.

*Fig.* 536.
PADLOCK.

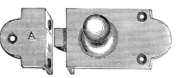

*Fig.* 537.
CUPBOARD-CATCH, OR FLUSH-BOLT.

*Fig.* 538.
CUPBOARD-LATCH.

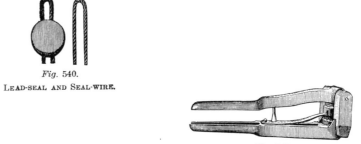

Fig. 540.

LEAD-SEAL AND SEAL-WIRE.

Fig. 541.

SEAL-PRESS.

Fig. 539.

LEAD-SEAL.

Fig. 542.

SEAL-HOOK.

*Fig. 543.*

EGG-SHAPED STOVE.

*Fig. 544.*

CYLINDRICAL-STOVE.

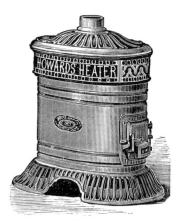

*Fig. 545.*

HOWARD-STOVE.

Fig. 546.

CHILSON CAR-STOVE.

Fig. 547.

WINSLOW CAR-STOVE.

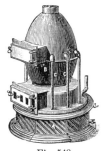

Fig. 548.

WINSLOW CAR-STOVE.

*Inside.*

Fig. 549.

STOVE-RING.

# SPEAR-HEATERS.

LIST OF NAMES OF THE PARTS OF SPEAR-HEATERS WHICH ARE DESIGNATED BY THE NUMBERS IN FIGS. 550–554:

1. *Hood.*
2. *Cold-air Pipe.*
3. *Hot-air Pipe.*
4. *Smoke-pipe.*
5. *Smoke-pipe Cap or Jack.*
6. *Deck-collar.*
7. *Screen, for Hood.*

8. *Smoke-pipe Casing.*
9. *Perforated Smoke-pipe Casing.*
10. *Outside Top-plate.*
11. *Inside Top-plate.*
12. *Fire-pot.*
13. *Ash-pit Base.*

14. *Bottom Stove-plate.*
15. *Inside-ring.*
16. *Casing.*
17. *Fire-door.*
18'. *Grate.*
18. *Fire-door Frame.*

19. *Grate-ring.*
20. *Grate-bar.*
21. *Base-plate.*
22. *Top-ring, of Base-Plate.*
23. *Ash-pit Front.*
24. *Ash-pit Door.*

*For list of names of the parts designated by the numbers in the engravings   see page 416.*

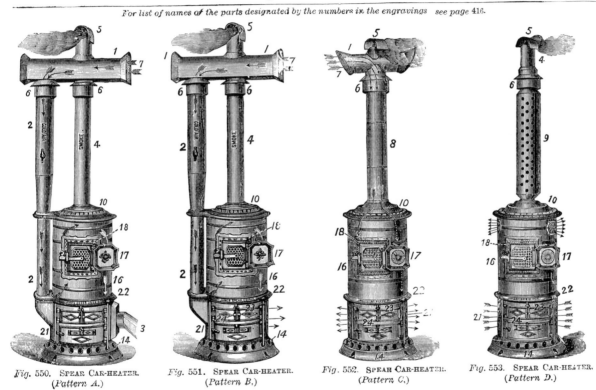

Fig. 550. SPEAR CAR-HEATER.
(*Pattern A.*)

Fig. 551. SPEAR CAR-HEATER.
(*Pattern B.*)

Fig. 552. SPEAR CAR-HEATER.
(*Pattern C.*)

Fig. 553. SPEAR CAR-HEATER.
(*Pattern D.*)

*For list of names of the parts designated by the numbers in the engravings, see page 410.*

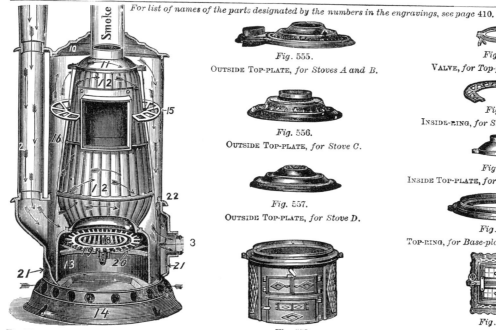

Fig. 554. SPEAR ANTI CLINKER CAR-HEATER.
*Section.*

*Fig. 555.*

OUTSIDE TOP-PLATE, *for Stoves A and B.*

*Fig. 556.*

OUTSIDE TOP-PLATE, *for Stove C.*

*Fig. 557.*

OUTSIDE TOP-PLATE, *for Stove D.*

*Fig. 558.*

BASE-PLATE, WITH TOP-RING, *for Stoves C and D.*

*Fig. 559.*

VALVE, *for Top-plate, for Stove G.*

*Fig. 560.*

INSIDE-RING, *for Stoves A, B, C and D.*

*Fig. 561.*

INSIDE TOP-PLATE, *for Stoves A, B, C and D.*

*Fig. 562.*

TOP-RING, *for Base-plate for Stoves C and D.*

*Fig. 563.*

FIRE-DOOR AND DOOR-FRAME,
*for Stoves A, B, C and D,*

Fig. 564. FIRE-POT, *for Stoves A, B, C and D.*

Fig. 565. ASH-PIT FRONT, *for Stoves A, B, C and D.*

Fig. 566. FIRE-DOOR FRAME, *for Stoves A, B, C and D.*

Fig. 567. FIRE-DOOR,

Fig. 568. ASH-PIT BASE, *for Stoves A, B, C and D.*

Fig. 569. BASE-PLATE SCREEN, *for Stoves C and D.*

Fig. 570. GRATE, *for Stoves A, B, C and D.*

Fig. 571. GRATE-BAR, *for Stoves A, B, C and D.*

Fig. 572. BOTTOM STOVE-PLATE, *for Stoves A, B, C and D.*

Fig. 573. BASE-PLATE, WITH TOP-RING, *for Stove A.*

Fig. 574. BASE-PLATE, WITH TOP-RING, *for Stove B.*

Fig. 575. FIRE-PROOF BOTTOM, *for Stoves A, B, C and D.*

Fig. 576. GRATE.

Fig. 577. GRATE-RING.

Fig. 578. POKE-HOLE FUNNEL.

Fig. 579. DOUBLE FIRE-DOOR.

# BAKER CAR-HEATER.

LIST OF NAMES OF THE PARTS OF THE BAKER CAR-HEATER, WHICH ARE DESIGNATED BY THE NUMBERS IN FIG. 581.

1. *Bottom-plate.*
2. *Ash-pit.*
3. *Grate.*
4. *Fire-pot.*
5. *Inside-casing.*
6. *Outside-casing.*
8. *Cast-iron Top.*
9. *Safety-grate.*
11. *Heat-guard.*
12. *Smoke-top.*
13. *Feed-door.*
16. *Rocking-bar, for Grate.*
18. *Ring, for Smoke-top.*
20. *Coil.*
23. *Circulating-drum.*
25. *Combination-cock.*
26. *Safety-valve.*
28. *Filling-funnel.*
30. *Pressure-gauge.*

*Fig.* 580. BAKER CAR-HEATER. *Perspective View.*

# Baker Car-heater.

*For list of names of the parts designated by the numbers in the engraving, see page 414.*

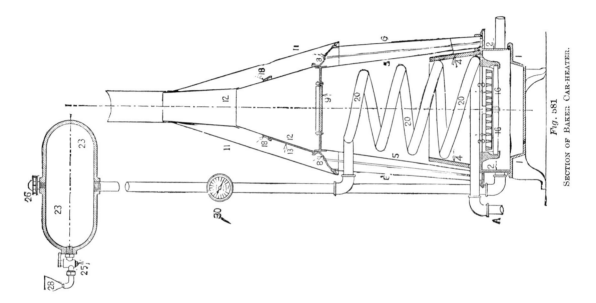

*Fig. 581.* Section of Baker Car-heater.

Fig. 582.
BOTTOM STOVE-PLATE.

Fig. 583.
ASH-PIT.

Fig. 584.
GRATE.

Fig. 585.
FIRE-POT.

Fig. 586.
INSIDE CASING.

Fig. 587.
OUTSIDE-CASING.

Fig. 588.
ASH-PIT DOOR.

Fig. 589.
CAST-IRON TOP.

Fig. 590.
SAFETY-GRATE.

Fig. 591.
SAFETY-GRATE SPRING.

Fig. 592.
HEAT GUARD.

Fig. 593.
SMOKE-TOP.

Fig. 594.
FEED-DOOR.

Fig. 595.
FEED-DOOR HANDLE.

Fig. 596.
SAFETY-GRATE LATCH.

Fig. 597.
ROCKING-BAR FOR GRATE.

Fig. 598.
ASH-PIT-DOOR HANDLE.

Fig. 599.
RING FOR SMOKE-TOP.

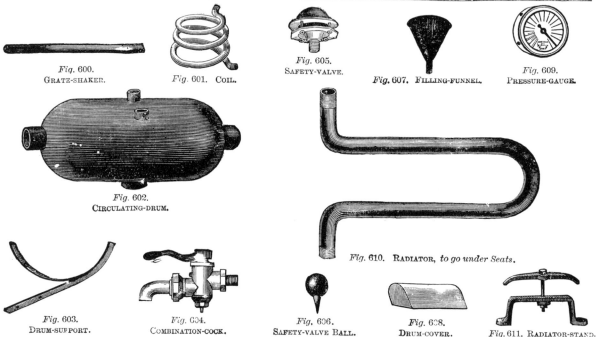

Fig. 600.
GRATE-SHAKER.

Fig. 601. COIL.

Fig. 605.
SAFETY-VALVE.

Fig. 607. FILLING-FUNNEL.

Fig. 609.
PRESSURE-GAUGE.

Fig. 602.
CIRCULATING-DRUM.

Fig. 610. RADIATOR, *to go under Seats.*

Fig. 603.
DRUM-SUPPORT.

Fig. 604.
COMBINATION-COCK.

Fig. 606.
SAFETY-VALVE BALL.

Fig. 608.
DRUM-COVER.

Fig. 611. RADIATOR-STAND.

*Fig. 612.*

PIPE-SUPPORT.

*Fig. 613.*

RADIATOR-STAND.

*Fig. 614.*

RADIATOR-STAND.

*Fig. 615.*

DOUBLE PIPE-STRAP AND BACK.

*Fig. 616.*

SINGLE PIPE-STRAP

*Fig. 617.*

CLOSE RETURN-BEND.

*Fig. 618.*

OPEN RETURN-BEND.

*Fig. 619.*

DRAW-OFF COCK.

*Fig. 620.*

ELBOW.

*Fig. 621.*

REDUCING-TEE.

*Fig. 622.*

NIPPLE.

*Fig. 623.*

PIPE-COUPLING.

*Fig. 624.*

BUSHING FOR PIPES.

*Fig. 625.*

PLUG.

*Fig. 626.*

TEE OR **T**.

*Fig. 627.*

REDUCING PIPE-COUPLING.

*Fig. 628.*

UNION-JOINT.

*For list of names of the parts designated by the numbers in the engraving, see page 421.*

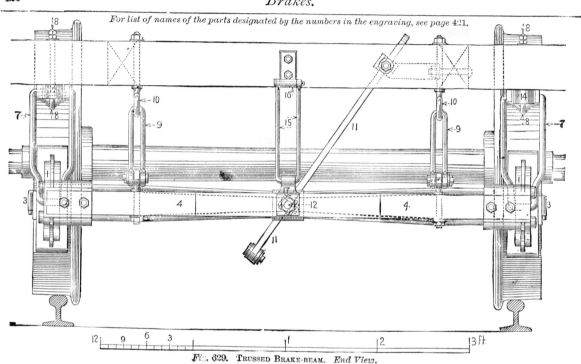

FIG. 629. TRUSSED BRAKE-BEAM. *End View.*

# BRAKES.

List of Names of the Parts of Brakes which are Designated by the Numbers in Figs. 629–631.

1. *Brake-block.*
2. *Brake-shoe.*
3. *Brake-shoe Key.*
4. *Trussed Brake-beam.*
5. *Brake-beam Truss-rod.*
6. *Brake-beam King-post.*
7. *Brake-hanger.*
8. *Brake-hanger Carrier.*
9. *Brake Safety-chain or Link.*
10. *Brake Safety-chain Eye-bolt.*
11. *Brake-lever.*
12. *Brake-lever Fulcrum.*
13. *Brake-lever Stop.*
14. *Brake-hanger Bearing.*
15. *Parallel Brake-hanger.*
16. *Parallel Brake-hanger Carrier.*
17. *Parallel Brake-hanger Eye.*

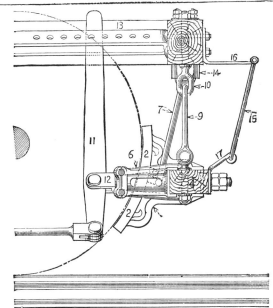

*Fig.* 630.
Trussed Brake-beam.
*Side View.*

*For list of names of the parts designated by the numbers in the engraving, see page 421.*

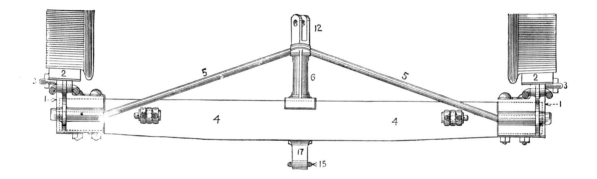

*Fig.* 631.
TRUSSED BRAKE-BEAM.
*Plan.*

*For list of names of the parts designated by the numbers in fig. 633, see page 421.*

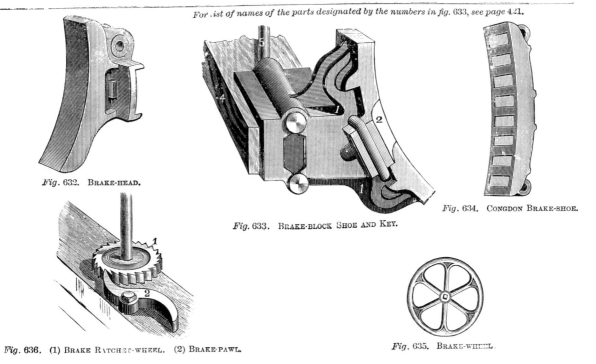

Fig. 632. BRAKE-HEAD.

Fig. 633. BRAKE-BLOCK SHOE AND KEY.

Fig. 634. CONGDON BRAKE-SHOE.

Fig. 636. (1) BRAKE RATCHET-WHEEL. (2) BRAKE-PAWL.

Fig. 635. BRAKE-WHEEL.

# BRAKES.

LIST OF NAMES OF THE PARTS OF BRAKES WHICH ARE DESIGNATED BY THE NUMBERS IN FIGS. 637–645.

1. Brake-beam.
2. Brake-lever.
3. Brake-shaft Chain.
4. Brake-shaft Connecting-rod.
5. Lower Brake-rod.
6. Secondary Brake-rod.
7. Floating-lever.
8. Floating Connection-rod.
9. Centre Brake-lever.
10. Centre Brake-lever Chain.
11. Centre Brake-lever Sheaves.
12. Long Brake-rod.

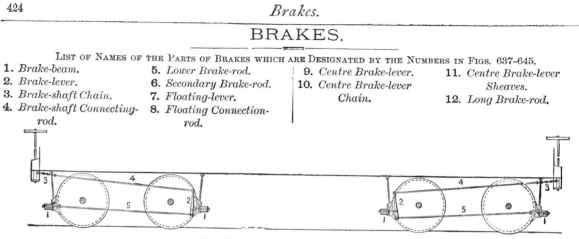

Fig. 637. SINGLE-LEVER BRAKE. *Side View.*

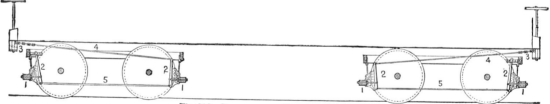

Fig. 638. DOUBLE-LEVER BRAKE *Side View.*

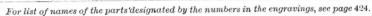

*For list of names of the parts designated by the numbers in the engravings, see page 424.*

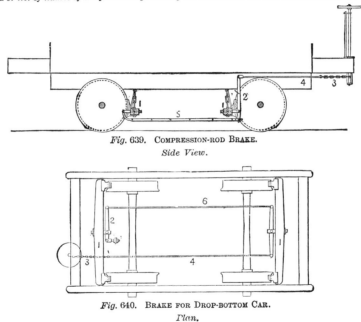

*Fig.* 639. COMPRESSION-ROD BRAKE.

*Side View.*

*Fig.* 640. BRAKE FOR DROP-BOTTOM CAR.

*Plan.*

*For list of names of the parts designated by the numbers in the engravings, see page 424.*

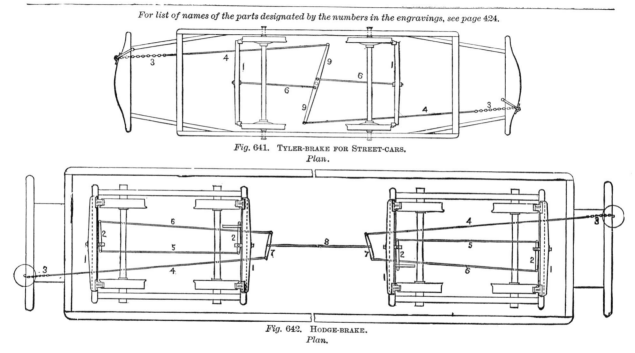

Fig. 641. Tyler-brake for Street-cars.
Plan.

Fig. 642. Hodge-brake.
Plan.

For list of names of the parts designated by the numbers in the engravings, see page 424.

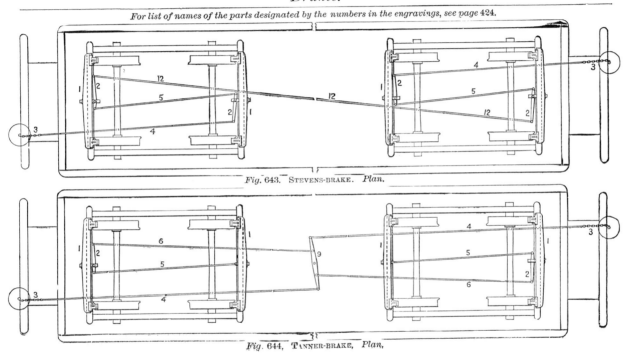

*Fig.* 643. Stevens-brake. *Plan.*

*Fig.* 644, Tanner-brake, *Plan,*

*For list of names of the parts designated by the numbers in the engraving, see page 424.*

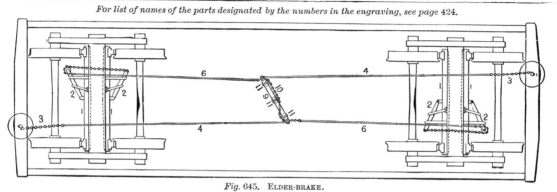

*Fig.* 645. ELDER-BRAKE.
*Plan.*

# CREAMER-BRAKE.

LIST OF NAMES OF THE PARTS OF THE CREAMER-BRAKE WHICH ARE DESIGNATED BY THE NUMBERS IN FIGS. 646-648.

**1.** *Drum.*
**2.** *Cross-bar.*
**3.** *Post-bracket.*
**4.** *Top-arm.*
**5.** *Jointed Top-pawl.*
**6** *Jointed Side-pawl.*

**7.** *Tripping-lever.*
**8.** *Connecting-rod.*
**9.** *Roof-lever.*
**10.** *Side-pawl.*
**11.** *Collar.*
**12.** *Drum-cover.*

**13.** *Stud, for Jointed Side-pawl.*
**14.** *Standard, for Cross-bar.*
**15.** *Bottom-ratchet of Drum.*
**16.** *Pipe-stay.*

**17.** *Brake-wheel.*
**18.** *Upper Brake-shaft Bearing.*
**19.** *Guard-pipe.*
**20.** *Chain-pulley.*

For list of names of the parts designated by the numbers in the engravings, see page 428.

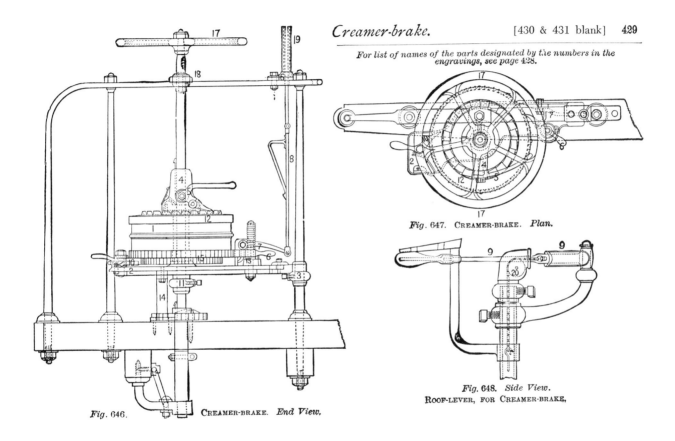

Fig. 646.   CREAMER-BRAKE.   *End View.*

*Fig.* 647.  CREAMER-BRAKE.  *Plan.*

*Fig.* 648.  *Side View.*
ROOF-LEVER, FOR CREAMER-BRAKE,

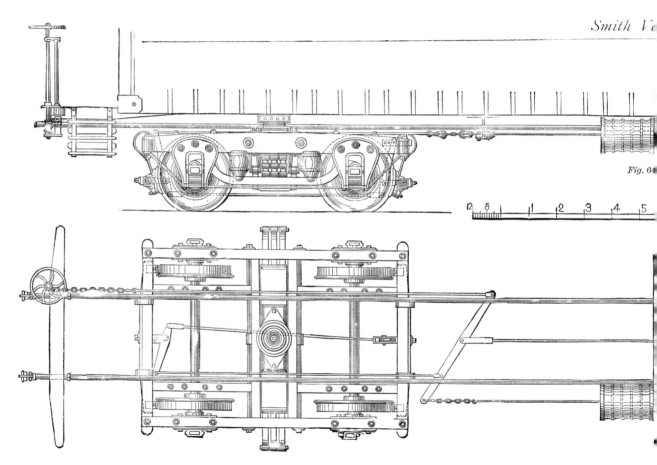

*Fig. 64*

12  6     1    2    3    4    5

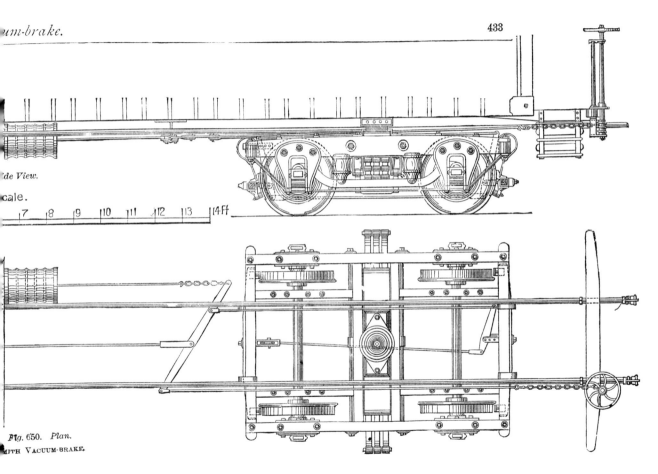

de View.

cale.

7  8  9  10  11  12  13  14ft

Fig. 650.  Plan.

MITH VACUUM-BRAKE.

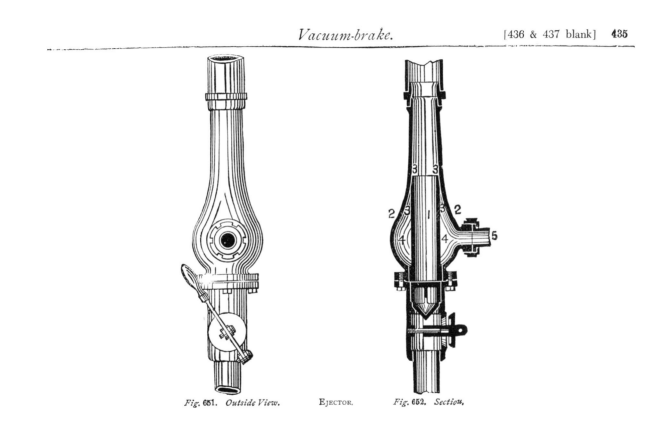

*Fig.* 651. *Outside View.*　　　Ejector.　　*Fig.* 652. *Section.*

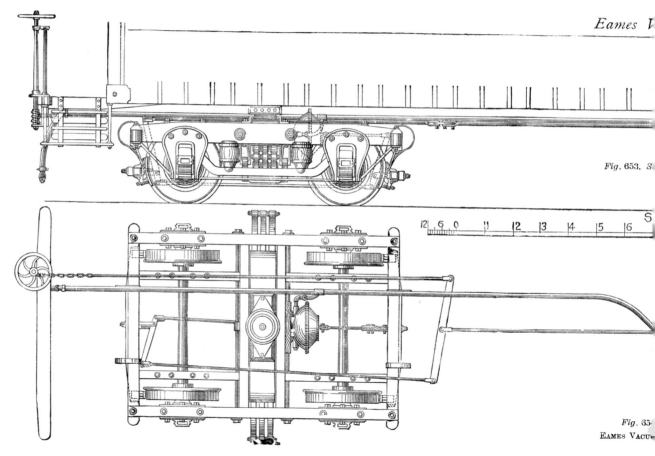

*Fig. 653. S*

12  6  0    11    12    13    14    15    16    S

*Fig. 65*

EAMES VACU

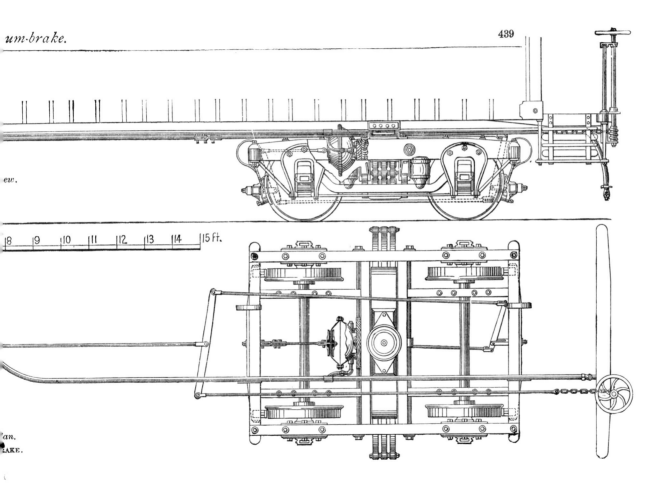

439

ew.

8  9  10  11  12  13  14  15 ft.

# WESTINGHOUSE-BRAKE.

LIST OF NAMES OF THE PARTS OF THE WESTINGHOUSE-BRAKE ATTACHED TO THE LOCOMOTIVE AND TENDER AND DESIGNATED BY THE NUMBERS IN FIGS. 655–657.

1. *Main Air-reservoir.*
2. *Brake-cylinder, for Tender-brake.*
3, 4. *Engine and Air-pump.*
3. *Steam-cylinder.*
4. *Air-cylinder.*

5. *Air-strainer.*
6. *Steam-pipe.*
7. *Exhaust-pipe.*
8. *Supply-pipe.*
9. *Discharge-pipe.*
10. *Three-way Cock.*
11. *Tender Brake-hose.*

12. *Driving-wheel Brake-cylinder.*
13. *Throttle-valve.*
14. *Brake-pipe.*
15. *Stop-cock.*
16. *Triple-valve.*

17. *Triple-valve Branch-pipe.*
18. *Auxiliary-reservoir.*
19. *Brake-cylinder Pipe.*
20. *Air-gauge.*
21. *Brake-block Tie-rod.*

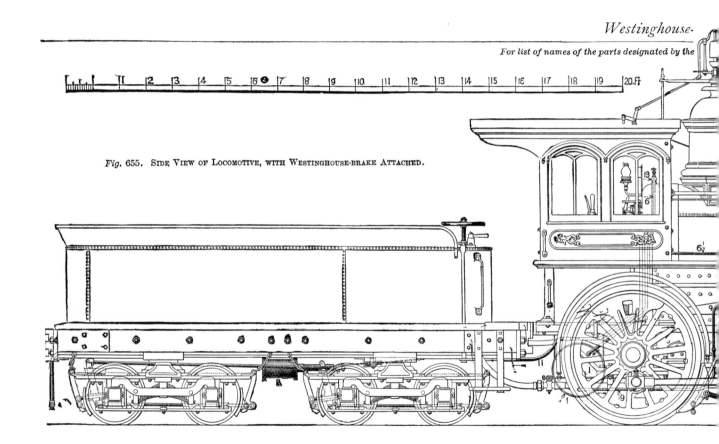

*Fig.* 655. Side View of Locomotive, with Westinghouse-brake Attached.

*umbers in the engraving, see page 442.*

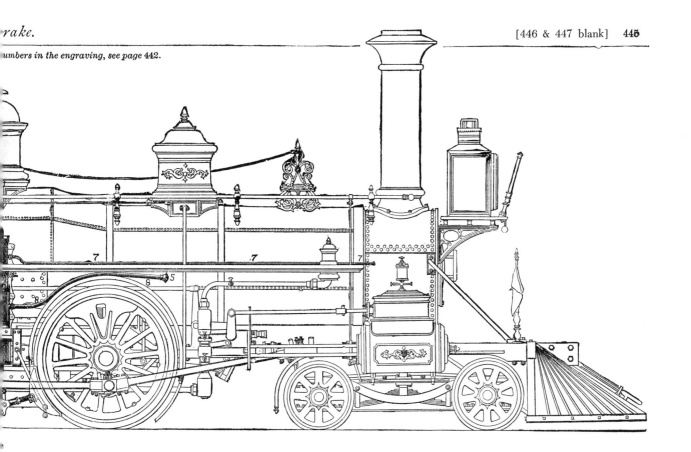

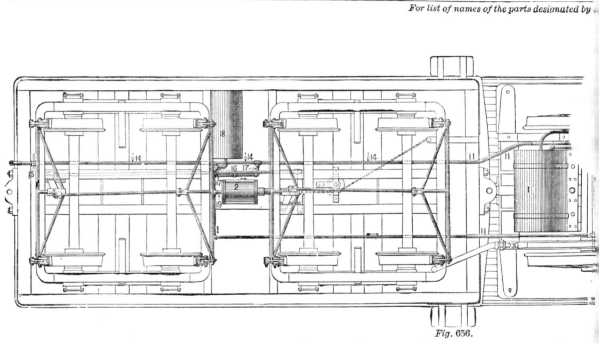

*Fig. 656.*

INVERTED PLAN OF ENGINE AND TENDER, WITH WESTINGHOUSE AUTOMATIC-BRAKE ATTA

*bers in the engravings, see page 441.*

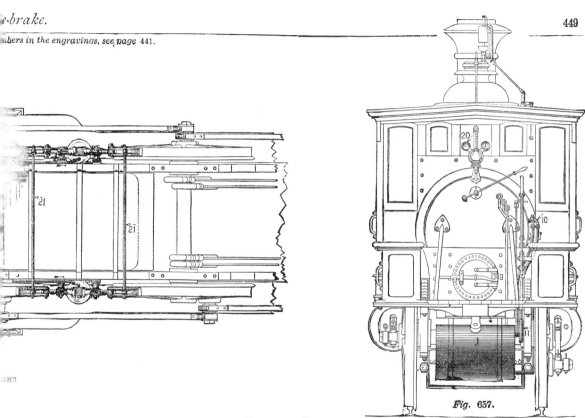

*Fig. 657.*

END VIEW OF LOCOMOTIVE, WITH WESTINGHOUSE AUTOMATIC-BRAKE ATTACHED.

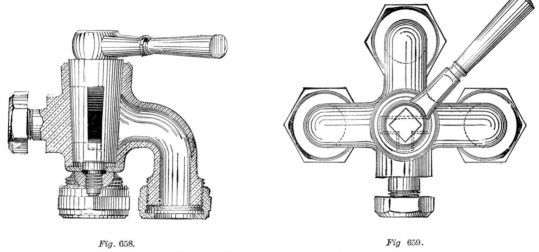

*Fig. 658.*      *Fig 659.*

*Section.*    THREE-WAY COCK, *for Westinghouse-brake.*    *Plan.*

# WESTINGHOUSE CAR-BRAKE.

List of Names of the Parts of the Westinghouse-brake Attached to the Cars and Designated by the Numbers in Figs. 660–663.

1. *Auxiliary-reservoir, for Car-brake.*
2. *Brake-cylinder, for Car-brake.*
3. *Cross-head.*
4. *Cylinder-lever Bracket.*
5. *Release-lever.*
6. *Release-lever Rod.*
7. *Release-spring Rod.*
8. *Release-spring.*
9. *Triple-valve.*
10. *Drain-cup.*
11. *Cylinder-levers.*
12. *Floating Connecting-rod.*
13. *Brake-shaft Connecting-rod.*
14. *Lower Brake-rod.*
15. *Brake-lever.*
16. *Floating-lever.*
17. *Secondary Brake-rod.*
18. *Cylinder-lever Tie-rod.*
19. *Cylinder-lever Support.*
20. *Brake-pipe.*
21. *Auxiliary-reservoir Bands.*
22. *Auxiliary-reservoir Beams.*
23. *Auxiliary-reservoir Nipple.*
24. *Triple-valve Branch-pipe.*
25. *Brake-cylinder Pipe.*
26. *Leakage-valve.*
27. *Conductor's-valve Pipe.*
28. *Conductor's-valve Dis-charge-pipe.*
29. *Stop-cock, for Brake-pipe.*
30. *Brake-hose.*

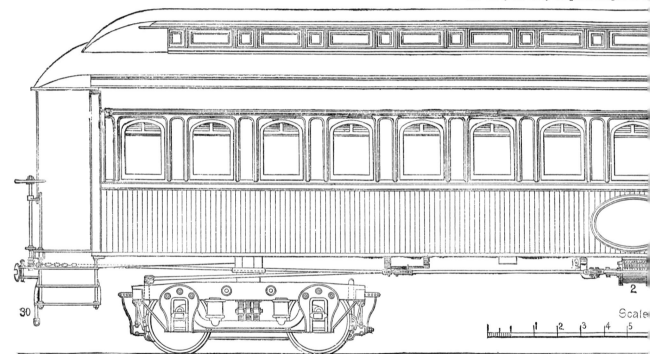

30

19

2

Scale

1  2  3  4  5

*Fig.* 660. SIDE VIEW OF CAR, WIT

*numbers in the engraving see page* 453.

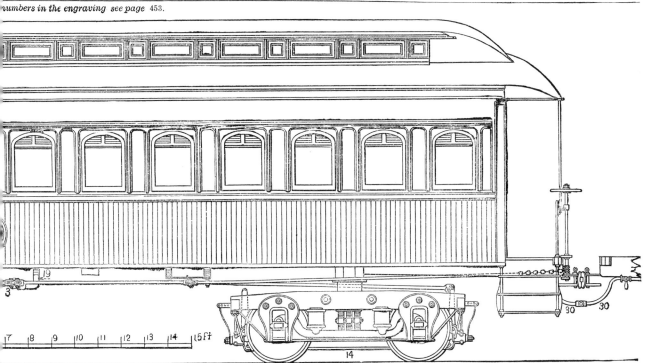

STINGHOUSE AUTOMATIC-BRAKE ATTACHED.

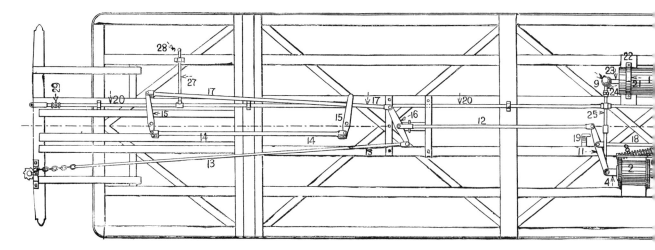

*Fig.* 661.

INVERTED PLAN OF CAR, WITH WESTINGHOUS

*numbers in the engraving, see page* 453.

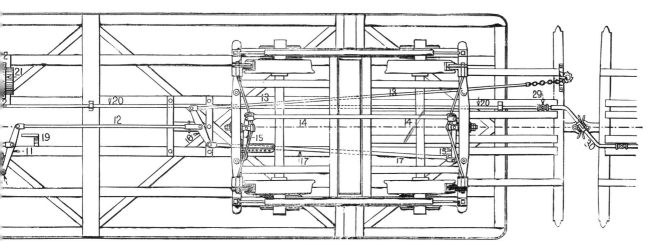

AUTOMATIC-BRAKE ATTACHED.

*For list of names of the parts designated by the numbers in the engraving, see page* 453.

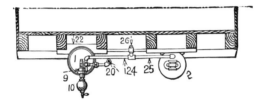

*Fig.* 663.

TRANSVERSE SECTION OF CAR, WITH WESTINGHOUSE
AUTOMATIC BRAKE ATTACHED.

# ENGINE AND AIR-PUMP, FOR WESTINGHOUSE-BRAKE.

LIST OF NAMES OF PARTS OF THE ENGINE AND AIR-PUMP OF WESTINGHOUSE-BRAKE DESIGNATED BY THE NUMBERS IN FIGS. 664–665.

2. *Steam Cylinder-head.*
3. *Steam-cylinder.*
4. *Centre-piece.*
5. *Air-cylinder.*
6. *Air-cylinder Head.*
7. *Steam-piston.*
7'. *Steam-piston Head.*
8. *Air-piston.*
9. *Packing-rings,* **for** *Steam-piston.*
9'. *Packing-rings, for Air-piston.*
10. *Reversing-valve Plate.*
12. *Reversing-valve Stem.*

13. *Reversing-valve.*
14. *Piston-head, for Upper Steam-valve.*
14'. *Piston-head, for Lower Steam-valve.*
15. *Piston Packing-ring, for Upper Steam-valve.*
16. *Piston Packing-ring, for Lower Steam-valve.*
17. *Upper Steam-valve Bushing.*
18. *Lower Steam-valve Bushing.*
19. *Reversing-cylinder.*

20. *Reversing-piston.*
21. *Piston Packing-ring, for Reversing-piston.*
22. *Reversing-cylinder Cap.*
23. *Reversing-valve Bushing.*
24. *Reversing-valve cap.*
25. *Piston-rod Nut.*
26. *Discharge-valve Stop-bolt.*
27. *Piston-rod Packing-nut.*
28. *Piston-rod Packing-gland.*
29. *Right Chamber-cap.*

30. *Left Chamber-cap.*
31. *Discharge-valve Seat.*
32. *Upper Discharge-valve.*
33. *Lower Discharge-valve.*
34. *Receiving-valve.*
35. *Union-joint, ½-inch.*
36. *Union-joint, ¾-inch.*
37. *Union-joint, 1¼-inch.*
44. *Drain-cock, of Engine.*
45. *Steam-pipe.*
46. *Exhaust-pipe.*
47. *Supply-pipe.*
48. *Discharge-pipe.*

*For list of names of the parts designated by the numbers in the engraving, see page 462.*

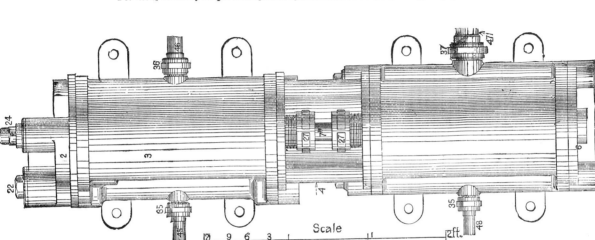

Scale

*Fig.* 664.

ENGINE AND AIR-PUMP COMPLETE, FOR WESTINGHOUSE-BRAKE.

*Side View.*

*For list of names of the parts designated by the numbers in the engraving, see page 462.*

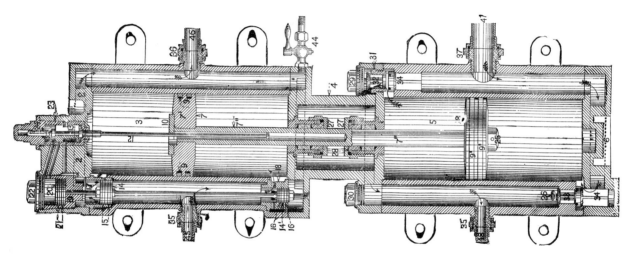

*Fig. 665.*

ENGINE AND AIR-PUMP COMPLETE, FOR WESTINGHOUSE-BRAKE.

*Section.*

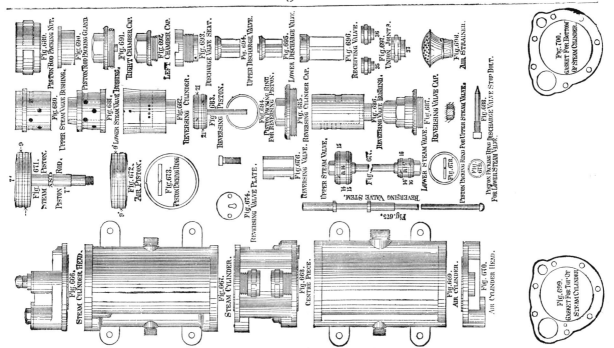

Fig. 689. Piston Rod Packing Nut.

Fig. 690. Piston Rod Packing Gland.

Fig. 691. Right Chamber Cap.

Fig. 692. Left Chamber Cap.

Fig. 693. Discharge Valve Seat.

Fig. 694. Upper Discharge Valve.

Fig. 695. Lower Discharge Valve.

Fig. 696. Receiving Valve.

Fig. 697. Union Joint.

Fig. 698. Air Strainer.

Fig. 700. Gasket for Bottom of Steam Cylinder.

Fig. 680. Upper Steam Valve Bushing.

Fig. 681. Lower Steam Valve Bushing.

Fig. 682. Reversing Cylinder.

Fig. 683. Reversing Piston.

Fig. 684. Piston Packing Ring for Reversing Pistons.

Fig. 685. Reversing Cylinder Cap.

Fig. 686. Reversing Valve Bushing.

Fig. 687. Reversing Valve Cap.

Fig. 688. Piston Packing Ring for Discharge Valve Stop Bolt.

Fig. 671. Steam Piston and Piston Rod.

Fig. 672. Air Piston.

Fig. 673. Piston Packing Ring.

Fig. 674. Reversing Valve Plate.

Fig. 676. Reversing Valve.

Fig. 677. Upper Steam Valve.

Fig. 678. Lower Steam Valve.

Fig. 679. Piston Packing Ring for Upper Steam Valve.

Fig. 675. Reversing Valve Stem.

Fig. 666. Steam Cylinder Head.

Fig. 667. Steam Cylinder.

Fig. 668. Centre Piece.

Fig. 669. Air Cylinder.

Fig. 670. Air Cylinder Head.

Fig. 699. Gasket for Top of Steam Cylinder.

*For list of names of the parts designated by the numbers in the engravings, see page 467.*

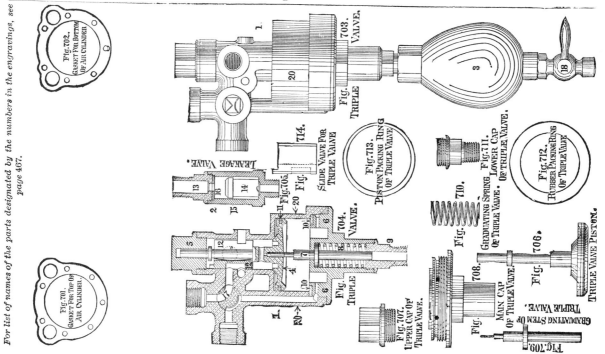

Fig. 702. Gasket For Bottom Of Air Cylinder.

Fig. 701. Gasket For Top Of Air Cylinder.

Fig. 703. Triple Valve.

Fig. 704. Triple Valve.

Fig. 705. Leakage Valve.

Fig. 714. Slide Valve For Triple Valve.

Fig. 713. Piston Packing Ring Of Triple Valve.

Fig. 711. Lower Cap Of Triple Valve.

Fig. 712. Rubber Packing Ring Of Triple Valve.

Fig. 710. Graduating Spring Of Triple Valve.

Fig. 706. Triple Valve Piston.

Fig. 707. Upper Cap Of Triple Valve.

Fig. 708. Main Cap Of Triple Valve.

Fig. 709. Graduating Stem Of Triple Valve.

# TRIPLE-VALVE, FOR WESTINGHOUSE-BRAKE.

LIST OF NAMES OF THE PARTS OF THE TRIPLE AND LEAKAGE VALVES OF THE WESTINGHOUSE-BRAKE DESIGNATED BY THE NUMBERS IN FIGS. 703–705.

1. *Triple-valve.*
2. *Leakage-valve.*
3. *Drain-cup.*
4. *Triple-valve Piston.*
5. *Upper-cap, of Triple-valve.*
6. *Main-cap.*
7. *Graduating-stem.*
8. *Graduating-spring.*
9. *Lower-cap.*
10. *Rubber Packing-ring.*
11. *Piston Packing-ring.*
12. *Slide-valve.*
13. *Leakage-valve Cap.*
14. *Leakage-valve Plug.*
15. *Leakage-valve Case.*
16. *Rubber-seat, for Leakage-valve.*
17. *Four-way-cock Plug, for Leakage-valve.*
18. *Drain-cock.*
20. *Triple-valve Case.*

# BRAKE-HOSE COUPLING, FOR WESTINGHOUSE-BRAKE.

LIST OF NAMES OF THE PARTS OF THE BRAKE-HOSE CLUTCH-COUPLINGS FOR WESTINGHOUSE-BRAKE DESIGNATED BY THE NUMBERS IN FIGS. 715 AND 716.

3. *Brake-hose Coupling-case.*
4. *Brake-hose Coupling-cap.*
5. *Brake-hose Coupling-valve.*
6. *Brake-hose Coupling-valve Spring.*
7. *Packing-ring Washer.*
8. *Packing-ring.*
10. *Brake-hose-coupling Packing-expander.*

*For list of names of the parts designated by the numbers in the engravings, see page 467.*

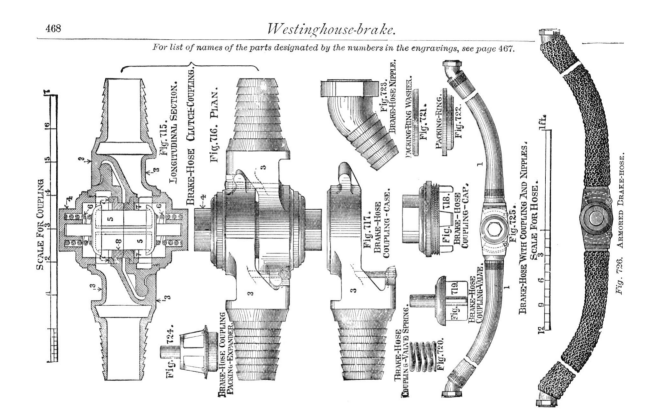

SCALE FOR COUPLING

Fig. 715. LONGITUDINAL SECTION.

BRAKE-HOSE CLUTCH-COUPLING.

Fig. 716. PLAN.

Fig. 724.

BRAKE-HOSE COUPLING PACKING-EXPANDER.

Fig. 717. BRAKE-HOSE COUPLING-CASE.

Fig. 723. BRAKE-HOSE NIPPLE.

Fig. 721. PACKING-RING WASHER.

Fig. 722. PACKING-RING.

Fig. 718. BRAKE-HOSE COUPLING-CAP.

Fig. 719. BRAKE-HOSE COUPLING-VALVE.

Fig. 720. BRAKE-HOSE COUPLING-VALVE SPRING.

Fig. 725. BRAKE-HOSE WITH COUPLING AND NIPPLES. SCALE FOR HOSE.

Fig. 726. ARMORED BRAKE-HOSE.

# WESTINGHOUSE TENDER-BRAKE CYLINDER.

List of Names of the Parts of the Brake-cylinder for Westinghouse Tender-brake Designated by the Numbers in Figs. 727 and 728.

2. *Cylinder-body, for Tender-brake.*

3. *Piston, for Tender-brake.*

3′. *Piston-head, for Tender-brake.*

3″. *Piston-rod, for Tender-brake.*

4. *Back Cylinder-head, for Tender-brake.*

5. *Front Cylinder-head, for Tender-brake.*

6. *Piston-sleeve, for Tender-brake.*

7. *Piston Follower-plate, for Tender-brake.*

8. *Piston Packing-leather, for Tender-brake.*

9. *Piston Follower-bolt for Tender-brake.*

10. *Piston-packing Expander, for Tender-brake.*

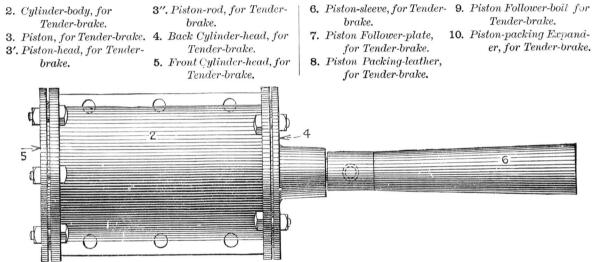

*Fig.* 727. Brake-cylinder, *for Westinghouse Automatic Tender-brake.*

*For list of names of the parts designated by the numbers in the engraving, see page 469.*

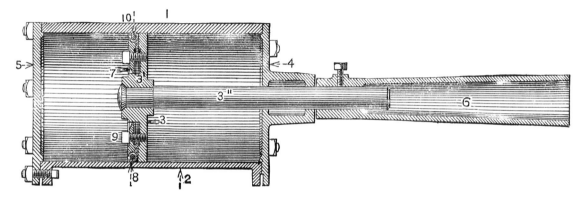

*Fig. 728.*
BRAKE-CYLINDER,
*For Westinghouse Automatic Tender-brake*
*Section.*

For list of names of the parts designated by the numbers in the engraving, see page 472.

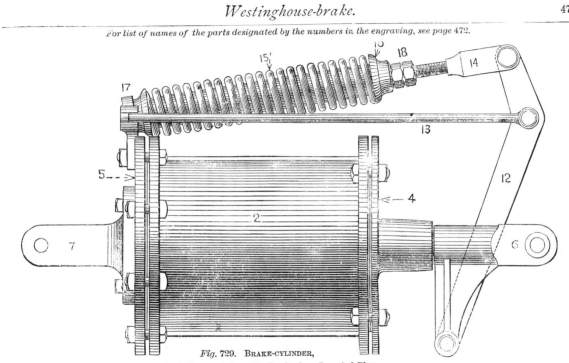

*Fig.* 729. BRAKE-CYLINDER,

*For Westinghouse Automatic Car-brake. Inverted Plan.*

# WESTINGHOUSE CAR-BRAKE CYLINDER.

LIST OF NAMES OF THE PARTS OF BRAKE-CYLINDERS FOR WESTINGHOUSE AUTOMATIC CAR-BRAKE, DESIGNATED BY THE NUMBERS IN FIGS. 729 AND 730.

**2.** *Cylinder-body, for Car-brake.*
**3.** *Piston, for Car-brake.*
**3'.** *Piston-head, for Car-brake.*
**3".** *Piston-rod, for Car-brake.*
**4.** *Back Cylinder-head, for Car-brake.*
**5.** *Front Cylinder-head, for Car-brake.*
**6.** *Cross-head, for Car-brake.*
**7.** *Cylinder-lever Bracket, for Car-brake.*
**8.** *Piston Follower-plate, for Car-brake.*
**9.** *Piston Packing-leather, for Car-brake.*
**10.** *Piston Packing-expander, for Car-brake.*
**11.** *Piston Follower-bolt, for Car-brake.*
**12.** *Release-lever, for Car-brake.*
**13.** *Release-lever Rod, for Car-brake.*
**14.** *Release-spring Rod, for Car-brake.*
**15.** *Release-spring, for Car-brake.*
**16.** *Release-spring Washer, for Car-brake.*
**17.** *Release-spring Bracket, for Car-brake.*
**18.** *Release-spring Nuts, for Car-brake.*

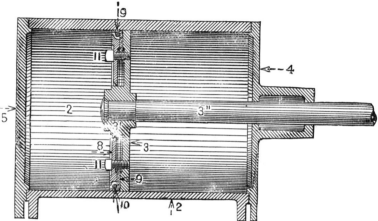

*Fig. 730.*

BRAKE-CYLINDER,

*For Westinghouse Automatic Car-brake.*

*Section.*

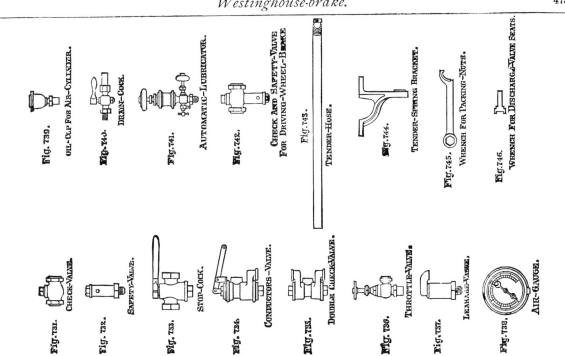

Fig. 739. Oil-Cup for Air-Cylinder.

Fig. 740. Drain-Cock.

Fig. 741. Automatic-Lubricator.

Fig. 742. Check and Safety-Valve for Driving-Wheel-Brake.

Fig. 743. Tender-Hose.

Fig. 744. Tender-Spring Bracket.

Fig. 745. Wrench for Packing-Nuts.

Fig. 746. Wrench for Discharge-Valve Seats.

Fig. 731. Check-Valve.

Fig. 732. Safety-Valve.

Fig. 733. Stop-Cock.

Fig. 734. Conductor's-Valve.

Fig. 735. Double Check-Valve.

Fig. 736. Throttle-Valve.

Fig. 737. Leakage-Valve.

Fig. 738. Air-Gauge.

# WESTINGHOUSE DRIVING-WHEEL BRAKE.

LIST OF NAMES OF THE PARTS OF WESTINGHOUSE DRIVING-WHEEL BRAKE DESIGNATED BY THE NUMBERS IN FIGS. 747–749.

1. Cylinder, for Driving-wheel Brake.
2. Cylinder-body, for Driving-wheel Brake.
3. Piston, for Driving-wheel Brake.
3'. Piston-head, for Driving-wheel Brake.
3''. Piston-rod, for Driving-wheel Brake.
4. Bottom Cylinder-head, for Driving-wheel Brake.
5. Top Cylinder-head, for Driving-wheel Brake.
6. Cross-head, for Driving-wheel Brake.

7. Piston follower, for Driving-wheel Brake.
8. Piston Packing-leather, for Driving-wheel Brake.
9. Piston Packing-expander, for Driving-wheel Brake.
10. Piston Follower-bolt, for Driving-wheel Brake.
11. Piston-rod Packing-nut, for Driving-wheel Brake.
12. Piston-rod Packing-leather, for Driving-wheel Brake.

13. Eccentric-lever, complete, for Driving-wheel Brake.
15. Eccentric-lever Casting, for Driving-wheel Brake.
16. Brake-shoe, for Driving-wheel Brake.
17. Brake-block, for Driving-wheel Brake.
18. Eccentric-lever Nut, for Driving-wheel Brake.
19. Eccentric-lever Stud, for Driving-wheel Brake.

23. Brake-block Suspending-link, for Driving-wheel Brake.
24. Brake-block Suspending-plate, for Driving-wheel Brake.
25. Brake-block Suspending-stud, for Driving-wheel Brake.
26. Brake-block Pin, for Driving-wheel Brake.
27. Brake-block Pin-rod, for Driving-wheel Brake.
28. Eccentric-lever Links, for Driving-wheel Brake.

For list of names of the parts designated by the numbers in the engravings, see page 474.

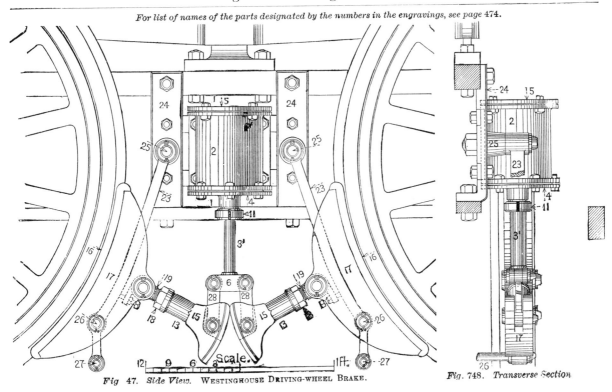

Fig 47. *Side View.* WESTINGHOUSE DRIVING-WHEEL BRAKE.

Fig. 748. *Transverse Section*

*For list of names of the parts designated by the numbers in the engraving, see page 474.*

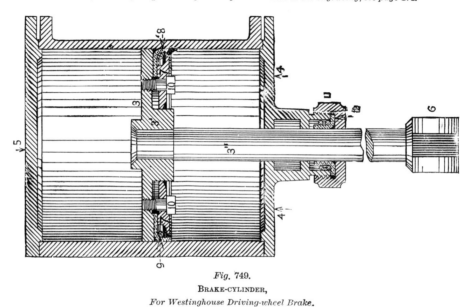

Fig. 749.

BRAKE-CYLINDER,

*For Westinghouse Driving-wheel Brake.*

Section.

# STREET-CARS.

LIST OF NAMES OF THE PARTS OF STREET-CARS DESIGNATED BY THE NUMBERS IN FIGS. 750–753.

1. *Street-car Wheel.*
2. *Street-car Axle.*
3. *Pedestal.*
4. *Journal-box.*
5. *Jaw-bit.*
6. *Side Journal-spring.*
7. *Spring-saddle.*
8. *Sill.*
9. *End-sill.*
10. *Transverse Floor-timber.*
11. *Sill Tie-rod.*
12. *Floor.*
13. *Wheel-box.*
14. *Wheel-box Button.*
15. *Window-post.*
16. *Stud.*
17. *Corner-post.*

18. *Door-post.*
19. *Belt-rail.*
20. *Belt-rail Band.*
21. *Fender-rail.*
22. *Fender-guard.*
23. *Inverted Body-truss-rod.*
24. *Inverted Body-queen-post.*
25. *Inverted Truss-rod-plate.*
26. *Turnbuckle.*
27. *Outside-panel.*
28. *Lower Outside-panel.*
29. *Upper End-panel.*
30. *Lower End-panel.*
31. *Inside Frieze-panel.*
32. *Panel-strip.*

33. *Panel-furring.*
34. *Seat-bottom, and Longitudinal seat.*
35. *Seat-leg.*
36. *Front Seat-rail.*
37. *Front Seat-bottom-rail.*
38. *Back Seat-bottom-rail.*
39. *Back Seat-rail.*
40. *Lower Seat-back-rail.*
41. *Upper Seat-back-rail.*
42. *Seat-back Board.*
43. *End Seat-panel.*
44. *Upper Belt-rail.*
45. *Window-ledge.*
46. *Letter-board.*
47. *Plate.*

48. *Eaves-moulding.*
49. *Window-blind Rest.*
50. *Window-sash Rest.*
51. *Outside Window-stop.*
52. *Inside Window-stop.*
53. *Carline.*
54. *End-carline.*
55. *Roof-boards.*
56—56. *Clear-story.*
57. *Clear-story Bottom-rail.*
58. *Clear-story Post.*
59. *Clear-story Window.*
60. *Clear-story Carline.*
61. *Clear-story End-ventilator.*
62. *End Roof-lights.*
63. *Ventilator-hood.*

64. *Window.*
65. *Window-rail.*
66. *Window-stile.*
67. *Window-lift.*
68. *Sash Parting-strip.*
69. *Window-blind.*
70. *Window-blind Stile.*
71. *Window-blind Rail.*
72. *Window-blind Mullion.*
73. *Window-blind Lift.*
74. *Lamp-case.*
75. *Lamp-case Door.*
76. *Lamp-case Chimney.*
77. *Window-guards.*
78. *Door-stile.*
79. *Door-mullion.*
80. *Door-window Mullion.*
81. *Middle or Lock Door-rail.*
82. *Top Door-rail.*
83. *Door-case Top-rail.*
84. *Door-case Intermediate-rail.*

85. *Door-case Top-panel.*
86. *Door-case Sash.*
87. *Door-case Sash-button.*
88. *Door Guard-band.*
89. *Fare-wicket and Fare-wicket Door.*
90. *Fare-wicket Door-case.*
91. *Sliding-door Handle.*
91.′ *Door-sheave.*
92. *Door-latch Plate.*
92.′ *Sliding-door Holder.*
93. *Door-sill.*
94. *Inside Hand-rail.*
95. *Inside Hand-rail Bracket.*
96. *Hand-straps.*
97. *Signal-bell.*
98. *Bell-strap.*
99. *Bell-strap Guide.*
99.′ *Bell-strap Guide, with Roller.*

100. *Draw-timber.*
102. *Platform-timber Clamps.*
103. *Platform End-timber.*
104. *Platform, or Platform-floor.*
105. *Platform-timber Band.*
106. *Draw-hook.*
107. *Helper-ring.*
108. *Platform-post.*
109. *Base-washer, for Platform-post.*
110. *Platform-rail.*
111. *Dash-guard.*
112. *Dash-guard Straps.*
113. *Body Hand-rail.*
114. *Platform-step, or Side-step.*
115. *Platform-hood.*
116. *Platform-hood Bow.*
117. *Platform-hood Car-line.*
118. *Platform-hood Knee.*

119. *Platform-hood Moulding.*
120. *Brake-shaft Crank.*
121. *Brake-shaft Crank-handle.*
122. *Brake-shaft.*
123. *Upper Brake-shaft Bearing.*
124. *Lower Brake-shaft Bearing.*
125. *Brake Ratchet-wheel.*
126. *Brake-pawl.*
127. *Brake-shaft Chain.*
128. *Brake-shaft Connecting-rod.*
129. *Centre Brake-lever.*
130. *Centre Brake-lever Spider.*
132. *Secondary Brake-rod.*
133. *Brake-beam.*
134. *Brake-hanger.*
135. *Brake-head.*
136. *Rubber-tread.*

For list of names of the parts designated by the numbers in the engraving, see page 477.

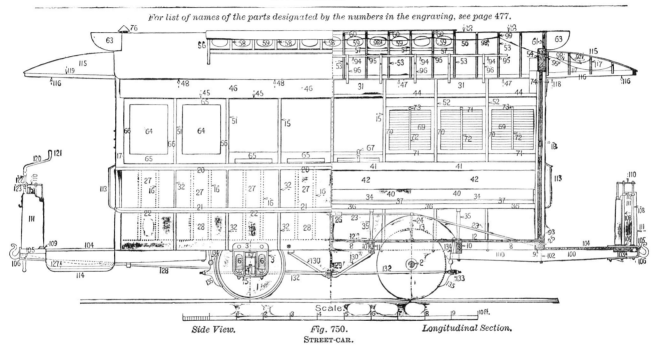

Side View.  Fig. 750.  Longitudinal Section.

STREET-CAR.

*For list of names of the parts designated by the numbers in the engraving, see page 477.*

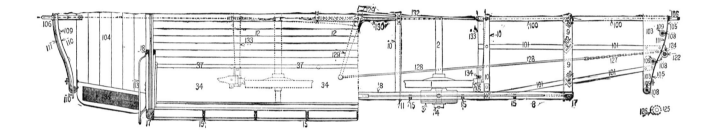

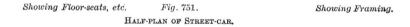

*Showing Floor-seats, etc.*     Fig. 751.          *Showing Framing.*

HALF-PLAN OF STREET-CAR.

*For list of names of the parts designated by the numbers in the engravings, see page 477.*

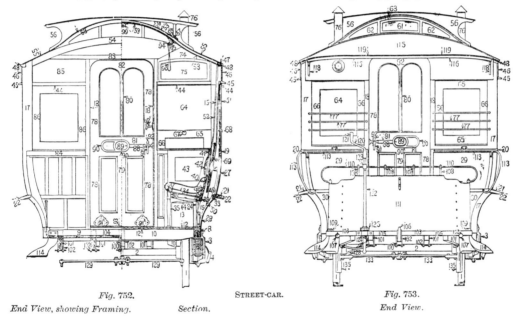

Fig. 752.

End View, showing Framing.　　　Section.　　　STREET-CAR.　　　Fig. 753.

End View.

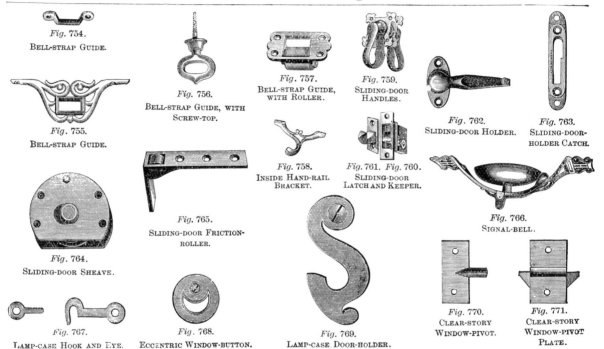

Fig. 754.
BELL-STRAP GUIDE.

Fig. 755.
BELL-STRAP GUIDE.

Fig. 756.
BELL-STRAP GUIDE, WITH
SCREW-TOP.

Fig. 757.
BELL-STRAP GUIDE,
WITH ROLLER.

Fig. 759.
SLIDING-DOOR
HANDLES.

Fig. 762.
SLIDING-DOOR HOLDER.

Fig. 763.
SLIDING-DOOR-
HOLDER CATCH.

Fig. 758.
INSIDE HAND-RAIL
BRACKET.

Fig. 761. Fig. 760.
SLIDING-DOOR
LATCH AND KEEPER.

Fig. 766.
SIGNAL-BELL.

Fig. 764.
SLIDING-DOOR SHEAVE.

Fig. 765.
SLIDING-DOOR FRICTION-
ROLLER.

Fig. 767.
LAMP-CASE HOOK AND EYE.

Fig. 768.
ECCENTRIC WINDOW-BUTTON.

Fig. 769.
LAMP-CASE DOOR-HOLDER.

Fig. 770.
CLEAR-STORY
WINDOW-PIVOT.

Fig. 771.
CLEAR-STORY
WINDOW-PIVOT
PLATE.

# HAND-CARS.

LIST OF NAMES OF THE PARTS OF HAND-CARS DESIGNATED BY THE NUMBERS IN FIGS. 772–775.

1. *Hand-car Wheel.*
2. *Axle.*
3. *Journal-box.*
4. *Pinion.*
5. *Gear-wheel.*
6. *Crank-shaft.*
7. *Crank-shaft Bearings.*
8. *Sills.*
9. *End-sills.*
10. *Floor-timbers.*
11. *Cross-frame Tie-timber.*
12. *Seat.*
13. *Seat-bracket.*
14. *Seat-bracket Brace.*
15. *Seat-riser.*
16. *Floor.*
17. *Lever-frame Post.*
18. *Lever-frame Cap.*
19. *Hand-car Lever.*
20. *Lever-handle.*
21. *Lever-shaft.*
22. *Lever-shaft Bearings.*
23. *Bell-crank.*
24. *Connecting-rod.*
25. *Lever-frame Tie-rod.*
26. *Hand-car Truss-rod.*
27. *Brake-beam.*
28. *Brake-beam Hanger.*
29. *Brake-head.*
30. *Brake-rod.*
31. *Brake-lever.*
32. *Brake-lever Fulcrum.*

*For list of names of the parts designated by the numbers in the engraving, see page 483.*

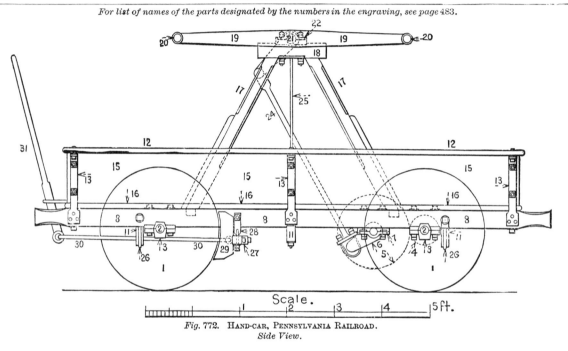

Scale.

*Fig. 772.* HAND-CAR, PENNSYLVANIA RAILROAD.
*Side View.*

For list of names of the parts designated by the numbers in the engraving, see page 483.

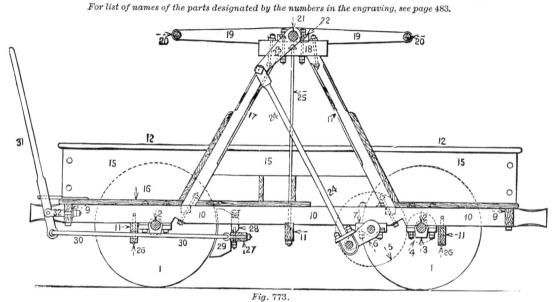

*Fig. 773.*

HAND-CAR, PENNSYLVANIA RAILROAD.

*Longitudinal Section.*

*For list of names of the parts designated by the numbers in the engraving, see page 483.*

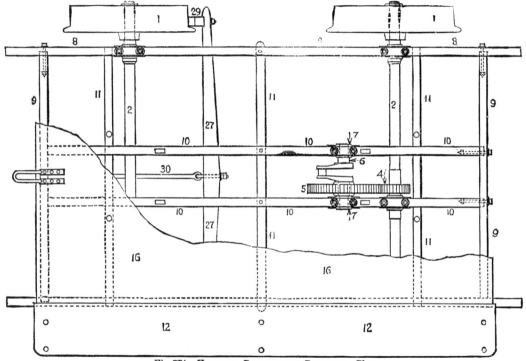

*Fig. 774.* HAND-CAR, PENNSYLVANIA RAILROAD. *Plan.*

*For list of names of the parts designated by the numbers in the engraving, see page 483.*

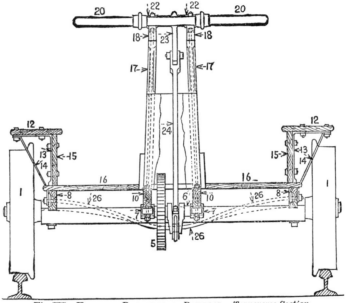

*Fig. 775.* HAND-CAR, PENNSYLVANIA RAILROAD. *Transverse Section.*

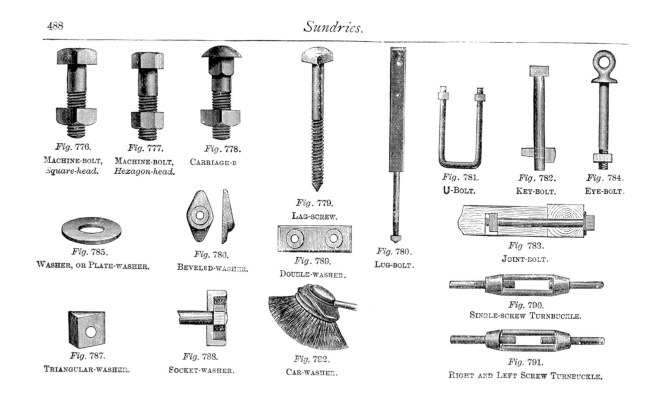

Fig. 776.
MACHINE-BOLT,
Square-head.

Fig. 777.
MACHINE-BOLT,
Hexagon-head.

Fig. 778.
CARRIAGE-B

Fig. 779.
LAG-SCREW.

Fig. 780.
LUG-BOLT.

Fig. 781.
U-BOLT.

Fig. 782.
KEY-BOLT.

Fig. 784.
EYE-BOLT.

Fig. 785.
WASHER, OR PLATE-WASHER.

Fig. 786.
BEVELED-WASHER.

Fig. 789.
DOUBLE-WASHER.

Fig 783.
JOINT-BOLT.

Fig. 787.
TRIANGULAR-WASHER.

Fig. 788.
SOCKET-WASHER.

Fig. 792.
CAR-WASHER.

Fig. 790.
SINGLE-SCREW TURNBUCKLE.

Fig. 791.
RIGHT AND LEFT SCREW TURNBUCKLE.

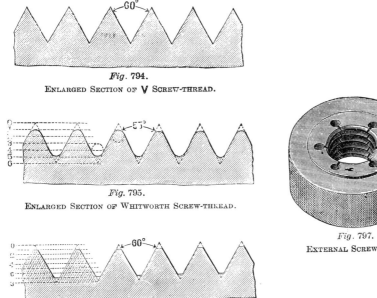

Fig. 794.

ENLARGED SECTION OF V SCREW-THREAD.

Fig. 795.

ENLARGED SECTION OF WHITWORTH SCREW-THREAD.

Fig. 796.

ENLARGED SECTION OF SELLERS SCREW-THREAD.

Fig. 797.

EXTERNAL SCREW-GAUGE.

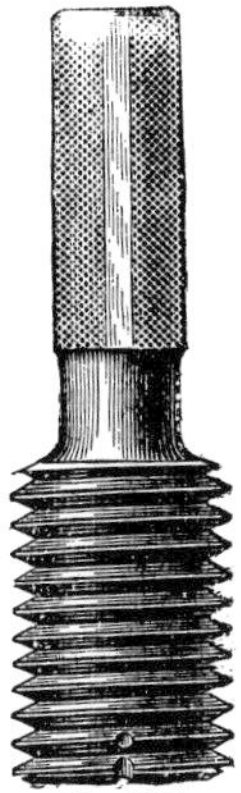

Fig. 798.

INTERNAL SCREW-GAUGE.

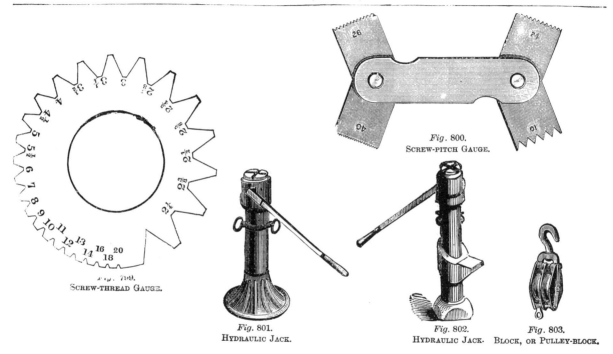

Fig. 800.
SCREW-PITCH GAUGE.

Fig. 799.
SCREW-THREAD GAUGE.

Fig. 801.
HYDRAULIC JACK.

Fig. 802.
HYDRAULIC JACK.

Fig. 803.
BLOCK, OR PULLEY-BLOCK.

# TRUSSES.

**List of the Names of the Parts of Trusses Designated by the Numbers in Figs. 804–811.**

1. *Truss-rod.*
2. *Truss-rod Washer.*
3. *Truss-rod Bearing.*
3.' *Truss-rod Saddle.*
4. *Truss-block.*
5. *King-post.*
6. *Queen-post.*
7. *Skew-back.*
8. *Brace.*
9. *Counter-brace.*
10. *Brace-rod.*
11. *Counter-brace Rod.*
12. *Post.*
13. *Top-chord.*
14. *Lower-chord.*
15. *Vertical-rod.*

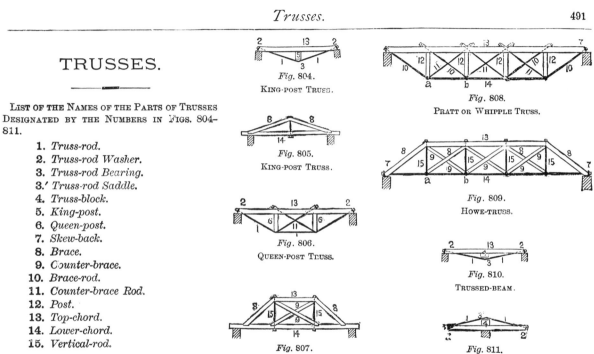

*Fig. 804.*
KING-POST TRUSS.

*Fig. 805.*
KING-POST TRUSS.

*Fig. 806.*
QUEEN-POST TRUSS.

*Fig. 807.*
QUEEN-POST TRUSS.

*Fig. 808.*
PRATT OR WHIPPLE TRUSS.

*Fig. 809.*
HOWE-TRUSS.

*Fig. 810.*
TRUSSED-BEAM.

*Fig. 811.*
TRUSSED-BEAM.

# ADVERTISEMENTS.

*[See the Index to Advertisements following the Preface.]*

The following cuts illustrate the working of Lead-Lined Bearings; the *heavy black line* showing the lead lining, which, in bearings for use, is best when made about one-sixteenth of an inch thick.

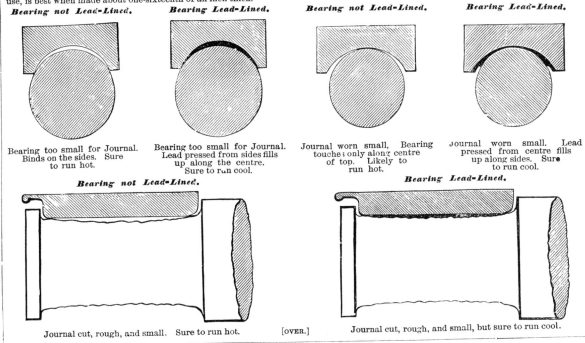

*Bearing not Lead-Lined.*

*Bearing Lead-Lined.*

*Bearing not Lead-Lined.*

*Bearing Lead-Lined.*

Bearing too small for Journal. Binds on the sides. Sure to run hot.

Bearing too small for Journal. Lead pressed from sides fills up along the centre. Sure to run cool.

Journal worn small, Bearing touches only along centre of top. Likely to run hot.

Journal worn small. Lead pressed from centre fills up along sides. Sure to run cool.

*Bearing not Lead-Lined.*

*Bearing Lead-Lined.*

Journal cut, rough, and small. Sure to run hot.

[OVER.]

Journal cut, rough, and small, but sure to run cool.

The following cuts illustrate a construction and form of journal-bearing and key by which, as compared with the bearing and key of usual construction, the following objects are secured, viz.: Diminished first cost of bearing, without decrease in its durability. Greatly reduced cost of renewing worn bearings. Exemption from ruinous cutting of the journal and breaking of the bearing in case of the journal becoming heated. Perfect alignment of the bearing with the journal from the first. Proper distribution of weight along the journal at all times, whether the journal-box does or does not tip. Diminished liability to heating of the journal, and greatly increased durability of the bearing. An essential reduction in power required to move trains.

## EXPLANATION OF ENGRAVINGS.

$K$ is the key, its back being made circular to fit a corresponding recess cast in the under side of the top of the box, while its under side has a rounded recess running across it for receiving the rounded ridge $R$ $R$, running across the back of the bearing, and upon which the load

 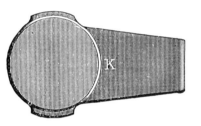

upon the bearing is always received, and thence properly distributed along the journal. Said key readily turns laterally with the bearing, to enable the latter to conform to the alignment of the journal. $I$ $B$ is the back or load-carrying part of the bearing, and is made of steel or of the strongest soft cast iron. In the bearing, $W$ $M$ is the wearing or anti-friction metal for the wear of the journal, and, as shown in this case, is a solid brass casting, with a flange at each end for the wear of the collars of the journal, until the intermediate part is worn cut by the journal. $A$ $B$ is the soft lining of the bearing, by which it is made self-fitting. At the end of the axle, $W$ $M$ is a removable plate of brass for receiving and restricting the end thrust of the axle, which is thereby kept within desirable limits. When the wearing metal, $W$ $M$, is worn out, a new one is substituted in its place, the same back, $I$ $B$, being used. Thousands of these backs are now in use, in which the wearing metal has been many times renewed. The pendant lip at the outer end of the bearing may be omitted when desirable. These *backs, made as above, never break.* Orders respectfully solicited and promptly filled by D. A. HOPKINS, 113 Liberty Street, New York, Patentee and Sole Manufacturer.

THE BEST CHEAP JOURNAL BEARINGS ever offered to the public are THE HOPKINS COMBINATION BEARINGS.

They appear to be just what they are, instead of being, like so-called cheap brass bearings, made up of a villainous mixture, in which every element of real excellence and reliability is sacrificed in the effort to make them appear like really good metal.

They wear the journal as little, if not less, than any others.

They are less likely to cause heating of the journal than the best brass bearings.

They do not break in pieces or spread out as solid brass bearings do, in case of the journal becoming extremely hot.

Their cost is only about one-half that of brass bearings.

They out-wear any brass bearings ever made.

They cost less to renew, when worn, than any others.

They are made to fit any form of journal-box, but cannot, with safety, be made as thin as brass bearings are sometimes made.

Before applying them, remove from the journal all rust and dried paint.

In ordering, send tracing of the journal (when new) for which they are wanted, as well as of brass bearings used.

*No* charge for trial sets.

Orders respectfully solicited and promptly filled by D. A. HOPKINS, 113 Liberty street, New York, Patentee and Sole Manufacturer.

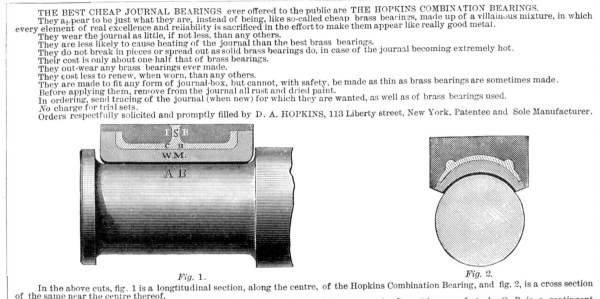

*Fig. 1.*                                    *Fig. 2.*

In the above cuts, fig. 1 is a longtitudinal section, along the centre, of the Hopkins Combination Bearing, and fig. 2, is a cross section of the same near the centre thereof.

*I, B,* is the back, or load-carrying part of the bearing, and is made of the strongest soft cast-iron, or of steel. *C, B,* is a contingent bearing made of the best brass for journal bearings, and is secured to said back by a spur *S,* riveted into the back. *W, M,* is the wearing (or anti-friction) metal, part of the bearing thoroughly held in its place, and designed to receive the principal wear of the journal. The dark heavy line, *A, B,* is the auxiliary, or self-fitting, part of the bearing. The wearing metal, *W M,* is a very hard and remarkably good anti-friction metal, requiring a red heat to melt it. In case of the journal becoming so extremely hot as to melt out the wearing metal (*W M*), the journal will be received and run upon the contingent (brass) bearing, which, being supported and held in place by the iron back, cannot be broken, or escape from its position, and will last to run thousands of miles.

# 3

# WILSON, WALKER & CO.,

## Works and Office, Twenty-ninth and Railroad Sts., Pittsburgh, Pa.

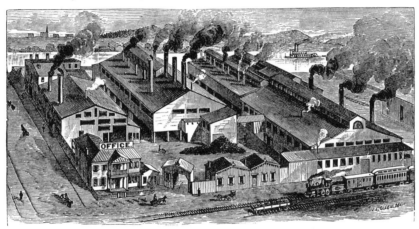

MANUFACTURERS OF ALL KINDS OF

Car and Locomotive Forgings, including Draw-bars, Locomotive Frames, Miller Hooks, Axles, Links, Pins, Diamond or Truck Irons, Universal Mill Plates for Bridges, Merchant Bar Iron, etc., etc.

# THE BUSHNELL SPRINGS,

PATENTED AND MANUFACTURED BY

## E. L. Bushnell, Poughkeepsie, N. Y.

These Springs are made of the best STEEL SPRING WIRE, coiled small enough so that a large number can be used in a seat, and made with four eyes at each end (as shown in the smaller engraving) by means of which they are closely and firmly connected together, forming a *smooth* and *continuous* surface, and making a **LIGHTER, SOFTER, STRONGER** and **CHEAPER** seat, seat-back, or bunk than any other. These Springs have been thoroughly tested by long use, and thousands of them are now in daily wear. They are in use on the following lines :

THE N. Y. CENTRAL & HUDSON RIVER R. R.
PENNSYLVANIA RAILROAD.
CENTRAL RAILROAD OF NEW JERSEY.
PULLMAN'S PALACE CAR CO.
WAGNER'S PALACE CAR CO.
MICHIGAN CENTRAL R. R.
DELAWARE, LACKAWANNA & WESTERN R. R.
PHILADELPHIA, WILMINGTON & BALTIMORE R. R.
NORTHERN CENTRAL R. R.
CAROLINA CENTRAL R. R.
CENTRAL VERMONT R. R.
INTERCOLONIAL RAILWAY CO.

DELAWARE & HUDSON CANAL CO.

## CAR BUILDERS.

GILBERT & BUSH CO., TROY, N. Y.
HARLAN & HOLLINGSWORTH CO., WILMINGTON, DEL.
BOWERS, DURE & CO., WILMINGTON, DEL.
JACKSON & SHARP CO., WILMINGTON, DEL.
BILLMEYER & SMALL CO., YORK, PA.
WASON MANUFACTURING CO., SPRINGFIELD. MASS.
ONTARIO CAR CO., LONDON, ONT., and others.

These Springs are made in strict conformity with Common-Sense Mechanical laws, and recommend themselves to all practical **men.**
BUNK SPRINGS, usual size, $5.00. SEAT SPRINGS, usual size, $1.50. BACK SPRINGS, usual size, $1.50.

11

# W. C. ALLISON & Co.,

MAIN OFFICE AND WORKS:

## 32d AND WALNUT STREETS,

PHILADELPHIA, PENNA.,

BRANCH OFFICE AND WAREHOUSE:

## 78 JOHN STREET,

NEW YORK,

MANUFACTURE

## All kinds of Freight, Construction and Hand Cars for Broad and Narrow Gauge Railroads, Portable Track and Plantation Cars;

ALSO

## ALL KINDS OF CAST AND WROUGHT IRON WORK, BOLTS, NUTS, WASHERS, ETC.,

FOR

## CARS, BUILDINGS AND BRIDGES,

AND FURNISH

## Wheels, Axles, Frogs, Switches, Fish Plates and General Railroad Supplies.

# WASON MANUFACTURING COMPANY

### (ESTABLISHED 1845.)

### SPRINGFIELD, MASSACHUSETTS,

Manufacturers of All Descriptions of Railway Cars, Car and Locomotive Wheels, Frogs, Switches and Railway Castings. Employ None But Experienced Workmen, and Have on Hand a Large and Complete Stock of Seasoned Lumber, Sufficient for Several Years' Consumption. Special Facilities for Furnishing Sectional Work for Exportation. Daily Capacity, One Passenger and Six Freight Cars. Shipments Made from New York or Boston.

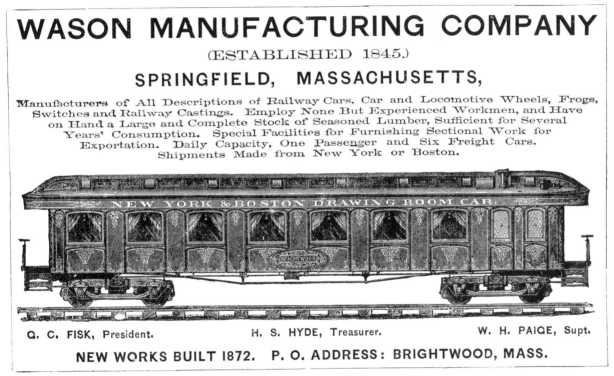

G. C. FISK, President.        H. S. HYDE, Treasurer.        W. H. PAIGE, Supt.

### NEW WORKS BUILT 1872. P. O. ADDRESS: BRIGHTWOOD, MASS.

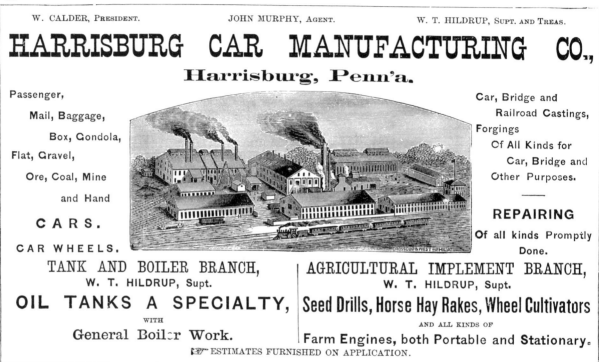

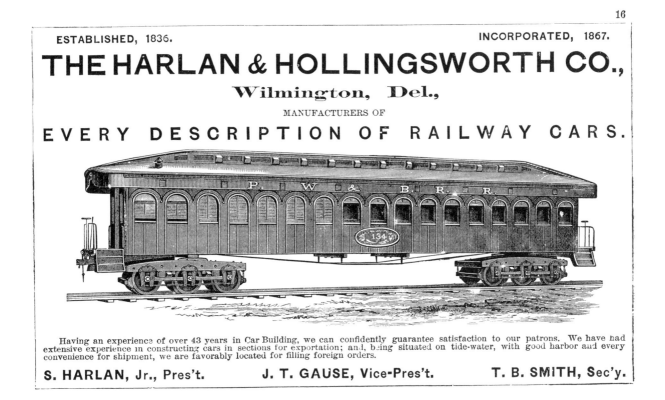

# SUPPLEMENT TO THE CAR-BUILDERS' DICTIONARY,

SUGGESTED BY

## MURPHY & CO., CAR-VARNISH MAKERS,

### Newark, N. J.

**A. B. C.** The beginning of wisdom and the foundation of car painting.

**Air-Brake.** A gag to be used when drummers get too windy—not Varnish drummers, of course.

**Blind.** None so blind as those who won't see—the economy of the Murphy Varnishes.

**Bolster.** Something used in lobbying.

**Box, A Hot.** The box a car painter gets into when his varnish goes seedy or specky and the maker won't take it back.

**Car-Spring.** Why wouldn't a car-*spring* be a good place for the Directors to water the stock?

**Coupling.** The best coupling is finish coupled with endurance, as found in the Murphy Varnishes.

**Cylinder.** Anything round.—*Webster*. Our drummers are generally *'round*. Why, then, are they not cylinders? Because they are all "on the square."

**Link Motion.** The link-by-link progress of the Darwinian development.

**Master Car Painter.** A master car painter who persists in the lead-and-oil system of priming, might be called one of the "old masters."

**Narrow-Gauge.** The idea that cheap varnishes are the cheapest.

**Paper Car Wheels.** Railroads are built on *paper* nowadays, and the RAILROAD GAZETTE sends out *paper* tracts—why not send *paper* wheels also?

**Rapid Transit.** From A. B. C. to P. D. B.

**Switch, A Misplaced.** The school-boy's notion of a birch rod applied in the rear. The switchman should also remember that the locomotive has a tender behind.

**Safety Platform.** The platform of the Murphy movement.

**Tie-Bar.** A place of retreat for Directors when there is a tie-vote.

**Truck.** Poor Varnish.

*Particular attention is called to the* **AUTOMATIC BRAKE,** *now largely adopted by the railways of this and other countries. The "Automatic" has proved itself to be the most efficient train and safety brake known. Its application is instantaneous; it can be operated from any car in the train, if desired, and, should the train separate or a hose or pipe fail, it is applied automatically to the entire train.*

*With the driving-wheel and tender brakes the engineer can handle an ordinary freight train better than can be done by brakemen. The saving in car-wheels and wages will therefore be apparent. On shifting or yard engines it is invaluable.*

*The special steam brake for freight engines is so made that the air brake apparatus can be added at any time. It furnishes, in the first instance, the cheapest kind of a brake for locomotives only. The special regulating-valve governs the pressure on the pistons, regardless of condensation. The pressure may be regulated or varied as desired.*

*The Company is prepared to contract for equipping the entire freight or passenger stock of any line on most favorable terms.*

*A guarantee is given customers against loss from patent suits on the apparatus sold them.*

## FULL INFORMATION FURNISHED ON APPLICATION.

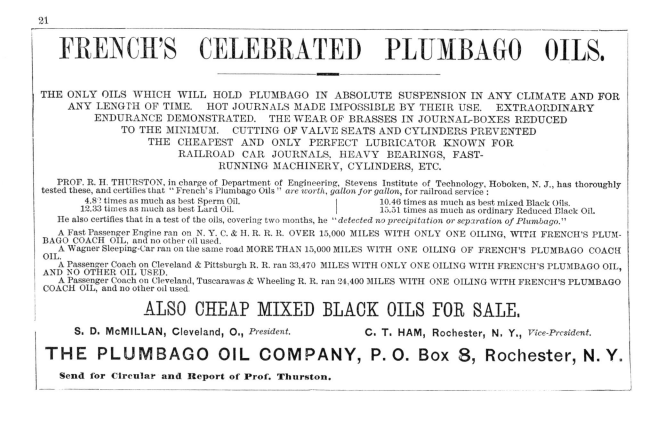

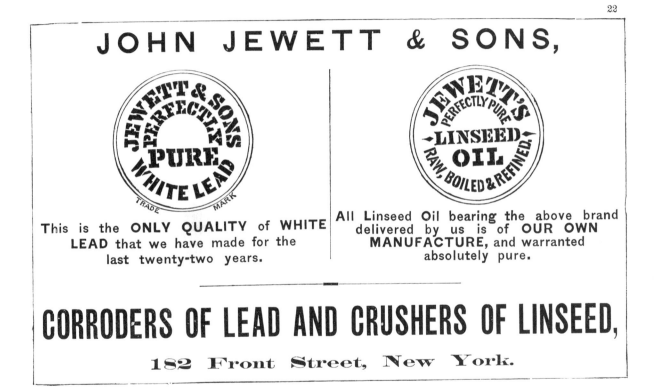

ESTABLISHED 1858.

# THRESHER & CO.,

MANUFACTURERS OF

## ALL KINDS OF

# RAILWAY VARNISHES,

## DAYTON, OHIO.

These Varnishes have an Established Reputation for Unsurpassed Durability, Uniform Quality and Superior Adaptation to Railway Wants. Their widely-extended and long-continued use upon leading Railroads of the Country ATTESTS THEIR EXCELLENCE.

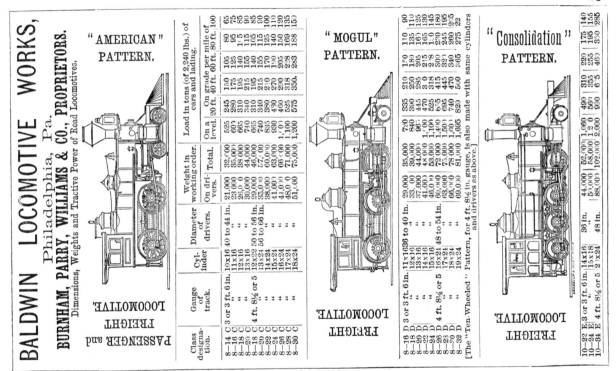

# BALDWIN LOCOMOTIVE WORKS,
### Philadelphia, Pa.
### BURNHAM, PARRY, WILLIAMS & CO., PROPRIETORS.
Dimensions, Weights and Tractive Power of Road Locomotives,

## "AMERICAN" PATTERN.
### PASSENGER and FREIGHT LOCOMOTIVE.

| Class designation. | Gauge of track. | Cylinder | Diameter of drivers. | Weight in working order. On drivers. | Total. | Load in tons (of 2,240 lbs.) of cars and lading. On a level | On grade per mile of 20 ft. | 40 ft. | 60 ft. | 80 ft. | 100 |
|---|---|---|---|---|---|---|---|---|---|---|---|
| 8—14 C | 3 or 3 ft. 6 in. | 10x16 | 40 to 44 in. | 21,000 | 32,000 | 525 | 245 | 150 | 105 | 80 | 65 |
| 8—16 C | " | 11x16 | " | 23,000 | 35,000 | 600 | 280 | 175 | 125 | 95 | 75 |
| 8—18 C | " | 12x16 | " | 26,0 0 | 38,000 | 665 | 310 | 195 | 145 | 115 | 85 |
| 8—20 C | " | 13x16 | " | 30,000 | 44,000 | 710 | 340 | 215 | 115 | 105 | 90 |
| 8—20 C | 4 ft. 8½ or 5 | 12x22 | 50 to 56 in. | 29,000 | 57,00 | 665 | 310 | 195 | 195 | 105 | 85 |
| 8—22 C | " | 13x24 | 56 to 66 in. | 35,0 0 | 60,000 | 740 | 340 | 210 | 155 | 115 | 100 |
| 8—24 C | " | 14x24 | " | 38,000 | 63,000 | 835 | 380 | 240 | 170 | 140 | 110 |
| 8—26 C | " | 15x24 | " | 41,00 | 66,000 | 980 | 430 | 270 | 205 | 150 | 120 |
| 8—28 C | " | 16x24 | " | 41,0 0 | 71,000 | 1,100 | 525 | 318 | 228 | 169 | 135 |
| 8—30 C | " | 17x24 | " | 48,0 0 | 75,000 | 1,200 | 575 | 350 | 283 | 188 | 150 |
| | | 18x24 | | 51,00 | | | | | | | |

## "MOGUL" PATTERN.
### FREIGHT LOCOMOTIVE.

| Class designation. | Gauge of track. | Cylinder | Diameter of drivers. | Weight in working order. On drivers. | Total. | On a level | 20 ft. | 40 ft. | 60 ft. | 80 ft. | 100 |
|---|---|---|---|---|---|---|---|---|---|---|---|
| 8—16 D | 3 or 3 ft. 6 in. | 11x16 | 36 to 40 in. | 29,000 | 35,000 | 720 | 335 | 210 | 150 | 110 | 90 |
| 8—18 D | " | 12x16 | " | 33,000 | 39,000 | 840 | 390 | 250 | 180 | 135 | 110 |
| 8—20 D | " | 13x16 | " | 37,000 | 44,00 | 960 | 445 | 285 | 215 | 160 | 175 |
| 8—22 D | " | 15x16 | " | 41,000 | 48,000 | 1,100 | 470 | 315 | 215 | 165 | 130 |
| 8—24 D | 4 ft. 8½ or 5 | 16x21 | 48 to 54 in. | 46,000 | 53,000 | 1,100 | 525 | 415 | 210 | 1 0 | 145 |
| 8—26 D | " | 16x21 | " | 60,000 | 72,000 | 1,490 | 675 | 505 | 300 | 230 | 180 |
| 8—28 D | " | 17x24 | " | 63,000 | 75,000 | 1,50 | 695 | 445 | 325 | 245 | 195 |
| 8—30 D | " | 18x24 | " | 66,000 | 78,000 | 1,60 | 740 | 470 | 340 | 260 | 205 |
| 8—32 D | " | 19x24 | " | 69,000 | 81,000 | 1,695 | 820 | 500 | 365 | 275 | 22 |

[The "Ten-Wheeled" Pattern, for 4 ft. 8½ in. gauge, is also made with same cylinders and drivers as above.]

## "Consolidation" PATTERN.
### FREIGHT LOCOMOTIVE.

| Class designation. | Gauge of track. | Cylinder | Diameter of drivers. | Weight in working order. On drivers. | Total. | On a level | 20 ft. | 40 ft. | 60 ft. | 80 ft. | 100 |
|---|---|---|---|---|---|---|---|---|---|---|---|
| 10—22 E | 3 or 3 ft. 6 in. | 14x16 | 36 in. | 44,000 | 52,000 | 1,060 | 490 | 310 | 220 | 175 | 140 |
| 10—24 E | " | 15x18 | " | 54,000 | 58,000 | 1,2 0 | 560 | 355 | 255 | 195 | 155 |
| 10—34 E | 4 ft. 8½ or 5 | 2 x24 | 48 in. | 88,000 | 102,000 | 2,000 | 990 | 6 5 | 46 | 350 | 285 |

# IRON CLAD PAINT.

TRADE

MARK.

Trade Mark Patented.   Paint Patented.   None genuine unless marked with above.
This Paint is used on nearly all the railroads in the country.   Used by L. S. & M. S., Wabash R'y, C., C., C. & I. R'y, C. & P. R'y, C., H. & D. R. R., Cincinnati Southern R'y, N. Y., L. E. & W. R'y (Erie), Southern Central R. R., Canada Southern, Mobile and Ohio, N. O. & Mobile, Macon & Brunswick, Penn. R. R., C., M. & St. P. R'y, A. & N. R'y, R. & D. R'y, Carolina Central, P., C. & St. L. R'y, P. & E. R. R., M. L. S. & W. R'y, K. & D. M. R'y, W. C. & A. R. R., M., I. & N. R'y, N. C. & St. L., N. I. & E. R. R., I. & G. N. R. R., etc., etc.   Adopted by U. S. Government for Iron Ships' Bottoms, also United States Lighthouses.   Dry and Ground in Oil same as Lead, for Roofs, Railroad Cars, Bridges and all kinds of Iron Work.

**IRON CLAD PAINT CO., Cleveland, Ohio.**

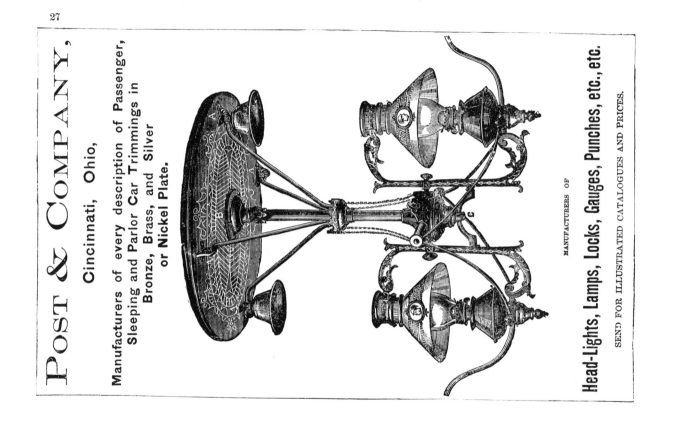

# SAFFORD'S SAFETY DRAW-BAR.

Victory over more than 30 Self-Couplers in the Master Car-Builders' Convention of June, 1876.   Also indorsement for safety in coupling by the Yard Masters, in their Convention, June, 1877, and by 300 others who were unable to attend the Convention, and 300 railroad officials who are residents in 28 States, and who admit its superiority over any other yet produced.

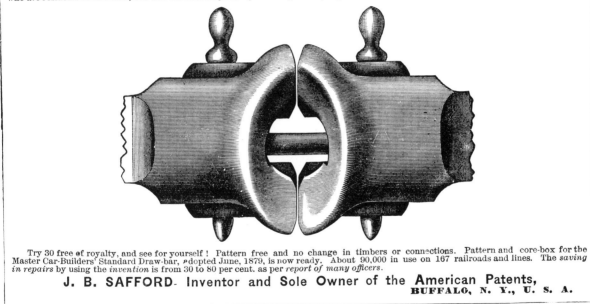

Try 30 free of royalty, and see for yourself !  Pattern free and no change in timbers or connections.  Pattern and  core-box for the Master Car-Builders' Standard Draw-bar, adopted June, 1879, is now ready.  About 90,000 in use on 167 railroads and lines.  The *saving in repairs* by using the *invention* is from 30 to 80 per cent. as per *report of many officers.*

**J. B. SAFFORD**- Inventor and Sole Owner of the **American Patents,**
**BUFFALO, N. Y., U. S. A.**

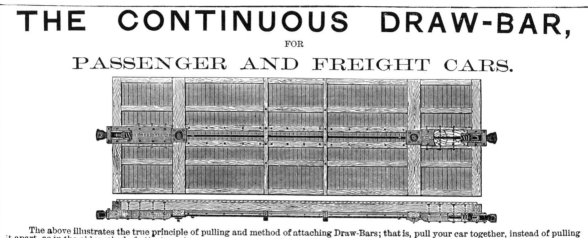

The engraving illustrates our new principle of connecting the Continuous Draw-Bar to Passenger Cars that are constructed with the Miller Platform. It will at once be seen, on examination of the cut, that we entirely avoid, by the introduction of the Continuous Rod, all lost motion between buffers, as the strain of draft, being applied at the rear end of each car, throws the timbers of each car into compression and so draws and holds the buffers of adjoining cars constantly against each other, to steady the train and entirely avoid sudden shocks and jars. To apply this arrangement, there is no alteration necessary to be made in the present style and shape of Miller hook or coupler, and the additional cost is but slight. It has now been in use for upward of four (4) years on a number of coaches, and is giving entire satisfaction.

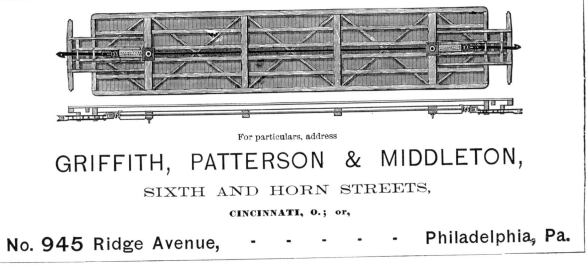

For particulars, address

# GRIFFITH, PATTERSON & MIDDLETON,

### SIXTH AND HORN STREETS,

**CINCINNATI, O.; or,**

## No. 945 Ridge Avenue, - - - - - Philadelphia, Pa.

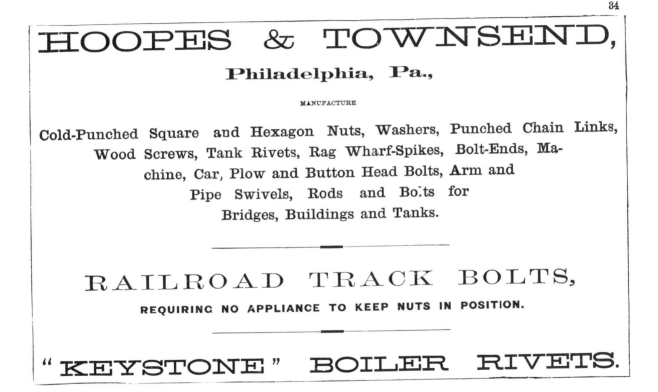

# HOOPES & TOWNSEND,

## Philadelphia, Pa.,

MANUFACTURE

Cold-Punched Square and Hexagon Nuts, Washers, Punched Chain Links, Wood Screws, Tank Rivets, Rag Wharf-Spikes, Bolt-Ends, Machine, Car, Plow and Button Head Bolts, Arm and Pipe Swivels, Rods and Bolts for Bridges, Buildings and Tanks.

---

# RAILROAD TRACK BOLTS,

### REQUIRING NO APPLIANCE TO KEEP NUTS IN POSITION.

---

# "KEYSTONE" BOILER RIVETS.

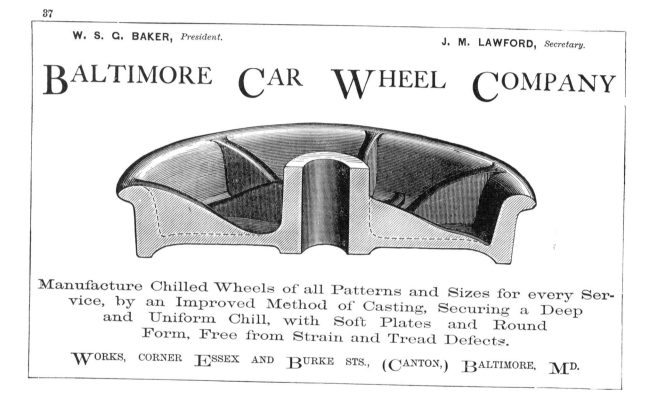

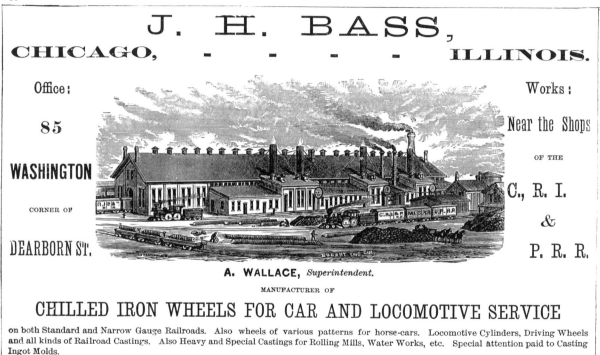

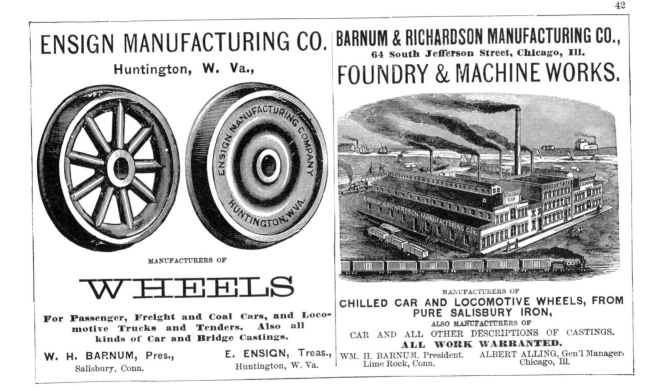

# WILLIAM SELLERS & CO.,

## PHILADELPHIA.

## IRON AND STEEL WORKING MACHINE TOOLS,

FOR RAILWAYS, MACHINE SHOPS, ROLLING MILLS, ETC.

Pivot Bridges. Shafting. Tweddle's Hydraulic Riveter.

THE 1876 INJECTOR BOILER-FEEDER. SIMPLE, RELIABLE AND EFFECTIVE.

Started, Regulated and Stopped by One Motion of a Lever.

NEW EXPANSION STEAM-TRAP. SUITS ANY LOCATION.

BRANCH OFFICE: 79 LIBERTY ST., NEW YORK.

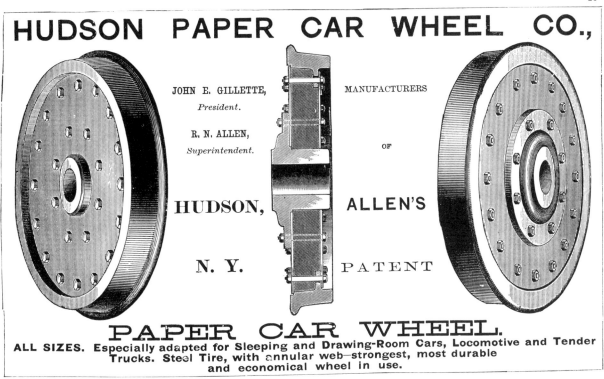

# CLEVELAND RUBBER COMPANY.

Our Company was incorporated in 1872, since which time it has never ceased operations for a single day for lack of orders, and although its capacity for manufacturing has been many times doubled since the start, yet to-day we find ourselves able to meet the demands made upon us only by working two forces of men. We will again enlarge our works this fall. We ask the trade and consumers to give our products a trial.

## RUBBER HOSE.

Our White Shield Fire-Engine Hose resists a pressure of 400 lbs. to the square inch Our Air Brake Hose, is made extra good, to insure strength and durability; ends capped. Our Steam Hose contains an extra heavy tube that resists the action of steam. All sizes of standard hose kept constantly in stock. Tank and Suction Hose of any size and length made to order.

## VALVES.

Pure Para Rubber Valves, and all sizes and styles of ordinary valves made to order

We are prepared to make iron moulds for casting rubber to any form.

## RUBBER BELTING.

Made of heavy cotton duck, coated with a smooth surface of india rubber Warranted.

## RUBBER SPRINGS.

Caoutchouc or India Rubber is the most elastic substance known to commerce. It is not affected by air, moisture or heat. It will not rust or rot. Its elasticity is absolutely indestructible, and its durability is greater than any part of that which it will save from wreck by vibration. These qualities make it better adapted for springs and cushions than any other nown article. We speak of good Rubber pring and not that " mixture," so called, which has been the means of throwing all rubber springs out of use to so large an extent. State what weight each spring is calculated to carry, and about how much they can settle and vibrate un er that weight, in ordering.

## GASKETS, ETC.

Ordinary kinds and sizes of Gaskets kept on hand ; special kinds or styles made to order in five days. Pure rubber tubing and tubing with cloth insertion, rubber cords and strips of any size and length, rubber rings of all kinds and rubber of any design or shape for any mechanical purpose, we are prepared to make as ordered, on short notice.

## PACKING.

Sheet Packing, two qualities and all thicknesses ; round and square packing, a superior article made of best cotton duck, kept on hand.

## RUBBER BLOCKS

for cushions, or rubber made in any required shape for springs or bumpers.

FACTORY, ON C & P. R. R.,
NEAR WOODLAND AV.

CLEVELAND,
O.

GENERAL OFFICE & STOREROOM,
No. 8 SOUTH WATER ST.

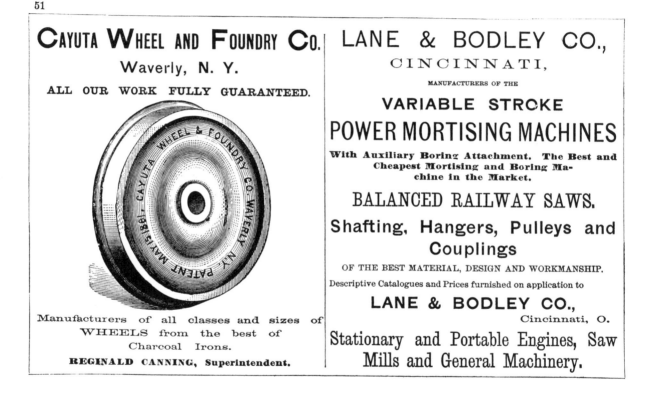

WOOD-WORKING MACHINERY

FOR

# RAILROAD SHOPS, CAR-BUILDERS,

Planing Mills, Bridge - Builders, Cabinet, Carriage, Sash, Door and Blind Makers.

SEND FOR NEW CATALOGUE.

GOODELL & WATERS,

31st and Chestnut Streets,    -   -   -   Philadelphia, Pa.

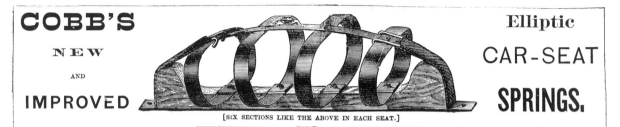

# THE THIELSEN TRUCK CO.

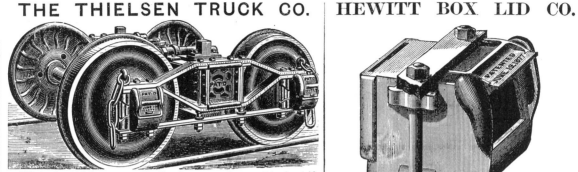

This truck, which is represented by the above engraving, consists of outside frames made entirely of iron, and instead of wooden cross pieces rolled channel bars are used, the ends of which are securely riveted to cast-iron end-pieces attached to the outside frames, as shown above.

This truck is cheaper and lighter than most of the wooden swing-beam trucks in use, and much more durable and economical, costing less for repairs, as there are no timbers to shrink or decay and no bolts to work loose. Owing to the secure manner in which the truck is held square, by the channel bars and castings, the frames are not so likely to get out of line as they are in other trucks, and consequently there is less liability of hot boxes. It has been adopted as the standard truck on the Michigan Central, Chicago, Burlington & Quincy, Flint & Pere Marquette, and Atchison, Topeka & Santa Fe Railroads, and has also recently been introduced on the Kansas City & St. Joe, Atchison & Nebraska, and several other prominent Western roads.

For information regarding its working we would refer to the following prominent railroad men, who have had it in use on their lines for several years:

J. C. McMULLIN, Chicago, Gen. Man. C. & A. R. R.; C. E. PERKINS, Chicago, Vice-Pres. C., B. & Q. R. R.; WM. B. STRONG, Gen. Man. A., T. & S. F. R. R.; H. B. LEDYARD, Detroit, Gen. Man. Mich. Cen. R. R.; G. H. NETTLETON, Kan. City, Gen. Man. K. C., S. F. & C. B. R. R.; L. W. TOWNE, Atchison, Gen. Supt. Atch. & Neb. R. R.; S. KELLER, East Saginaw, Supt. F. & P. M. R. R.

For information respecting terms, specifications, estimates, etc., apply to the

**THIELSEN TRUCK CO., 122 Randolph St., Chicago, Ill.**

# HEWITT BOX LID CO.

## ITS ADVANTAGES ARE:

FIRST.—It cannot be taken off.

SECOND.—That it is always in place and always closed when the car is in motion.

THIRD.—Its simplicity and easy adjustment, which commend it at once to all oilers and yard-men.

FOURTH.—Its tightness, and the AVOIDANCE OF ANY NUTS OR FASTENINGS TO LOOSEN.

It is now in use on many prominent Railroads, and universally indorsed as being the best and most economical cover in use. Address

**HEWITT BOX LID CO.,**
**122 Randolph St.,** **CHICAGO.**

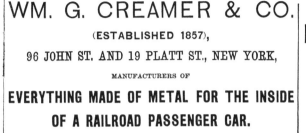

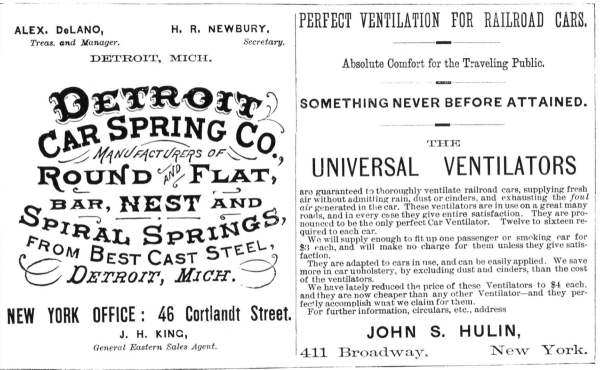

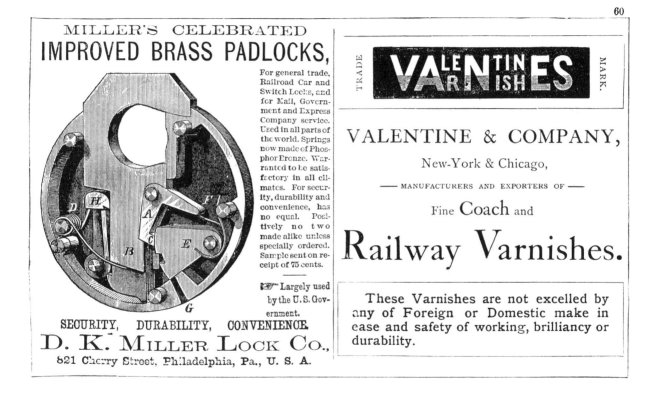

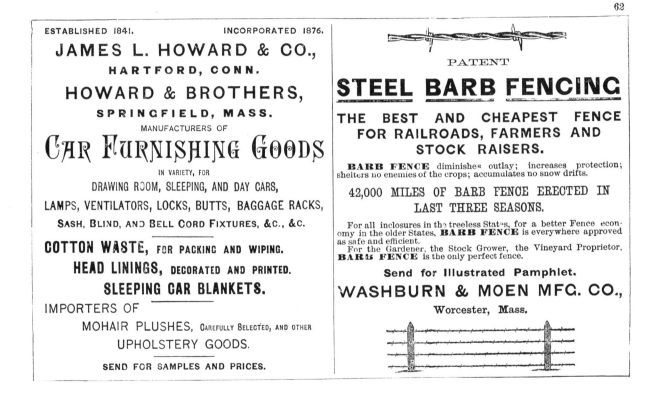

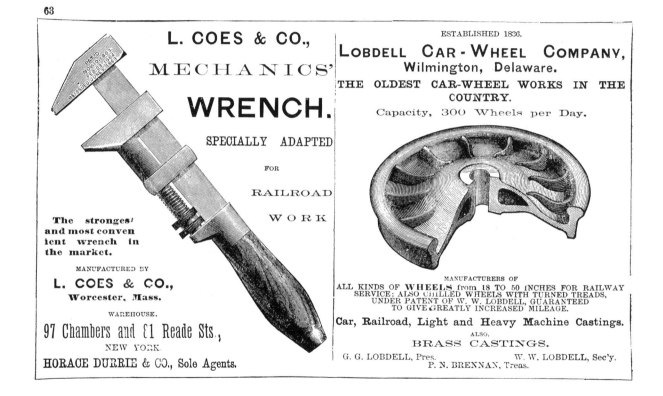

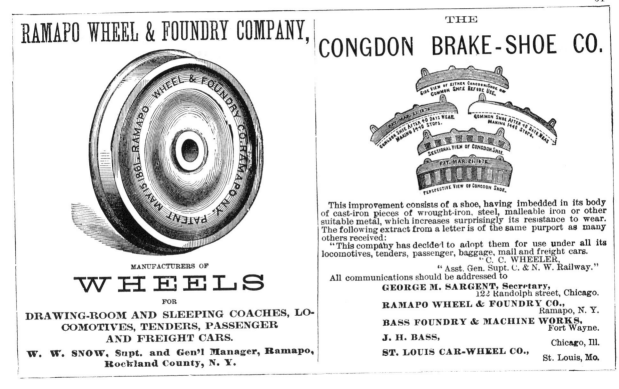

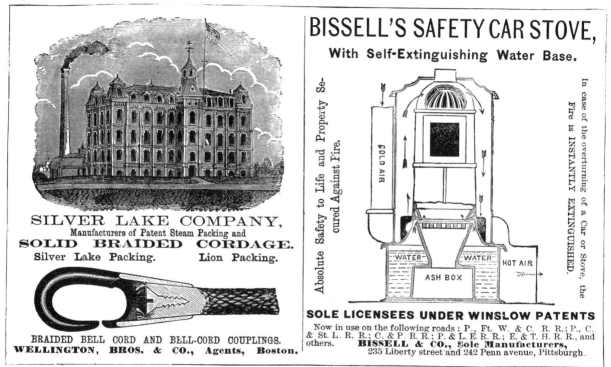

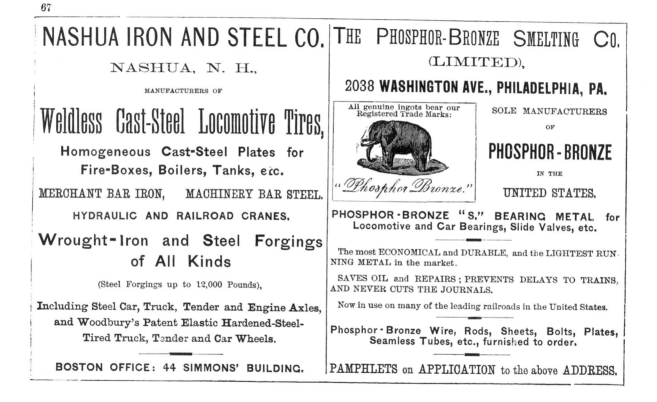

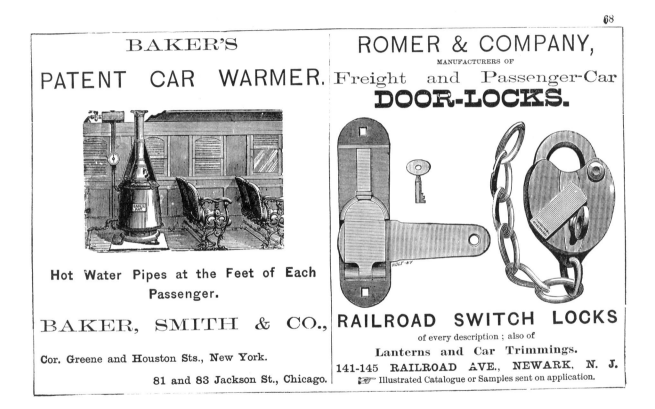

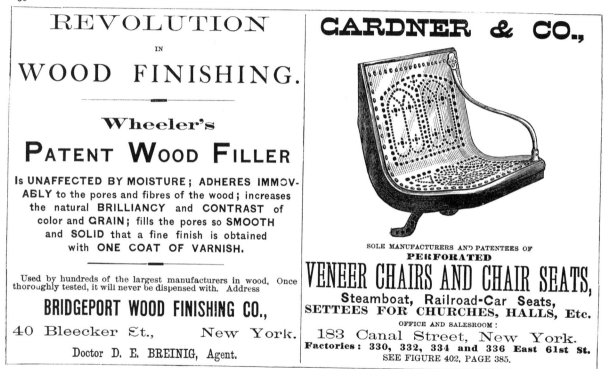

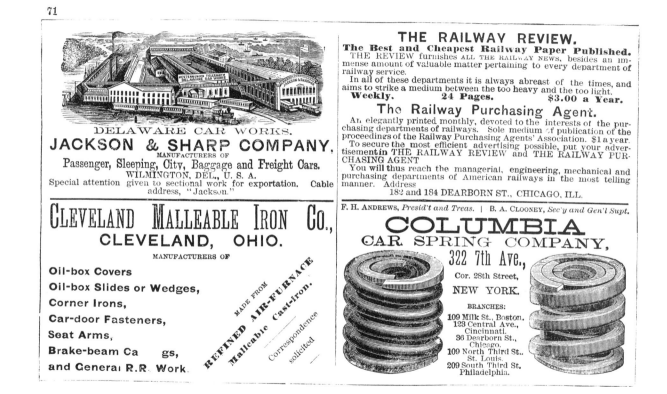

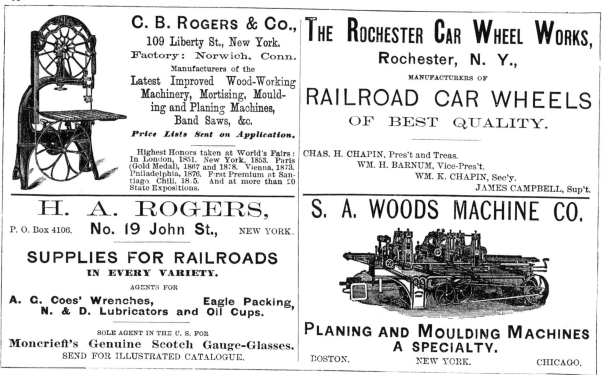

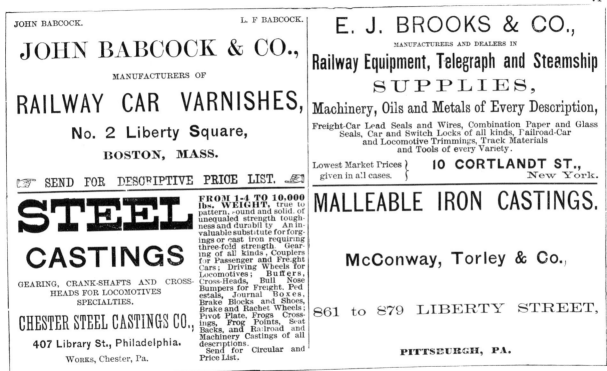

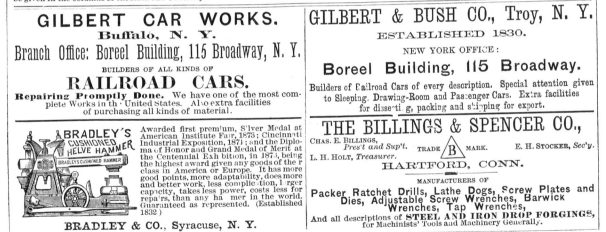

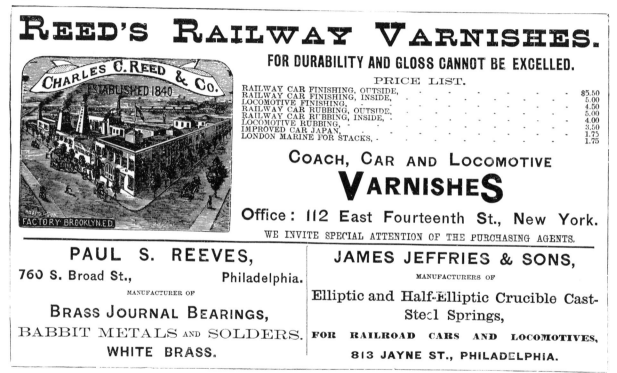

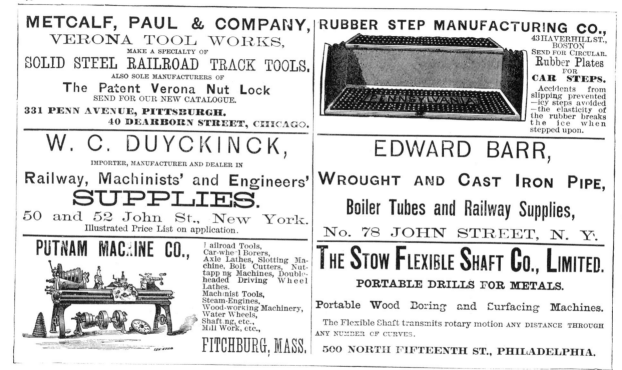

# THE TAYLOR IRON WORKS,

MANUFACTURERS OF

## CHILLED AND STEEL-TIRED CAR WHEELS,

## CAR AXLES, CAR HOOKS AND FORGINGS.

Principal Office and Works at High Bridge, N. J.

### NEW YORK OFFICE, 91 LIBERTY STREET.

LEWIS H. TAYLOR, *Pres't.*     JAMES H. WALKER, *Sec'y and Treas.*     SAMUEL P. RABER, *Supt.*

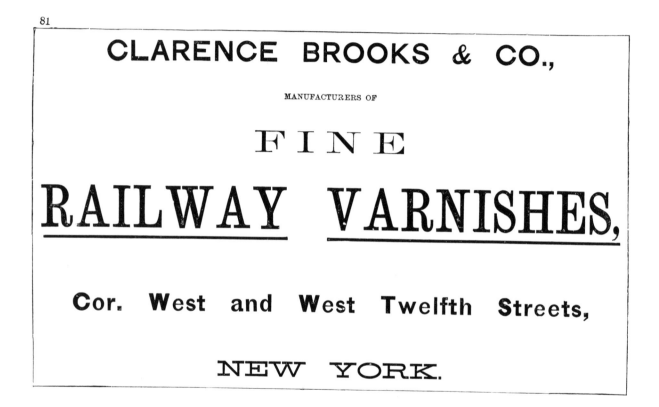

**CLARENCE BROOKS & CO.,**

MANUFACTURERS OF

FINE

**RAILWAY VARNISHES,**

**Cor. West and West Twelfth Streets,**

NEW YORK.

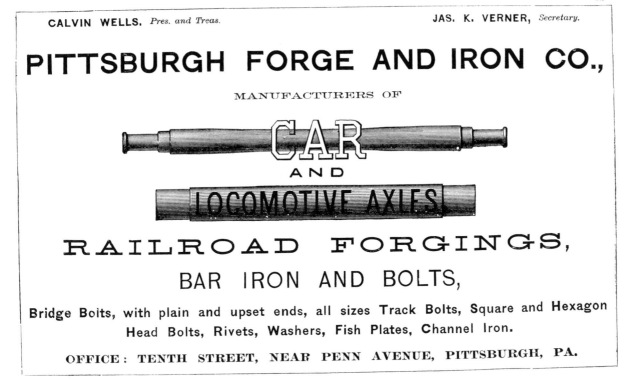

# BARNEY & SMITH MANUFACTURING CO.,
## Manufacturers of Rolling Stock for Railroads, Frogs, Car Wheels and all Kinds of Castings.

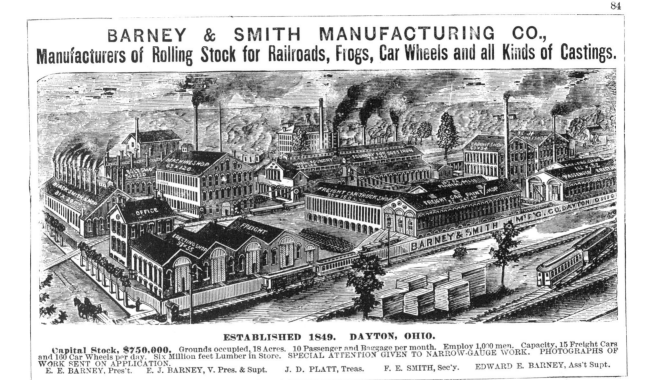

## ESTABLISHED 1849. DAYTON, OHIO.

**Capital Stock, $750,000.** Grounds occupied, 18 Acres. 10 Passenger and Baggage per month. Employ 1,000 men. Capacity, 15 Freight Cars and 160 Car Wheels per day. Six Million feet Lumber in Store. SPECIAL ATTENTION GIVEN TO NARROW-GAUGE WORK. PHOTOGRAPHS OF WORK SENT ON APPLICATION.

E. E. BARNEY, Pres't.    E. J. BARNEY, V. Pres. & Supt.    J. D. PLATT, Treas.    F. E. SMITH, Sec'y.    EDWARD E. BARNEY, Ass't Supt.